Windows® Command Line Administration
Instant Reference

John Paul Mueller

WILEY

Wiley Publishing, Inc.

Acquisitions Editor: Agatha Kim
Development Editor: Jennifer Leland
Technical Editor: Russ Mullen
Production Editor: Liz Britten, Eric Charbonneau
Copy Editor: Cheryl Hauser
Editorial Manager: Pete Gaughan
Production Manager: Tim Tate
Vice President and Executive Group Publisher: Richard Swadley
Vice President and Publisher: Neil Edde
Book Designer: Maureen Forys, Happenstance Type-O-Rama
Compositor: JoAnn Kolonick, Happenstance Type-O-Rama
Proofreader: Jen Larsen, Word One
Indexer: Ted Laux
Project Coordinator, Cover: Lynsey Stanford
Cover Designer: Ryan Sneed
Cover Image: iStockphoto

Library of Congress Cataloging-in-Publication Data
Mueller, John, 1958-
  Windows command line administration instant reference / John Paul Mueller.
      p. cm.
  Includes bibliographical references and index.
  ISBN 978-0-470-65046-2 (pbk.), ISBN: 978-0-470-93107-3 (ebk),
  ISBN: 978-0-470-93090-8 (ebk), ISBN: 978-0-470-93086-1 (ebk)

1. Command languages (Computer science)—Handbooks, manuals, etc. 2. Microsoft Windows
(Computer file)—Handbooks, manuals, etc. 3. Operating systems (Computers)—Handbooks,
manuals, etc. I. Title.
  QA76.7.M79 2010
  005.4'46—dc22
                                    2010032265

Dear Reader,

Thank you for choosing *Windows Command Line Administration Instant Reference*. This book is part of a family of premium-quality Sybex books, all of which are written by outstanding authors who combine practical experience with a gift for teaching.

Sybex was founded in 1976. More than 30 years later, we're still committed to producing consistently exceptional books. With each of our titles, we're working hard to set a new standard for the industry. From the paper we print on, to the authors we work with, our goal is to bring you the best books available.

I hope you see all that reflected in these pages. I'd be very interested to hear your comments and get your feedback on how we're doing. Feel free to let me know what you think about this or any other Sybex book by sending me an email at nedde@wiley.com. If you think you've found a technical error in this book, please visit http://sybex.custhelp.com. Customer feedback is critical to our efforts at Sybex.

Best regards,

Neil Edde
Vice President and Publisher
Sybex, an Imprint of Wiley

This book is dedicated to Claudia Meyer, who has taught me a great deal about human spirit and the ability to come back after a crisis. She has been an inspiration to me.

Acknowledgments

Thanks to my wife, Rebecca, for working with me to get this book completed. I really don't know what I would have done without her help in researching and compiling some of the information that appears in this book. She also did a fine job of proofreading my rough draft and page proofing the result. Rebecca also keeps the house running while I'm buried in work.

Russ Mullen deserves thanks for his technical edit of this book. He greatly added to the accuracy and depth of the material you see here. Russ is always providing me with great URLs for new products and ideas. However, it's the testing Russ does that helps most. He's the sanity check for my work. Russ also has different computer equipment from mine, so he's able to point out flaws that I might not otherwise notice.

Matt Wagner, my agent, deserves credit for helping me get the contract in the first place and taking care of all the details that most authors don't really consider. I always appreciate his assistance. It's good to know that someone wants to help.

A number of people read all or part of this book to help me refine the approach, test the coding examples, and generally provide input that all readers wish they could have. These unpaid volunteers helped in ways too numerous to mention here. I especially appreciate the efforts of Eva Beattie, Jonathan S. Weissman, and Osvaldo Téllez Almirall who provided general input, read the entire book, and selflessly devoted themselves to this project.

Finally, I would like to thank Pete Gaughan, Agatha Kim, Jennifer Leland, Liz Britten, Cheryl Hauser, and the rest of the editorial and production staff at Sybex for their assistance in bringing this book to print. It's always nice to work with such a great group of professionals and I very much appreciate the friendship we've built over the few years.

About the Author

John Mueller is a freelance author and technical editor. He has writing in his blood, having produced 86 books and over 300 articles to date. The topics range from networking to artificial intelligence and from database management to heads-down programming. Some of his current books include a Windows command line reference, books on VBA and Visio 2007, a C# design and development manual, and an IronPython programmer's guide. His technical editing skills have helped over 52 authors refine the content of their manuscripts. John has provided technical editing services to both *Data Based Advisor* and *Coast Compute* magazines. He's also contributed articles to magazines like *DevSource, InformIT, SQL Server Professional, Visual C++ Developer, Hard Core Visual Basic, asp.netPRO, Software Test and Performance,* and *Visual Basic Developer.* Be sure to read John's blog at

http://www.amazon.com/gp/blog/id/AQOA2QP4X1YWP

When John isn't working at the computer, you can find him in his workshop. He's an avid woodworker and candle maker. On any given afternoon, you can find him working at a lathe or putting the finishing touches on a bookcase. He also likes making glycerin soap and candles, which comes in handy for gift baskets. You can reach John on the Internet at JMueller@mwt.net. John is also setting up a Web site at http://www.mwt.net/~jmueller/. Feel free to look and make suggestions on how he can improve it. One of his current projects is creating book FAQ sheets that should help you find the book information you need much faster.

Contents

Introduction

Let's face it, while GUI applications are nice and they do provide significant levels of hand holding, they're cumbersome and inefficient. The command line is an essential part of the administrator experience—at least, if the administrator wants to go home at night and spend weekends somewhere other than work. Using the command line can often provide faster results with far less effort. In addition, the command line lends itself to easy automation, so you might not need to manually perform some tasks at all; you can let the computer do them while you have a cup of coffee and gab with a friend in the next cubicle. However, no one can memorize every command, or even a significant subset of them, so *Windows Command-Line Administration Instant Reference* provides you with a quick reference for the common commands and provides examples of their use to help you avoid potential errors. In short, if you want to spend time doing something other than adding users to the server, you need this book!

Work Faster and More Efficiently

Have you looked at the Administrative Tools folder of the Control Panel lately? It typically contains fourteen or more links to consoles that you use to administer Windows using a GUI. Finding the right console isn't always straightforward. For example, most people would be tempted to look for hardware settings in System Configuration, but they really appear in Computer Management. Some of the consoles don't even appear in the Administrative Tools folder. A typical Windows setup includes 21 consoles, so one-third of the consoles are missing—you need to know they exist in order to use them. If you want to set a group policy, you need to know that you have to use GPEdit.MSC (the Group Policy Editor) to change them, but don't count on Windows helping you. In short, the GUI is disorganized and difficult to use. On the other hand, if you want to use the command line, you open one item—the command prompt. How much simpler can things get?

Speaking of group policies, it requires a single command at the command line to change any group policy. Yes, changing the policy requires that you create the command, but there is help to do that.

Changing a policy such as a Domain Profile for Windows Firewall using Group Policy Editor, however, requires that you dig down six levels, figure out which of the policies will actually do what you want, and then perform upward of five additional steps in order to change the policy. Now, imagine that you have to change a lot of policies on a number of machines. When working with the command line, you can create a batch file that performs the task on every machine on your network. The batch file will likely require an hour or so to create and test, while using the GUI may very well require days because the Group Policy Editor lacks automation.

The command line is great for more than just changing settings. Have you ever wanted to discover all of the files associated with a particular application and been frustrated in your efforts? The command line supports a nifty utility called FindStr that lets you look inside files for copyright statements and other strings. If you have some idea of what to look for, FindStr will faithfully search every file on the hard drive for that string—no matter where the file might appear. You can't even perform this task using the GUI because Microsoft thinks it knows better than you how to find things. The GUI doesn't even index the inside of every file, just those that Microsoft thinks you should search. In short, if you want to find anything anywhere, you need the command line, not a GUI.

It would be easy to go on and on about the benefits of the command line, but you have an entire book to convince you of the incredible value of using the command line in place of the GUI in most situations. Of course, every good thing comes with caveats and the command line is no different. The command line does require that you be able to type commands accurately in order to obtain accurate results. That's why you need *Windows Command-Line Administration Instant Reference*. This book uses a task-based approach to make it easy for you to type just the command you need. It's packed with hundreds of example commands, some of which will meet your needs with little or no change. If you want to get more out of your day, you need to use the command line with *Windows Command-Line Administration Instant Reference*.

Goals for Writing This Book

I want you to be able to get started using the command line today to perform useful work. Starting with the first chapter you'll find that you can immediately begin using the command line to work faster and more efficiently. Suddenly, the system that felt so slow just a few minutes earlier will accomplish work quickly because you'll take command using a time proven interface. The first and most important goal of this book is to get you to work now.

Most people don't realize the immense number of commands and utilities available at the command line. In fact, there are commands and utilities to perform some extremely esoteric tasks and you won't see them covered in this book. Instead, this book exposes you to the commands and utilities that you'll commonly use; 149 of them. That's right! You have access to 149 commands and utilities that can make it faster and more efficient to administer the systems under your control. Some of these commands and utilities, such as Windows Management Interface Command line (WMIC) are so powerful that you might decide never to use the GUI again. The second goal for this book is to expose you to the most useful commands and utilities that the command line has to offer. Look at Appendices A and B to see lists of these commands and utilities.

Automation is one of the major benefits of working at the command line. If you need to perform a particular task often, there isn't any reason to keep doing it manually when you can tell the computer to perform the task for you instead. Using a GUI makes many people think that it's normal to manually perform the same repetitious work over and over again until your eyes glaze over and you fall asleep out of sheer boredom. Work shouldn't be boring and the automation that the command line can provide relieves you of boredom. Many administrators have the mistaken idea that they have to become programmers to use automation, but this book shows you that you can create perfectly acceptable batch files to automate tasks without becoming even close to a programmer. So the third major goal of this book is to help you understand how automation comes into play using batch files.

Of course, you may find that batch files are limited and after working with batch files for a while, you might decide that a little programming isn't so bad after all. The fourth goal of this book is to demonstrate that scripting is not only powerful, but that it isn't very hard either. Imagine how nice it would be to get all of your work done in half or even a quarter of the time you do now. Working at the command line and using the full scope of automation it can provide will help you move toward that goal. So, the final goal for this book is to help you understand the benefits of scripting. You won't actually learn how to script using this book—that's the topic of another tome, but you'll get enough information to decide whether scripting is right for you. In addition, you'll see some pretty nifty scripts that will definitely save you time.

Who Should Read This Book?

This book is designed to meet the needs of administrators who are tired of letting the GUI slow them down and who want the productivity advantage of working at the command line. More and more administrators are moving to the command line because it lets them perform tasks quickly. In addition, the command line lends itself to automation, so that you don't spend hours performing precisely the same boring task over and over again.

Power users will also appreciate this book because it gives them the edge needed to work quickly in today's competitive market. There isn't any reason to spend hours mousing about when you can complete the task in a matter of seconds at the command line. For that matter, by using some of the scheduling techniques found in this book, you can automate some tasks completely so that you won't actually perform them manually again. This book is all about letting the computer do as much for you as it possibly can so you can spend more time watching the game, reading a book, or doing something else that's a bit more interesting than sitting in front of the computer.

I'm assuming that you already know how to use Windows quite well and that you've performed administration tasks in the past. This book presents you with instructions for performing common tasks at the command line and the information you need to customize these tasks to meet your specific needs. However, the complete novice won't be able to keep up with the pace of this book.

What You Need to Use This Book

You'll very likely want to set up a test machine when working through the examples in this book. A production machine simply isn't the right environment in which to learn how to work at the command line. I used Windows 7 and Windows Server 2008 while writing this book. If you have some other version of Windows, you may find that your system doesn't have some of the features I discuss. You'll still find plenty to interest you.

I recommend that you set up the hardware required for a two-machine network as part of your test setup. Otherwise, you really won't see how some of the client-side tasks are supposed to work. Using a virtual machine setup may work acceptably, but I opted for using two physical machines so that the interactions would work just as they do on your network. There are advantages to using two physical machines, because virtual machines sometimes lack the differences in environment that two physical machines provide.

The book contains descriptions of numerous utilities that you can download and use free for the most part. You may prefer other utilities, but I used these utilities to create the content for the book. If you find a technique useful, download the utility that goes with it and try it too. I'm always on the lookout for new utilities, so please be sure to tell me about your utilities at `JMueller@mwt.net`.

Conventions Used in This Book

It always helps to know what the special text means in a book. The following table provides a list of standard usage conventions. These conventions make it easier for you to understand what a particular text element means.

Table 1.1: Standard Usage Conventions

Convention	Explanation
`Inline Code`	Some code will appear in the text of the book to help explain application functionality. The code appears in a special font that makes it easy to see. This monospaced font also makes the code easier to read.
`Inline Variable`	As with source code, variable source code information that appears inline will also appear in a special font that makes it stand out from the rest of the text. When you see monospaced text in an italic typeface, you can be sure it's a variable of some type. Replace this variable with a specific value. The text will always provide examples of specific values that you might use.
`[Optional Code]` or `[`*`Optional Variable`*`]`	In some cases, a command or utility provides an optional entry. The code form of this entry appears in square brackets. Both code entries and variables can be optional. Whenever you see the square brackets, remember that you have a choice to make about typing the code or variables within the square brackets.
`User Input`	Sometimes I'll ask you to type something. For example, you might need to type a particular value into the field of a dialog box. This special font helps you see what you need to type.

Table 1.1: Standard Usage Conventions *(continued)*

Convention	Explanation
Filename	A variable name is a value that you need to replace with something else. For example, you might need to provide the name of your server as part of a command line argument. Because I don't know the name of your server, I'll provide a variable name instead. The variable name you'll see usually provides a clue as to what kind of information you need to supply. In this case, you'll need to provide a filename. Although the book doesn't provide examples of every variable that you might encounter, it does provide enough so that you know how to use them with a particular command.
[Filename]	When you see square brackets around a value, switch, or command, it means that this is an optional component. You don't have to include it as part of the command line or dialog field unless you want the additional functionality that the value, switch, or command provides.
File ➢ Open	Menus and the selections on them appear with a special menu arrow symbol. "File ➢ Open" means "Access the File menu and choose Open."
italic	You'll normally see words in italic if they have special meaning or if this is the first use of the term and the text provides a definition for it. Always pay special attention to words in italic because they're unique in some way.
Monospace	Some words appear in a monospaced font because they're easier to see or require emphasis of some type. For example, all filenames in the book appear in a monospaced font to make them easier to read.
URLs	URLs will normally appear in a monospaced font so that you can see them with greater ease. The URLs in this book provide sources of additional information designed to improve your development experience. URLs often provide sources of interesting information as well.
➡	This is the code continuation arrow. It tells you when a single line of code in a file actually appears on multiple lines in the book. You don't type the code continuation arrow when you use the code from the book in your own code. Rather, you continue typing the code in the book on a single line in your code. For example, you would type the following code on a single line, even though it appears on multiple lines here.

```
<add connectionString=➡
    "Server=MAINVISTA\SQLEXPRESS;➡
    Database=ReportServer$SQLExpress;➡
    Integrated Security=true" ➡
    name="MySQLConnection" />
```

The book also uses a number of special text entries. These special entries provide you with additional information about the task at hand. The following list describes each of these special text entries.

NOTE   Notes provide general ancillary information that doesn't fit within the confines of the text. For example, a note might tell you about a Web site where you can find additional information. A note can also provide amplifying information, such as the use of a special technique with a particular command or utility. Generally, you can ignore notes if you want, but reading the notes will definitely help you get more out of the book.

WARNING   Warnings are especially important to read because they tell you about things that can go wrong when you use a particular command or utility. In fact, not reading warnings can be harmful to your data (and then your career). This book uses warnings to emphasize text—a warning says "Watch out! Danger ahead!" Always read the warnings in the book before you use the associated command or utility. In addition, if you don't feel you fully understand the warning, be sure you do some additional research before you use the command or utility. Feel free to contact me at `JMueller@mwt.net` about any warnings you don't understand.

Interesting Side Topics

You'll see a number of fascinating side topics in the book. Sometimes these sidebars are appealing to read on their own. You may have a few minutes to kill, which is a good time to thumb through the book looking for these interesting tidbits. Sidebars always contain helpful and pertinent information. This is extra information that's designed to make your use of the command line better in some way, but you can just as easily skip the information if you want. Treat sidebars as you would articles that you read online. They'll always provide something of importance, but not always a topic that's essential for performance of the task at hand.

PART I

Command Line Basics

IN THIS PART ▶

1

Configuring the Local Machine

IN THIS CHAPTER, YOU WILL LEARN TO:

▶ **CONFIGURE THE COMMAND WINDOW** (Pages 4-10)

- Set the Window Options (Page 4)
- Change the Font (Page 7)
- Choose a Window Layout (Page 8)
- Define the Text Colors (Page 9)

▶ **SET THE ENVIRONMENT** (Pages 10-15)

- Manage Environment Variables with the *Set* Command (Page 10)
- Manage Environment Variables with the *SetX* Utility (Page 13)

▶ **PERFORM COMMON TASKS** (Pages 16-20)

- Clear the Display (Page 16)
- Determine the Operating System Version (Page 16)
- Start an Application (Page 16)
- Work with Services (Page 18)
- Shut Down the System (Page 19)

▶ **OBTAIN COMMAND LINE HELP** (Pages 20-21)

Y ou can access the command line anytime you want. Issuing commands will work just fine without doing anything special. However, if you want to have the best possible experience at the command line, then you need to perform a few configuration tasks before you proceed. This chapter describes basic configuration procedures you can use to enhance your command line experience and make it better.

Configure the Command Window

Many users start the command window, see the typical command prompt, and just assume that they'll never see anything else. Fortunately, you can easily configure the command window to appear as you want, at least within limits.

You can access these features using these steps:

1. Click the box in the upper left corner of the command window and choose Properties from the context menu. You'll see a properties dialog box with four tabs.

2. Set the properties on each tab to meet specific needs, such as displaying the text in another color. Each of these tabs is described in the sections that follow.

Set the Window Options

The Options tab shown in Figure 1.1 defines how the command window reacts when you open it. The Cursor Size option controls the size of the cursor, with small being the default. The Large option provides a block cursor that's very easy to see. The Display Options determine whether you see the command window full screen or as a window. Using the full screen mode when you have a number of tasks to perform is easier on the eyes.

Figure 1.1: The Options tab helps you control the appearance and behavior of the command window.

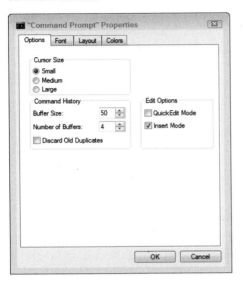

NOTE   Older versions of Windows let you change the display mode through a property setting. However, Server Core (the version of Windows Server 2008 that comes without the usual GUI and relies exclusively on the command line for configuration) doesn't let you run the command window in full screen mode by changing the Display Options setting. This particular option is missing when you view the dialog box shown in Figure 1.1. In most cases, you don't want to run the command window in full screen mode when working with Server Core because the few graphical elements it provides can become inaccessible and it's already possible to maximize the screen real estate by maximizing the window. Without a Start menu, taskbar, or other graphical elements to consume space, using Windows shouldn't cause any problems. (If you really must work in full screen mode, you must modify the registry to do it.)

The Command History is especially important. The Buffer Size option determines the number of commands the buffer will store. Every command requires memory, so increasing this number increases the amount of memory the command prompt requires. Increase this number when you plan to perform a number of complex commands. A smaller number will save memory for larger command line applications. The Number of Buffers Option controls the number of individual histories. You need one history for each command process (application environment) you create. Generally, the four buffers that Figure 1.1 show work fine.

To better understand how buffers work, try this experiment:

1. Open a command window.

2. Type a command such as **CLS** or **Dir** and press Enter.

3. Press the Up arrow.

   You should see the command you just typed—there's the buffer. The command you typed appears in the first buffer. Remember that you have four buffers that you can use at the command processor when using the default settings.

4. Press Esc. The command processor clears the command from the prompt so you have a blank prompt to use.

5. Type **Cmd** and press Enter. You've just created a new command processor. This command processor uses the second buffer.

6. Press the Up arrow. You don't see anything because this command processor is using its own buffer.

7. Now, type a different command (such as **CLS** or **Dir**) and press Enter.

8. Press the Up arrow. You'll see the command you just typed, but not any of the commands from the previous command processor.

9. Press Esc to clear the command.

10. Type **Exit** and press Enter to close the current command processor. You're back to the previous command processor.

11. Press the Up arrow twice and you'll see whatever command you typed earlier because this command processor is using the first buffer.

12. Press Esc to clear the command.

13. Type **Cmd** and press Enter. This action creates a new command processor that will use the second buffer.

14. Press the Up arrow.

Wait, what are you seeing here? You see the Exit command. Press the Up arrow again and you'll see the command you typed in step 7 for the second buffer. Each buffer retains its content, even if you close the command processor.

15. Type **Exit** and press Enter. You return to the first command processor.

16. Type **Exit** again and press Enter; the command processor window closes.

The Edit Options determine how you interact with the command window. Check the QuickEdit Mode when you want to use the mouse to work with the entries directly. The only problem with using this feature is that it can interfere with some commands such as Edit that have a mouse interface of their own. The Insert Mode option lets you paste text into the command window without replacing the text currently there. For example, you might copy some information from a Windows application and paste it as an argument for a command.

Change the Font

The Font tab shown in Figure 1.2 controls the font used to display text. The font size automatically changes when you resize the window, but you can also control the font size directly using this tab. The raster fonts give the typical command line font appearance that works well for most quick tasks. The Lucida Console font works better in a windowed environment. It's easier on the eyes because it's smoother, but you might find that some applications won't work well with it if they create "text graphics" using some of the extended ASCII characters. The extended ASCII characters include corners and lines that a developer can use to draw boxes and add visual detail.

Figure 1.2: Use the Font tab to control the size of the text in the command window.

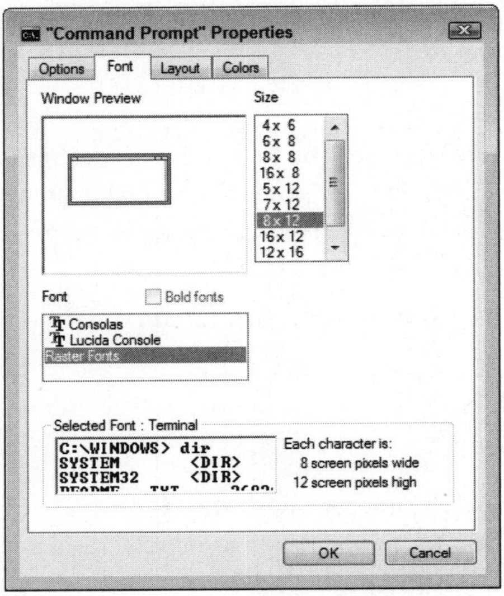

Choose a Window Layout

The Layout tab shown in Figure 1.3 has the potential to affect your use of the command window greatly when working in windowed mode. The Screen Buffer Size controls the width and height of the screen buffer, the total area used to display information. When the Window Size setting is smaller than the Screen Buffer Size, Windows provides scroll bars so you can move the window around within the buffer area and view all it contains. Some commands require a great deal of space for display purposes. Adjusting the Screen Buffer Size and Window Size can help you view all of the information these commands provide.

The Window Position determines where Windows places the command window when you first open it. Some people prefer a specific position on the screen so they always know where a new command window will appear. However, it's generally safe to check Let System

Position Window to allow Windows to place the command window on screen. Each command window will appear at a different, randomly chosen, position on screen.

Figure 1.3: Change the size and positioning of the command window using the Layout tab.

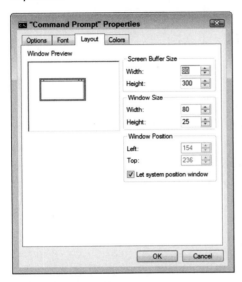

Define the Text Colors

Microsoft assumes that you want a black background with light gray letters for the command window. Although DOS used this setting all those years ago, today, many people want a choice. The Color tab lets you choose different foreground, background, and pop-up colors for the command window (even though Figure 1.4 doesn't show the colors, it does present the dialog box layout). You can modify the window to use any of the 16 standard color combinations for any of the text options. Use the Select Color Values options to create custom colors.

Figure 1.4: Modify the text colors for an optimal display using the Colors tab.

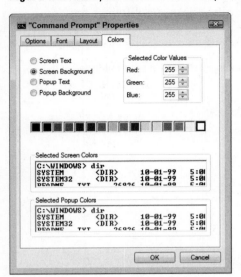

Set the Environment

The command line environment is important because it controls how the command processor works and also changes the way the commands and utilities work in many cases. Configuring the command line lets you perform work faster and with greater ease. For example, you might need to create an environment variable to ensure that a command or utility can locate files or data that it needs. The following sections describe how to control the command line environment so that everything works as you anticipate.

Manage Environment Variables with the *Set* Command

Environment variables are important because they let you define the value of something. An environment variable acts as a storage container that the command processor or you can later access to work more efficiently. For example, the PATH environment variable contains a list of locations to search for executable files. The command processor uses the PATH environment variable to locate the commands you want to execute. The following sections tell how to work with environment variables.

Display Environment Variables

The operating system automatically creates some environment variables when you open a command prompt. To see a list of these environment variables, type **Set** and press Enter. Figure 1.5 shows typical output from this command.

Figure 1.5: Display every environment variable using the Set command.

All of the environment variables shown in Figure 1.5 are defined by default—you don't create any of them. To display a single environment variable, you can use either of the following commands.

	Set *VariableName*

or

	Echo *%VariableName%*

In both cases, you type the command, followed by the name of the variable you want to see. For example, if you want to see the value of the PATH environment variable, you type either **Set PATH** or **Echo %PATH%** and press Enter. The second form relies on variable expansion. You tell the command processor to expand an environment variable by surrounding the environment variable name with percent signs (%). Environment variable expansion has a lot of uses, but you normally use it when systems have the same setting with a different setting value. For example, the location of the Windows directory can differ between machines, but every machine will have a Windows directory. Using environment variable expansion makes it possible to find the Windows directory location on each machine.

NOTE   The PATH environment variable provides a third display method that isn't available to other environment variables. You can simply type **PATH** and press Enter to display the path.

Create or Change an Environment Variable

In some cases, you must create or change an environment variable. To create or change an environment variable temporarily, use the following command line syntax.

```
Set VariableName=Value
```

The *VariableName* defines the name of the variable you want to create or change, while Value defines the content of the variable. If you type the name of an existing variable, the command processor changes its value. When you need to make more permanent changes, you must use the SetX utility described in the "Manage Environment Variables with the SetX Utility" section of the chapter instead.

Expand an Environment Variable

Several applications can share an environment variable. The most common example of a shared environment variable is PATH, but there are other examples. You may find that you need to expand the environment variable content, rather than change it. For example, you might need to add another path to the PATH environment variable. In this case, you expand the current environment variable content and add it to the new content using this approach:

```
Set VariableName = %VariableName%;Value
```

or

```
Set VariableName = Value;%VariableName%
```

For example, let's say you want to add C:\ to the beginning of the existing PATH environment variable. In this case, you type **Set PATH=C:\;%PATH%** and press Enter (remember that paths are separated in the PATH environment variable using semicolons). Using %PATH% expands the content of the PATH environment variable, just as if you had typed **Echo %PATH%**. Likewise, if you want to add C:\ to the end of the PATH environment variable, you type **Set PATH= %PATH%;C:** and press Enter.

Use Equations in Environment Variables

Normally, the command process places the precise value you type in the environment variable. For example, if you type **Set MyVar=2*3** and press Enter, MyVar will contain the value 2*3. However, if you type **Set /A MyVar=2*3** and press Enter, MyVar will contain the value 6 instead. The /A command line switch tells Set to interpret the value as an equation.

Get User Input

You might not know what value to place in an environment variable when you create a batch file. In this case, you can prompt the user to obtain the value. For example, if you want to provide a value for MyVar, you might type **Set /P MyVar="Type a value for MyVar "** and press Enter. In this case, the user sees the prompt "Type a value for MyVar" at the command line. To add a value to MyVar, the user types it at the command line and presses Enter.

Manage Environment Variables with the *SetX* Utility

Any environment variable that you create or change using the Set command is only valid for the current session. The moment that you close the command prompt, the environment variable changes back to its original value or it disappears entirely. You can create or change environment variables permanently using the Environment Variables dialog box shown in Figure 1.6 (accessed by clicking Environment Variables on the Advanced tab of the System Properties dialog box). Unfortunately, having to manually change permanent environment variables using this approach won't work when you need to automate tasks. The SetX utility makes it possible to make such changes from the command prompt.

Figure 1.6: The Environment Variables dialog box shows permanent environment variables.

As you can see from Figure 1.6, permanent environment variables can affect either a single user or the system as a whole. The SetX utility can create or change environment variables at either level. Use the Set command to display the environment variables you create using the SetX utility. You can also use the SetX utility to change environment variables on other machines. The following sections tell how to use the SetX utility.

Change the User-Level Environment

User-level environment variables affect only the current user. The system stores them in the HKEY_CURRENT_USER hive of the registry. To create a permanent user-level environment variable, use the following command line syntax.

    SetX *VariableName Value*

As with the Set command, VariableName contains the name of the variable you want to create, while Value contains the information you want to place within the variable. Unlike the Set command, there's no equals sign between VariableName and Value. The environment variable you create won't affect the current session—to create an environment variable for the current session, you must also use the Set command.

Change the System-Level Environment

System-level environment variables affect every user of a particular machine. The system stores them in the HKEY_LOCAL_MACHINE hive of the registry. To create a permanent system-level environment variable, use the following command line syntax.

```
SetX /M VariableName Value
```

The /M command line switch tells SetX to create a system-level (also known as a machine-level) environment variable. As before, VariableName contains the name of the variable you want to create, while Value contains the information you want to place within the variable. The new environment variable only affects future sessions. You must use the Set command to create an environment variable for the current session.

Set Environment Variables on Other Machines

There's a whole class of commands and utilities that perform tasks on other machines from a local machine. Administrators can use the commands and utilities to interact with client systems without actually going to the client system. In general, you must supply these values:

- Machine name (/S command line switch)
- Username (/U command line switch)
- (Optional) Password (/P command line switch)

The machine name is the fully qualified name of the machine you want to access. The username must be an account that the person using the command can access. Adding the password to a batch file is a security risk. Consequently, you should always omit the password. However, the command won't execute sometimes if you omit the /P command line switch. To get around this problem, you can use /P *, which isn't documented, but always works.

As an example, let's say you want to add a system-level environment variable named NewVar to a machine named WinMachine using the Administrator credentials. In this case, you type **SetX /S WinMachine /U Administrator /P * /M NewVar Value** and press Enter. The SetX utility prompts you for the Administrator password. Type the password and press Enter to complete the task.

Perform Common Tasks

Several common tasks performed at the command line don't necessarily involve the work you're trying to accomplish. For example, when the screen becomes cluttered with too much old information, you might want to clear it so that all of your new commands are easier to see. The following sections describe a few of these common tasks.

Clear the Display

After you execute a number of commands, you might find that the display is getting cluttered. Too much information on the screen can slow you down, so cleaning up every once in a while is a good idea. To clear the display, type **CLS** and press Enter. There isn't any way to just clear part of the display—you must clear the entire display. However, clearing the display doesn't clear the command history. You can still press the Up and Down arrows to move between previously typed commands.

Determine the Operating System Version

Not every version of the command processor supports every command and utility. Consequently, you often need to know which version of the command processor is present on the user's machine. To perform this task, type **Ver** and press Enter. You'll see an operating system version number, such as Microsoft Windows [Version 6.1.7600], which indirectly tells you which version of the command processor is installed. (The command prompt also displays the version number automatically when you open the window.)

Start an Application

Sometimes you want to start a command line application in a separate window. Perhaps this application requires a special environment to run and you don't want to change the current environment to support it. In many other cases, the command line application requires enhanced rights to run or has some other requirement that makes it impossible or seriously irresponsible to run it in the current window. For example, you don't want to run commands that modify the registry in a window with user-level access—using a separate window is more secure. It's also possible to run an application with a higher priority or assign it to a specific processor to help spread the load among processors on a multi-processor system. The Start utility provides the answer to all of these needs.

You can use the Start utility with either command line or Windows GUI applications. For example, if you want to start a separate window to execute the Ver command, you'd type **Start Ver** and press Enter. The command processor will open a separate window, execute the Ver command in it, and wait for you to close the window before continuing. Of course, you might not want the command to execute in a separate window, in which case you'd type **Start /B Ver** and press Enter. The /B command line switch tells the command processor to use the existing window. The difference is that using /B disables Ctrl+C usage; you must issue a break command using Ctrl+Break instead.

It's also possible to start Windows applications using the Start utility. In fact, you have a wide range of ways to use the Start utility to start a Windows application. The easiest method is to simply use the name of the application, such as Notepad. For example, if you want to start a copy of Notepad, you'd type **Start Notepad** and press Enter. Unlike a command line utility, Start automatically resumes once it starts the Windows application unless you use the /Wait command line switch. For example, if you type **Start /Wait Notepad** and press Enter, the Start utility will wait until you exit Notepad before it begins the next step of a batch file or returns control to the command prompt. You can also start Windows applications as minimized using the /Min command line switch or maximized using the /Max command line switch.

Start can also provide some file-related alternatives for starting applications. For example, if you type **Start Test.TXT** and press Enter, the command processor will look in the registry for the default application for opening files that have a TXT extension, start that application, and pass the name of the file to it. In this case, you'll likely see a copy of Notepad open with Test.TXT loaded in it. When you want to be sure that the command process uses a specific application, you provide the name of the application and the file. For example, let's say you want to open a specific URL in Firefox. In this case, you might type **Start "C:\ Program Files\Mozilla Firefox\Firefox" http://antwrp.gsfc.nasa. gov/apod/** and press Enter. The command processor will open the URL at http://antwrp.gsfc.nasa.gov/apod/ in Firefox.

Work with Services

The Service Control (SC) utility provides a number of methods for interacting with services on a system. In fact, there are enough ways that you're unlikely to use them all. Most administrators need to know how to start, stop, pause, continue, and view a service. The following sections describe how to perform common SC tasks.

View Service Status

SC provides an amazing 10 ways to query information about a service. The most common way is to use the Query or QueryEx options because they provide you with basic information about the service status and the features it supports. For example, if you want to see the status of the W32Time service, you type **SC Query W32Time** and press Enter. The output will tell you about the service type, whether it's running, the commands it supports (such as Pause), and some flag information that can prove useful at times when troubleshooting a particular service (you'd need documentation about these flags before the flag information becomes useful).

Sometimes you need a little more information. For example, you might want to know the service description. In this case, you type **SC QDescription W32Time** and press Enter. You see the service name and the full description provided for it in the Services console. A more practical bit of information are the privileges the service requires to work properly. In this case, you type **SC QPrivs W32Time** and press Enter. The output provides a list of privileges that you can decipher at http:// svchost-exe.net/. Of course, administration normally means knowing how a service is configured. To see the configuration for a service, type **SC QC W32Time** and press Enter. The output contains the content of the TYPE, START_TYPE, ERROR_CONTROL, BINARY_PATH_NAME, LOAD_ORDER_GROUP, TAG, DISPLAY_NAME, DEPENDENCIES, and SERVICE_START_NAME fields.

Start, Pause, Continue, or Stop a Service

Administrators commonly need to perform four common tasks with services: start, pause, continue, and stop. Pausing a service differs from stopping a service in that the service retains all of its data. When you continue the service after a pause, the service begins right where it left off. Stopping a service requires that you issue a Start command to reload it, which means that the service begins from scratch. Almost every service supports starting and stopping—pause support requires special programming. Here are typical examples of the four service status changing commands.

- SC Start WinMgmt

- SC Pause WinMgmt

- SC Continue WinMgmt

- SC Stop WinMgmt

In all four cases, the SC utility either displays an error message, such as "[SC] StartService FAILED 1056: An instance of the service is already running" or it displays a success message that basically repeats the output of the Query switch. The important field of a successful command is STATE, which tells you the current operational state of the service.

Shut Down the System

Administrators often need to perform a shutdown of the system using something other than the standard GUI. For example, the system may require a shutdown after running a script or batch file that performs an update. Fortunately, the ShutDown utility provides the means of performing both local and remote shutdowns as described in the following sections.

Log Off the System

Logging off the system simply means that you end the current session. The system remains operational and someone else can log into it. This is the most common use of ShutDown for administrators because it lets the administrator log off the system after performing maintenance and lets the user take over. To log off a system, type **ShutDown \L** and press Enter.

Perform a Shutdown

In some cases, you need to perform a system shutdown, such as after installing a new application. In this case, you have a number of choices. The easiest method is to simply type **ShutDown /S** and press Enter. The system will perform an orderly shutdown after 30 seconds. If you want to shut down a remote system, you must also provide the machine name such as, **ShutDown /S /M \\RemoteComputer**, and press Enter.

The larger your organization is, the greater the need to provide a reason for the shutdown. Of course, you have the three major categories: Planned, Unexpected, and Expected. The three major categories have a major and minor subcategory associated with them. For example, when you install a new application, the major category is 4 and the minor category is 2. You can see a list of these codes at http://ss64.com/nt/shutdown.html. These codes feed into the Shutdown Event Tracker, which creates events that you can see in the Event Viewer (the article at http://www.topbits.com/the-shutdown-event-tracker.html provides some excellent information about the Shutdown Event Tracker). To shut down a system with an event, use the /D command line switch. For example, to show that the system is being shut down as the result of an application installation, you'd type **ShutDown /S /D P:4:2** and press Enter.

A 30-second shutdown is standard. However, you might find that you need to perform an immediate shutdown in some cases. To perform an immediate shutdown, type **ShutDown /S /T:0** and press Enter. The /T command line switch provides a timeout interval for the shutdown—a value of 0 means that the shutdown is immediate.

Shut Down and Restart the System

A shutdown actually turns off the computer in most cases. If you want to use the computer after the shutdown occurs, then you need to perform a shutdown and restart. The ShutDown utility provides two forms of restart. The standard restart simply starts up Windows as a fresh session. To perform this kind of restart, type **ShutDown /R** and press Enter.

In some cases, you might want to restore the Windows applications that were open at the time of the shutdown. In this case, you type **ShutDown /G** and press Enter. Most applications will automatically reopen when the system restarts.

Obtain Command Line Help

There are a number of ways to obtain help at the command line. In most cases, you'll type the name of a command or utility, followed by the /? command line switch to learn more about it. For example, to discover more about the Start utility, type **Start /?** and press Enter. Some utilities provide layered help. For example, the Net utility provides multiple layers. If you type **Net /?** and press Enter, you see the top layer that lists the subcommands you can type. To discover more about the Accounts subcommand, type **Net Accounts /?** and press Enter.

Unfortunately, Microsoft decided to make things difficult in some cases. For example, some utilities require that you use the /Help command line switch instead or you might have to use the Help utility to learn more about the command or utility in question. To see a list of commands and utilities that Help supports, type **Help** and press Enter. You could then learn more about a specific command, such as Ver. In this case, you'd type **Help Ver** and press Enter

The help supplied at the command line isn't always complete or accurate. For example, the Start utility seems to indicate that you can run 16-bit applications in a separate memory space using the /Separate command line switch. However, the /Separate command line switch is only useful when you're working with 32-bit Windows. The 64-bit version of Windows won't run 16-bit applications, even if you use the /Separate command line switch.

Command Line Basics

PART I

2

Making Remote Connections

IN THIS CHAPTER, YOU WILL LEARN TO:

M ost administration takes place on machines other than the one the administrator uses, which means making and managing a remote connection. The command line offers two ways to obtain a remote connection. For those commands that support it, you can specify which machine to interact with directly at the command line. This book shows several examples of this type of remote connectivity, such as the SetX technique described in the "Set Environment Variables on Other Machines" section of Chapter 1. This chapter uses a different approach, the Remote Desktop.

The Remote Desktop offers a number of advantages over using commands specifically designed for remote execution. The first advantage is that you have access to the full array of command line commands and utilities, even those that don't support remote access. The second advantage is that you don't have to figure out how to execute the command or utility in a remote context, so using the Remote Desktop can be simpler than using special command line syntaxes. Of course, using the Remote Desktop requires some additional setup, and you can't use the Remote Desktop when automation is required (such as using a BAT file or a script). Consequently, each form of remote access has its place. The following sections describe how to configure and use Remote Desktop to perform command line tasks.

NOTE   All newer versions of Windows support remote connections. However, if you still have an ancient copy of Windows on one of your systems, you might find the remote connections don't work. This chapter uses Windows 7 as the basis for making remote connections—remote connections for other versions of Windows may display slight differences from the version described in this chapter.

Configure the Remote System

Before you begin working with Remote Desktop, you might have to perform some configuration. At a minimum, you must ensure that the remote system allows for access by the Remote Desktop. Some configuration tasks occur on some machines, but not others. For example, when working with Windows Server 2003, you have access to the root directory, but you don't have such access in Windows Server 2008 and you might require it to perform some tasks. In addition, you might have to perform some continuing configuration tasks as you work with the remote system. Security issues are a special concern. The following sections describe the essential configuration tasks.

Change Security and Basic Setup

Security occurs at a number of levels in Windows. This section isn't a comprehensive treatment of the topic—it only gets you started. Of course, the first task you'll complete is to add an account for yourself to the system and use shares to make resources available. You can perform this task by relying on GUI tools such as Computer Management and Windows Explorer. However, many administrators don't want to perform tasks manually because they set up a considerable number of machines—automation is a better approach. The command line offers a way to automate configuration tasks such as adding accounts and setting security so that you can use Remote Desktop.

The following steps describe a typical setup scenario that you can modify to meet your specific needs (these steps also include some basic computer configuration used to make the system easier to access and more secure):

1. Type **Net User** *YourLoginName YourPassword* **/Add** and press Enter.

   (The Net utility is one of the more useful utilities at your disposal and you'll find it documented in Chapter 8.) This step sets up an account for you. Of course, you won't have administrator level privileges. If you're using this setup on a workgroup, you'll need to add your account to the Administrator group using a LocalGroup. If you're working on a domain, then you'll need to add your account to the Administrator group using a Group instead.

2. Type **Net LocalGroup "Administrators"** *YourLoginName* **/Add** and press Enter.

   You now are part of the Administrator group and can log in under your own name to the system. More importantly, you've just gained the ability to access the server remotely using Remote Desktop without having to perform a significant amount of configuration. You'll want to know what to call the computer, so you need to change the name of it next.

3. Type `WMIC ComputerSystem Where Name="%COMPUTERNAME%" Call Rename Name="`*`NewName`*`"` and press Enter.

   Make sure you choose a name that will work with your work-group or domain setup. Of course, the computer isn't part of the workgroup or domain yet, so that's what you need to do next.

NOTE The `WMIC` command is one of the most powerful configuration features of the command line. Because `WMIC` is so incredibly powerful, you'll find it in several chapters of the book. Chapter 3 shows how to use `WMIC` when configuring print jobs. Chapter 11 shows how to use `WMIC` with Active Directory. Chapter 15 shows how to use `WMIC` to perform maintenance tasks.

---

4. Type `WMIC ComputerSystem Where Name="%COMPUTERNAME%" Call JoinDomainOrWorkgroup Name="`*`NameOfWorkgroup`*`"` and press Enter.

   At this point, you have an account on the system and you're part of the Administrator group. Your computer has an easy-to-type name that you know and it's part of your workgroup. At this point, you need to set it up for remote access. (This section shows the command line technique for granting remote access—the "Setup Remote Administrator" section shows the GUI technique.)

5. Type `WMIC RDToggle Where ServerName="%COMPUTERNAME%" Call SetAllowTSConnections AllowTSConnections="1"` and press Enter.

   After you reboot the system, it provides Remote Desktop capability. However, the firewall prevents you from making a connection, so you need to open a port for the Remote Desktop.

6. Type `NetSH Firewall Set PortOpening TCP 3389 "Remote Desktop"` and press Enter.

   (You'll use the `NetSH` utility for more than just the firewall configuration; see the "Script Networking Solutions" section of Chapter 24 for more details.) The firewall now permits you access to the server. It's important for some tasks to have access to the C drive as well, so you need to create a share. The default share automatically provides the required permissions.

7. Type `Net Share "Drive_C"=C:\` and press Enter.

Everyone now has access to the C drive. You can refine the permissions later. However, now you have the required account, permissions, computer name, workgroup, remote access, and drive access. Many of the commands you'll work with in this book are actually scripts. The default scripting engine is WScript—Microsoft uses the graphical engine for compatibility purposes, but the graphical engine doesn't work very well in a command line environment. The next step changes the default scripting engine to the command line equivalent.

8. Type CScript //H:CScript and press Enter.

   (The CScript utility always uses a double slash for its own command line arguments; learn more about this utility in the "Run Scripts with the CScript and WScript Utilities" section of Chapter 22.) You'll see a message that tells you that the default scripting engine is now CScript. You should activate your copy of Server Core using the next step. However, you can skip this step and go right to step 10 if you prefer.

9. Type SLMGR -ATO and press Enter.

   The activation process seems to take forever. However, get a cup of coffee, and when you get back, you should see a confirmation message. (When using WScript instead of CScript, you'll see a confirmation dialog box that you'll need to dismiss by clicking OK.) It's time to reboot the system to ensure all of the changes occur.

10. Type Shutdown /r and press Enter.

    (The Shutdown command provides a number of useful command line switches that you can discover in the "Shutdown the System" section of Chapter 1.) You'll see a message telling you that the system will shut down in a few seconds. The system will reboot and you'll find all of the changes you've made in place. You should also be able to access the system using Remote Desktop at this point.

NOTE Sometimes the WMIC RDToggle command won't work properly with older clients. In this case, type SCRegEdit / CS 0 and press Enter. You'll see a message that the script has changed the proper registry entry. You must reboot the system after making this change using the Shutdown /r command.

Setup Remote Administrator

You may not want to use the manual approach for configuring your server as described in the "Change Security and Basic Setup" of this chapter. In fact, very often you'll accomplish many of the tasks described in that section during the installation process. However, you still need to enable remote access to ensure you can use Remote Desktop with the machine you want to configure.

The following steps describe the GUI approach for obtaining remote access.

1. Choose Start ➢ Control Panel or Start ➢ Settings ➢ Control Panel to display the Control Panel.

2. Click System and Security, and then Allow Remote Access in the System group when using a workstation. If you're using the classic view of the Control Panel, double click the System applet and then choose the Remote tab of the System Properties dialog box. In both cases, you see the Remote tab of the System Properties dialog box as shown in Figure 2.1.

Figure 2.1: The Remote tab of the System Properties dialog box contains the remote access setting.

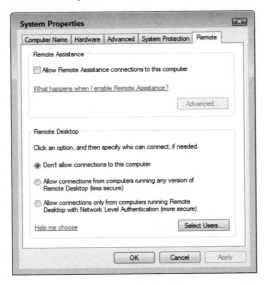

3. On older systems, check the Enable Remote Desktop on This Computer option. On newer systems check the Allow Connections from Computers Running Any Version of Remote Desktop option.

   If you have the required software on every system in your workplace, you could always use the Network Level Authentication option, but most environments don't include the required software on every system.

4. Click OK. Windows makes Remote Desktop access available to administrators.

If you want to allow other accounts to use Remote Desktop (always a poor choice if you don't actually need it), then you must configure these other users by clicking Select Users on the Remote tab of the System Properties dialog box. In this case, you see the Remote Desktop Users dialog box shown in Figure 2.2. Click Add to add the new user and select the user you want to add. Use this feature with extreme care because anything that compromises the account you add could also compromise the machines the account can access using Remote Desktop.

Figure 2.2: Add users who aren't administrators for Remote Desktop access with extreme care.

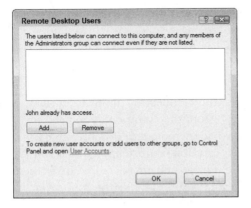

Use the Remote Desktop Connection Application

The Remote Desktop Connection application provides the means to connect to a Windows system for remote management. You only need this application when you want to access the command prompt on the other machine. For example, you won't need this application when you want to use a console to create a remote connection or when you want to use a command line utility from a local machine to make the connection. The Remote Desktop Connection application is exceptionally useful because it does let you create a direct connection to the server. You can monitor events and manage the system directly, which reduces one potential cause of failure (making the remote connection every time you want to perform a task). Select Start ➢ All Programs ➢ Accessories ➢ Remote Desktop Connection or Start ➢ Programs ➢ Accessories ➢ Communications ➢ Remote Desktop Connection to start the Remote Desktop Connection application. The following sections describe how to use this application.

NOTE You must make any changes you want to the Remote Desktop Connection application configuration before you connect to the remote server. Once you make the connection, you can't change the configuration. Consequently, it's always a good idea to create a complete configuration first, save it to disk, and then reopen it as needed for a particular server. Otherwise, you'll spend a lot of time reconfiguring the Remote Desktop Connection every time you want to use it.

Create a Connection

Before you can use the Remote Desktop Connection application (I'll refer to it simply as Remote Desktop from this point on), you need to configure the remote machine to provide remote access connectivity. The "Configure the Remote System" section of this chapter tells you how to perform this task. Once the remote machine is ready for a connection, you must configure Remote Desktop to make the connection. The following procedure helps you make the connection.

NOTE Some versions of Remote Desktop have additional fields on some of the tabs. The procedure includes information for these additional fields. However, if you don't see the additional field, simply skip that step. The screenshots show the Windows 7 version of Remote Desktop. Your screenshots will vary from those shown in the book when working with other versions of Windows.

1. Start the application and click Options.

   Remote Desktop expands to show the complete list of options that you can access with it. The General tab shows the connection options as shown in Figure 2.3.

Figure 2.3: Set the connection parameters for the connection you want to normally make.

2. Type the server name or select it from the drop-down list in the Computer field.

3. Type your account name on the server in the User Name field.

   If you're working on a domain, make sure you include the domain name, followed by a backslash, followed by your name, such as WinServer\John.

4. (Optional) Type your password in the Password field (when this field is supported).

   Make sure you use the password for your account on the remote system.

5. (Optional) Type the name of the server in the Domain field when using a workgroup setup.

   If you're using a domain setup, then type the name of the domain in the Domain field.

6. (Optional) Check Allow Me to Save Credentials (or Save My Password) if you want Remote Desktop to save your password for future use.

   This feature even works if you provide your password while making the connection.

7. Select the Display tab.

   You see display settings like those shown in Figure 2.4. Set the Display Configuration setting to the size you think you'll need.

Figure 2.4: Configure the display so you can see the remote desktop comfortably.

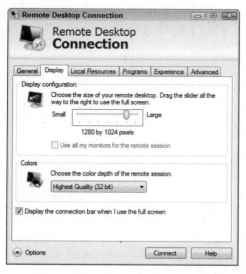

Command line users can usually get by using the 1024 by 768 pixels setting to save screen real estate on the local machine. In addition, a smaller screen makes Remote Desktop faster, something you definitely want, to enhance productivity. Setting the number of colors lower will also produce a performance enhancement. See the "Set the Display" section of the chapter for additional display settings changes you can make.

8. (Optional) Select the Local Resource tab. Make any settings changes required to work with the remote system properly.

   In most cases, you won't need audio. However, you may want to use local drives on the remote system. See the "Access Local Resources" section of the chapter for details for modifying the use of local resources with the remote computer.

9. (Optional) Select the Programs tab. Check Start the Following Program on Connection. Type a location for the program in the Program Path and Filename field. Type a starting location for the program in the Start in the Following Folder field.

   See the "Run a Configuration Program" section of the chapter for additional details.

10. Select the Experience tab. Choose the connection speed for your connection to the remote system.

    The connection speed is important because it defines how your system will interact with the remote system.

11. Clear the checkmarks next to every feature you don't really need, to improve performance.

    For example, most administrators won't require Desktop Composition for any purpose, especially not the command line. See the "Optimize Performance" section of the chapter for additional information.

12. Select the Advanced tab, if your version of Remote Desktop provides it. Choose an option that defines what you want to do when Server Authentication fails.

    The best option is to ask Remote Desktop to warn you about the problem. It's never a good option to choose Connect and Don't Warn Me because you could end up with a less secure connection.

13. (Optional) Click Settings in the Connect from Anywhere section. Use administrator - provided settings to configure the Remote Desktop Gateway settings. In most cases, the default settings will work fine and you should keep them in place unless you have a specific reason for making a change.

14. (Optional) Select the General tab. Click Save As. You'll see a Save As dialog box. If you want to save this setup as the default connection, then click Save. Otherwise, type a name for the setup in the File Name field and click Save.

   You can save as many setups as needed for the machines you want to access. Use the default setup for the machine you access most often.

15. Click Connect. You'll see Remote Desktop performing all of the required connection tasks. Eventually, you'll see a Remote Desktop window like the one shown in Figure 2.5.

Figure 2.5: The remote connection appears in a special Remote Desktop window.

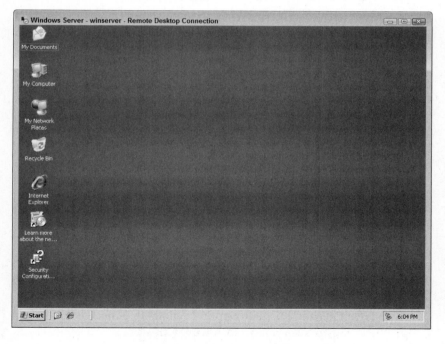

Use a Saved Connection

After you create the initial connection, Remote Desktop opens with the default connection already set up. If you want to use the default connection, all you need to do is click Connect when Remote Desktop starts. Otherwise, you can follow these steps:

1. Click Options to display the list of options shown in Figure 2.3.

2. Click Open to display the Open dialog box.

3. Choose the connection you want to use from the Open dialog box and then click Open to open the connection.

4. Click Connect to make the connection. You won't need to create a setup more than once if you save it to disk.

It's also possible to double click the RDP file containing a connection in Windows Explorer to make the connection to the server, so you can simply place the RDP file on your desktop to make the connection instantly accessible.

Set the Display

The display settings you use affect how much screen real estate you have for performing tasks and also affect performance. Using a larger screen size gives you more space to work. However, a larger screen size also requires more network bandwidth to transmit the data. Consequently, you must weigh the need to see as much as possible on the remote server against the performance requirements for your task. Figure 2.6 shows the display settings.

The Remote Desktop Size slider lets you change the size of the window, with the smallest size being 640 x 480 pixels, which is normally too small to work with a GUI system, but can work just fine with the command line. If you want to use your entire display to work with the remote system, move the slider all the way to the right. The size will change to Full Screen and the display will take up your entire display area. In fact, it will look like you're working directly at the remote console, rather than using Remote Desktop.

Figure 2.6: Define a display size that works best for the task you need to perform.

NOTE   If you want to continue working with your local system while managing the remote system, make sure you check the Display the Connection Bar When in Full Screen Mode option. Otherwise, you might need to log out every time you want to regain access to the local system.

Performance isn't only affected by screen size. Notice that you can also modify the number of colors that Remote Desktop displays. More colors translate into a better display, but also reduce performance because Remote Desktop has to transfer more data for the additional colors. Because the command line lacks a GUI, you'll experience a performance gain by setting the number of colors to 256. In most cases, you won't even notice the difference in appearance, but you will notice the difference in performance.

Access Local Resources

Remote Desktop makes it possible to map your local hardware to respond to events on the remote machine. Figure 2.7 shows the settings you can use to map resources as needed. The following list describes each of the resource mapping areas.

Figure 2.7: Perform automatic resource mapping to make local resources available for use.

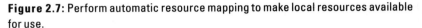

Remote Computer Sound   Lets you bring sounds from the remote machine to your local machine. This setting has three options. You can choose to play the remote sound locally, not play the remote sound at all (effectively muting the remote system), or play the sound at the remote location.

Keyboard   Controls the use of control key combinations. For example, when you press Alt+Tab, this setting controls whether you switch between applications on the local machine or the remote machine. This setting only affects Remote Desktop when you have it selected when working in windowed mode. If you press Alt+Tab when Remote Desktop is working in a window and you don't have Remote Desktop selected, then the Alt+Tab combination always affects the local machine, even when you choose the On the Remote Computer option. Normally, any control key combinations only go to the remote machine when you use Remote Desktop in full screen mode.

Local Devices   Determines which local devices you can access from the remote machine. This may sound like a very odd consideration, but when you're working with the remote machine, Remote Desktop shuts off access to local resources such as disk drives, printers, and serial ports. Only your display, keyboard, and mouse are active on the remote machine unless you tell Remote Desktop to perform the required mapping. Check any of these options to make the resources on your local machine available when working at the remote machine.

Run a Configuration Program

You might find that you want to run a configuration program on the remote machine when you create the connection. This program can perform any task and you can use both batch and script files, in addition to standard applications. Figure 2.8 shows the Programs tab. The options work much like a remote profile. When you want to use a remote program, check Start the Following Program on Connection, type the name of the application you want to use (including the full path), and tell Remote Desktop which folder you want to use as a starting point.

Figure 2.8: Use a configuration application as needed to automate Remote Desktop tasks.

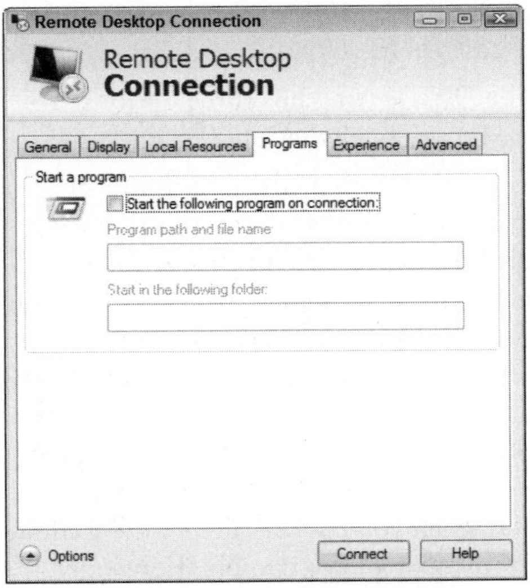

Optimize Performance

The connection you use to create a Remote Desktop is important. You can't expect the same performance from a dial-up connection that you do from a high-speed internal network. Consequently, Remote Desktop provides a method for telling it what to expect in the way of connection in order to optimize connection performance as shown in Figure 2.9.

Figure 2.9: Use only the resources you actually need to obtain good performance.

Choosing one of the default options, such as LAN (10 Mbps or Higher), automatically sets the options that Remote Desktop uses. When working with a newer setup, such as the one found in Windows 7, you have the option of clearing or adding features such as Desktop Composition. Always use the fewest features possible to enhance the performance of the connection.

When working with an older copy of Remote Desktop, you can choose Custom from the list and configure the options you want to use. Most systems actually work best with the Custom setting, even if you're working across a LAN. For example, most systems don't provide Menu and Window Animation, so you can clear this option. You'll probably want to clear the Themes and Show Contents of Window While Dragging options as well.

Terminate a Session

At some point, you'll want to end (terminate) your session with Remote Desktop. You don't actually use the Remote Desktop utility to perform this task. Instead, you rely on the resources of the remote system to tell Remote Desktop when the session is over. The following sections describe how to terminate a session.

Use the Start Menu

By far the easiest way to terminate a session is to use the Start menu. Simply choose Start ➤ Log Off. The remote system will perform the normal logoff procedure, at which point Remote Desktop will close. If you intend to turn the remote system off or reboot it after you complete maintenance, you can also choose the Start ➤ Shutdown or Start ➤ Restart commands as needed.

Use the Logoff Utility

The Logoff utility can provide an alternative for logging off the system if you're working at the command prompt and don't really want to access the GUI. In addition, the Logoff utility can provide you with additional information about the logoff procedure if you think there's a problem during this process. To perform a standard logoff, type **Logoff** and press Enter. The system will perform a standard logoff procedure, at which point Remote Desktop will end as usual. To perform a logoff where you can verify the process that the remote machine is following, type **Logoff /V** and press Enter. You'll see additional information about the logoff process that you can use for diagnostic purposes.

3

Automating Tasks

IN THIS CHAPTER, YOU WILL LEARN TO:

O ne of the best reasons to work at the command line is to automate tasks. It's not that you can forget about the task completely, but you don't have to worry about whether the task is scheduled for completion either. Barring a major problem, such as a power outage, the computer faithfully starts and completes the task for you automatically. Now, you may very well have to interpret the results later, but that's not the point—the point is that the task is automatically performed as far as the computer can complete it for you, relieving you of the burden of completing it manually.

This chapter examines task automation from a command line perspective. The goal is to configure the computer's automation to perform any task that it can complete automatically. Before you get the idea that automation somehow entails programming, you can use automation for anything. If you want the computer to perform a backup automatically, it can do it for you. Likewise, you can tell the computer to display a reminder or anything else that you'd normally use an application to perform. However, it's true that you can also use automation with any scripts you create, but automation and scripting aren't reliant on each other in any way.

View and Manage Tasks Using Scheduled Tasks

The Task Scheduler console resides in the Administrative Tools folder of the Control Panel. It pays to have a familiarity with the Task Scheduler console before you execute commands at the command line so you have a better idea of just how Task Scheduler works. The following sections discuss Task Scheduler as a service and then provide a quick overview of performing basic tasks using the GUI.

NOTE   This book assumes that you have the Administrative Tools folder displayed on both the All Programs menu and Start menu. To configure Windows to display the Administrative Tools folder this way, right-click the taskbar and choose Properties from the context menu. Select the Start Menu tab of the taskbar and Start Menu Properties dialog box and click Customize. Scroll down to the System Administrative Tools entry of the Customize Start Menu dialog box and select the Display on the All Programs Menu and the Start Menu option. Click OK twice to close both dialog boxes.

Configure the Task Scheduler

Task Scheduler is a service, not an application as most people would think about applications. The applications used to access Task Scheduler interact with the service; they don't perform any tasks directly. Consequently, you can also interact with Task Scheduler using the Service Control (SC) utility described in the "Work with Services" section of Chapter 1. Any service-related task you normally perform with SC also works with Task Scheduler. The following sections describe three tasks that you commonly perform on Task Scheduler using SC.

Start the Task Scheduler

As a safety precaution, it's a good idea to set the service to manual and manually start it as needed. To set the Task Scheduler to start manually, type **SC Config Schedule Start= Demand** and press Enter. Notice the space between the equals sign (=) and the value. Of course, if you're running tasks every day, the automatic start option makes more sense. In this case, you type **SC Config Schedule Start= Auto** and press Enter.

When you want to determine the Task Scheduler status, type **SC QueryEx Schedule** and press Enter. Use QueryEx, rather than Query, so that you obtain the Process Identifier (PID) as part of the output—many command line utilities require the PID as input. To start the Task Scheduler, type **SC Start Schedule** and press Enter.

Stop the Task Scheduler

When you finish using Task Scheduler for a particular task and you know that no other part of the operating system relies on it, you can stop Task Scheduler to save processing cycles and to make your system a bit more secure. To stop Task Scheduler type **SC Stop Schedule** and press Enter.

Set Task Scheduler Security

The Task Scheduler logs on using the Local System account. Normally, this account provides more than sufficient rights for local activities. However, when you automatically perform tasks on remote machines, you might need to change the account to handle the increased security requirements. Always make sure you have the Task Scheduler service running when you need to execute applications automatically. To change the password to another account, type **SC Config Schedule Obj= ".\AccountName" Password= "AccountPassword"** and press Enter.

Notice that the account name includes both the domain and the username. The use of a period indicates the location machine.

Never give Task Scheduler more rights than it actually requires when you perform the intended tasks. Use the Local System account whenever possible. To change the service account back to Local System, type **SC Config Schedule Obj= ".\LocalSystem" Password= ""** and press Enter. It's important to note that newer versions of Windows tighten security considerably, so you need to consider the effect of the new security measures on any tasks you want to perform. In many cases, you'll need to change the security settings of any jobs that you want to move from other servers to the local server to ensure they'll run correctly.

View Tasks

Before you add any new tasks, you must know which tasks are already configured on a system.

Use these steps to view the current list of tasks:

1. Choose Start ➤ Administrative Tools ➤ Task Scheduler. You see the Task Scheduler console shown in Figure 3.1.

Figure 3.1: The Task Scheduler console is one method of accessing the underlying service.

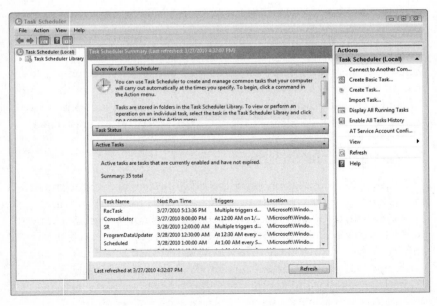

2. Click the down arrow next to Active Tasks to see the list of tasks configured on the machine.

   As shown in Figure 3.1, the demonstration system has several tasks configured on it.

3. (Optional) Click Display All Running Tasks in the Actions pane.

   You see the list of tasks that are currently running on the system as shown in Figure 3.2. You must stop these tasks before you can delete them.

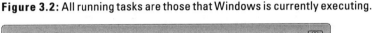

Figure 3.2: All running tasks are those that Windows is currently executing.

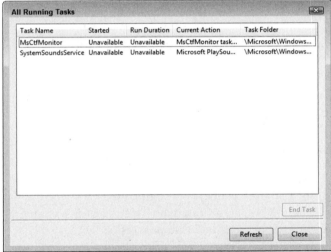

4. (Optional) Click the down arrow next to Task Status.

   This list tells you which tasks have executed and whether they succeeded. Failed tasks require interaction on your part to fix so that they run properly. In some cases, this means deleting the task because it can't succeed due to a lack of resources or a system configuration issue.

NOTE   Windows supports an alternative form of tasks that were used in older versions of Windows. These Automated Tasks (AT) originally appeared as part of the Unix operating system and are extremely limited in what they can do for you. You can create these tasks using the AT command. It's also possible to manage them using the Windows Management Instrumentation (WMI) Command line (WMIC) utility using the Job alias. (Chapters 11 and 15 tell you more about practical uses for WMIC, which are many.) The Task Scheduler GUI lets you see these tasks, but it doesn't let you create them. It's also possible to use Task Scheduler to configure the AT service account. In general, because the AT service is so limited (and ancient), you should avoid using it unless you already have a number of batch files that rely on this older technology. For this reason, the AT command and WMIC Job alias aren't discussed in this book. You can learn more about the AT command at http://support.microsoft.com/kb/313565. The WMIC Job alias isn't well documented online, so you'll need to learn about it by reading a book such as *Administering Windows Server 2008 Server Core* (Sybex, 2008).

Create New Tasks

Eventually, you want to create new tasks. One way to do this is to rely on the GUI. You can also use the SCHTasks command as described in the "Manage Tasks Using the SCHTasks Command" section of this chapter. In short, you have no lack of ways to create new tasks.

The following steps describe the GUI method of creating a basic task:

1. Use the technique described in the "View Tasks" section to ensure the task isn't already created.

2. Click Create Task in the Actions pane. You see the Create Task dialog box shown in Figure 3.3.

3. Type a name for the task in the Name field.

4. Type a task description in the Description field.

   Make sure you provide enough details so you know why you created the task, what purpose it serves, and what a successful result should accomplish.

Figure 3.3: The Create Task dialog box contains all the options for creating a new task.

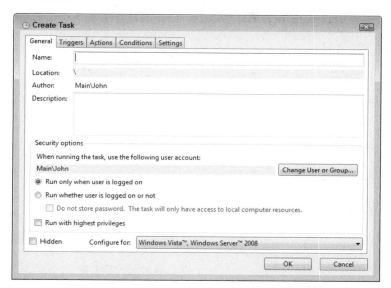

5. Choose a running option.

   Administrative tasks are normally run whether or not the user is logged on. Only user configuration or user-specific tasks require that the user is logged on because the task might need to configure the system for that particular user.

6. Choose a Configure For option.

   For maximum compatibility, select the Windows Server 2003, Windows XP, or Windows 2000 option. If you want to ensure the task runs with the best security and can access Window 7 or Windows Server 2008 R2 features, select the Windows 7, Windows Server 2008 R2 option.

7. Select the Triggers tab. Click New.

   You see the New Trigger dialog box shown in Figure 3.4. A trigger defines when to run the task, and you can configure as many triggers as needed to ensure the task runs when you need it to. Task Scheduler supports a host of trigger methods, such as on a schedule or when the user logs onto the system. You can even select specific system events.

8. Configure the trigger and click OK.

Figure 3.4: Define one or more triggers as needed to determine when to run the task.

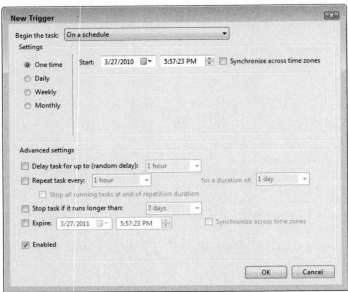

9. Repeat steps 7 and 8 to configure all of the required triggers. You should end up with one or more triggers on the Triggers tab as shown in Figure 3.5.

Figure 3.5: Every task requires at least one enabled trigger or it will never run.

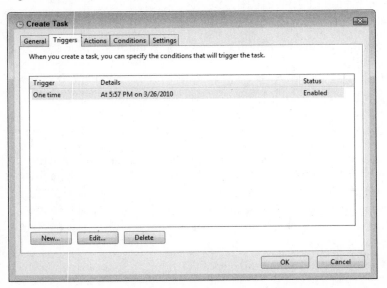

10. Select the Actions tab.

This tab shows the actions that the task will perform—you can perform more than one task at a time, such as running multiple applications. Click New. You see the New Action dialog box shown in Figure 3.6.

Figure 3.6: Actions determine what the task will perform.

11. Select one of the actions from the Action drop-down list box.

You can choose from starting a program (the most common action), sending an e-mail, or displaying a message. Fill out the fields required to perform the task and click OK.

12. Repeat steps 10 and 11 as often as necessary to define all of the actions required to complete the task. You should end up with one or more actions, as shown in Figure 3.7.

Figure 3.7: The list of actions you define determines what the task accomplishes.

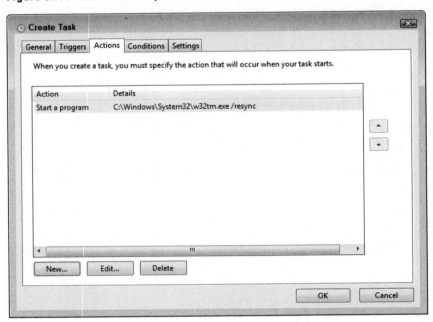

13. (Optional) Select the Conditions tab. Configure any required conditions for running that task. The default options normally work fine.

14. (Optional) Select the Settings tab. Define any required settings, such as letting the task run on demand (rather than on a schedule). The default options on this tab normally work well.

15. Click OK.

    Task Scheduler checks the task for potential errors. If the task has a trigger that schedules it to run, you see it added to the Active Tasks list shown in Figure 3.1. The task is added to the Task Scheduler Library if it isn't configured to run immediately.

Delete Existing Tasks

At some point, you'll want to remove tasks that you no longer need. To remove a task, highlight its entry in any of the lists and click Delete in the Actions pane. Task Scheduler will ask whether you're certain that you want to remove the task. Click Yes and Task Scheduler will delete the task from the list.

WARNING   Task deletion is a one-way process—there isn't any way to undo this action. Be certain that you actually do want to delete a task before you click Yes. Even though creating a task isn't difficult, it can become time consuming when you have a lot of triggers or options to configure. A good safeguard is to export the task before you delete it by clicking Export in the Actions pane and saving the task as an XML file. You can always import the XML file to recreate the task later.

Manage Tasks Using the *SchTasks* Command

The SchTasks command replicates the functionality of the Task Scheduler console using a command line interface rather than a GUI. The advantage of using SchTasks is that you can manage tasks using scripts or batch files. Because tasks have to be created on each machine individually, the SchTasks command makes it possible to automate the process of adding required tasks to a group of machines. The following sections describe how to perform Task Scheduler management using the SchTasks command.

Use the */Create* Switch

The /Create switch lets you create new tasks, just like using the Task Scheduler console. The only real difference is that you use command line switches to perform the task, which means you can enter a single command at the command prompt to create a task, rather than go through an entire series of complicated steps. The important thing to remember is that if you don't supply a command line switch, the SchTasks command assumes that you want to use a default value. When working with SchTasks, you should create a list of command line switches using the same steps as you would when you work with the GUI. The only required command line switches are /TN, which gives the task a name; /TR, which provides the name of an application to run; and /SC, which defines when to run the task.

Here's a procedure you can use to create a simple task:

1. Define the task name using the /TN *Taskname* switch, where *Taskname* is the name of the task.

2. Define the application to run using the /TR *ApplicationPath* switch, where *ApplicationPath* is the full path to the application. The arguments for the application appear after the full application path, such as /TR "Dir *.*". Notice the use of double quotes around the application name and the application arguments (*.* in this case).

3. Define a trigger using the /SC *Type* switch, where *Type* is one of the following selections:

   - Minute
   - Hourly
   - Daily
   - Weekly
   - Monthly
   - Once
   - OnStart
   - OnLogon
   - OnIdle
   - OnEvent

4. Define a schedule that's consistent with the selected trigger. The two most common switches are /ST *StartTime* and /SD *StartDate*, which define a start time and a start date.

5. (Optional) Define an interval for repeating tasks using the /RI *Interval* switch, where *Interval* is a selected interval. You can't define an interval for the Minute, Hourly, Onstart, OnLogon, OnIdle, and Onevent schedule types. The valid interval range is 1 to 599,940 minutes, with a default of 10 minutes. For example, if you want to run a task once a week, you define the interval as 1,440 minutes.

Using this procedure, you could combine a number of switches together to create a task using the following command:

```
SchTasks /Create /TN "My Special Task" /TR "Dir *.*" /SC
Once /ST "14:00:00"
```

This command creates a task named My Special Task that executes the
Dir *.* command once at 2 PM on the current day. The SchTasks command provides support for every feature that the GUI does. All you need
to do is combine the required command line switches. To see the full list
of command line switches, type **SchTasks /Create /?** and press Enter.

Use the /*Delete* Switch

When you finish using a task, you'll want to delete it. To remove a
task from the list, simply type **SchTasks /Delete /TN** *Taskname*, where
Taskname is the name of the task you want to remove.

The SchTasks command normally asks whether you're certain that
you want to delete a particular task before it actually performs the
task. Unfortunately, you might not want to interact with SchTasks from
within a batch file. In this case, add the /F command line switch—
SchTasks will delete the task without asking whether you're certain.

Use the /*Query* Switch

You use the /Query switch in a number of ways. The primary use is to
determine which tasks are running on a particular system. When you
want to view these tasks manually, type **SchTasks /Query | More**. This
form of the command obtains all of the current tasks, pipes them to the
More command, and displays them one page at a time.

Sometimes, you need to process the list of tasks. For example,
you might want to check the machine setup to ensure it has all of the
required tasks. In this case, you'll probably want the output to appear
in a file and in a form that's easier to process with a script or batch file.
In this case, you type (or add to a batch file) **SchTasks /Query /FO CSV >
Output.TXT**. The /FO switch outputs the list of tasks as Comma Separated
Values (CSV), to make processing easier. The redirection operator (>)
sends the result to Output.TXT.

A query may also include looking for a particular task. In this case,
you use the SchTasks /Query /TN *Taskname* command, where Taskname
is the name of the task you want to find. As with other forms of query,
you'll see the next scheduled run and whether the task is ready to run.

Use the /*Change* Switch

The /Change switch works just like the /Create switch. The only difference is that instead of creating a new task, you're modifying an existing task. In this case, the task must already exist or you'll see an error message. In addition, only the values you supply are changed—existing properties retain their values.

NOTE   The /Change command line switch has one limitation. You can't use this switch to change the task name. If you want to change the task name, you must use the GUI. As an alternative, you can delete the old task and then create a new one with the same values and a different name.

Use the /*Run* Switch

The /Run command line switch lets you run a task whenever you want. Simply use the SchTasks /Run /TN Taskname command, where Taskname is the name of the task you want to run.

Use the /*End* Switch

The /End command line switch lets you end a running task. Simply use the SchTasks /End /TN Taskname command, where Taskname is the name of the task you want to end. An odd output of this command is that it always reports success as long as the task exists, even if the task isn't running at the time. Consequently, a success message doesn't necessarily mean that you ended a running task—simply that the task isn't running once the command completes.

PART II
Managing Data

IN THIS PART ▶

Managing Data

PART II

4

Working with File and Directory Objects

Managing Data

PART II

F older and directory objects consume a considerable amount of the administrator's time because they're the focus of user activity. The user doesn't care much about the application that manipulates the data, but rather focuses on the data itself, which resides in files. The user doesn't understand that double-clicking a file starts a process where Windows looks for the appropriate application to open the file within the registry and that security issues, incorrect registry entries, and other problems can prevent Windows from opening the file. In short, the commands and utilities described in this chapter probably have one of the most visible effects on the way the user perceives Windows and how well you're doing your job. The following sections describe many of the directory and file management tools you can access at the command line.

Manage Directory Objects

Directory objects act as storage containers for files. The directory structure begins with the root directory that's normally specified simply with a backslash (\). Consequently, when you see C:\, you're seeing a reference to the root directory. Directories can hold other directories and files. The list of directories begins with the ultimate parent, which is the root, and ends with the bottom directory, the child. Any directory contained within another directory is the child of the directory and the container directory is the parent. You can always access the parent by using two periods (..) as a reference. The overall hierarchical structure of directories (also known as a directory tree) is hidden from user view in most cases because of the way that Windows handles directories and files. However, you must be constantly aware of the directory structure as you perform the management tasks described in the following sections.

Find Directories

Most administrators are aware that the Dir command can help locate files. However, when you use the /AD command line switch, you can use the Dir command to locate directories with ease. For example, if you type **Dir /AD C:\Windows** and press Enter, you'll see the children of the C:\Windows directory. If you further extend the command by typing **Dir /AD /S C:\Windows** and press Enter, you'll obtain a complete directory tree of the C:\Windows directory. Unfortunately, the directory tree is large and it'll pass you by at light speed. Consequently, you need some way to

slow things down. Either of the following commands will let you see the
C:\Windows directory tree at a more reasonable pace.

- `Dir /AD /S C:\Windows | More`
- `Dir /AD /S C:\Windows > WindowsTree.TXT`

In the first case, the command pipes the output of the Dir command
to the More command, which displays the output one screen at a time.
This form is useful when you simply need to locate a particular child in
the C:\Windows directory tree. In the second case, the command redirects
the output from the console window to the WindowsTree.TXT file. You
won't actually see the command execute on screen. This form is useful
when you need a more permanent record of the directory tree or if you
need to perform additional processing on the output.

Find Directories Using Patterns

Directory names might not be absolute or you might not precisely
remember the name of a directory when you search for it. For example,
many applications add version information to the directory name so
different versions of the application can reside on the same hard drive.
When this problem occurs, you can use patterns to help locate the directory. The Dir command supports the ? (single character replacement) and
* (multiple character replacement) wildcard characters that you can use to
search for directories. For example, the command Dir Win* /AD /S would
locate any directory that begins with Win starting from the current location.
Likewise, the command Dir /AD /S "Microsoft Visual Studio *.?" will
find the directory entries for any version of Microsoft Visual Studio when
executed from the root directory. Notice the use of double quotes around
search patterns that include spaces in them.

Every Windows system has environment variables defined in it and you
can define additional environment variables as needed. Some environment
variables, such as WinDir, provide path information. This path information can vary by machine, but the name of the environment variable is
always the same because Windows defines it for you. Consequently, if
you want to perform a directory listing of the Windows directory, but you
don't know where that is, you can type **Dir %WinDir%** and press Enter. The
%WinDir% part of the command expands to the Windows directory, wher-
ever that directory might be on the host machine. The environment variable must contain just one directory for this technique to work, but it's a
useful technique.

Managing Data

PART II

View the Current Directory

The command prompt normally tells you the current directory. If it doesn't, then type **Prompt PG** and press Enter. The $P tells Prompt to display the current path, while $G tells it to display a greater than (>) sign. However, you might not always be able to see the current directory, such as during the execution of a batch file. In this case, type **CD** or **ChDir** and press Enter to display the current directory. If you want to output the directory information to a file for processing within a batch file, you can always use the CD > CurDir.TXT command, which places the directory information in CurDir.TXT using redirection.

Change the Current Directory

Executing commands in the directory that contains the command or data that you need to manipulate is more efficient than trying to execute all of the commands from a single directory. The reason is simple—using paths is cumbersome and error prone. To move from the current directory to another directory, use the CD *NewDirectory* or ChDir *NewDirectory* command, where *NewDirectory* is the path that you want to use.

Paths are either absolute, such as C:\Windows or relative. Relative paths come in two forms:

- **Parent:** Type .. to move to the parent level of the current directory.

- **Child:** Type the directory name without a backslash to move to the child directory of the current directory.

Here are examples of the three directory change types:

```
CD C:\Users\John
CD ..\..
CD Windows\System32
```

In this first case, the directory will change to C:\Users\John (assuming this directory exists) no matter where you type the command because the command relies on an absolute directory location. In the second case, the directory will change to the parent of the parent of the current directory. For example, if you're at C:\Users\John, then the directory will change to the root directory because the root directory is the parent of C:\Users. In the third case, the directory changes to the C:\Windows\System32 directory assuming that you're in the root directory of the C drive.

It's also possible to combine relative forms to make moving from one directory to another more efficient. For example, if you're already in the C:\Users\John directory and want to move to the C:\Users\Amy directory, then you type **CD ..\Amy** and press Enter. The first part of the command moves to C:\Users (the parent of C:\Users\John) and the second part of the command moves to the Amy subdirectory.

Create Directories

To create a new directory, use the MD *NewDirectory* or MkDir *NewDirectory* command, where *NewDirectory* is the path of the directory you want create. In many cases, the new directory is simply a child of the current directory. For example, if you want to create MyDirectory as a child of the current directory, you type **MD MyDirectory** and press Enter. The MD and MkDir commands can use both absolute and relative directory paths. See the "Change the Current Directory" section for a description of these path types.

Move Directories

To move a directory to a new location, use the Move *OriginalPath NewPath* command, where *OriginalPath* is the absolute or relative path of the directory you want to move and NewPath is the original or relative path to the new location. For example, if you want to move MyDir from its current location to C:\Temp, you'd type **Move MyDir C:\Temp\MyDir** and press Enter. Notice that the new location must include the original directory name or Move will register an error that it can't rename an existing directory. The Move command automatically moves any files or subdirectories contained in the original directory to the new location. See the "Change the Current Directory" section for a description of the absolute and relative path types.

Rename Directories

To rename a directory, use the Move *OriginalName NewName* command, where *OriginalName* is the original name (and optionally the path) of the directory and NewName is the new name of the directory. For example, if you want to rename MyDir to MyNewDir, you'd type **Move MyDir MyNewDir** and press Enter. See the "Change the Current Directory" section for a description of the absolute and relative path types.

Managing Data

PART II

The Move command does allow you to combine move and rename tasks into a single command. To move MyDir to C:\Temp and rename it to MyNewDir, you'd type **Move MyDir C:\Temp\MyNewDir** and press Enter.

Remove a Directory

When a directory is no longer needed and contains no files or subdirectories, you can remove it from the system using the RD *DirName* or RmDir *DirName* command, where *DirName* is the absolute or relative path of the directory you want to remove. (See the "Change the Current Directory" section for a description of the absolute and relative path types.) Of course, the directory might not be empty or you might not be certain about its content.

Use the following procedure to ensure you remove directories only when you don't actually need them. (The procedure uses *DirName* to represent the directory path you want to remove.)

1. Type **Dir DirName /S /B** and press Enter.

   You see a listing of any files in the directory you want to remove. As with most command and utilities, the /S command line switch tells Dir to search all of the subdirectories. Using the /B command line switch displays the files in bare format, which means that you don't see the usual headers and other extraneous information that could clutter up the list.

2. Review the file list to make sure you don't need any of the files.

3. Type **Del DirName /S /Q** and press Enter.

   The Del command displays a list of the files it has deleted. Using the /Q command line switch tells Del to remove the files without asking you first. Otherwise, you have to answer a question about deleting each of the files.

4. Type **RD DirName /S /Q** and press Enter.

   The RD command removes the specified directory and all its subdirectories.

Display a Directory Structure

Directory structures can become complex and hard to understand, so it's good to know how to display them in a comprehensible form. The Tree utility provides a means of seeing the directory structure from any starting point on your hard drive. Simply use the Tree *StartingPath* command, where *StartingPath* is an absolute or relative path. (See the "Change the Current Directory" section for a description of the absolute and relative path types.) The output uses ASCII graphics to help you understand the directory structure. For example, Figure 4.1 shows the directory structure of a test directory, MyDir.

Figure 4.1: The Task Scheduler console is one method of accessing the underlying service.

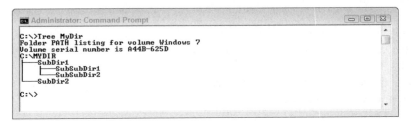

Manage File Objects

As you might expect, file objects use many of the same command forms that directory objects do. The command prompt does provide significantly more options for working with files though because drives have far more files than directories and files come in more forms. The following sections describe how to extend what you know about directory commands and utilities to files. (As with directories, finding files often involves working with absolute and relative paths. See the "Change the Current Directory" section for a description of the absolute and relative path types.)

Find Files

The Dir command provides a host of ways to locate files on your hard drive. Because Dir can check the entire drive, the results are often more accurate than provided with the Windows search mechanisms. In addition, you can sort files as needed (see the "Find Files in Sorted Order" section for details) and locate files based on their attributes (see the "Find Files by Attribute" section for details). The Dir command also supports a number of display options, such as the /X command line switch that shows you the 8.3 (8 dot 3) display name for files used in the registry. Type **Dir /?** and press Enter to see a complete list of options.

Use these steps to perform a basic search for files. (The example helps you build a command line by following each of the steps.)

1. Type **Dir** *Filename*, where *Filename* is the name of the file you want to locate.

   (You can optionally add an absolute or relative path to the file specification.)

2. (Optional) Type **/S** if the file is in a subdirectory.

3. (Optional) Type **/B** if you want the file listing displayed without the usual header information.

4. (Optional) Type **/P** if you expect to see more than one screen of file listings and want the Dir command to pause after each screen.

5. (Optional) Type **/Q** if you want to see the owner of the file.

6. (Optional) Type **/R** if you want to see the alternate streams in a file that contains multiple streams.

   (Multiple stream files contain data in a sectionalized manner and are somewhat rare, even in newer systems.)

7. (Optional) Type **/W** if you want to see just a list of filenames in the shortest space possible (in tabular format, three to six filenames across).

8. (Optional) Type **/X** if you want to see the 8.3 filenames alongside the longer filenames.

   For example, the Program Files directory becomes PROGRA~1 in 8.3 format and My Interesting File.TXT becomes MYINTE~1.TXT. Files such as Desktop.INI are already in 8.3 format, so they don't have an 8.3 equivalent.

9. Press Enter.

   The Dir command shows zero or more files using the criteria you selected. Of course, you only see a file displayed if the file exists.

Find Files in Sorted Order

When you display a directory listing, the files appear in the order in which the hard drive stores their entries, which may not always be very helpful when you need to locate a file. To obtain a sorted list of directories and files, use the `Dir /OOrder Filename` command, where `Order` is an ordering switch.

Now that you have some idea of how to use file ordering, it's time to look at the methods available for sorting. The following list describes each of the sort orders:

- /OD: Sort in date/time order with the oldest dates and times first.
- /OE: Sort by extension in alphabetic order, from A to Z.
- /OG: Place directories first in the sort order.
- /ON: Sort by name in alphabetic order, from A to Z.
- /OS: Sort by size with smallest files first.
- /O-Order: Reverse the order of the sort. For example, /O-D sorts the files and directories in date/time order with the newest dates and times first.

In some cases, a single sort won't provide the information in the required order. You can combine multiple order switches to obtain the desired effect. For example, if you want to sort by size first, and then by name, type `Dir /OS /ON` and press Enter.

Find Files by Attribute

File attributes describe files in specific ways. For example, the read-only attribute defines a file that can't be written—only read. Directories use a special directory attribute that sets them apart from files. The `Dir /AAttribute Filename` command, where `Attribute` is the attribute you want to search for, helps you locate specific kinds of files.

Now that you have some idea of how to find files using an attribute, it's time to look at the available attributes. The following list describes each of the standard attributes:

- /AA: Locates files that are ready for archiving.
- /AD: Locates directory entries.
- /AH: Locates hidden files (these are sometimes visible within Windows Explorer without any special setup).
- /AI: Displays files that aren't indexed for use in Windows Search.

Managing Data

PART II

- /AL: Displays file entries that include reparse points. A *reparse point* is special data associated with the file that defines it in a special way using custom data that's managed by a filter (such as the properties set on a Word document that you see on the Details tab of the file's Properties dialog box). You can read about reparse points at http://msdn.microsoft.com/library/aa365503.aspx.

- /AR: Locates read-only files.

- /AS: Locates system files.

- /A-*Attribute*: A prefix used to negate a standard attribute. For example, if you want to find all entries except for directories, you type **Dir /A-D** and press Enter.

The attributes are important for another reason. The Dir command won't display hidden files unless you add the /AH switch. Consequently, you might not even see some files without using an attribute switch. You can combine switches to obtain specific effects. For example, the hidden and system switches are commonly used together for operating system files. If you want to find just the operating system files on a hard drive, you can type **Dir *.* /AH /AS /S** and press Enter.

Find Files Using Patterns

Locating files using patterns is much the same as locating directories. Everything described for directories in this section of the chapter also works for files. However, you can take file processing to an entirely new level using batch files (see Part VII of the book for a description of creating batch files at the command line). Listing 4.1 shows an example of a batch file that parses the PATH environment variable and locates every LOG file in that listing.

Listing 4.1: Batch File for Processing a List of Directories

```
@ECHO OFF

@REM Obtain the current path.
Set DirPath=%PATH%

@REM Process each directory entry in turn.
:LOOP
```

```
@REM Keep processing entries until finished, and then exit.
If "%DirPath%"=="" GoTo EXIT

@REM Obtain the directory listing in the top directory.
For /F "tokens=1* delims=;" %%a in ("%DirPath%") Do Dir
%%a\*.LOG

@REM Place the remaining directory entries in DirPath.
For /F "tokens=1* delims=;" %%a in ("%DirPath%") Do Set
DirPath=%%b

@REM Process the next entry.
GoTo LOOP

@REM Exit the batch file.
:EXIT
@ECHO ON
```

In this case, the batch file creates a new environment variable named DirPath that contains the content of the PATH environment variable at the outset. However, every time the batch file processes a directory, it removes that directory from DirPath. Eventually, DirPath will equal "" (nothing) and the batch file exits.

The entries in the PATH environment variable are separated using semi-colons (;), so it's possible to use the For command to parse (separate) the individual entries. You'll discover more about the For command in Chapter 21, but the first For statement essentially tells the system to grab the first directory entry and perform a Dir *.LOG command with it. The second For statement takes everything but the first directory entry and places it in DirPath (making DirPath one directory entry shorter).

The GoTo LOOP statement simply tells the batch file to go back up to the :LOOP label. The batch file checks DirPath for any additional directory entries and processes the next directory entry or exits the batch file. Figure 4.2 shows typical results (your exact results will vary). The point of this example is that you can create any level of complexity for locating files on your system. It's possible to change this batch file to look for any file type in the path or using any other complex environment variable of your choice.

Managing Data

PART II

Figure 4.2: Batch files and pattern searches combined can make it possible to find any file with ease.

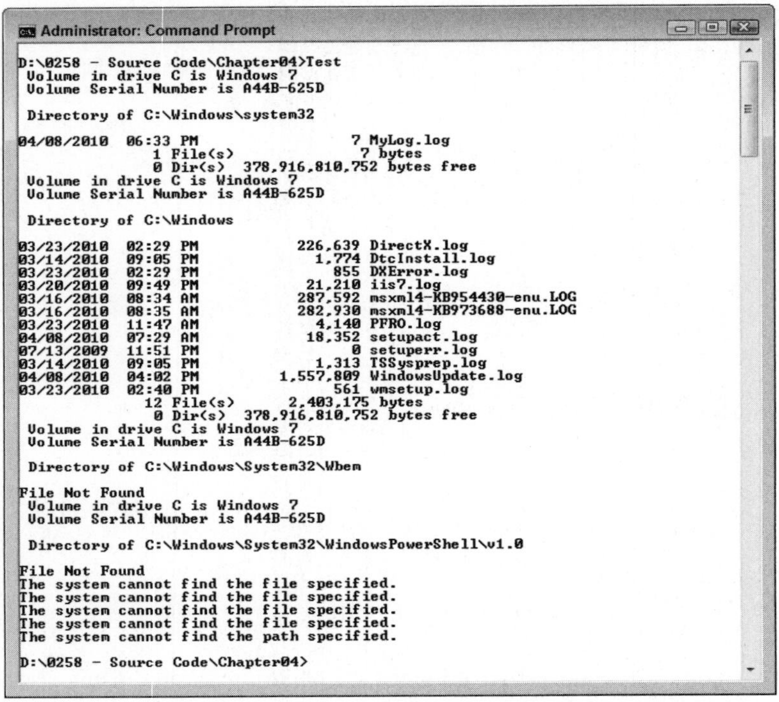

```
Administrator: Command Prompt

D:\0258 - Source Code\Chapter04>Test
 Volume in drive C is Windows 7
 Volume Serial Number is A44B-625D

 Directory of C:\Windows\system32

04/08/2010  06:33 PM                 7 MyLog.log
               1 File(s)              7 bytes
               0 Dir(s)  378,916,810,752 bytes free
 Volume in drive C is Windows 7
 Volume Serial Number is A44B-625D

 Directory of C:\Windows

03/23/2010  02:29 PM           226,639 DirectX.log
03/14/2010  09:05 PM             1,774 DtcInstall.log
03/23/2010  02:29 PM               855 DXError.log
03/20/2010  09:49 PM            21,210 iis7.log
03/16/2010  08:34 AM           287,592 msxml4-KB954430-enu.LOG
03/16/2010  08:35 AM           282,930 msxml4-KB973688-enu.LOG
03/23/2010  11:47 AM             4,140 PFRO.log
04/08/2010  07:29 AM            18,352 setupact.log
07/13/2009  11:51 AM                 0 setuperr.log
03/14/2010  09:05 PM             1,313 TSSysprep.log
04/08/2010  04:02 PM         1,557,809 WindowsUpdate.log
03/23/2010  02:40 PM               561 wmsetup.log
              12 File(s)       2,403,175 bytes
               0 Dir(s)  378,916,810,752 bytes free
 Volume in drive C is Windows 7
 Volume Serial Number is A44B-625D

 Directory of C:\Windows\System32\Wbem

File Not Found
 Volume in drive C is Windows 7
 Volume Serial Number is A44B-625D

 Directory of C:\Windows\System32\WindowsPowerShell\v1.0

File Not Found
The system cannot find the file specified.
The system cannot find the file specified.
The system cannot find the file specified.
The system cannot find the file specified.
The system cannot find the path specified.

D:\0258 - Source Code\Chapter04>
```

Copy Files

Generally, you perform file copies using Windows Explorer when you plan to perform the task manually because it's often less work to do so. However, file copying is handy within a batch process or a script. The automated process may work with file locally, but then you need to copy it to a networked or other shared location.

The following steps define what you need to consider when using the Copy command. (The example helps you build a command line by following each of the steps.)

1. Type **Copy** *SourceFile* *DestinationFile* where *SourceFile* is the original filename plus the absolute or relative path as needed and *DestinationFile* is the target filename plus the absolute or relative path of the destination.

2. Type **/V** to ensure that the copy process is verified.

Otherwise, you won't know whether the destination has a good copy of the file.

3. (Optional) Type **/D** if the source file is encrypted and you want to be sure the file is decrypted at the destination.

4. (Optional) Type **/Y** to suppress overwrite messages.

   If you don't include this command line switch, the batch file could stop in the middle of a process as it waits for user input, so you normally do include this command line switch.

5. Press Enter.

   The Copy command performs the copying process and provides notification of success or errors.

Perform Bulk File Transfers

Windows provides several utilities for performing bulk transfers of files. The most popular of these utilities is XCopy. Of course, you can also use XCopy to perform a basic file copy. XCopy is a relatively complex command line utility—type **XCopy /?** and press Enter to see a full list of command line options.

The following steps define what you need to consider when creating an XCopy command line. (The example helps you build a command line by following each of the steps.)

1. Type **XCopy** *SourceFile DestinationFile* where *SourceFile* is the original filename plus the absolute or relative path as needed and *DestinationFile* is the target filename plus the absolute or relative path of the destination.

2. Type **/V** to ensure that the copy process is verified. Otherwise, you won't know whether the destination has a good copy of the file.

3. (Optional) Type **/M** to copy only files that have the archive bit set.

   You can use this option to perform a simple type of backup. Copying the file resets the archive bit. (Use the /A command line switch if you want to leave the archive bit unchanged.)

4. (Optional) Type **/D:*m-d-y***, where *m* is the month, *d* is the day, and *y* is the year to copy only the files that were created after the specified date.

5. (Optional) Type **/S** to copy all of the files in subdirectories as well as those in the source directory.

This command line switch preserves the directory structure to create a perfect copy of complex directory setups. (If you want to also copy empty subdirectories, use the /E command line switch.)

6. (Optional) Type **/C** to continue copying files, even if an error occurs.

This command line switch helps you overcome the Windows Explorer limitation where the copy stops immediately after the first error.

7. (Optional) Type **/Q** if you want to hide the names of the files as XCopy copies them.

(Use the /F command line switch if you want to display the full path for each copied file instead of just the filename.)

8. (Optional) Type **/G** to copy encrypted files to a destination that doesn't support encryption.

9. (Optional) Type **/H** to copy hidden and system files from the source directory to the target.

10. (Optional) Type **/R** to overwrite read-only files in the target directory. Type **/K** if you want to preserve the attributes of the source files as you copy them to the target directory (normally, XCopy resets the read-only attribute).

11. (Optional) Type **/O** to copy files with full ownership and Access Control List (ACL) security information intact.

(If you also want to copy the audit settings, use the /X command line switch instead.)

12. (Optional) Type **/Y** to suppress overwrite messages.

If you don't include this command line switch, the batch file could stop in the middle of a process as it waits for user input, so you normally do include this command line switch.

13. Press Enter.

XCopy copies the files from the source directory to the target.

Remove Files

To delete files you no longer need from the hard drive, use the Del *Filename* or Erase *Filename* command, where *Filename* is the name (and optionally the path) of the file you want to remove. Unlike deleting files in Windows, this form of file deletion is permanent unless you use a file recovery program—the file doesn't go to the Recycle Bin. For example, to remove a file named MyTrashFile.TXT, you'd type Del **MyTrashFile. TXT** and press Enter.

Move Files

Moving a file performs two operations. First, the file is copied from the current directory to the target directory. Second, the file is deleted from the current directory. The result is that a single command moves the file from current directory to the target directory. To move a file, use the Move *Filename Target* command, where *Filename* is the path and name of the file you want to move and *Target* is the path and name of the file in its new location. For example, to move Temp.TXT from the current directory to C:\Temp\Temp.TXT, you'd type **Move Temp.TXT C:\Temp** and press Enter. Unless you plan to rename the file, as well as move it, you only need to supply the target directory.

Rename a File

To rename a file, use the Ren *OldName NewName* command, where *OldName* is the current name of the file and *NewName* is the new name of the file. For example, if you wanted to rename Temp.TXT to NewName.TXT, you'd type **Ren Temp.TXT NewName.TXT** and press Enter.

Set File Attributes

Special file and directory attributes control how the system views these resources and what you can do with them. To set file attributes, use the Set *AttributeSet Target* command, where *AttributeSet* is one or more attributes and *Target* is the file or directory that will receive the attribute change. To add an attribute, you precede the attribute letter with a plus sign (+). Likewise, to remove an attribute, you precede the attribute letter with a minus sign (–). For example, if you wanted to remove the system attribute from Temp.TXT, you'd type **Attrib –S Temp.TXT** and press Enter. Here's a list of the attributes you can use with the Attrib command.

- **R**: Read-only file attribute
- **A**: Archive file attribute

Managing Data

- S: System file attribute
- H: Hidden file attribute
- I: Don't index content file attribute

Work with File Associations and Types

Strictly speaking, you don't need to know anything about file associations or file types to work with files from the command prompt. However, Windows does need to know this information when working with files in the GUI. Whenever a user double-clicks a file, Windows looks up the file association based on the file extension, locates the file type information, and then executes an application to load the file based on what it finds. Consequently, knowing something about the file associations and types on your system is important, but it isn't something that you'll use from the command prompt.

Windows provides two commands for working with file associations and types. You use the Assoc command to determine and set the file associations. The file association connects a specific file type with an extension. The FType command defines the file type information. For example, you can specify what happens when a particular file type receives a request to open a file. The file types all rely on verbs, action words, to define specific tasks. The most common of these verbs are open and print, but depending on the file type, you might find many others.

The Assoc and the FType commands work together to show the relationships between file extensions and file types, and to allow you to modify these relationships. For example, an administrator could create a batch file to set up a user machine to use specific applications to handle certain kinds of files. The following sections describe these two commands.

Determine File Associations

To determine a file association, use the Assoc *FileExtension* command, where *FileExtension* is the extension you want to check. The FileExtension must include the period. For example, to check the file association for a TXT file, you type **Assoc** .**TXT** and press Enter.

Create File Associations

To create a new file association, use the `Assoc` `FileExtension=FileType` command, where `FileType` is the kind of file you want to associate with the extension. The `FileType` must exist within the registry (create it if necessary using the `FType` command). Always place an equals sign (=) between the file extension and type. For example, to associate the .TXT extension with the `txtfile` type, you'd type **Assoc .TXT=txtfile** and press Enter at the command line.

Determine File Types

To determine a file type, use the `FType` `FileType` command, where `FileType` is the kind of file you want to view. A `FileType` always includes the file type name and the associated action. For example, if you type **FType txtfile** at the command prompt and press Enter, the `FType` command responds with `txtfile=%SystemRoot%\system32\NOTEPAD.EXE %1` on a system using the default setup. In this case, `txtfile` is the file type. The action appears after the equals sign. The `%SystemRoot%` environment variable points to the Windows directory on your machine. The System32 directory contains many of the executable files including both EXEs and DLLs. The application that Windows starts to load is a text file in Notepad. The `%1` after Notepad is a placeholder for the file. You can include as many placeholders as required by the application. The action can also include any command line switches that the application requires to handle the file type.

NOTE   The FType command can display the open verb action or set the action for this verb for any file type on your system. You can also use it to create new file types as needed to express a specific file requirement. The FType command only works with the open verb, not any of the other verbs (such as `print`) that the file type might contain. Even so, this command is invaluable in setting up a system quickly.

Create File Types

To create a new file type, use the `FType` `FileType=OpenCommandString` command, where `OpenCommandString` is the location of the executable and parameters required to open a file type.

Now that you understand how to create a file type, let's build one. Use the following procedure to create a new file type:

1. Type **FType**, followed by the file type name, such as txtfile.

2. Type = to begin the open verb command line string.

3. Type a path to the command.

   Whenever possible, use an expansion variable such as %System-Root% that contains only one path entry, such as C:\Windows, as the starting point to ensure the command string works across machines. Add as much path information as needed to point directly to the application.

4. Type the application name, including extension, such as **Notepad.EXE**.

   If the application opens using a host, such as RunDLL32.EXE, supply the host application name first, the host parameters, and then the application name, and parameters as required by the host application. Remember to consider security requirements, which may mean using RunAs.EXE as the starting application, rather than starting the application directly.

5. Type **%1**, which is always the full name and path of the file as supplied by Windows.

   Windows supplies only one variable input argument.

6. Type any required application command line switches.

7. Press Enter.

   FType creates the new file type for you. Remember that creating a file type doesn't provide an association between the file type and the file extension. Use the Assoc command to perform this task.

Make Data Links

Data links create links between an existing file or directory and another location. The data link makes it appear as if the data is available from the linked location, when it physically exists in another location. The main purpose for data links is for compatibility. A directory or file might have had another name at one time, but now it has a new name, so the data link makes older programs think that the old file still exists. Data links also make it possible for a group to share a single file or to create other kinds of sharing situations. For example, you might want to make it possible for a group of people to view a file without being able to change it—the data link can have read-only rights from a shared folder, while the actual file retains read/write privileges from the original folder.

Create Simple Hard Links

Hard links make it possible to create multiple directory entries for a single file. You could use this feature for creating an entry for a shared file in each user's My Documents folder. Every user would see the same information (say a list of contacts) and it would appear that the information is in their folder, but the file itself could exist in another location. A hard link is limited to a single volume. For example, you can't create a hard link between C:\MyData.TXT and Z:\MyData.TXT, but you can create a hard link between C:\MyData\MyData.TXT and C:\AnotherLocation\MyData.TXT. There's no requirement for the names of the hard links to be the same. For example, you can create a hard link between ABC.TXT and XYZ.TXT.

To create a simple hard link, use the FSUtil Hardlink Create *NewLink OriginalFile* command, where *NewLink* is the path and filename of the new directory entry you want to create and *OriginalFile* is the path and filename of the original file. For example, if you want to create a hard link named HardLink.TXT to Temp.TXT, then you'd type *FSUtil Hardlink Create HardLink.TXT Temp.TXT* and press Enter.

View Simple Hard Links

It pays to know where hard links appear on the hard drive. To view the list of hard links associated with a particular file, use the FSUtil Hardlink List *Filename* command, where *Filename* is the name of the file that you suspect has a hard link. If the file doesn't have any hard links associated with it, the command executes without outputting any information. For example, if you wanted to see the hard links associated with Temp.TXT, you'd type **FSUtil Hardlink List Temp.TXT** and press Enter.

Delete Simple Hard Links

When you finish using a hard link, you should delete it from the hard drive. You can remove hard links in any order. To remove a hard link, use the Del *Filename* or Erase *Filename* command, where *Filename* is the name of the hard link you want to remove. Unlike a standard file delete, the file content remains accessible as long as at least one directory entry is associated with the file. For example, to remove a hard link named Hardlink.TXT, you'd type **Del Hardlink.TXT** and press Enter.

Create Hard Links Using the New Technique

The MKLink utility helps you create symbolic or hard links. You use these links to make it appear that the link is actually part of the system. Unlike the FSUtil utility, you can't use MKLink to view symbolic or hard links, or junctions.

NOTE   Junctions, another type of link, provide a connection between a nonexistent directory and an existing directory. For example, Windows Server 2008 uses a junction to provide support for the Documents and Settings folder that used to appear in Windows. The real directory is now the Users folder.

To create a hard link using the MKLink utility, use the MKLink /H NewLink OriginalFile command, where NewLink is the path and filename of the new directory entry you want to create and OriginalFile is the path and filename of the original file. For example, if you want to create a hard link named HardLink.TXT to Temp.TXT, then you'd type **MKLink /H HardLink.TXT Temp.TXT** and press Enter.

Create Symbolic Links

To create a symbolic link between two files, use the MKLink NewLink Target command where NewLink is the path of the new link and Target is the path to the original file. For example, if you wanted to create a symbolic link named SymLink.TXT to Temp.TXT, then you'd type **MKLink SymLink.TXT Temp.TXT** and press Enter.

Working with directories is a little different from files. To create a directory symbolic link on the hard drive, use the MKLink /D NewLink Target command, where **Target** is the path to the original directory. For example, if you wanted to create a symbolic directory link named SymDir to SubDir1, then you'd type **MKLink /D SymDir SubDir1** and press Enter.

Unlike hard links, symbolic links are exceptionally easy to see in the directory listing. The Dir command shows symbolic file links as <SYMLINK>, with the name of the linked file in square brackets after the link name, such as SymLink.TXT [Temp.TXT]. Directory symbolic links are similar—the directory entry shows as <SYMLINKD> (rather than <DIR>)

with the name of the linked directory in square brackets after the link name, such as SymDir [SubDir1].

Symbolic links are the most flexible type of link. For example, you can create both absolute and relative symbolic links. Symbolic links can also include complex components such as junctions or mounted folders. You can learn more about symbolic links at http://msdn.microsoft.com/library/aa365680.aspx.

Create Junctions

Junctions are a kind of soft link. They work much like hard links do, except that you have a little more freedom when you work with them. For example, links can appear on different volumes. The only requirement is that junctions must reference resources on the same computer, so you can't use a junction to create a link to a resource on another machine.

To create a junction between two resources, use the MKLink /J *NewLink Target* command, where *NewLink* is the path of the new link and *Target* is the path of the file or directory for which you want to create the link. For example, if you wanted to create a junction between JuncDir and SubDir1, you'd type **MKLink /J JuncDir SubDir1** and press Enter. Likewise, to create a junction between JuncLink.TXT and Temp.TXT, you'd type **MKLink /J JuncLink.TXT Temp.TXT** and press Enter.

Like symbolic links, junctions appear differently from standard files and directories in the directory listing provided by the Dir command. You see <JUNCTION> for either files or directories. In addition, the entry shows the name of the linked file or directory in square brackets after the link name, such as JuncDir [C:\MyDir\SubDir1] or JuncLink.TXT [C:\MyDir\Temp.TXT]. Notice that a junction entry always includes the full path to the linked file or directory.

Managing Data

PART II

5

Administering File and Directory Content

IN THIS CHAPTER, YOU WILL LEARN TO:

Managing Data

PART II

C hapter 4 discusses the file and directory structure—the physical presence of storage on the hard drive and its hierarchical organization. This chapter goes a step further by describing the content of the storage, which isn't always data—it can also be other files, directories, executable code, settings, and a wealth of other content types.

It's important to separate structure from content as you administer the hard drives and other storage devices on a system. Structure ensures the security of the content. It also makes the content easier to find and facilitates group activities. A good structure makes it possible to manipulate content with greater ease and create new content as needed.

Execute Applications Anywhere

When working in Windows, you rely on the Start menu shortcuts to start applications. However, at the command prompt, you must tell the command processor where to locate applications in most cases. (Both Windows and the command line share the ability to use file associations to start applications). Every time you request an application, the command processor begins by looking for the application in the current directory. When it doesn't find the application in the current directory, it reviews the content of the PATH environment variable and looks in every directory it finds listed there for the application. Consequently, it's important to know how to manage the PATH environment variable.

View Application Paths

Before you add any new application paths, you should view the current PATH environment variable to ensure it requires the addition. To see the current path, simply type **Path** and press Enter. However, if you're working within a batch file or script, you can type **Echo %Path%** and press Enter instead to see the path. The PATH environment variable consists of a series of directory entries, such as C:\Windows, separated by semicolons.

Set Application Paths

The positioning of a directory entry in the PATH environment variable is important. The command processor begins at the front of the list and continues until the last entry when looking for applications. The search through directories that don't contain the requested application can become time consuming. Therefore, you want to place the directories you use most often at the front of the list and those that are used least often at the back of the list. In addition, you want to periodically remove entries that aren't required from the list.

To add a new directory to the beginning of the list, type **Path=DirectoryPath;%Path%** and press Enter. DirectoryPath is the full path, including drive letter, to the directory you want to add. To add a new directory to the end of the list, type **Path=%Path%DirectoryPath;** and press Enter. Make sure you watch the PATH environment variable for potentially problematic entries. The PATH environment variable should always end with a semicolon. If you don't see one, make sure to add a semicolon to the command like this, Path=%Path%;DirectoryPath;.

Locate Information in Files

Administrators normally look for different kinds of information from other users. Even though the information appears in files, they're often files that Windows Search doesn't support. For example, an administrator might try to find executable files with a certain vendor name or phrase in them, which wouldn't be indexed by Windows Search. Sometimes, searching from the command line simply returns better results. The following sections describe some of the ways that you can use to search through files at the command line.

Find Simple Strings

Use the Find utility when your search needs are simple and you want the fastest possible response. To use the Find utility, use the Find *"Search String" FileSpecification* command, where *"Search String"* is a string that you want to find (always place the string in double quotes) and *FileSpecification* is the name of the file you want to search, such as *.TXT (you can also search single files, of course). If you want to perform a case insensitive search, add the /I command line switch. The output shows the name of each file with a matching string and the lines within the file that contain the string. If you want only a list of filenames and the number of hits within each file, use the /C command line switch.

Find Complex Strings

The Find utility is limited to simple searches where the string is straightforward. If you want to perform a complex search, you need the FindStr utility, which can perform standard, case insensitive, wildcard, and regular expression searches. For example, to find TXT files that have words that begin with H and end with o, you can type **FindStr "H*o" *.TXT** and press Enter. In this case, the asterisk (*) acts as a wildcard character. Likewise, if you wanted to find TXT files that contain the words Hello or World (or both), you can type **FindStr "Hello World" *.TXT** and press Enter. If the file must contain both words as a discrete string, then you use the /C command line switch by typing **FindStr /C:"Hello World" *.TXT** and pressing Enter.

Regular expressions are an impressive FindStr feature. For example, if you want to find TXT files that contain Hello at the beginning of the line and World at the end of the line, you'd type **FindStr "^Hello $World" *.TXT** and press Enter. The caret (^) indicates that Hello must appear at the beginning of the line and the dollar sign ($) indicates that World must appear at the end of the line. As with many utilities, type **FindStr /?** and press Enter to obtain a full list of features.

Display Files Containing Strings

Normally, FindStr displays the lines within the file that contain the text. If you want only a list of filenames (especially important when the strings gain in complexity) use the /M command line switch. For example, if you type **FindStr /M "Hello World" *.TXT** and press Enter, you see just a list of filenames that contain either Hello or World.

Unlike the Find utility, you can also use FindStr to search a directory tree. Simply add the /S command line switch to search all of the child directories of the directory that you specify. When you combine this feature with redirection, you can create unique file listings for future reference. For example, to find all of the EXE files on a hard drive that contain a Microsoft copyright and place that list in a text file for future reference, type **FindStr /M /S "Microsoft" *.EXE > MicrosoftEXE.TXT** and press Enter. The resulting listing does come in handy when you need to find the location of a specific executable later. The same technique works for other copyrighted files. You may want to locate all of the files from a specific vendor in order to completely remove a stubborn application from a hard drive. This technique is a good first step in the right direction.

Perform Case Insensitive Searches

Many administrative searches are case sensitive. If you perform a case insensitive search, you may have to wait a very long time for the search to complete due to all of the permutations of capitalization found in some types of files. However, there are times where you must perform a case insensitive search. In this case, use the /I command line switch. For example, to find all of the TXT files that contain the phrase hello world, no matter how the phrase is capitalized, you'd type FindStr /I /C:"hello world" *.TXT and press Enter.

Monitor the File System with the *FSUtil* Command

The File System Utility (FSUtil) is one of the more important utilities to know about when administering a system. This single utility can perform a host of tasks on any drive. You'll find yourself using it relatively often. In fact, you've already seen one use of the FSUtil in the "Make Data Links" section of Chapter 4. The following sections provide a description of how to use basic FSUtil features. To see a complete list of FSUtil features, type **FSUtil** and press Enter. Display help for a particular command by using the FSUtil *Command* /?, where *Command* is the name of the command you want to see, such as Volume.

Control File System Behavior

The FSUtil Behavior command controls how the file system works. For example, you can modify the use of the older DOS 8-character filename, with a 3-character file extension. Each setting acts as an on/off switch for a particular file system behavior. The following sections tell how to query and set common behaviors.

Control Extended Character Use

The AllowExtChar setting determines whether you can use extended characters, including diacritic characters used for languages other than English, in the short filenames on New Technology File System (NTFS) volumes. The default configuration doesn't provide a value for this option. Setting the value to 1, or true, allows you to use the extended character set. To view the current AllowExtChar setting, type **FSUtil Behavior Query AllowExtChar** and press Enter. To allow use of extended characters, type **FSUtil Behavior Set AllowExtChar 1** and press Enter.

Check for Errors

The BugcheckOnCorrupt setting tells the system to check for bugs on the NTFS volumes. (This feature first appeared in Vista and isn't available with older versions of Windows.) The system issues a 0x00000024 stop error when it encounters corruptions on the volume. This setting keeps NTFS from silently deleting files when it encounters corruption—letting the administrator perform a backup of data before self-healing takes place. Unfortunately, the BugcheckOnCorrupt setting is disabled by default. To view the current BugcheckOnCorrupt setting, type **FSUtil Behavior Query BugcheckOnCorrupt** and press Enter.

Use these steps to set NTFS to provide the 0x00000024 stop error:

1. Type **FSUtil Behavior Set BugcheckOnCorrupt 1** and press Enter.

2. Reboot the computer after you make the settings change or it won't take effect.

3. Type **FSUtil Repair Set C: 0x10** and press Enter to set the C drive to use the BugcheckOnCorrupt setting.

4. Repeat step 3 for the other drives you want to protect. Substitute the appropriate drive letter for other drives.

Configure 8.3 Filename Support

The Disable8dot3 setting determines whether Windows supports older DOS naming conventions or uses extended filenames exclusively. The older DOS naming conventions relied on an 8-character filename and a 3-character file extension. Disabling this support could cause some applications to fail because the 8.3 naming convention is easier to use reliably within applications and applications don't really care that much about long filenames.

The default value is 0, or false, which means that the older DOS naming convention is available. To view the current Disable8dot3 setting on a pre-Windows 7 system, type **FSUtil Behavior Query Disable8dot3** and press Enter. To allow use of 8.3 character filenames on pre-Windows 7 systems, type **FSUtil Behavior Set Disable8dot3 0** and press Enter.

Windows 7 adds a new wrinkle to the Disable8dot3 setting that you need to be careful about. When you type **FSUtil Behavior Query Disable8dot3** and press Enter, you can see any of the following values:

- 0: Short name creation enabled for the entire file system
- 1: Short name creation disabled for the entire file system
- 2: Short name creation per volume
- 3: Short name creation on the system volume only

The use of per-volume settings on Windows 7 changes how you work with 8.3 names. The default value on a Windows 7 system is 2, which lets you set 8.3 support for each volume. When working with a Windows 7 machine, type **FSUtil Behavior Query Disable8dot3 C:** (where C: is the volume you want to check) and press Enter to see the current 8.3 name support status. To set an individual volume's 8.3 name support, type **FSUtil Behavior Set Disable8dot3 C: 0** (where C: is the volume you want to set) and press Enter. If you want to disable 8.3 name support on a particular volume, type **FSUtil Behavior Set Disable8dot3 C: 1** (where C: is the volume you want to set) and press Enter.

Configure Compression

The DisableCompression setting configures compression for the affected file system object. The default value is 0, or false, which means that compression is available. To view the current DisableCompression setting, type **FSUtil Behavior Query DisableCompression** and press Enter. To allow use of file compression, type **FSUtil Behavior Set DisableCompression 0** and press Enter.

Configure Encryption

The DisableEncryption setting configures encryption for the affected file system object. The default value is 0, or false, which means that encryption is available. To view the current DisableEncryption setting, type **FSUtil Behavior Query DisableEncryption** and press Enter. To allow use of file compression, type **FSUtil Behavior Set DisableEncryption 0** and press Enter.

Managing Data

PART II

Control the Last Access Attribute

The DisableLastAccess setting determines whether Windows changes the last access time stamp for a directory or file each time you list the directory contents on an NTFS volume. The default setting doesn't provide a value for this option under older versions of Windows (Windows 7 automatically configures this setting to 1). Setting this option to 1, or true, will increase disk performance slightly, but then you'll lack last access time statistics when working with the drive. To view the current DisableLastAccess setting, type **FSUtil Behavior Query DisableLastAccess** and press Enter. To ensure the system provides last access time statistics, type **FSUtil Behavior Set DisableLastAccess 0** and press Enter.

Encrypt the Paging File

The EncryptPagingFile setting determines whether the system encrypts the paging file to ensure third parties can't obtain information about your system by reading it. For example, it may be possible to read passwords as part of the paging file under certain conditions. Using this setting incurs a significant performance penalty. The default value is 0, or false, which means that the paging file isn't encrypted. To view the current EncryptPagingFile setting, type **FSUtil Behavior Query EncryptPagingFile** and press Enter. To keep the system from encrypting the paging file, type **FSUtil Behavior Set EncryptPagingFile 0** and press Enter.

Manage the Volume Dirty Bit

The FSUtil Dirty command checks or sets the dirty bit for a volume. The system automatically performs an AutoChk (a boot time ChkDsk equivalent) whenever it detects the dirty bit during startup. The AutoChk utility looks for drive errors. You can repair drive errors using the FSUtil Repair command.

Query Dirty Bit Status

The Query command determines whether the specified volume is dirty (requires a check). To view the current status of a volume, type **FSUtil Dirty Query C:** and press Enter (where C: is the volume you want to check). The output tells whether or not the specified volume is dirty.

Set the Dirty Bit

The Set command lets you set the dirty bit for the specified volume. You can use this command when you suspect a volume contains errors and want to check it during the next boot cycle. To set the dirty bit, type **FSUtil Dirty Query C:** and press Enter (where C: is the volume you want to AutoChk). After you set the dirty bit, you can't clear it, so setting the dirty bit always results in a drive check during the next boot cycle.

Obtain the File System Information Using *FSInfo*

The FSUtil FSInfo command is one of the more interesting and immediately usable commands. It provides you with statistics regarding the file system. For example, you can use it to obtain a list of active drives on the current system. You could redirect this list to a text file for use with a script or output it to a batch file to perform a task on every attached drive. The following sections describe this command in more detail.

List the Drives

The Drives command displays the current list of active drives on the system. To see a list of all current drives (both local and remote), type **FSUtil FSInfo Drives** and press Enter.

Get the Drive Type

The Drivetype command displays the drive information for the specified volume. You must specify a volume letter. The output is a generic term for the drive type such as Fixed Drive or CD-ROM Drive. For example, if you type **FSUtil FSInfo Drivetype C:** and press Enter, the utility will likely tell you that C: is a fixed drive.

Discover the General Volume Information

The VolumeInfo command displays statistics about the specified volume including the volume name, volume serial number, maximum component length, and file system name. In addition, the output tells whether the drive supports case sensitive filenames, Unicode in filenames, file-based compression, disk quotas, sparse files, reparse points, object identifiers, the encrypted file system, and named streams. Finally, you can determine whether the volume preserves the case of filenames, and if it

Managing Data

PART II

preserves and enforces Access Control Lists (ACLs). For example, if you type **FSUtil FSInfo VolumeInfo C:** and press Enter, you see the statistics for the C drive.

Discover the NTFS Volume Information

The NTFSInfo command displays the low-level statistics about the NTFS volume. This information includes NTFS version, number of sectors, total clusters, free clusters, total reserved clusters, bytes per sector, bytes per cluster, bytes per file record segment, and clusters per file record segment. In addition, you can learn the following MFT statistics: valid data length, start location (MFT1 and MFT2), zone start, and zone end. For example, if you type **FSUtil FSInfo NTFSInfo C:** and press Enter, you see the NTFS statistics for the C drive.

Get the Drive Statistics

The Statistics command displays a list of the operational statistics for the specified volume. The statistics include the following user information: UserFileReads, UserFileReadBytes, UserDiskReads, UserFileWrites, UserFileWriteBytes, and UserDiskWrites. These are all standard counters, so you can also access them using the Performance console. In addition to user information, you can obtain metadata, MFT, root file, and log file statistics. For example, if you type **FSUtil FSInfo Statistics C:** and press Enter, you see the drive statistics for the C drive.

Manage Quotas

Quotas help keep resource usage under control on systems with multiple users. Each user receives a specific amount of disk space to use for personal needs. Every file that has the user as an owner counts against the total. When the user exceeds their quota, the system informs both the user and the administrator (using a system of violation notifications). The following sections describe how to perform quota-related tasks.

Enforce Quotas

The Enforce command enables quota enforcement for the specified resource. This option doesn't enable tracking. To configure quotas, you follow a procedure similar to this one (which configures quotas for a volume named C: and sets a quota for user John of 20 GB with a warning at the 80 percent level):

1. Type FSUtil Quota Track C: and press Enter.

2. Type FSUtil Quota Enforce C: and press Enter.

3. Type FSUtil Quota Modify C: 21474836480 17179869184 John and press Enter.

   The first number, 21474836480 (or 20 GB), is the quota in bytes, while the second number, 17179869184 (or 16 GB), is the threshold at which the user receives a warning in bytes.

4. Perform step 3 for each of the users you want to configure.

5. Type FSUtil Quota Query C: and press Enter. You see a list of the quotas set on the system.

6. Verify that each of the quotas is set correctly.

See Existing Quotas

The Query command displays the query settings for the specified resource. In addition to the actual quota settings, this command displays the per user settings. This information includes the user SID, change time, quota used, quota threshold, and quota limit. For example, if you type FSUtil Quota Query C: and press Enter, you see the current quota settings for the C drive.

Track Quotas

The Track command enables quota tracking for the specified resource. This option doesn't enable enforcement of any rules you have in place. For example, if you type FSUtil Quota Track C: and press Enter, you enable quota tracking for the C drive.

View Quota Violations

The Violations command displays a list of quota violations found in the event log. If the event log doesn't have any quota violations, the utility displays a "No quota violations detected" message. The utility checks both the system and application logs for both quota threshold and quota

Managing Data

limit violations. To see a list of quota violations, type FSUtil Quota
Violations and press Enter.

Modify Quotas

The Modify command changes the quota settings for a particular user.
You must supply the drive, threshold, limit, and user name when using
this command. For example, if you want to change the settings for user
John to support a 20 GB quota limit and a 16 GB warning threshold on
drive C, you'd type FSUtil Quota Modify C: 21474836480 17179869184
John and press Enter.

Disable Quotas

The Disable command stops quota tracking and enforcement for the
specified resource. For example, if you type FSUtil Quota Disable C:
and press Enter, you disable quotas for the C drive.

Set the Notification Interval

The FSUtil Behavior QuotaNotify command defines the interval between
disk quota violation checks on an NTFS drive. The disk quota system
ensures that a user doesn't use more resources than the administrator
allows. The default setting is 3,600 seconds or 1 hour when you enable
the quota system. You can supply any value between 1 second and
4,294,967,295 seconds. Longer intervals enhance system performance,
but could result in more quota violations. To determine the current
interval, type FSUtil Behavior Query QuotaNotify and press Enter. To
change the current setting, type FSUtil Behavior Set QuotaNotify 3600
(where 3600 is an interval in seconds) and press Enter. You must reboot
the system for this change to take effect.

Repair File System Errors

The FSUtil Repair command lets you repair a file system object from
the command line. You use it to place the system object in a known
good state. In some cases, repairing the system object could mean data
loss because the object is broken in such a way that repairing it means
losing the data (perhaps due to a pointer or other problem).

Query Volume Status

The Query command determines the repair status of the specified volume. The repair status defines what kinds of repairs you can perform on the volume.

The status includes any of the following values:

0x01 The volume supports general repair (also known as self-healing).

0x08 The volume warns about potential data loss when performing a repair.

0x10 (Windows Vista and Above) The volume disables automatic repairs after it encounters corruption for the first time and provides a 0x00000024 stop error (see the "Check for Errors" section of this chapter for details).

To query the status of a drive, type **FSUtil Repair Query C:** and press Enter, where C: is the volume you want to check. You'll see a list of flags set for the volume.

Set the Volume Flags

The Set command changes the repair status of the specified volume. To set the repair status, type **FSUtil Repair Set C: 1** (self-heals silently), **FSUtil Repair Set C: 9** (self-heals with warnings of data loss), or **FSUtil Repair Set C: 0x10** (warns of corruption and disables self-healing) and press Enter (where C: is the volume you want to change). The number supplied with the command (the flag) contains a number that specifies the repair status. See the "Query Volume Status" section for a list of acceptable values.

Initiate a Repair

The Initiate command performs a repair of the specified file on the referenced volume. To use this feature, you must provide the segment number of the file, which means having a detailed knowledge of the disk organization. For example, to fix a file having a segment number of 0x001600000000123D on drive C, you'd type **FSUtil Repair Initiate C: 0x001600000000123D** and press Enter. Normally, you receive the segment number as output from another repair utility such as ChkDsk.

Managing Data

PART II

Display Data Files

Normally, you rely on special applications to see the content of data files. However, administrators don't always have a special application installed when they need it—they may need to see a file quickly before a system is up and running. Some types of data are also impromptu and temporary in nature, which means that you need to see it now and probably won't need it later. In either case, the administrator can rely on a number of techniques to obtain the desired results as described in the following sections.

Display a Data File on Screen

The Type command is one of the simplest commands you can use. It attempts to display any file you feed it, including executable files. In fact, except for some beeping and strange visual effects, it's quite possible to scan an executable file using just the Type command. To display any file using the Type command, use the Type Filename command, where Filename is the name of any file. For example, to see Temp.TXT, you type **Type Temp.TXT** and press Enter. The Type command doesn't provide any filtering, so you normally need to combine it with some type of data redirection (described in the "Employ Data Redirection" section of the chapter) or the More utility (described in the "Display Data One Page at a Time" section of the chapter).

Employ Data Redirection

Data redirection is the process of sending data from one command or utility to another command or utility. You can also redirect command or utility output to a device (see the "Understanding Command Line Devices" sidebar in this chapter for details on standard devices) or a file. Redirection provides the means for sending output to a location other than the standard output device (the console), obtaining input from a device other than standard input (the keyboard), and using something other than the standard error device (usually the console) to report problems. The command line supports three forms of redirection: input, output, and pipe. Each requires use of specialized symbols.

Understanding Command Line Devices

You can access a number of devices from the command line. Some devices accept input, others output, and some accept both. These devices always reference a physical device of some type. In some cases, the device isn't attached to your machine, but it's accessible from your machine, such as a network printer. Many commands and utilities let you use a device in place of a drive letter as an argument. For example, the Copy command lets you use input from a device to create a file. You can also use a file as output to a device. Here's the standard list of command line devices.

CON   The system console, which is the combination of keyboard and monitor used to access the computer system. Input comes from the keyboard and output goes to the monitor.

PRN   The default printer. You must configure network printers to provide a port to support a command line device. The port appears on the Ports tab of the network printer's Properties dialog box. Even if your printer can provide bidirectional communication, the PRN device is only capable of output.

LPT1 through LPT4   The printer attached to the first through fourth printer (parallel) ports. The device need not physically attach to the parallel port; Windows can redirect the output to the physical device for you. You must configure network printers to provide a port to provide a command line device. The port appears on the Ports tab of the network printer's Properties dialog box. Even if your printer can provide bidirectional communication, the LPT devices are only capable of output.

AUX   The auxiliary device; the one serviced by the first serial port (COM1). It's usually better to reference COM1 directly for readability in batch files. The AUX device is a holdover from the early days of DOS.

NUL   The output doesn't go anywhere. The NUL(L) device is also known as the bit bucket.

**CLOCK$**   This device is supposed to access the real-time clock. In reality, the device normally doesn't work in modern systems and Windows makes no effort to provide required redirection. You should avoid using the CLOCK$ device.

COM1 through COM4   The communication device attached to the first through fourth serial ports. Although standard outputs for this port include modems, you can connect printers as well. The serial port can act as both an input and an output device. You can configure network printers to use a COM port instead of an LPT port using the Ports tab of the network printer's Properties dialog box.

Managing Data

PART II

One of the most common forms of redirection is the pipe and it uses the pipe symbol (|) that appears over the backslash on most keyboards. In fact, the pipe is much older than the PC and appears in the earliest Unix operating systems (see the history at http://www.linfo.org/pipes.html for details). The pipe accomplishes what its name implies; it acts as a pipe between small applications. You connect the applications using the pipe and data flows between the applications using the pipe. For example, you can temporarily connect the Dir command to the Sort command to create a customized directory output using a command like this:

```
Dir /A-D | Sort /+13
```

The resulting command obtains a listing of the current directory without the directory entries, and sorts them by the time column. Figure 5.1 shows the results of this command.

Figure 5.1: Combining commands and utilities makes the command prompt extremely flexible.

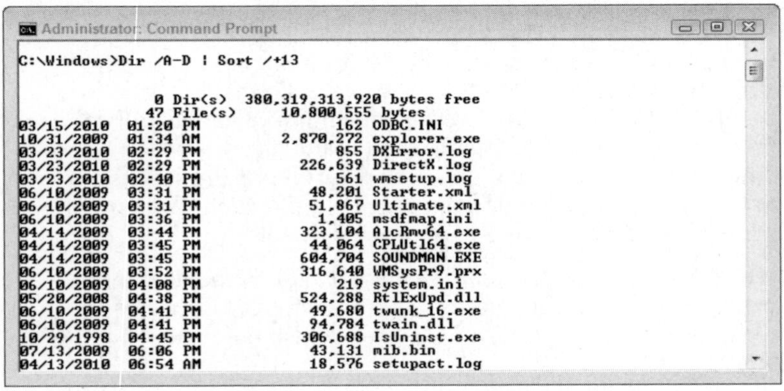

Redirection always works with a file or other streaming device. You never use redirection with another command. The two types of redirection are input and output, with output being the most commonly used. To output the results of a command such as Dir or Sort to a file, you use a greater than sign (>) or output redirection pointer. Windows clears the file if it exists and places the command output in it. However, you might want to place the results of several commands into a file. In this case, you use two greater than signs (>>). A double output redirection pointer always appends the output of a command to the existing file. Here's an example of sending the output of the Dir command to a file:

```
Dir *.TXT > MyFile.TXT
```

In this case, you'd end up with a file called MyFile.TXT that contains a list of all of the text files in the current directory.

Input relies on the less than symbol (<) or input redirection pointer. You can always use a file as input to a command that's expecting text or record data. In some cases, you can use file input to generate commands as well. The point is that a file or other streaming device acts as input. Although it's extremely uncommon, you also have access to a double input redirection pointer (<<). This symbol appends input to previous input for a command.

The combination of an output redirection pointer and an input redirection pointer can be the same as a pipe. Here's an example of the two forms of redirection used together:

```
Dir /A-D > MyFile.TXT
Sort /+13 < MyFile.TXT
```

In this case, the output of the Dir command appears in MyFile.TXT. The second command uses MyFile.TXT as input to the Sort command. The result is the same as the pipe example shown in Figure 5.1.

Although you can only include one redirection symbol on a command line, you can use as many pipes as needed to accomplish a task. This means that you can create a series of pipes to connect any number of commands and create some interesting command sequences. For example, you can combine the Dir, Sort, and More commands as shown here to provide output where you see one display at a time (see the "Display Data One Page at a Time" section for details on the More utility).

```
Dir /A-D | Sort /+13 | More
```

Display Data One Page at a Time

In many cases, the output of a command spans more than a single page on the console. If the output is short enough, you can always scroll forward or backward to see the information. However, the output is often so long that the display buffer fills and the old information is lost, making

Managing Data

PART II

it impossible to see the results of the entire command. The More utility
makes it possible to see the output a single screen at a time. All you do is
redirect the output of any command, even help, to the More utility using
the pipe. For example, if you want to redirect the output of the Dir com-
mand to the More utility, you type **Dir | More** and press Enter.

The More utility includes an extended mode that you enable using
the /E command line switch. The extended mode provides additional
functionality to make it easier to work with output files. For example,
you can display a few additional lines to see part of a continuation of
data in a file.

The following list describes the extended mode commands, which
you can type at the More prompt:

P *n* Displays the next *n* lines of the file. Type the **P** command.
You'll see a Lines prompt. Type the number of lines to display and
press Enter.

S *n* Skips the next *n* lines of the file (doesn't display them). Type
the **S** command. You'll see a Lines prompt. Type the number of lines
to display and press Enter.

F Displays the next file in the list. If there's no next file, the More
utility ends. This action doesn't necessarily end the previous application in the pipe. Press Ctrl+C to end the previous command (such
as Type) as necessary.

Q Quits the More utility without displaying any additional data.
This action doesn't necessarily end the previous application in the
pipe. Press Ctrl+C to end the previous command (such as Type) as
necessary.

= Shows the number of the current line of text. For example, if the
More utility is currently displaying the 49th line in the file, you'll
see Line: 49 as part of the More prompt.

? Shows the list of extended commands.

<space> Displays the next page of the file.

<enter> Displays the next line of text in the file.

The More utility provides a simple prompt at the bottom of the command window for entering display commands. You can only move forward in a file, not backward. Whenever you enter a command, the More
prompt extends to request any additional information. Figure 5.2 shows

the More prompt after typing the **P** command. Notice that the prompt contains the Lines: entry that lets you input the number of lines to display.

Figure 5.2: Using the More utility in extended mode makes it easy to manipulate the on-screen display.

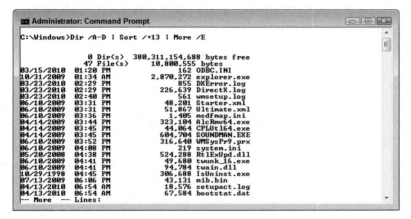

Managing Data

PART II

6

Managing the Hard Drive

IN THIS CHAPTER, YOU WILL LEARN TO:

Managing Data

PART II

A s the primary means of data storage and also the only mechanical part of consequence in most computers, the hard drive merits special attention on the part of the administrator. The mechanical nature of current hard drive technology means that it has a higher failure rate than just about any other part in the system (fans also fail, but let's face it—a failed fan is hardly going to cause lost sleep). Over time, administrators have come up with all kinds of methods for mitigating some of the reliability concerns of hard drives. One of those techniques is to maintain the hard drive in such a way as to find hard drive errors before they become a problem.

Because a hard drive is all about storage, it must also be managed appropriately to ensure that everyone gets their fair share. Given the low cost of storage today, it might seem as if allocating storage would be the smallest administrator worry, but even with the low cost, ensuring that everyone has enough space for their ever-expanding data is a problem for many administrators.

This chapter focuses on techniques you can use to work with hard drives at the command prompt. Of course, you'll need additional techniques that aren't found in this book to perform tasks such as managing your Redundant Array of Inexpensive Disks (RAID). The techniques in this chapter are more general in nature and will help you work with just about any hard drive setup to improve both reliability and accessibility.

NOTE   Many administrators will falsely assume that "hard drive" refers just to the spinning disks in a system. However, the hard drive utilities in this chapter also work with solid state drives. Of course, you must consider the kind of drive when using a utility. For example, thumb drives (those that plug into a USB port) usually use the File Allocation Table (FAT) file system, rather than the New Technology File System (NTFS) that Windows typically uses for a spinning hard drive. As a consequence, you must use the utilities in the same way that you would with a FAT system when working with a thumb drive. Removable media also benefits from these utilities. For example, you can use many of these utilities with your erasable DVD drive. In short, if you have a doubt, at least try the utility with your newer technology drive to see if the utility will work.

Save Hard Drive Space

In the day and age of the cheap hard drive, where almost no one seems to even compress their hard drive any longer, it seems almost silly to discuss saving hard drive space. However, the reality for most companies is that users still find ways to fill all of the available space on a server's drive with seemingly limitless quantities of data of dubious worth. The Compact utility makes it possible to compress and uncompress data as needed. Perhaps there's a temporary space crunch and you want to compress the largest files to make room.

NOTE   Some administrators look only at the most obvious use of the Compact utility, which is to save space on the hard drive. However, compressing data on the hard drive can have a useful side effect, which is to improve hard drive performance. A compressed file (one where the compression is high) requires less time to read from the hard drive and decompressing it on the fly requires only a few processing cycles. The biggest performance boost occurs on large files that compress well. Of course, if the file doesn't compress very much, it may still require the same amount of time to read from the hard drive, but now there's the additional overhead of decompressing it. Consequently, in some cases, file compression can also reduce performance. A good general rule of thumb is that graphics and other data files compress well and provide a reasonable performance boost when compressed, while executables tend not to compress well and will actually cause a performance hit.

Compress Data

It's possible to compress everything from a single file to a directory to an entire hard drive using a single command. To compress data, use the Compact /C *Object* command where *Object* is a file or directory. If you want to compress an entire directory tree, include the /S command line switch. In some cases, errors will occur when you try to compress files that aren't normally compressed, such as system files. To ensure your batch file or script works as anticipated, use the /I command line switch, which tells Compact to ignore the error. For example, to compress the C:\MyDir directory and its subdirectories regardless of errors, you'd type **Compact /C /S /I C:\MyDir*.*** and press Enter.

Managing Data

PART II

Unlike using the GUI, the Compact utility actually provides you with useful information as output when you type a command. You see the compression ratios of each file as the utility compresses them, along with the overall compression ratio for the entire process. This information helps you make the decision as to whether compression is a good option for the directory and its content.

Uncompress Data

At some point, you may decide to uncompress data. For example, you might not achieve the performance boost that you thought you might when using file compression. To uncompress data use the Compact /U *Object* command, where *Object* is a file or directory. If you want to uncompress an entire directory tree, include the /S command line switch. For example, to uncompress the C:\MyDir directory and its subdirectories, you'd type **Compact /U /S C:\MyDir*.*** and press Enter. The output from this command simply tells you whether the file or directory uncompressed successfully.

View Compression Status

You can set Windows Explorer to display compressed files and directories in a different color from other files and directories. However, you can't tell whether or not a file or directory is compressed at the command line without issuing a command. To determine the compressed status of a file or directory, use the Compact *Object* command, where *Object* is a file or directory. If you want to check the status of subdirectories as well, use the /S command line switch. For example, to check the status of the C:\MyDir directory and its subdirectories, you'd type **Compact /S C:\MyDir*.*** and press Enter. The output shows the current compression ratio of files. In addition, you can see whether new files added to a directory are automatically compressed.

Manage the Volume

Hard drive management is one of the more important administrative tasks and you can perform most (if not all) of these tasks at the command line. Management means everything from making the hard drive more accessible to ensuring that the data remains safe (both secure and reliably accessible). Of course, you have to maintain security and reliability without overly encumbering the hard drive—making it perform poorly. The following sections describe many of the hard drive management tasks you can perform at the command line—from the simple to the complex.

Get Volume Information

The Vol command is quite simple. To use it, simply type **Vol** and press Enter. The output shows the volume name and serial number. The volume name (or label) can be blank, but the serial number always has a value associated with it.

Someone can easily tamper with the volume name, but the serial number remains the same until the next time you format the drive unless you write a special application to make the change (see the article at www.codeproject.com/KB/system/change_drive_sn.aspx as an example). Although the serial number isn't guaranteed to be unique (it's normally based on the date you format the drive), you can use it as a means of validating precisely which drive you're working with in any given organization, assuming no one goes around and purposely changes the serial numbers.

Manage Volume Labels

The Label command makes it easy to give a volume a meaningful name. For example, if accounting has its own hard drive, you might want to label that hard drive **Accounting**. To use the Label command, type **Label** followed by the name you want to assign, and then press Enter. For example, if you want to make drive D the Accounting drive, then you'd type **Label D: Accounting** and press Enter. You can change the label of a hard drive at any time. In addition, if you use the Label command without supplying a volume name, the command erases the current label from the hard drive. You can also use the Label command to label mount points by specifying the /M command line switch.

Format a Disk

Formatting a disk prepares it for use by setting down control tracks that the drive uses to locate, read, and write data. You can use the Format utility with any permanent media such as a hard drive. The following sections describe basic use of the Format utility.

Perform a Quick Format

Many drives are so large now that performing a full format can require hours. Drives are now tested during the manufacturing process and have become more reliable as well, making a full format unnecessary in many cases. A quick format makes the drive ready for use in just a few seconds. To perform a quick format, use the Format /Q *DriveLetter* command, where *DriveLetter* is the letter of the drive you want to format. For example, if you want to format the C drive, you type **Format /Q C:** and press Enter.

Create Drives with Specific Characteristics

The Format utility can create drives with a vast array of characteristics that can do everything from improve compatibility with other systems, increase storage potential, and enhance security. To improve compatibility, you can use the /FS:FileSystem command line switch, which determines the file system used by Format. The current version of the utility supports FAT, FAT32, exFAT, NTFS, and UDF (Universal Disk Format). When working with UDF, you can also specify a UDF version number of 1.02, 1.50, 2.00, 2.01, or 2.50 using the /R:Revision command line switch.

Storage potential depends on how allocation units are used. For example, if you store a 1 byte file in a 4,096 byte allocation unit, the hard drive has 4,095 bytes of wasted space. Tuning the allocation size to meet the storage demands of the data on the hard drive can improve storage capacity. To tune the allocation units, you use the /A:*Size* command line switch with the appropriate allocation unit size. For example, NTFS supports allocation unit sizes of 512, 1,024, 2,048, 4,096, 8,192, 16K, 32K, and 64K.

The /P:*Passes* command line switch is actually a security feature. This command line switch writes zeros to every sector on the hard drive for the number of passes you specify. The more passes you use, the less likely it is that anyone can ever retrieve any of the information on the hard drive. Of course, using this command line switch also imposes a performance penalty because you have to wait for the drive to write all those zeros.

Mount a Volume

Simply having a volume available doesn't mean you can use it. In order to use a volume, you must mount it. At one time, mounting was a physical process in which the administrator would physically place a volume on the spindle for reading. Now it's a logical process—mounting the drive simply means to make it available for use. Generally, Windows automatically mounts all of the volumes on a system during startup. To disable automatic volume mounting, type **MountVol /N** and press Enter. When you want to reenable automatic mounting, type **MountVol /E** and press Enter. You dismount the volume to perform certain forms of maintenance on it and then mount it when you're finished.

List the Volumes

Many administrators associate a volume with a drive letter. However, this isn't the case when it comes to MountVol. What you really need is the volume's Globally Unique Identifier (GUID) as it appears in the registry. In order to get this number, you type **MountVol** and press Enter. The beginning of the output shows help information for MountVol, but what you need is at the end of the output, which shows a list of registry volume entries. These entries appear as:

```
\\?\Volume{b28876a5-2fd6-11df-9582-806e6f6e6963}\
```

If the volume is mounted, then you also see a drive letter after the volume listing. Otherwise, you see a message of:

```
*** NO MOUNT POINTS ***
```

Add a Volume

To add (mount) a new volume, you create an association between a drive letter and a volume entry. For example, let's say that you have a volume with a volume entry of \\?\Volume{b28876a5-2fd6-11df-9582-806e6f6e6963}\ and you want to associate it with F:. In this case, you type **MountVol F: \\?\Volume{b28876a5-2fd6-11df-9582-806e6f6e6963}** and press Enter. You won't see any output when the command is successful. As soon as the drive is mounted, you can begin using it.

Remove a Volume

To remove (dismount) a volume, you remove the association between the drive letter and the volume entry. This process disassociates the two and makes the drive inaccessible so that you can perform certain types of maintenance on it. The /D command line switch dismounts the volume. For example, if you want to dismount the F drive, you type **MountVol F: /D** and press Enter.

Maintain the Volume

The data on a hard drive represents an enormous investment for your organization. Of course, you'll perform the usual backups and use technologies such as RAID to guard that investment. However, you can also perform some standard maintenance tasks that can often tell you that the hard drive is going to fail long before it actually does. The following sections describe how to perform volume maintenance.

Determine File and Directory Status

The ChkDsk utility can check entire drives when working with any file system. However, it can also check directories and even individual files when working with the FAT file system. To check a file system, use the ChkDsk Volume command, where Volume is a drive letter followed by a colon, such as C:. If you add the /V command line switch, you see additional information that depends on the kind of volume that you're checking. An NTFS volume displays additional cleanup information. For example, to perform a full check of the E drive, you'd type **ChkDsk /V E:** and press Enter. Figure 6.1 shows typical output.

Figure 6.1: ChkDsk provides you with detailed information about file and directory status.

```
C:\>ChkDsk /V E:
The type of the file system is NTFS.
Volume label is Data.

WARNING!  F parameter not specified.
Running CHKDSK in read-only mode.

CHKDSK is verifying files (stage 1 of 3)...
  19456 file records processed.
File verification completed.
  0 large file records processed.
  0 bad file records processed.
  0 EA records processed.
  0 reparse records processed.
CHKDSK is verifying indexes (stage 2 of 3)...
  19578 index entries processed.
Index verification completed.
  0 unindexed files scanned.
  0 unindexed files recovered.
CHKDSK is verifying security descriptors (stage 3 of 3)...
  19456 file SDs/SIDs processed.
Index $SII of file 9 contains 30 unused index entries.
Index $SDH of file 9 contains 30 unused index entries.
There are 30 unused security descriptors.
Security descriptor verification completed.
  62 data files processed.
CHKDSK is verifying Usn Journal...
  3911968 USN bytes processed.
Usn Journal verification completed.
Windows has checked the file system and found no problems.

  626280447 KB total disk space.
    7281944 KB in 237 files.
        140 KB in 63 indexes.
          0 KB in bad sectors.
     108627 KB in use by the system.
      65536 KB occupied by the log file.
  618889736 KB available on disk.

       4096 bytes in each allocation unit.
  156570111 total allocation units on disk.
  154722434 allocation units available on disk.

C:\>
```

If this volume had any bad sectors, missing data, incorrect file entries, or any other errors, they would appear in the output messages. In this case, the volume is error free, so you don't see anything other than the status messages of the utility so that you know what task it has performed. The most important line appears about two-thirds down: "Windows has checked the file system and found no problems."

Locate Bad Sectors

Using ChkDsk in read-only mode as described in the "Determine File and Directory Status" provides status information about a volume, but it doesn't fix anything. In order to fix something, you must choose the level of repair you want to perform. The following list tells you about the command line switches used to repair a volume in order of depth.

- **/F**: Repairs the basic errors encountered on a volume.

- **/R**: Locates any bad sectors on the volume and recovers information from them whenever possible. This option also implies the /F level of repair.

- **/B**: (NTFS-only) Reevaluates the bad sectors on the volume and restores them if possible. This option also implies both the /F and /R levels of repair.

Some volumes require that you dismount them first. If you try to run ChkDsk for repairs and find that the utility displays an error message about not being able to use read/write mode, use the /X command line switch to dismount the volume. Using the /X command line switch automatically invokes the /F command line switch as well.

It's not advisable to use the ChkDsk utility in read/write mode directly. Instead, you should follow a careful process of diagnosis and repair. For example, let's say you think there's a problem with the E volume, which relies on NTFS formatting. You would follow these steps to repair it:

1. Type **C:** and press Enter to set the drive to the C volume.

2. Type **MD Temp** and press Enter to create a temporary directory you can use to store information about the repair.

3. Type **ChkDsk /V E: > C:\Temp\Error.TXT** and press Enter to determine whether the volume has errors.

   Redirecting the output to Error.TXT will let you see errors that will potentially scroll off the screen otherwise. Using a directory on a different volume will minimize potential disruption of files on the

Managing Data

PART II

volume with errors. If the volume doesn't have errors, exit this procedure—your volume is safe to use.

4. Perform a backup of the volume.

   Make sure you back up the entire volume file by file, rather than making a mirror image of the volume. Creating a mirror image will simply move the error from the volume to the backup. You have to assume that the backup will lack some files currently found on the volume, that you may see errors during the backup process, and that some data loss will occur. The backup simply helps you to save as much data as possible before the repair process occurs.

5. Determine a level of repair suitable for the drive.

   If the initial check simply shows a few file errors, you can use the /F command line switch. Otherwise, you should use either the /R or /B command line switch (using /B on NTFS volumes is preferred).

6. Type **ChkDsk /F E: > C:\Temp\Repairs.TXT** or **ChkDsk /B E: > C:\ Temp\Repairs.TXT** and press Enter.

   This step starts the repair process. Redirecting the output to Repairs.TXT will let you see all of the changes the ChkDsk makes to the volume.

7. Perform step 6 until ChkDsk reports that all of the errors are repaired.

8. Depending on the repair results, you can attempt to restore missing or damaged files from earlier backups or the backup you make in step 4.

Perform Boot-Time Disk Checks

Some volumes aren't easily checked with ChkDsk. For example, you can't check the boot volume using ChkDsk because the system requires the boot volume for services and can't dismount it. The best you can hope to achieve is to obtain status information as described in the "Determine File and Directory Status" section of the chapter. In these situations, you can use the ChkNTFS utility to perform a boot-time check of the drive. To determine whether a drive is already scheduled for a check, use the ChkNTFS Volume command, where Volume is the volume letter followed by a colon, such as C:. The ChkNTFS utility reports whether the volume is dirty (requires a boot-time check) or not.

To schedule a volume for a boot-time check, use the ChkNTFS /C *Volume* command. This command sets the volume's dirty bit. For example, if you want to check the E volume, you'd type **ChkNTFS /C E:** and press Enter. The next time you boot the system ChkNTFS will automatically run and perform a check of the drive before the operating system has started (ensuring you get the most accurate results).

Improve Disk Access Performance

Disk fragmentation is a terrible problem, even on today's hard drives, because it robs the system of performance in the one area where performance is already poor. Your system already spends considerable time waiting for the hard drive to fetch data. When the hard drive is fragmented, the fetch process takes even longer. In fact, Microsoft recognizes disk fragmentation as a serious problem and configures Windows 7 to automatically schedule disk defragmentation on a regular basis. If your organization turns off this feature, you need to defragment the drive manually at a time when the process won't affect user productivity.

Analyze the Disk

Before you defragment all of the drives on a system, it's best to know whether the drives are actually fragmented. To determine which drives are fragmented, type **Defrag /A /C /H** and press Enter. The /A command line switch starts the analysis process. The /C command line switch performs the task on all of the drives in the system. The /H command line switch tells Defrag to operate at normal priority so that the analysis completes in a timely manner (the default priority is low). Otherwise, you'll wait a very long time for the results.

Figure 6.2: To save time, analyze the drives on a system before you defragment them.

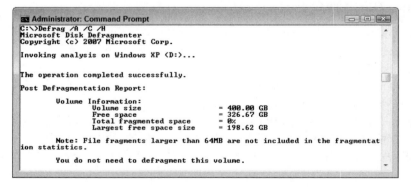

When the analysis is done, you see a report similar to the one shown in Figure 6.2 that tells you the status of each drive. In this case, the drive is 0 percent fragmented, so you don't need to defragment it. Generally, levels of fragmentation 2 percent or less won't require action on your part.

Defragment the Disk

After a drive becomes fragmented, you need to defragment it to ensure that it continues to perform acceptably. Let's say that the D and E drives are both fragmented. In this case, you'd type **Defrag D: E: /M /H** and press Enter. The Defrag utility accepts all of the volumes that require defragmentation as part of a single command. The /M command line switch tells Defrag to perform the task on all volumes in parallel, which makes far better use of your system's resources that performing the task on one disk at a time. The /H command line switch performs the task at normal priority to ensure that the task completes within a reasonable amount of time. If you want to perform free space consolidation (making larger spaces for new files), simply add the /X command line switch.

Manage Partitions

Managing partitions isn't something you do very often on a computer system. For one thing, changing the partitions after configuring the computer could have undesired results. However, every administrator has to work with partitions at some point during the configuration process and during updates. The DiskPart utility is an essential tool for managing partitions, especially during those times when the usual GUI tools simply aren't available. The following sections describe some common DiskPart tasks.

Start *DiskPart*

You can use DiskPart with direct command line input or supply a text file that contains a script of actions for DiskPart to perform. The text file will simply contain one command per line. You'll usually have a better experience with DiskPart if you create a script to perform the required tasks. Using a script reduces the potential for error. Use the DiskPart /s ScriptName command to start a script, where ScriptName is the name of the text file that contains the commands. For example, to use the MyScript.TXT file, you'd type **DiskPart /s MyScript.TXT** and press Enter.

It's also possible to type commands manually. To start the command line version of DiskPart, type **DiskPart** and press Enter. You'll see the DISKPART> prompt where you enter specific subcommands. Because DiskPart is so complex, it comes with its own help system. Simply type **Help** and press Enter to see a full list of DiskPart subcommands.

List the Objects

Before you can interact with the disks on a system, you need to know about them. To see the physical disks (not to be confused with volumes), type **List Disk** and press Enter. You'll see a list of the disks installed and detected for the current machine. The output includes the disk number, disk status, total disk size, amount of free space, whether the disk is basic or dynamic, and the GPT style. The disk with the asterisk (*) is the one with focus.

You can also see a list of volumes for the current machine. Volumes are the logical partitions created on a disk. To see the volumes, type **List Volume** and press Enter. You'll see a list of all the volumes on all disks for the current machine. The output includes the volume number, volume drive letter, volume label, file system used to support the volume, volume type (such as partition, DVD-ROM, or CD-ROM), the volume size, the volume status, and information about the volume purpose (such as a system or a boot drive). The volume with the asterisk (*) is the one with focus.

It's also possible to see partitions for the current system. However, you can't see the partitions immediately. First, you must select a disk. Let's say you want to see the partitions for the first disk on the system. In this case, you'd use this procedure:

1. Type **List Disk** and press Enter.

    You'll see a list of disks for the system. Make sure you select a disk that has a status of Online (normally Disk 0, which is the assumption for this procedure).

2. Type **Select Disk 0** and press Enter. DiskPart will now report that Disk 0 is the selected disk. In fact, if you type **List Disk** again, you'll see an asterisk next to its entry.

3. Type **List Partition**.

    You'll see a list of the partitions for Disk 0. The output includes the partition number, the partition size, the partition type, and the offset of the partition from the beginning of the disk. On dynamic disks, these partitions may not correspond to the dynamic volumes on the disk. This discrepancy occurs because dynamic disks contain entries in the partition table for the system volume or boot volume (if present on the disk). The partition with the asterisk (*) is the one with focus.

See Object Details

After you see an object of interest, you probably want to know the details about it. Starting at the disk level, you can type **Detail Disk** and press Enter to see low-level information about the disk drive as shown in Figure 6.3. The disk details provide more information about the disk type, which is a RAID in this case. In addition, you get a listing of volumes on the disk.

Figure 6.3: Disk details tell you how the disk is used and more about the kind of disk.

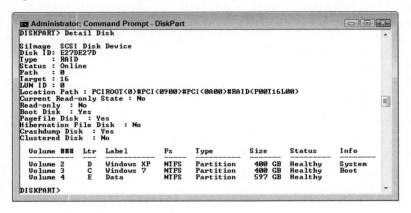

The next level of information is specific volumes. However, you can't access this information without performing a few extra steps:

1. Choose a volume to view from the list of volumes obtained using either Detail Disk or List Volume.

This example assumes Volume 2, as shown in Figure 6.3.

2. Type **Select Volume 2** (or the number of the volume you want to see) and press Enter.

DiskPart will tell you that the volume you chose is the selected volume.

3. Type **Detail Volume** and press Enter.

You see volume specifics as shown in Figure 6.4. In this case, the information is for Windows 7. The information you receive from earlier versions of Windows will differ. One of the more important pieces of information you receive is what disks the volume resides on, which is especially important when working with certain kinds of volume configurations such as spanned volumes.

After you select a volume to view, you can see the details of the partition associated with it. Simply type **Detail Partition** and press Enter to see the partition information. You'll discover the partition type, whether the partition is hidden, the partition's active state, the offset of the partition from the beginning of the disk, and partition-specific information such as the drive letter and file system.

Figure 6.4: Volume details tell you information such as whether the volume is hidden from view.

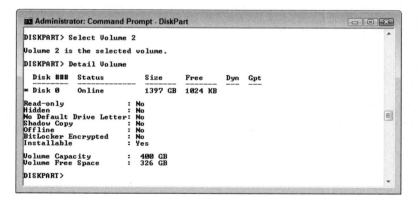

Select an Object

Before you can do something with an object, you must select it. DiskPart supports three object types:

- Disk
- Volume
- Partition

To select a particular object, you use the `Select ObjectType ObjectNumber` command, where `ObjectType` is `Disk`, `Volume`, or `Partition`, and `ObjectNumber` is the number of the object you want to work with. For example, to select the first volume, you type **Select Volume 0** and press Enter.

Rescan a Computer for Objects

In some cases, you might have to scan the computer for new objects. For example, if you change removable media, the change may not appear until after you perform a new scan. To perform this task, type **Rescan** and press Enter. `DiskPart` will display two messages. First, it will tell you to wait while it scans the computer for new devices. Second, you'll see a completion message that tells you the scan is finished.

Create a Partition

The `Create Partition` command helps you create a new partition on a disk. However, before you can create a partition, you must use the `Select Disk Number` command to select a disk (where `Number` is the number of the disk that will contain the new partition). For example, if you want to create a new partition on Disk 0, then you'd type **Select Disk 0** and press Enter. The disk must have sufficient space to hold the new partition or the `Create Partition` command will fail.

Create a Primary Partition

A primary partition is a bootable partition on the drive. You can use it to hold the operating system. To create a new primary partition, use the `Create Partition Primary Size Offset ID Align NoError` command, where `Size` is the size of the partition in MB, `Offset` is the location of the partition from the beginning of the drive, `ID` is an identifier, `Align` is the alignment value, and `NoError` is a Boolean value that indicates whether `DiskPart` should continue processing a script. Here is a more detailed description of the arguments:

- **Size:** The utility gives the new partition the focus once the system creates it. The system snaps the partition size to the cylinder size. For example, if you specify a size of 500 MB, the system rounds up the size of the partition to 504 MB. The system uses all of the free space on the disk when you don't define a partition size.

- **Offset:** The offset only affects Master Boot Record (MBR) disks. The offset defines the byte offset of the partition. If you don't specify an offset, the partition begins at the beginning of the extended partition. The offset you specify must allow enough room for the partition defined by the size argument.

- **ID:** Microsoft sets the ID argument aside for OEMs. Never specify an ID for a GUID Partition Table (GPT) disk. Use the Create Partition EFI and Create Partition MSR as needed to set up GPT disks. When working with an MBR disk, you can use the ID to set the disk type. The MBR values include C12A7328-F81F-11D2-BA4B-00A0C93EC93B (EFI system partition), E3C9E316-0B5C-4DB8-817D-F92DF00215AE (MSR partition), EBD0A0A2-B9E5-4433-87C0-68B6B72699C7 (basic data partition), 5808C8AA-7E8F-42E0-85D2-E1E90434CFB3 (LDM Metadata partition on a dynamic disk), and AF9B60A0-1431-4F62-BC68-3311714A69AD (LDM Data partition on a dynamic disk).

- **Align:** The align argument specifies the alignment of the primary partition on a disk that isn't cylinder aligned. You normally use this value for hardware RAID setups to improve performance. The value is the number of kilobytes from the beginning of the disk to the closest alignment boundary.

- **NoError:** Normally, DiskPart will stop performing any processing the moment it encounters an error to prevent potential data loss or disk errors. However, when performing a batch process, stopping may not be an ideal solution, so you add this argument to the command line to ensure processing continues.

Create an Extended Partition

An extended partition is a primary partition that can contain multiple secondary partitions—each of which can have a drive letter. A disk can contain only one extended partition. Use the Create Partition Extended *Size Offset NoError* to create an extended partition, where *Size* is the size of the partition in MB, *Offset* is the location of the partition from the beginning of the drive, and *NoError* is a Boolean value that indicates whether DiskPart should continue processing a script.

The utility gives the new partition the focus once the system creates it. A disk can only have one extended partition. You must create an extended partition before you can create logical drives. As with the primary partition, the size argument defines the size of the partition. For example, if you specify a size of 500 MB, the system rounds the size of the partition up to 504 MB. The system uses all of the free space on the disk when you don't define a partition size.

The offset only affects MBR disks. The offset defines the byte offset of the partition. If you don't specify an offset, the partition begins at the beginning of the free space on the disk. The system snaps the partition size to the cylinder size; it rounds the offset to the closest cylinder boundary. For example, if you specify an offset that's 27 MB and the cylinder size is 8 MB, the system rounds the offset to the 24 MB boundary.

Create a Logical Partition

A logical partition is a secondary partition of an extended partition. In other words, you must first create an extended partition before you can create a logical partition. After you create the extended partition, you select it using the `Select Partition` command as explained in the "Select an Object" section of the chapter. Only after you perform these initial tasks can you use the `Create Partition Logical` *Size Offset NoError* command to create a logical partition (where *Size* is the size of the partition in MB, *Offset* is the location of the partition from the beginning of the drive, and *NoError* is a Boolean value that indicates whether `DiskPart` should continue processing a script).

The utility gives the new partition the focus once the system creates it. The system snaps the partition size to the cylinder size. As with primary and extended partitions, if you specify a size of 500 MB, the system rounds up the size of the partition to 504 MB. The system uses all of the free space on the disk when you don't define a partition size.

The offset only affects MBR disks. The offset defines the byte offset of the partition. If you don't specify an offset, the partition begins at the beginning of the extended partition. The offset you specify must allow enough room for the partition defined by the size argument. If the offset won't allow enough space, the system changes the offset so that the logical disk can fit within the extended partition.

Create a Volume

The `DiskPart` utility can create a number of volume types. However, modern systems normally implement RAID in hardware. Consequently, you normally limit yourself to creating simple volumes using the Create Volume Simple *Size* *Disk* *NoError* command, where *Size* is the size of the volume in MB, *Disk* is the number of disk to use for the volume, and *NoError* is a Boolean value that indicates whether DiskPart should continue processing a script.

The utility automatically changes focus to the new volume once the system creates it. The size argument defines the size of the volume in megabytes. The utility uses the entire free space on the disk when you don't specify the size argument.

The disk argument specifies the disk to receive the new volume. The utility uses the current disk when you don't specify the disk option.

Clean a Drive

You may want to clean a drive before removing it from the system or reformatting it for another use. The Clean command removes the partition and volume formatting on the disk with focus. The system overwrites the MBR partitioning information and hidden section information on MBR disks. The system overwrites the GPT partitioning information, including the Protective MBR, on GPT disks. A GPT disk doesn't include hidden sector information. The system completely erases the disk when you use the Clean All command.

Mark a Partition as Active

The active partition is the one that the system uses to boot. You can only use primary partitions for boot purposes and only one primary partition is marked as active at any given time. If you fail to mark a partition that contains system files as being active, the system may not boot. DiskPart doesn't check your partition selection for accuracy.

Use these steps to mark a partition active. The example assumes that you're setting Partition 1 on Disk 0 active:

1. Type **Select Disk 0** (or whatever disk number you want to use) and press Enter. DiskPart tells you that it has selected Disk 0.

2. Type **Select Partition 1** (or whatever partition on the selected disk that you want to mark active) and press Enter. DiskPart tells you that it has selected Partition 1.

3. Type **Active** and press Enter. DiskPart tells you that the partition is marked as active.

Mark a Partition as Inactive

The Inactive command marks the current MBR disk partition inactive, which means you can no longer boot from the partition. When the computer reboots, the system starts using the next available boot option specified in the BIOS such as a CD-ROM drive or a Pre-Boot eXecution Environment (PXE)–based boot environment. A PXE can include Remote Installation Services (RIS). Some computers won't restart without an active partition, so use this command with care. If you're unable to start your computer after marking the system or boot partition as inactive, insert the Setup CD in the CD-ROM drive, restart the computer, and repair the partition using the FixMBR and FixBoot utilities from the Recovery Console.

Use the following steps to use this command. The example assumes that you're setting Partition 1 on Disk 0 inactive:

1. Type **Select Disk 0** (or whatever disk number you want to use) and press Enter. DiskPart tells you that it has selected Disk 0.

2. Type **Select Partition 1** (or whatever partition on the selected disk that you want to mark inactive) and press Enter. DiskPart tells you that it has selected Partition 1.

3. Type **Inactive** and press Enter. DiskPart tells you that the partition is marked as inactive.

Assign a Drive Letter

The Assign command assigns a drive letter or mount point to the volume with focus. If you don't specify a drive letter or mount point, the utility uses the next available drive letter. The utility generates an error when you attempt to assign an existing drive letter to the volume. The system won't allow you to assign drive letters to system volumes, boot volumes, or volumes that contain the paging file. In addition, you can't assign a drive letter to an OEM partition or any GPT partition other than a basic data partition.

The following steps show how to assign a drive letter to a volume. The example assumes that you're assigning C to Volume 1 on Disk 0:

1. Type **Select Disk 0** (or whatever disk number you want to use) and press Enter. DiskPart tells you that it has selected Disk 0.

2. Type `Select Volume 1` (or whatever volume on the selected disk that you want to assign a drive letter to) and press Enter. DiskPart tells you that it has selected Volume 1.

3. Type `Assign Letter=C` (or whatever letter you want to assign to the selected volume) and press Enter. DiskPart tells you it has assigned the new drive letter. If you assign a letter to a volume that already has a letter, the new letter replaces the existing letter. You can't assign two different letters to the same volume.

Remove a Drive Letter

The Remove command removes a drive letter or mount point from the volume with focus. If you don't specify a drive letter or mount point, the utility removes the first drive letter or mount point that it encounters. You can't remove the drive letters on system, boot, or paging volumes, OEM partitions, any GPT partition with an unrecognized GUID, or any of the special, nondata GPT partitions such as the EFI system partition.

The following steps show how to remove a drive letter from a volume. The example assumes that you're removing C from Volume 1 on Disk 0:

1. Type `Select Disk 0` (or whatever disk number you want to use) and press Enter. DiskPart tells you that it has selected Disk 0.

2. Type `Select Volume 1` (or whatever volume on the selected disk from which you want to remove a drive letter) and press Enter. DiskPart tells you that it has selected Volume 1.

   Type `Remove Letter=C` (or whatever letter you want to remove from the selected volume) and press Enter. DiskPart tells you it has removed the existing drive letter. If you remove a letter from a volume, the volume still exists, but it has no drive letter, making it inaccessible from Windows using standard techniques.

Extend a Volume

When you work with an NTFS volume, you can extend it into the next contiguous unallocated space to increase the volume size. The unallocated space must appear on the same disk. The unallocated space must also appear after the current partition; the sector number of the unallocated space must be higher than the sector number of the currently selected volume.

Use the Extend *Size Disk NoError* command to perform this task, where *Size* defines the amount of space to add to the current partition, *Disk* specifies a dynamic disk to use, and *NoError* is a Boolean value that indicates whether DiskPart should continue processing a script. If you don't specify the *Size* argument, the system uses all of the contiguous unallocated space. The *Disk* argument applies to dynamic disks. Use this argument to specify the dynamic disk to use to extend the volume. If you don't specify the *Disk* argument, the system uses the current disk.

Delete an Object

When you no longer need a disk configuration, volume, or partition, you can delete it. Type **Delete Disk**, **Delete Volume**, or **Delete Partition**, and press Enter. The command deletes the currently selected disk, volume, or partition as appropriate.

You can't delete the system volume, boot volume, or any volume that contains the active paging file or crash dump (memory dump). Likewise, you can't delete the system partition, boot partition, or any partition that contains the active paging file or crash dump (memory dump). Use the Override argument to allow DiskPart to remove disks, volumes, or partitions of any type on a drive.

Exit *DiskPart*

After you finish using DiskPart, you'll want to end the application gracefully to ensure that none of your changes is missed. Type **Exit** and press Enter to end the DiskPart utility.

7

Securing the Data

IN THIS CHAPTER, YOU WILL LEARN TO:

Managing Data

PART II

Security takes many forms on computer systems. There are entire books written about securing the system itself, securing the user, and securing applications. This chapter describes another category of security—securing the data. Although the techniques in this chapter won't provide a complete protective bubble around your data that's both virus and user proof, it does give you a good start. In fact, you might be a little surprised at how much you can do to protect your data using just the command line utilities supplied with Windows.

Protect Data

The Cipher utility makes it possible to encrypt the files that hold data on a hard drive. After encryption, only the user whose key fits the file can open it for viewing. The encryption and decryption process doesn't require any extra work on the user's part—it all happens in the background. The files do consume a little extra space on the hard drive and there's a small performance hit when opening and closing the file due to the encryption and decryption process. The following sections describe how to perform essential Cipher utility tasks.

Encrypt a File or Directory

It's possible to encrypt specific directories or files without affecting the rest of the files on a hard drive. In fact, because of the size and performance penalties of using encrypting, most administrators will target data files, rather than all of the files on a hard drive. To encrypt a directory or file, use the Cipher /E Name command, where Name is the directory or filename. For example, if you want to encrypt C:\MyDir, you'd type **Cipher /E C:\MyDir** and press Enter. However, this command only encrypts the directory. If you want to encrypt all of the files and subdirectories within C:\MyDir, then you use these steps:

1. Type **Cipher /E /S:C:\MyDir** and press Enter.

   The Cipher utility displays each file and directory that it encrypts and a status message so that you know it was successfully encrypted. Notice that there's a colon between the /S command line switch and the directory specification. This command format differs from other utilities.

2. Type **Cipher /W:C:\MyDir** and press Enter.

This second command removes artifacts of plain text from the directory. Otherwise, you might leave bits of plain text behind that someone could read. This second command will take a few minutes to complete, but it's an important part of the process, so be patient.

No matter how you encrypt a file or directory, if this is the first time you've performed an encryption, make sure you back up your key to removable media. In fact, Windows 7 users will see a notification to perform the task in the Notification Area. The "Backup Recovery Keys and Certificates" section describes how to perform this task from the command line.

View Encrypted Files and Directories

It's useful to know whether a file or directory is encrypted. To determine the encryption status, you view it using the Cipher utility using the Cipher Name command, where Name is the file or directory you wish to view. When you view a directory, you simply see an E for encrypted or U for unencrypted. For example, if you want to see the status of C:\MyDir, you type **Cipher C:\MyDir** and press Enter. The output displays U or E followed by the name of the directory. The output also tells you whether any new files and subdirectories are automatically encrypted.

As with directories, files display an E or U depending on their encrypted or unencrypted state. For example, to see the status of all of the files and subdirectories of the C:\MyDir directory, you type **Cipher /S:C:\MyDir** and press Enter. Figure 7.1 shows typical results. Notice that each of the subdirectories tells whether files and directories added to it are automatically encrypted.

In some cases, you want more information than just knowing whether or not a file is encrypted. In this case, you rely on the Cipher /C Name command, where Name is the name of the file or directory. For example, if you want to know more information about the encryption of C:\MyDir, you'd type **Cipher /C C:\MyDir** and press Enter. Figure 7.2 shows typical output from this command. As you can see, the information includes the compatibility level, encryption algorithm, and key size. Most importantly, the output tells you which users can decrypt the file.

Managing Data

PART II

Figure 7.1: An E or U tells you the status of a file or subdirectory.

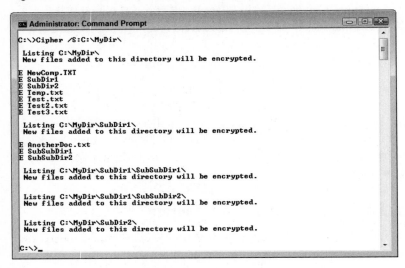

Figure 7.2: The /C command line switch provides detailed Cipher information.

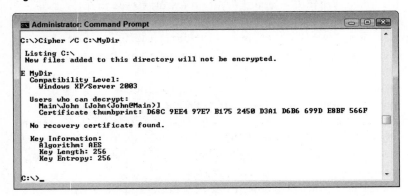

Encrypt Hidden Files

Normally, the Cipher utility doesn't do anything with hidden and system files. Fortunately, the /H command line switch makes hidden and system files visible so that you can encrypt them. For example, if you want to encrypt the files and subdirectories with the hidden or system attribute enabled (in addition to all of the regular files) in C:\MyDir, you'd type **Cipher /H /E /S:C:\MyDir** and press Enter.

WARNING You must use the /H command line switch with special care. Encrypting a hidden or system file that the system needs to boot will make the system unbootable. Generally, you won't need to work with hidden or system files unless you specifically set the file attributes as hidden or system.

Back Up Recovery Keys and Certificates

One of the most important things to do when you encrypt files is to back up your recovery key and certificate. Otherwise, a major system error could make your data permanently inaccessible. The data might be just fine, but the encryption would prevent you from accessing it, making the data just as useless as if it had been damaged.

Use the following procedure to create a backup of your recovery key and certificate:

1. Log in as the user whose key you want to back up.

2. Type **Cipher /R:*Filename***, where *Filename* is the name of the recovery key and certificate.

   Only supply a filename, such as JohnKey, and not an extension. The output will actually contain two files: a CER file that contains the user's certificate and a PFX file that contains the certificate and private key.

3. Type a password for the file and press Enter when asked.

   Make sure you choose a complex password or the private key will become easy to access.

4. Retype the password and press Enter when asked.

5. Copy the resulting CER and PFX files to removable media such as a flash drive.

Add a User to a File or Directory

You may find that you need to add a user to a file or directory. For example, you might want to encrypt a shared directory. In this case, each user's credentials would need to be able to encrypt or decrypt the files independently of the other users. The easiest way to add a user is to generate a recovery key and certificate for the user using the procedure found in the "Backup Recovery Keys and Certificates" section of the chapter.

Once you have the CER file, you can use it to add that user to an encrypted file or directory. Simply use the Cipher /AddUser /CertFile:*Keyname* command, where *Keyname* is the filename of a CER file. For example, let's say you have the JohnKey.CER file of a particular user and you want to add the user to C:\MyDir. In this case, you'd type **Cipher /AddUser /CertFile:JohnKey.CER C:\MyDir** and press Enter. The user will now have access to C:\MyDir. Of course, you can use the /S command line switch to add the user to all files and subdirectories of a particular directory.

Remove a User from a File or Directory

At some point, you may have to remove a user from a file or directory. Use the following steps to remove a user from a file or directory (the example assumes that you're working with C:\MyDir):

1. Type **Cipher /C C:\MyDir** (or the file or directory with which you want to work).

   This command provides a detailed listing of the users who can access the file or directory. Figure 7.3 shows an example of a directory that contains two user entries—the example uses the John entry.

Figure 7.3: Obtain a list of the users who can access the target file or directory.

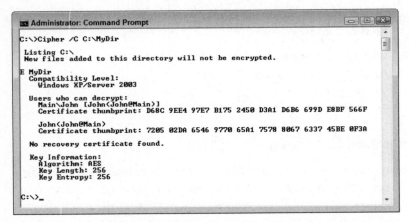

2. Right-click the command window and choose Mark from the context menu. Highlight the Certificate Thumbprint entry for the user you want to remove and press Enter.

   In the case of the example, you'd select 7205 02DA 6546 9770 65A1 7578 8067 6337 45BE 0F3A, which is John's entry.

3. Type `Cipher /RemoveUser /CertHash:`". Right-click the command window and choose Paste from the context menu. You see the certification hash code pasted into the window. Type " `C:\MyDir`. (The whole command should now read as `Cipher /RemoveUser / CertHash:`"7205 02DA 6546 9770 65A1 7578 8067 6337 45BE 0 F3A" `C:\MyDir`.) Press Enter. The `Cipher` utility removes the user from the list of users that can access the directory or file.

Decrypt a File or Directory

Decrypting a file or directory is just as easy as encrypting it, as long as the account that you're using has the right key associated with it. To decrypt a directory or file, use the `Cipher /D` *Name* command, where *Name* is the directory or filename. For example, if you want to decrypt `C:\MyDir`, you'd type `Cipher /D C:\MyDir` and press Enter. However, this command only encrypts the directory. If you want to encrypt all of the files and subdirectories within `C:\MyDir`, then you'd type `Cipher /D /S:C:\MyDir` and press Enter.

Change File and Directory Access

File and directory access are essential to maintaining data security. Of course, you can set file and directory access security using the GUI, but the ICACLS utility can make automating the task significantly easier. The following sections describe basic tasks you can perform using ICACLS.

Obtain the DACL

ICACLS is focused on the Discretionary Access Control List (DACL)—the part of the security setup that controls access, rather than the System Access Control List (SACL), which helps the administrator monitor user activity. Use the ICACLS *Name* command, where *Name* is the file or directory you want to check, to obtain the DACL. For example, if you wanted to check the C:\MyDir directory DACL, then you'd type **ICACLS C:\MyDir** and press Enter. Figure 7.4 shows typical output from the command.

Figure 7.4: The ICACLS utility helps you see the DACL for any file or directory.

Notice the letters in parentheses next to each of the names in the output. These letters tell you the access rights for that person or group. The rights are grouped into three categories: simple rights, specific rights, and inheritance rights. Table 7.1 describes each of the simple rights, Table 7.2 describes each of the specific rights, and Table 7.3 describes each of the inheritance rights. When a specific right conflicts with a simple right, the specific right normally takes precedence.

Table 7.1: Simple DACL Rights

Letter	Right
N	No access
F	Full access (the user can read, write, delete, or execute files or directories)
M	Modify access (the user can read, write, and delete the file or directory)
RX	Read and execute access
R	Read-only access
W	Write-only access
D	Delete access

Table 7.2: Specific DACL Rights

Letter	Right
DE	Delete
RC	Read control
WDAC	Write DAC (specifies the user has the right to modify the DACL)
WO	Write owner
S	Synchronize
AS	Access system security
MA	Maximum allowed
GR	Generic read
GW	Generic write
GE	Generic execute
GA	Generic all
RD	Read data/list directory
WD	Write data/add file
AD	Append data/add subdirectory
REA	Read extended attributes
WEA	Write extended attributes
X	Execute/traverse
DC	Delete child
RA	Read attributes
WA	Write attributes

Table 7.3: Inheritance Rights

Letter	Inheritance
OI	Object inherit
CI	Container inherit
IO	Inherit only
NP	Don't propagate inherit
I	Permission inherited from parent container

Looking at Figure 7.4, you can see that user John has inherited rights to this container from the parent container and that he has full access to C:\MyDir. However, when you look at the built-in Users account, you see that most users only have read and execute rights.

Find an SID

It's sometimes helpful to know whether a file or directory has a particular Security Identifier (SID) associated with it. For example, you may want to know whether a particular user already has rights to a file or directory. The ICACLS *Location* /FindSID *SID* command, where *Location* is the file or directory you want to check and *SID* is the SID of the user or group, helps you locate which users and groups have rights to specific files and directories.

Most administrators associate SIDs with the numeric version, such as S-1-0. In fact, you can see a list of well-known SIDs at support. microsoft.com/kb/243330. Every user on the system does have a numeric SID. Unfortunately, they're extremely hard to use, so the ICACLS utility also lets you use common SIDs, essentially, the logon name of the user or group you want to work with. For example, if you want to determine whether user John has access to C:\MyDir, you'd type **ICACLS C:\MyDir / FindSID John** and press Enter. An output of "SID Found" tells you that the user has rights to the specified directory.

Grant Permission

Before a user or group can access a file or directory, you must grant them permission. The ICACLS *Location* /Grant *SID*:(*Rights*) command (where *Location* is the target file or directory, *SID* is the SID for the user or group, and *Rights* are the permissions you want to grant) gives permission. Tables 7.1, 7.2, and 7.3 contain a list of rights that you can grant. Each of these rights is separated by a comma. For example, if you want to give user Joe read and write access to C:\Dir, you'd type **ICACLS C:\MyDir /Grant Joe:(R,W)** and press Enter.

Deny Permission

The total rights that a user has are a combination of inherited, granted, and denied rights. Rights from a parent directory flow down to child directories and files. You can also specifically grant rights using the technique described in the "Grant Permission" section of the chapter. Denying rights specifically removes permissions from the list of permissions that a user or group would normally have. Use the ICACLS *Location* /Deny *SID:(Rights)* command (where *Location* is the target file or directory, *SID* is the SID for the user or group, and *Rights* are the permissions you want to deny) to deny permission. Tables 7.1, 7.2, and 7.3 contain a list of rights that you can grant. Each of these rights is separated by a comma. For example, if you want to deny user Joe read and write access to C:\Dir, you'd type **ICACLS C:\MyDir /Deny Joe:(R,W)** and press Enter. Even if a user would normally have rights to a file or directory, specifically denying those rights takes precedence.

Remove Permission

Removing permission is not the same as denying permission. When you remove permission, it actually clears the Access Control Entries (ACEs) from the DACL. The ICACLS *Location* /Remove *SID* command (where *Location* is the target file or directory and *SID* is the SID for the user or group) actually removes all of the ACEs for the specified SID. Consequently, if you type **ICACLS C:\MyDir /Remove Joe** and press Enter, Joe's rights to C:\MyDir revert to his inherited rights to the directory.

You don't have to remove all of the permissions. It's possible to remove just the grant entries or just the deny entries. In this case, you combine the /Remove command line switch with a :G or a :D. For example, if you want to remove just the deny rights for Joe, you'd type **ICACLS C:\MyDir /Remove:D Joe** and press Enter.

Set the Owner

You can use ICACLS to safely set the owner of a file or directory. This is a cooperative change—it won't force a change that isn't supported by the user's current rights. In order to force a change, you must use the TakeOwn utility described in the "Take Ownership of Files" section of the chapter. To change the owner of a file or directory, use the ICACLS *Location* /SetOwner *SID* command, where *Location* is the target file or directory and *SID* is the SID for the user or group. For example, if you want to give user John ownership of C:\MyDir, you'd type **ICACLS C:\ MyDir /SetOwner John** and press Enter.

Verify Security

Sometimes the ACEs contained within the DACL for a particular resource become confused or incorrect—especially if someone has been tampering with them. Trojans and viruses often make themselves felt through errant entries, even if you can't see them in other ways. Use the ICACLS *Location* /Verify command, where *Location* is the target file, to verify the ACEs and ensure they're correct. For example, if you want to verify that the ACEs for C:\MyDir are correct, type **ICACLS C:\MyDir /Verify** and press Enter. If there are any errors, ICACLS will display a list of them for you.

Detect Shared Open Files

There are many different ways to detect open files on a system. However, one of the easiest ways to perform this task is to use the OpenFiles utility. The following sections describe this utility in more detail.

Use the Query Option

To see which files are opened on a particular system, type **OpenFiles / Query** and press Enter. You'll see a list of open files that include the file ID, the account accessing the file, the kind of access performed (normally Windows), and the filename. The list is probably going to be pretty long on a typical file server, so you'll want to combine this command with the More utility by typing **OpenFiles /Query | More** and pressing Enter.

From a practical perspective, even if you use the More utility, the list of files is going to be long and hard to search. Consequently, most administrators will want to output the list of open files to a text file for parsing within an application. One way to do this is to output the data in Comma Separated Value (CSV) format without a header. To do so, you type **OpenFiles /Query /FO CSV /NH > OpenFiles.CSV** and press Enter. This command will output the list of files to OpenFiles.CSV so that you can import them into an application for further review.

You probably won't access the server console directly unless you're using Remote Desktop. In this case, you can use the /S, /U, and /P command line switches to obtain the information from the server. For example, let's say the server name is MyServer, your name is Amy, and your password is Hello. In this case, you might type **OpenFiles /Query /S MyServer /U Amy /P Hello** and press Enter.

Use the Disconnect Option

In extremely rare conditions, you might need to disconnect a user from a file. For example, the user's machine might lock up and leave the file open. When the user tries to access the file after rebooting the machine, the file won't open because the file server already thinks that it's open. In this case, a manual disconnect is warranted. However, in most cases, you don't want to disconnect a user from a file because data loss could occur.

The safest way to disconnect a user from a file is using the file ID. To obtain the file ID, you begin by querying the files as described in the "Use the Query Option" section. Once you have the ID, you use the OpenFiles /Disconnect /ID *ID* command, where *ID* is the file identifier, to perform the task. For example, you might want to disconnect the file identified by number 22. In this case, you'd type **OpenFiles /Disconnect /ID 22** and press Enter.

A user might sometimes open multiple copies of the same file. If a lockup occurs, all of those copies will remain open. In this case, you can clear all of the open entries using the OpenFiles /Disconnect /OP *Filename* command, where *Filename* is the full path and filename of the file you want to disconnect. For example, let's say the user has multiple copies of C:\MyDir\MyFile.TXT open. In this case, you'd type **OpenFiles / Disconnect /OP C:\MyDir\MyFile.TXT** and press Enter.

Managing Data

PART II

Use the Local Option

The OpenFiles utility normally doesn't track files that are opened locally because doing so would bloat the output list. However, you might choose to list the local files as part of a security check or simply to verify that the server is closing a specific file after using it. Tracking local files is also useful on workstations where you may not have any shared file use to worry about. In this case, you type **OpenFiles /Local On** and press Enter. You must reboot the machine for the change to take effect.

To check the status of the local option, type **OpenFiles /Local** and press Enter. The OpenFiles utility will tell you whether or not it's tracking local file usage. If you want to stop tracking local files, simply type **OpenFiles /Local Off** and press Enter.

Take Ownership of Files

The person who creates a file owns the file. Consequently, all of the files that the Windows Setup application creates during installation are owned by the administrator. All of your personal data is owned by you. In most cases, the case for a particular ownership is clear. However, you may encounter situations where you must change the ownership of a file. For example, a manager who owns a group of shared files may leave the company and you'll need to assign those files to the new manager. The TakeOwn utility makes it possible to force ownership changes even if the change normally wouldn't work due to security rules. Consequently, you have to use this utility with care. The following sections describe the TakeOwn utility in more detail.

Set Administrator Ownership

The Administrator account is the easiest account to use when assigning ownership. The TakeOwn /A /F *Location* command, where *Location* is the file or directory that you want to assign, makes it easy to change the ownership of any file or directory. For example, if you want to assign ownership of C:\MyDir to the administrator, you'd type **TakeOwn /A /F C:\MyDir** and press Enter.

Assigning ownership of a directory to the administrator doesn't change the ownership of any files or subdirectories that the directory contains. In order to make this change, you must use the /R command line switch. For example, using the previous example as a starting point, you'd type **TakeOwn /A /R /F C:\MyDir** and press Enter. It's important to note that TakeOwn doesn't use the /S command line switch as most utilities do for subdirectories.

Set Other User Ownership

The TakeOwn utility normally uses the current user account for ownership purposes. In other words, if you want to assign ownership of a directory or group of files to a particular user, you must log in as that user. Consequently, if you want to give user John ownership of all of the files in C:\MyDir, you'd first log in as John, and then type **TakeOwn /R /F C:\MyDir** and press Enter. You'll see that the ownership changes automatically to user John.

Fortunately, you don't have to leave your desk to change ownership on another system. You can use the /S, /U, and /P command line switches to log onto another system from your desk and make the appropriate change. For example, if you want to give user Amy ownership of C:\MyDir on MyServer, then you'd type **TakeOwn /S MyServer /U Amy /P Hello /R /F C:\MyDir** and press Enter.

PART III

Managing the Network

IN THIS PART ▶

Managing the Network

PART III

8

Managing the Network

IN THIS CHAPTER, YOU WILL LEARN TO:

▷ **GET THE MEDIA ACCESS CONTROL INFORMATION (Page 140)**

▷ **INTERACT WITH THE NETWORK USING THE *NET* UTILITY (Pages 141-163)**

Managing the Network

PART III

E ntire books are written about network management because networks are incredibly complex. An administrator must consider the network hardware, protocols, operating systems, peripheral devices, application software, and services. In fact, some services, such as Exchange Server, require entire books by themselves (and even those books are incomplete in some regard).

This single chapter can't possibly hope to provide complete coverage of every networking need. It does, however, provide useful information for managing the network from the Windows command prompt. The sections that follow address the requirements of working with networks using just the features offered at the command line without the use of any other administration software. Even though these offerings might appear inconsequential at first, you'll be amazed at how many tasks you can perform using them. The goal of these sections is to make you aware of the network at a basic level, rather than the monitoring of any specific piece of hardware or software.

Get the Media Access Control Information

The Media Access Control (MAC) address is a unique identifier that's provided as part of the hardware for a Network Interface Card (NIC) or other device with direct network access. By querying the MAC address, you can ensure that you're actually working with a particular machine. The unique identifier makes system identification easy. To obtain the MAC address for any given machine, use the GetMAC command for the local machine and the GetMAC /S *System* /U *User* /P *Password* command for a remote system, where *System* is the name of the remote machine, *User* is the user account to use, and *Password* is the password for the user account. For example, to obtain the MAC address of each device on MyMachine using Sandra's account with the password ThePassword, you'd type **GetMAC /S MyMachine /U Sandra /P ThePassword** and press Enter.

The output of the GetMAC utility contains one MAC address for each NIC or other network device installed. The output also provides the transport attached to the device. If the device is present, but not connected to the network, then you see Media Disconnected for the transport entry.

Interact with the Network Using the *Net* Utility

The Net utility includes a host of subcommands that help you interact with the network software. For example, you can use the Net utility to add, view, edit, and delete users. To obtain a complete list of Net subcommands, type **Net /?** and press Enter. To obtain help on using a specific Net subcommand, use the Net *Subcommand* /? command, where *Subcommand* is the subcommand that you want to use. For example, to learn more about the Accounts subcommand, you'd type **Net Accounts /?** and press Enter. The following sections describe how to perform common tasks using the Net utility.

Manage Users

One of the most common tasks you perform using the Net utility is managing users. In fact, when you have a lot of users to add, it's not uncommon to automate this task so the computer performs the majority of the work. The following sections describe three common user management tasks.

NOTE   You can also use the WMIC UserAccount utility to work with user accounts. There isn't much difference between it and the Net User utility. Chapter 15 discusses the WMIC utility in more detail.

Add a User

Theoretically, you can use the Net User /Add command to add one or more users at a time. The safest way to add new users is to add them one command at a time, rather than try to add a group using a single command. For example, to add user Sam to the computer with a password of D3stiny!, you'd type **Net User Sam D3stiny! /Add** and press Enter. The Net utility does allow you to set a number of optional user account arguments, such as whether the user must supply a password and whether the user can change their password. However, user account details such as address and telephone number aren't available. In order to change these details you must rely on the WMIC utility.

Managing the Network

PART III

For security reasons, you normally include the /LogonPasswordChg:Yes command line switch to ensure the user changes their password during the initial logon. Otherwise, the user can rely on the default password you provided, which represents a security risk and opens the company to all kinds of privacy and other legal issues. In short, you normally type something like **Net User Sam D3stiny! /Add /LogonPasswordChg:Yes** and press Enter.

View a User

Viewing a particular user account is easy using the Net User *Username* command, where *Username* is the name of the user you want to view. For example, you might want to see Sam's account, so you'd type *Net User* **Sam** and press Enter. Figure 8.1 shows typical output from this command.

Figure 8.1: The user information includes every setting you can change and a few statistics.

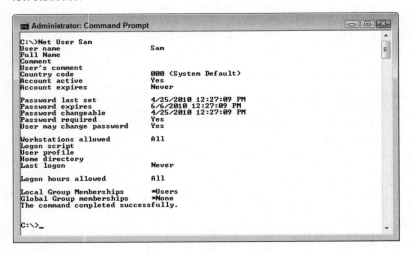

Figure 8.1 shows everything that the Net User command provides, including all of the settings you can change, such as a user account comment. One of the more important statistics shown in Figure 8.1 is Password Last Set, which tells you about the user's password habits. If you see that the user is waiting too long to change the password, you may want to modify system policies to require a shorter change interval.

Delete a User

You can use the Net User *Username* /Delete command (where *Username* is the user you want to delete) to remove users you no longer need. For example, to remove user Sam's account, you'd type **Net User Sam /Delete** and press Enter. The Net utility will tell you that the command completed successfully when it finds the name in the list of users.

WARNING Deleting a user is permanent. You can't undo the action. In addition, there isn't any way to export the user account information before you perform a deletion so that you can simply import an accidental deletion later. Consequently, you need to make sure you actually want to delete an account before you delete it. If you accidentally delete an account, you must re-create it from scratch. Unfortunately, even re-creating the account won't create the same account—the account SID and other security features will be different, so issues such as losing access to encrypted files will still be a problem. The only complete cure for the problem is to ensure you have backups of the user's certificates (see the "Back Up Recovery Keys and Certificates" section of Chapter 7 for details).

Manage Accounts

The Net Accounts subcommand helps you perform two tasks: force a logoff and manage overall password requirements. When you type **Net Accounts** and press Enter, you see the current settings for both automatically forcing a logoff and the system password requirements as shown in Figure 8.2. The following sections tell how to perform both tasks.

Figure 8.2: Use the Net Accounts subcommand to view forced logoff and password settings.

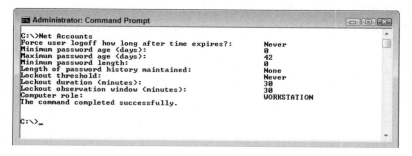

```
Administrator: Command Prompt

C:\>Net Accounts
Force user logoff how long after time expires?:      Never
Minimum password age (days):                         0
Maximum password age (days):                         42
Minimum password length:                             0
Length of password history maintained:               None
Lockout threshold:                                   Never
Lockout duration (minutes):                          30
Lockout observation window (minutes):                30
Computer role:                                       WORKSTATION
The command completed successfully.

C:\>_
```

Managing the Network

PART III

Force a Logoff

When you configure a user account, you can define what hours the user can access the computer. Configuring user hours prevents users from accessing the computer during off hours and could help reduce security risks. In addition, setting user hours also helps manage shared resources so that users don't access these resources during hours when other users need them. Of course, some users will try to work past their normal work hours. In order to manage the account and the resources it uses, you must force a logoff. The forced logoff setting answers the question of how long the system should wait for the user to voluntarily log off before forcing a logoff.

NOTE   Make sure you set a policy for user accounts to avoid inadvertently setting the user's access times incorrectly. One administrator could set the user access hours strictly based on the user's standard work hours, while another administrator gives the user 24-hour access to the system. Inconsistent policies and policies that don't reflect actual user needs can cause a wealth of problems, including security holes.

To set a forced logoff interval, use the Net Accounts /ForceLogoff: *Minutes* subcommand, where *Minutes* is the number of minutes to wait before forcing the user to log off. This setting affects every account on the system. For example, if you feel that it's reasonable to wait 30 minutes for users to log off, then you'd type **Net Accounts /ForceLogoff:30** and press Enter. On the other hand, if you don't want to force logoffs, then you'd type **Net Accounts /ForceLogoff:No** and press Enter.

Configure the Password Requirements

Configuring password requirements can be difficult. For example, setting a long interval between password changes tends to reduce support costs because users are less likely to forget their password, but using a long interval also gives outsiders a longer time to use compromised passwords to access your system. (Most security experts recommend you change your password every 30 to 90 days.) Longer passwords are more secure, but also harder to remember. Users are likely to write down long passwords, which means that your company is open to various sorts of social engineering and physical attacks (such as an office cleaner lifting the passwords off the user's monitor). The article at http://technet.

microsoft.com/library/cc784090.aspx provides some best practices that you can use to configure passwords on your system. Password requirements affect every user of a machine.

The following procedure helps you construct a Net Accounts subcommand that configures passwords:

1. Type **Net Accounts** to start the subcommand.

2. (Optional) Type **/MinPWLen:*Length***, where *Length* is the number of characters the user must supply for a password as a minimum.

    The default setting varies by Windows version. For example, Windows 7 has a minimum password length of 0. If you don't want to set a minimum password length, type **/MinPWLen:0**.

3. (Optional) Type **/MaxPWAge:*Days***, where *Days* is the maximum number of days the user can use a password before changing it.

    If you don't want to set a maximum password age, type **/MaxPWAge:Unlimited** instead. The default setting is 42 days for Windows 7.

4. (Optional) Type **/MinPWAge:*Days***, where *Days* is the minimum number of days that must pass before a user can change their password.

    This setting comes in handy if you have a user who changes their password often, but tends to forget the new password. Generally, more password changes are better, but too often can raise support costs. If you don't care how often the user changes their password, type **/MinPWAge:0**.

5. (Optional) Type **/UniquePW:*Number***, where *Number* is the number of unique passwords that the user must provide before repeating an old password.

    This setting prevents users from recycling the same two passwords. The maximum number of passwords that Windows 7 will track is 24. If you don't care how often the user relies on the same password when changing passwords, type **/UniquePW:0**.

6. (Optional) Type **/Domain** if you want the command to modify the domain controller settings, rather than the local machine settings.

7. Press Enter.

    The Net Accounts subcommand makes the required changes. For example, if you want the user to change their password at least every 90 days but no more than once a month, use a password of

Managing the Network

PART III

seven characters, and provide at least five unique passwords, you'd type **Net Accounts /MinPWLen:7 /MaxPWAge:90 /MinPWAge:30 / UniquePW:5** and press Enter.

Manage Domains and Local Groups

Groups come in two forms for the Net utility. You can either work with groups at the domain level using the Net Group subcommand or the local level using the Net LocalGroup subcommand. Both subcommands provide precisely the same features, so working with one is the same as working with the other. The examples in the sections that follow assume you're working with a local group, but remember that the same commands will work with a domain group if you substitute the Net Group subcommand for the Net LocalGroup subcommand.

NOTE The Net Group and Net LocalGroup subcommands both assume you're working at the local machine, which is probably your workstation and not the domain controller. Consequently, if you execute the Net Group subcommand, it always displays an error telling you it can only execute on a Windows domain controller (error 3515). Use the /Domain command line switch to execute Net Group and Net LocalGroup subcommands on the domain controller (for the current domain), rather than on the local machine. If you need to perform group management on a different domain, you must log onto an account for that domain. The Net utility doesn't support the /S, /U, and /P command line switches supported by some other utilities.

Add a Group

Groups make it simpler to manage security and perform other user-related tasks by categorizing individuals with like needs together. Use the following procedure to add a new group:

1. Determine whether you want to create a local group or a domain group. Type **Net LocalGroup** to create a local group or **Net Group** to create a domain group.

2. Type the group name.

3. (Optional) Type **/Comment:*String***, where *String* is a comment you want to associate with the group.

Place multi-word comments within double quotes, such as /Comment:"This is a sample group."

4. Type **/Add**.

5. Type **/Domain** if you want to create the group on the domain controller rather than the local machine.

6. Press Enter.

The Net LocalGroup or Net Group subcommand creates the new group for you. For example, if you want to create the local group, MyGroup, with an appropriate comment, you'd type **Net Local-Group MyGroup /Comment:"This is a sample group." /Add** and press Enter.

View a Group

At some point, you'll want to know who is a member of a particular group. To begin, you need to know the names of the groups on a system. For example, to see all of the local groups, you type **Net LocalGroup** and press Enter. Figure 8.3 shows typical results. The output simply provides a list of groups on the machine.

Figure 8.3: Determine which groups appear on the machine before querying a specific group.

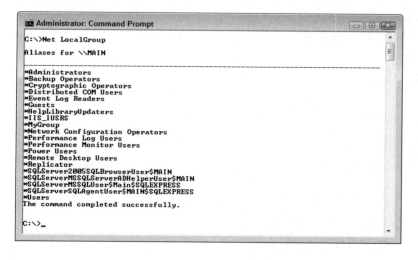

```
C:\>Net LocalGroup

Aliases for \\MAIN

-------------------------------------------------------------------------
*Administrators
*Backup Operators
*Cryptographic Operators
*Distributed COM Users
*Event Log Readers
*Guests
*HelpLibraryUpdaters
*IIS_IUSRS
*MyGroup
*Network Configuration Operators
*Performance Log Users
*Performance Monitor Users
*Power Users
*Remote Desktop Users
*Replicator
*SQLServer2005SQLBrowserUser$MAIN
*SQLServerMSSQLServerADHelperUser$MAIN
*SQLServerMSSQLUser$Main$SQLEXPRESS
*SQLServerSQLAgentUser$MAIN$SQLEXPRESS
*Users
The command completed successfully.

C:\>_
```

Managing the Network

PART III

Once you know the name of the group you want to query, you can request information about that group using the Net LocalGroup *GroupName* command where *GroupName* is the name of the group. For example, if you want to learn more about MyGroup, you'd type **Net LocalGroup MyGroup** and press Enter. Figure 8.4 shows typical output from this subcommand. The output contains the group name, comment, and a list of members.

Figure 8.4: Obtain specifics about a particular group.

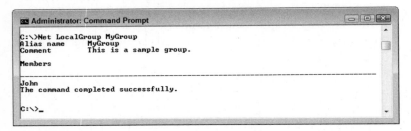

Delete a Group

Eventually, groups become useless. Perhaps the project has finished or the company has reorganized the people who relied on the group. When a group outlives its usefulness, you should remove it from the system to reduce security risks. Use the Net LocalGroup *GroupName* /Delete command, where *GroupName* is the name of the group, to remove a group you no longer need. For example, if you wanted to remove MyGroup, you'd type **Net LocalGroup MyGroup /Delete** and press Enter.

Add a User to a Group

Groups don't become useful until they contain members. In order to add a new member to a group, you use the Net LocalGroup *GroupName* *UserName* /Add command, where *GroupName* is the name of the group and *UserName* is the name of the user. For example, to add user John to MyGroup you'd type **Net LocalGroup MyGroup John /Add** and press Enter.

Delete a User from a Group

When users no longer require access to a group, you should remove them to ensure the system remains secure. In order to delete a member from a group, you use the Net LocalGroup *GroupName* *UserName* /Delete command, where *GroupName* is the name of the group and *UserName* is the name of the user. For example, to delete user John from MyGroup you'd type **Net LocalGroup MyGroup John /Delete** and press Enter.

Manage Computers

Administrators use the Net Computer subcommand only on domain controllers where they use it to add and remove computers from the domain controller's list. The following sections describe how to add and remove computers from a domain controller.

Add a Computer

Normally, the server automatically detects any new computers on the domain. However, you might find that the automatic detection doesn't work, especially as the network gets larger. In this case, you can use the Net Computer *UNCName* /Add subcommand, where *UNCName* is the Universal Naming Convention (UNC) name of the computer, to add the computer to the domain controller. For example, if you want to add MyComputer to the domain controller, you'd type **Net Computer \\ MyComputer /Add** and press Enter.

Remove a Computer

A domain controller will often fail to remove from its list old systems when they become unavailable. The main reason is that it's difficult for the domain controller to determine whether the computer is actually gone or whether it's simply offline. To remove a computer from the domain controller, use the Net Computer *UNCName* /Delete subcommand, where *UNCName* is the UNC name of the computer you want to remove. For example, if you want to remove MyComputer from the domain controller, you'd type **Net Computer \\MyComputer /Delete** and press Enter.

View and Close Sessions

The Net Session subcommand makes it possible to view and control sessions on any computer. The sessions listed are those with external connections to the computer, not the local connection you're using. Consequently, unless you share resources on your workstation with others on the network, you're unlikely to see anything listed for a typical workstation—this subcommand is more applicable to servers. The

Managing the Network

PART III

following sections describe common tasks you perform using the Net Session subcommand.

View All Sessions

Before you view a specific session, you normally check which sessions are available by viewing all of the sessions. To view all of the sessions, type **Net Session** and press Enter. You'll see an overview of all of the current sessions that include the computer name or TCP/IP address, the username, the client type, the number of open resources, and the system's idle time. The idle time tells you how much time has elapsed since the computer has performed any action, which you can use to determine when computers have crashed and are no longer connected to the server. Deleting those sessions is normally safe after you verify that the user is no longer connected.

View a Specific Session

Once you know the specific session you want to view, you use the Net Session *ComputerName* subcommand, where *ComputerName* is either the name or the TCP/IP address of the computer you want to view, to see the specifics. For example, you want to see the specifics of the computer at TCP/IP address 192.168.0.244, you'd type **Net Session \\192.168.0.244** and press Enter. The output displays the username, computer name, whether the session is a guest logon, the client type, the idle time, the total session time, and the number of resources opened on each of the server's shares (such as the number of files open on a disk drive).

Delete a Session

Deleting a session essentially disconnects the user from the host machine. The most common reason for deleting a session is that the client machine has frozen or otherwise become unable to use the session. The server still has the session open because it doesn't know that the session is no longer in use. Use the Net Session *ComputerName* /Delete subcommand, where *ComputerName* is the name or the TCP/IP address of the computer you want to work with, to delete the session. For example, if you want to delete the session for the computer at TCP/IP address 192.168.0.244, you'd type **Net Session \\192.168.0.244 /Delete** and press Enter.

Perform Server Configuration

The Net Config Server subcommand provides the means to access the server part of any machine. The machine could be a workstation that shares resources or a full-fledged domain controller. As long as the machine is running the Server service, you can configure the server elements on it using this subcommand. In fact, you can see the current configuration by typing Net Config Server and pressing Enter. You'll see statistics like the ones shown in Figure 8.5. The following sections describe server-related tasks you can perform using this subcommand.

Figure 8.5: Any machine that runs the Server service is a server you can configure using this subcommand.

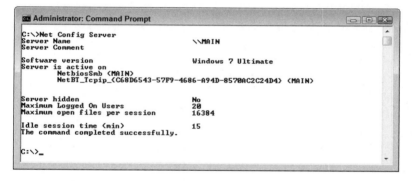

Setting the Autodisconnect Time

The automatic disconnect time controls when the server automatically disconnects a client that's been idle for too long. For example, this setting will automatically delete a session for a client that's frozen or otherwise become unavailable. Use the Net Config Server / Autodisconnect:Time command, where Time is the number of minutes to wait, to set the automatic disconnect time. For example, if you want to automatically disconnect clients after 15 minutes, you'd type **Net Config Server /Autodisconnect:15** and press Enter.

Managing the Network

PART III

NOTE Idle time is essentially inactivity. If the user or application isn't using processing cycles, then the system considers the application idle. An automatic disconnect works well if you want to ensure that documents are closed prior to a maintenance action, such as a backup. However, the side effect is that the user can lose the connection to the server and there is a chance of data loss if the user has left the application open without saving the local copy of any data changes. If you have users who consistently leave their systems on and documents open overnight, an automatic disconnect might not work as you intend it to. Make sure you set automatic disconnects to match company policy regarding application usage.

Setting a Comment

Comments help users identify the correct server on a network. Even if you're configuring a workstation that shares resources, you should provide a server comment to make it easier for users to locate the server. Use the `Net Config Server /SrvComment:Text` command, where *Text* is a string that contains the server comment, to add a comment to the server. For example, if you want to add a comment to a workstation that shares a printer for a workgroup, you might type **Net Config Server /SrvComment:"Workgroup Printer Server"** and press Enter. If you want to remove the comment from a server and not provide anything, you can type **Net Config Server /SrvComment:""** and press Enter.

Hiding the Server

In some cases, you need to run the Server service on a workstation, but you don't want anyone to actually use the workstation to share resources. For example, you might provide a network backup for all of the workstations on the network. Having every workstation appear as a potential source of resources would be confusing, so you'd hide the workstations that don't have shareable resources from view. Type **Net Config Server /Hidden:Yes** and press Enter to hide a server from view. To make the server visible again, you'd type **Net Config Server Hidden:No** and press Enter.

WARNING Hiding a server from view doesn't make it inaccessible—it simply means that you must know the name of the server and its resources to access it. In short, the server isn't really any more secure than it was before you hid it, but someone would need to perform additional work to find the server first.

View Workstation Configuration

The Net utility doesn't provide any means of configuring a workstation—the client portion of the machine setup. However, you can use the Net utility to view the workstation configuration. Simply type **Net Config Workstation** and press Enter. You'll see some workstation essentials, as shown in Figure 8.6.

Figure 8.6: The Net utility provides you with some details about workstation configuration.

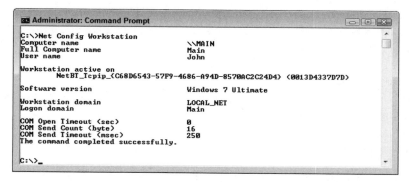

Manage Services

Windows services provide background processing. Much of the "magic" that users see when working with Windows is due to services that detect an event and then react to it. Of course, services can't do anything for you when they aren't running. It's important to start, stop, pause, and continue services at the right time to ensure Windows performs as expected. The following sections describe how to use the Net utility to interact with services.

View Started Services

Generally, you need to know what services are already running before you make any changes. That said, telling a service to start when it's already started won't do any harm to the system, nor will it generate an error message. All that you'll see is a message saying that the service is already started. To see which services are already started, type **Net Start** and press Enter. You'll see an alphabetical list of started services (but not all of the services installed on the machine).

Start Service Processing

Starting a service means that the Windows loads the executable file that supports the service and runs it. In many cases, this means running a .DLL within the SvcHost.EXE application. However, all you need to know is the name of the service. To start the service, use the Net Start *ServiceName* subcommand, where *ServiceName* is the name of the service as it appears in the Services console found in the Administrative Tools folder of the Control Panel. For example, to start the Bluetooth Support Service (BthServ), you'd type **Net Start "Bluetooth Support Service"** and press Enter.

Stop Service Processing

Stopping a service means unloading the service from memory and deallocating all of the resources used by the service. In order to use the service again, you must restart it, which means starting any processing from scratch. Make sure you want to actually stop the service, rather than pause the service so that processing can resume. To stop a service, use the Net Stop *ServiceName* subcommand, where *ServiceName* is the name of the service as it appears in the Services console found in the Administrative Tools folder of the Control Panel. For example, to stop the Bluetooth Support Service (BthServ), you'd type **Net Stop "Bluetooth Support Service"** and press Enter.

WARNING   Never stop a service until you have determined whether any other services are dependent on it. Stopping a service with dependencies will also stop the dependent services, which could cause unforeseen problems on the host system.

Pause Service Processing

Pausing a service means that Windows will put the process to sleep until you need it again. The service state is saved and any resources it uses will remain in use. When you continue (rather that start) using the service, the service will begin processing right where it left off, so nothing is lost when you pause the service. You'll normally stop a service, rather than pause it, when a service error occurs to ensure that any data errors or other problems are solved. To pause a service, use the Net Pause *ServiceName* subcommand, where *ServiceName* is the name of the service as it appears in the Services console found in the Administrative Tools folder of the Control Panel. For example, to pause the Bluetooth Support Service (BthServ), you'd type **Net Pause "Bluetooth Support Service"** and press Enter.

Continue Service Processing

You can only continue using a service after pausing it. If the service is stopped, then you must start it to use it. To continue a service, use the Net Continue *ServiceName* subcommand, where *ServiceName* is the name of the service as it appears in the Services console found in the Administrative Tools folder of the Control Panel. For example, to continue using the Bluetooth Support Service (BthServ), you'd type **Net Continue "Bluetooth Support Service"** and press Enter.

Manage Files

The Net File subcommand helps you to manage files opened by a client. This subcommand won't display any locally opened files. The following sections describe the three tasks you can perform using this subcommand.

View Files

You'll normally begin managing files by determining which files are opened. To see a complete list of the files opened by a client on a server, type **Net File** and press Enter. The output of this subcommand displays the file ID, the full path for the open file, the name of the user who has the file open, and the number of locks (if any) on the file. Locks are used to keep other users from accessing the file, so locked files are often a problem that an administrator must address when one user leaves a file that another user requires in the locked state.

View a File in Detail

In some cases, you need to learn more about an open file before you can do anything with it. To see file details, use the Net File *FileID* subcommand, where *FileID* is an identifier of an open file. For example, to see the details of file number 22, you'd type **Net File 22** and press Enter. The most important addition to the output is the permissions that the user has to the file. Often, permissions tell you what a user can do with the file and why the user is experiencing problems with it (you can't modify a file opened as read only).

Close Files

If a client workstation freezes or otherwise becomes unavailable, it can leave files in the open and locked state. Subsequent attempts to open the file for writing will fail because of the locks. In this case, you use the Net File *FileID* /Close subcommand, where *FileID* is an identifier of an open file, to close the file. For example, if you want to close file number 22, you'd type **Net File 22 /Close** and press Enter.

Obtain Help for the *Net* Utility

The Net /? command and its derivatives leave something to be desired when it comes to information. All that these commands really do is remind you of the command syntax. Because the Net utility is so complex, Microsoft actually provides special help commands for using it. The following sections describe these special forms of help.

Use *Help*

If you want to obtain detailed information about any Net subcommand, use the Net Help *Subcommand* command, where *Subcommand* is the subcommand that you want to learn about. For example, if you want to learn more about the Net File subcommand, you'd type **Net Help File** and press Enter. You'll see the complete command line syntax and details about each of the command line switches that the subcommand supports.

In some cases, such as the Net Config Server subcommand, you can go several layers deep in the Net Help subcommand. Simply type the additional levels as needed. For example, in this case, you'd type **Net Help Config Server** and press Enter to obtain the required help.

Use *Helpmsg*

Whenever the Net utility experiences an error, it provides you with a general error message. Unfortunately, the general information might not be enough for you to understand the error. In this case, you use the Net Helpmsg *Number* command, where *Number* is the error number you received, to discover additional information. For example, when you try to start a service that's already started, you see an error number of 2182. To learn more about this error, you type **Net Helpmsg 2182** and press Enter. The Net utility provides additional information about the error for you.

Manage Print Jobs

The Net Print subcommand helps you work with printers connected to your system. You can use this subcommand to manage print jobs at the command line, rather than rely on the GUI. The following sections describe how to manage print jobs using the Net Print subcommand.

NOTE   The Net Print subcommand may not be available with some newer versions of Windows such as Windows 7. In this case, you can rely on the WMIC PrintJob subcommand to manage print jobs instead. You can learn more about working with WMIC in Chapter 15.

View Jobs

Before you can do anything with the print jobs associated with a printer, you have to have a list of the pending jobs. To see the list of jobs, use the Net Print *ComputerName**ShareName* command, where *ComputerName* is the name of the computer and *ShareName* is the name of the printer share (not necessarily the same as the name of the printer). For example, to see the print jobs on the HP LaserJet 5 queue of WinServer, you'd type **Net Print "\\WinServer\HP LaserJet 5"** and press Enter.

The output shows a list of print jobs that includes the print job name, number, and size. A fourth column shows the job status. The print job number is the most important part of the list because you use it to change the print job status.

Hold a Job

In some cases, you might need to hold a job to let higher priority jobs complete first. To hold a job, you use the Net Print *ComputerName JobNumber* /Hold command, where *ComputerName* is the name of the computer and *JobNumber* is the number of the print job. For example, to hold print job 4 on WinServer, you'd type **Net Print \\WinServer 4 /Hold** and press Enter.

Release a Job

When all of the high priority jobs complete, you can release any lower priority jobs that you held earlier so that they can complete. To release a job, you use the Net Print *ComputerName JobNumber* /Release command, where *ComputerName* is the name of the computer and *JobNumber* is the number of the print job. For example, to release print job 4 on WinServer, you'd type **Net Print \\WinServer 4 /Release** and press Enter.

Delete a Job

Just about everyone prints something by mistake. Of course, you don't want to print something that no one needs, so you delete it from the queue. To delete a job, you use the Net Print *ComputerName JobNumber* / Delete command, where *ComputerName* is the name of the computer and *JobNumber* is the number of the print job. For example, to delete print job 4 on WinServer, you'd type **Net Print \\WinServer 4 /Delete** and press Enter.

Manage Resources

Sharing resources (also called simply a share) is one of the more important reasons to have a network. Therefore, it isn't any surprise that managing those resources is a top administrator goal. Although the Net utility doesn't provide complete resource management, it does provide some good rudimentary management features that will help you work with network resources with greater efficiency.

View Resources

Many administrators are unaware of the fact that there are many default resources on a system—shares that Windows actually creates during the setup process and never asks you about. Consequently, one of the first things you should do when working with a new system is to view these default shares before you add anything new. To see any existing shares, type **Net Share** and press Enter. Figure 8.7 shows a typical list of default shares with one addition for the printer.

Figure 8.7: Windows provides a number of default shares as part of the setup process.

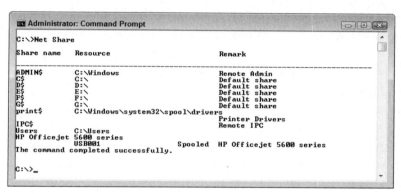

```
Administrator: Command Prompt

C:\>Net Share

Share name    Resource                            Remark

-------------------------------------------------------------------------------
ADMIN$        C:\Windows                          Remote Admin
C$            C:\                                 Default share
D$            D:\                                 Default share
E$            E:\                                 Default share
F$            F:\                                 Default share
G$            G:\                                 Default share
print$        C:\Windows\system32\spool\drivers
                                                  Printer Drivers
IPC$                                              Remote IPC
Users         C:\Users
HP Officejet 5600 series
              USB001                   Spooled    HP Officejet 5600 series
The command completed successfully.

C:\>_
```

A shared resource, such as C$, is called an administrative share because it's commonly used for administrative tasks and not defined for general use. When you look at the permissions for such a resource, you find that only the Administrators group can even access them. The output from the Net Share subcommand shows the share name, the resource it accesses, and a remark that tells you more about the resource.

The simple list shown in Figure 8.7 isn't enough to know who has access to a resource. To obtain detailed resource information, use the Net Share *ShareName* command, where *ShareName* is the name of the share, such as C$. For example, if you want to find out who can access the C$ resource, you'd type **Net Share C$** and press Enter. The detailed listing also provides you with the maximum number of users, the users who have access to the share, and the kind of caching used with the resource.

Share Resources

To provide access to a resource, you must create a share for it. You could create one monster subcommand to perform this task, but it's actually easier to perform the task in steps. Using the stepped approach also makes it easier to fix mistakes. The following steps create a share for the

Managing the Network

PART III

C drive on a system. In this case, the procedure grants full access to the Administrators group and full access to an individual user named John.

1. Type `Net Share Drive_C=C:\ /Grant:Administrators,Full /Grant:John,Full` and press Enter.

   This command creates the share. Of course, you can give the share any useful name—the example simply uses Drive_C as the share name. You must grant access to the share at the time you create it using the `/Grant` command line switch. The `/Grant` command line switch can appear any number of times and you can assign rights to both groups and individuals. The list of rights is: Full, Change, and Read. If you don't assign specific rights for the share, the Everyone group gets Read access.

2. (Optional) Type `Net Share Drive_C /Remark:"Provides access to the C drive."` and press Enter.

   Any time you create a share, you should assign a remark to it to make it easier for others to locate and understand the purpose of the share. The remark can be anything that users will find useful.

3. (Optional) Type `Net Share Drive_C /Cache:None` and press Enter.

   Caching determines how fast a user can access the resource in many cases. You have a choice of Manual, Documents, Programs, BranchCache, and None.

4. (Optional) Type `Net Share Drive_C /Users:5` and press Enter.

   This subcommand determines the maximum number of users for the resource. If you don't set a maximum number of users, an unlimited number of users can access the resource. While unlimited access is fine for a server in most cases, you'll want to limit shared resource access on a workstation to keep the workstation usable as a local resource.

Use Resources

After you create a share, you'll want to use it. The `Net Use` subcommand makes it possible to access a share on another system. To create access to a share, use the `Net Use LocalDevice RemoteShare` subcommand, where *LocalDevice* is the name of a local device that will receive the share and *RemoteShare* is the name of the share on the remote machine. For example, if you want to assign \\WinServer\C$ to the N drive on the local machine, you'd type **Net Use N: \\WinServer\C$** and press Enter. If you want to be sure that the resource will be available the next time you boot the system, you add the /Persistent:Yes command line switch, so you'd type **Net Use N: \\WinServer\C$ / Persistent:Yes** and press Enter instead.

If you later decide that you don't need the resource, then you'd delete it from the workstation. In this case, you'd type **Net Use N: /Delete** to remove resource access.

Remove Resources

Eventually a shared resource outlives its usefulness and you delete it. To remove a resource, you use the Net Share *ShareName* /Delete command, where *ShareName* is the name of the share. For example, to delete a shared resource named Drive_C, you'd type **Net Share Drive_C /Delete** and press Enter.

Obtain Statistics

The Net utility provides a few interesting statistics for both the server and workstation (client) portion of a machine. For example, when working with a server, you can see how many permission errors have occurred. The following sections describe how to view statistics using the Net utility.

View Server Statistics

The server statistics don't let you modify or configure anything, but they do tell you a few useful facts about the server portion of a machine. To see these statistics, type **Net Statistics Server** and press Enter. Figure 8.8 shows typical output from this subcommand. These statistics tell you about the overall health of your server. For example, a large number of permission errors can tell you that there are security issues you need to confront. A large number of timed out sessions can tell you about network issues or workstation configuration problems.

Managing the Network

PART III

Figure 8.8: Server statistics tell you how many connections are made and other interesting facts.

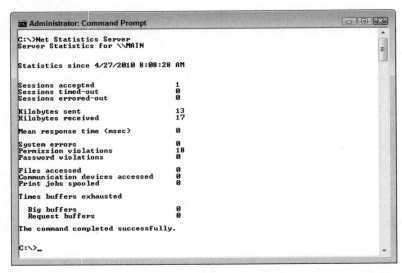

Figure 8.9: Workstation statistics can help you discover the overall health of the client.

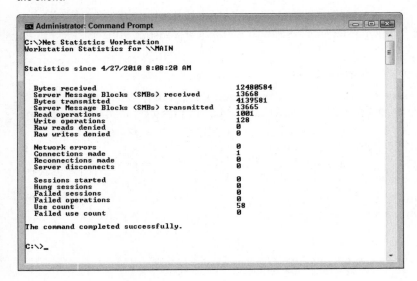

View Workstation Statistics

The workstation statistics tell you about the client portion of a machine. You can discover how much data the workstation is reading and writing. A more important statistic is the number of network errors the workstation is encountering. In a perfect environment, the workstation wouldn't encounter any network errors. To see the workstation statistics, type **Net Statistics Workstation** and press Enter. Figure 8.9 shows typical output from this subcommand.

Configure Time Synchronization

The Net Time subcommand lets you see and set local time based on another machine on the network. If you want to use an Internet time source, you need the W32Tm utility described in Chapter 15. The following sections describe how to use this subcommand.

View Time Source

If you want to view the current time on another computer, you can check it by accessing the computer by name. Simply use the Net Time *ComputerName* command, where *ComputerName* is the name of the remote computer you want to access. For example, to check the time on WinServer, you'd type **Net Time \\WinServer** and press Enter. You can also access the time on a domain controller by using the / Domain:ComputerName command line switch or a Reliable Time Source using the /RTSDomain:ComputerName command line switch.

Set Time Source

When you decide to reset your local clock using a remote computer as a source, you add the /Set command line switch. For example, to reset your computer's clock based on the time on WinServer, you'd type **Net Time \\WinServer /Set** and press Enter. The Net utility will ask if you're sure you want to reset your local clock based on the time on WinServer. Type **Y** and press Enter to complete the task.

Managing the Network

PART III

9

Working with TCP/IP

IN THIS CHAPTER, YOU WILL LEARN TO:

Managing the Network

PART III

A t one time, a wide range of network protocols were in use for PC networks. However, the vast majority of networks today use TCP/IP for their networking protocol because TCP/IP offers so many benefits and is ubiquitous—it's the standard that everyone seems to rely on today. For example, the Internet won't work without TCP/IP. This chapter explores how you can manage TCP/IP networks at the command line. Even though the coverage isn't complete, you'll find that the command line has a lot to offer when it comes to general management tasks.

Manage the Internet Protocol

The IPConfig utility is probably one of the most used on workstations to fix common TCP/IP problems. The precise functionality of IPConfig depends on the version of Windows that you use, because Microsoft has put a lot of effort into updating this command line utility to meet the needs of today's networks. Of course, the biggest issue to consider today is support for Internet Protocol version 6 (IPv6) because many companies are moving in that direction. Whether you believe that the world will run out of IPv4 addresses sooner, the Internet will eventually embrace IPv6, if for no other reason than the government will mandate it.

The following sections highlight the IPConfig features available to Windows 7 and Windows 2008 administrators. Most of these features are also available with older versions of Windows, but you'll definitely see differences if you use an older version of Windows—especially when it comes to IPv6 support.

Display the IP Information

Most administrators need basic information about their network, such as which adapters are active and what IP address they have assigned to them. In this case, type **IPConfig** and press Enter. You'll see information similar to the information shown in Figure 9.1. The physical adapters normally appear first, followed by the tunnel adapters. In this case, the tunnel adapters are used by IPv6 to IPv4 connectivity and you don't really need to worry about them. You might also see entries for a Virtual Private Network (VPN) if you have one set up. The physical adapter information includes the IPv4 and IPv6 addresses, along with the Domain Name System (DNS) suffix, which is mshome.net when you configure a workgroup.

Figure 9.1: The basic IPConfig information provides everything needed for an overview of the network.

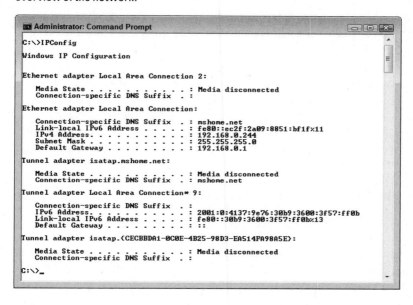

Figure 9.2: Getting all of the IPConfig information can be overwhelming.

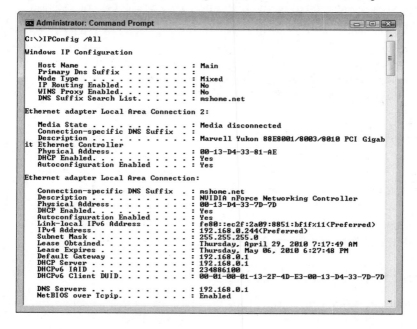

In some cases, you do need additional information. To obtain all of the information that IPConfig has to offer, type IPConfig /All and press Enter. Figure 9.2 shows a sample of the additional information you receive, which is substantial (the screenshot would have to be quite large to show everything for the sample system). For example, you now get complete DNS and Dynamic Host Configuration Protocol (DHCP) information. You also get the physical adapter's name and incidentals like the lease times.

Fortunately, IPConfig offers some intermediate levels of information between these two extremes. For example, you can type **IPConfig / DisplayDNS** and press Enter to see the contents of the DNS resolver cache. Type **IPConfig /?** and press Enter to see a complete list of display options.

Renew Addresses for an Adapter

Normally, the system takes care of renewing addresses automatically and the administrator doesn't have to think about it. In some cases, the network will suddenly stop working. One of the techniques for reestablishing contact (among many) is to try to renew the addresses for the network adapter. The fastest way to accomplish this task is to renew all of the adapters for a system, rather than renewing them one at a time. To perform this task at the IPv4 level, type **IPConfig /Renew** and press Enter. If you want to renew the IPv6 addresses, type **IPConfig /Renew6** and press Enter.

NOTE In most cases, you release an address before you renew it using the IPConfig /Release command. See the "Release a Connection" section for additional details.

On the rare occasion that you want to renew a particular connection, use the IPConfig /Renew *ConnectionName* or IPConfig / Renew6 *ConnectionName* command, where *ConnectionName* is the name of the connection as it appears in the IPConfig output. For example, Local Area Connection is one of the connections shown in Figure 9.1. Consequently, if you want to renew the IPv4 address for this connection, you'd type **IPConfig /Renew "Local Area Connection"** and press Enter.

Clear the DNS Resolver Cache

In some cases, you run into a problem where the DNS resolver cache on a system becomes corrupted or outdated. The DNS resolver cache is where the system stores IP addresses of URLs that the user visits. If the IP address of the URL changes before the DNS resolver cache purges itself, the user may find it impossible to get to the Web site or other resource. Type `IPConfig /FlushDNS` and press Enter to purge the content of the DNS resolver cache to correct errors of this sort.

The DNS resolver cache can also show where the user has gone on the Internet. To see how the DNS resolver cache is working and where the user has been, type `IPConfig /DisplayDNS | More` and press Enter (the DNS resolver cache normally contains so many entries that you need to pipe the output to `More` to see it). Each entry contains a record name, record type (see http://en.wikipedia.org/wiki/List_of_DNS_record_types for a list of standard record types), time to live (the amount of time that the DNS resolver cache will hold the record), the data length, section, and record data (normally an IP address or canonical name).

Renew DHCP Addresses and Register DNS Names

Normally, the system updates DHCP addresses and registers the client DNS name automatically. However, in some cases, you may find that the system can't find the client, the client can't find the network, or that some other miscommunication occurs. Type `IPConfig /RegisterDNS` and press Enter to correct problems where the server loses track of the client. If you think that the problem only exists for one adapter, you can use the `IPConfig /RegisterDNS` *Adapter* command, where *Adapter* is the name of the adapter to register.

NOTE Most `IPConfig` command line switches accept wild-card characters. For example, if you want to register all of the connections that begin with Local Area, you'd type `IPConfig / RegisterDNS "Local Area*"` and press Enter. The asterisk (*) represents any number of characters, while the question mark (?) represents a single character.

Release a Connection

If you no longer need a connection or need to perform some trouble-shooting, you can release it. In most cases, you'll use the `IPConfig / Release` *Adapter* command, where *Adapter* is the name of an adapter, to release just one adapter. For example, to release the connection for Local Area Connection 2, you'd type `IPConfig /Release "Local Area Connection 2"` and press Enter. Releasing a connection results in loss of network connectivity if the connection is active.

Managing the Network

PART III

Use Basic Diagnostics

Network connectivity can be notoriously difficult to maintain and trouble-shoot when it fails. After you check the physical connection and ensure all of the correct drivers are in place, you begin looking for other potential sources of the problem. The command line provides access to a number of diagnostic aids that can make troubleshooting easier. The following sections provide an overview of the most important troubleshooting aids.

Check Connections

The Packet Internet Groper (PING) utility makes it possible to check connectivity to a specific resource. For example, if you want to check the connection to a machine on the network named WinServer, you'd type **PING WinServer** and press Enter. When everything is working correctly, you see four tests of the connection as shown in Figure 9.3. The output shows the IP address of the remote connection, the amount of data sent to it, and how long the connection took to complete. At the end of the test you see statistics, such as the number of tests run and how many times the test failed. PING even provides times so that you can use it to detect slow connections.

Figure 9.3: The default PING configuration provides a simple way to test any connection.

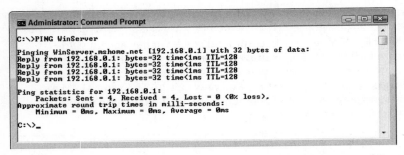

The basic test provides most of what administrators need to simply check a connection. However, PING provides command line switches to vary the size and number of tests. In fact, you can use the PING *RemoteAddress* -t command, where *RemoteAddress* is the name or IP address of the remote systems, to run PING continuously until you press Ctrl+C to stop the test.

The default test uses IPv4 unless you have IPv4 disabled on the sending machine. If you want to specifically test IPv6 connectivity, use the PING *RemoteAddress* -6 command. PING provides a wealth of other command line switches that modify the default test. Type PING /? and press Enter to learn more.

Trace Transmission Paths

Networks are complex and sometimes a packet doesn't take a direct path to a destination. In fact, if you're working with an Internet connection, it's almost certain that the path is indirect. A slow connection can simply mean a problem with one of the intermediate locations. Each of these intermediate connections is a hop. The PathPing utility will trace the connections between two endpoints up to 30 hops. For example, let's say you want to see the path between a client and www.mwt.net. You'd type **PathPing www.mwt.net** and press Enter. Figure 9.4 shows typical output from PathPing.

NOTE Don't include a protocol when working with PathPing or other path resolution utilities that work with a domain name. For example, if you type **PathPing http://www.mwt.net** and press Enter, you'll see an error message, "Unable to resolve target system name http://www.mwt.net" because you've included a protocol. PathPing and other utilities require only the domain name as input. This book will always include the protocol as part of an URL when the protocol is needed to avoid potential confusion.

Figure 9.4: Using PathPing shows you the path between the client machine and any other location.

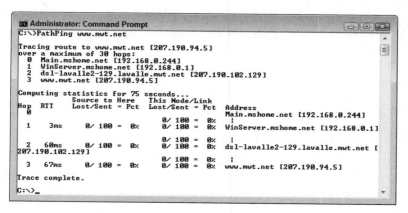

The output begins by creating a basic trace between two endpoints. In this case, the trace requires three hops (the first entry in the output is always the starting endpoint). Next, PathPing computes statistics for the various hops. In this case, none of the hops lost data. It takes 3 ms to send the packet between the starting endpoint and WinServer.mshome. net, another 60 ms to go to dsl-lavalle2-129.lavalle.mwt.net, and 67 ms to finally reach www.mwt.net. If you'd seen a significant amount of data loss or excessive transmission times for any of these hops, you would have found the point of potential data loss and the reason a connection is slow.

PathPing supports a number of additional features that you can see by typing **PathPing /?** and pressing Enter. For example, you can force PathPing to perform an IPv6 test by using the -6 command line switch.

Track the Network Path

The PathPing utility can be a little slow to use, especially when it comes to computing the network statistics. The TraceRt utility provides a simple version of the same utility. In this case, all you see is the path between two endpoints and the time required to traverse those endpoints. For example, if you want to check the connection between a client and www.mwt.net, you'd type **TraceRt www.mwt.net** and press Enter. Figure 9.5 shows typical output from this utility.

Figure 9.5: TraceRt is a simplified version of the PathPing utility.

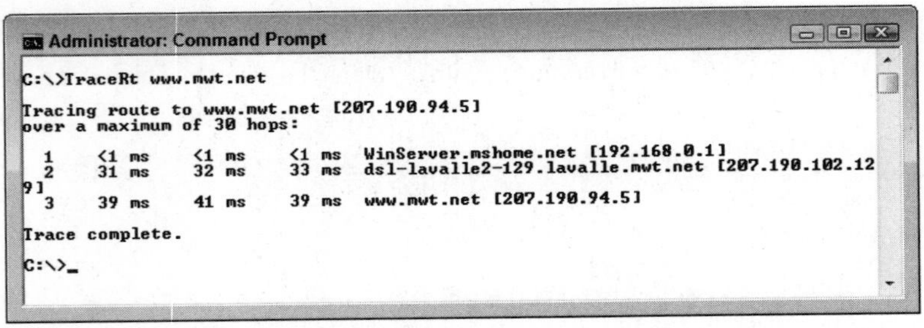

Using RPCPing and Other Special Connectivity Utilities

Many specialty connection utilities are available, such as RPCPing, which is commonly used to check connectivity with Exchange Server and other COM servers (see the Knowledge Base article at http://support.microsoft.com/kb/831051 for details). Even if you have a good connection to the server, the Remote Procedure Call (RPC) functionality required by these applications might not always work. RPCPing provides a means of performing a connectivity check using RPC, rather than IP packets.

The connectivity you're checking is with a particular server that relies on RPC. For example, you wouldn't use RPCPing to check connectivity to a server named WinServer, but you would use RPCPing to check connectivity to the Exchange Server installed on WinServer. In short, RPCPing is a second-level tool— the one you use after you make the initial check using PING, PathPing, or TraceRt.

In order to create a command line syntax for RPCPing, you must know something about the remote server and then choose command line switches that provide the information that the server needs. Type **RPCPing /?** and press Enter to see a list of these command line switches. Because RPCPing and other second-level tools of this sort are so specialized, discussing them in detail in this book isn't possible, but you should be aware of their presence and use them whenever possible to locate the source of application connectivity problems.

Managing the Network

PART III

Perform Detailed Network Diagnostics

The NetDiag utility can help you perform detailed network tests that locate specific issues, such as checking DNS for problems. In fact, NetDiag is one of those utilities that every administrator should know about and use regularly because it has the potential to save you a great deal of time, yet is free of charge. Unfortunately, newer versions of Windows don't come with NetDiag installed— you have to download and install it separately, so the first section that follows tells how to obtain this useful utility. The sections that follow describe how to use NetDiag to perform network diagnostics.

Obtain a Copy of *NetDiag*

Newer versions of Windows don't provide support for the NetDiag utility by default. (If you perform an upgrade install from Windows 2003 or older, you'll still find it on your system.) Use the following steps to obtain a copy of NetDiag for your own use:

1. Download a copy of the utility from http://www.microsoft.com/downloads/details.aspx?familyid=49AE8576-9BB9-4126-9761-BA8011FABF38 or http://www.microsoft.com/downloads/details.aspx?familyid=1EA70814-7E6C-46E5-8C8C-3C439A732E9F.

   Of the two downloads, the Windows XP version (the first URL) works better with newer versions of Windows. In some cases, you may find that you obtain better results by running this utility at a client, rather than at the server, due to the security features of Windows Server 2008.

2. Double-click the WindowsXP-KB838079-SupportTools-ENU.EXE or NetDiag_Setup.EXE file and follow the installation instructions.

   The Windows XP version of the download will detect the operating system you're using. Use these additional steps to install this version.

   a. Install the Windows XP Support Tools first on a Windows XP system.

   b. Locate the NetDiag.EXE file in the \Program Files\Support Tools folder.

   c. Copy the NetDiag.EXE file to the machine where you want to use it.

3. Open a command prompt in Administrator mode by right-clicking the Command Prompt shortcut and choosing Run As Administrator from the context menu.

   You may have to provide a password to use the command prompt with the higher level credentials.

4. Add the NetDiag.EXE file location to the path by using the PATH=*NetDiagPath*;%PATH% command, where *NetDiagPath* is the location of NetDiag.EXE.

   For example, if you use the default Windows XP Support Tools path, you'd type **PATH=C:\Program Files\Support Tools;%PATH%** and press Enter. Likewise, if you use the default Windows

Server 2000 path, you'd type **PATH=C:\Program Files\Resource Kit\;%PATH%** and press Enter. Make sure you modify the path to meet your specific installation needs.

Perform a Test

NetDiag provides a number of tests. In order to run these tests, simply type **NetDiag** and press Enter. You might decide that you want the utility to output more or less information. In this case, you type **NetDiag** followed by one of the verbosity command line switches in the following list, and then press Enter:

- **/L:** Doesn't output any information at all, except to tell you when the test is done. The output goes to the NetDiag.LOG file instead.

- **/Q:** Output only the error information to screen.

- **/V:** Output error information, the standard test information, and supplemental test information. The supplemental test information tells you about each test step and also includes details about adapters such as the adapter statistics.

- **/Debug:** Outputs all of the information supplied with /V, plus service-related information for each adapter card. This is the maximum amount of information you can receive.

Understand Diagnostics

Generally, the utility performs all tests in an attempt to locate all networking problems on the first pass. You must bind TCP/IP to one or more adapters before running any of the tests (Windows generally performs this task automatically for you during installation, but some versions of Windows, such as Windows Server 2008 Server Core, may require manual setup). If you're simply checking the system for problems, then performing all of the tests is a very good idea, especially if you can perform the tests during a scheduled system maintenance time.

There are situations where you may already have a good idea of what is wrong with the network or you might need to run specific tests in the interest of saving time. In this case, you can either run specific tests using the NetDiag /Test:TestName command or skip specific tests using the NetDiag /Skip:TestName command, where TestName is the name of one of the tests in Table 9.1. For example, if you want to perform just the IPConfig test, you type **NetDiag /Test:IpConfig** and press Enter.

Table 9.1: NetDiag Test Listing

Test Name at Command Line	Full Name
Autonet	Automatic Private IP Addressing (APIPA) address test
Bindings	Bindings test
Browser	Redir and Browser test
DcList	Domain controller list test
DefGw	Default gateway test
DNS	DNS test
DsGetDc	Domain controller discovery test
IpConfig	IP address configuration test
IpLoopBk	IP address loopback ping test
IPX	IPX test
Kerberos	Kerberos test
Ldap	LDAP test
Member	Domain membership test
Modem	Modem diagnostics test
NbtNm	NetBT name test
Ndis	Netcard queries test
NetBTTransports	NetBT transports test
Netstat	Netstat information test
Netware	Netware test
Route	Routing table test
Trust	Trust relationship test
WAN	WAN configuration test
WINS	WINS service test
Winsock	Winsock test

Locate and Fix Minor Problems

The NetDiag utility can fix minor network problems automatically. To check the network completely and automatically fix minor problems, type **NetDiag /Fix** and press Enter. You can also combine the /Fix command line switch with any level of verbosity and with switches that limit the number of tests that NetDiag runs.

Get Network Statistics

Network statistics can often point out hard-to-locate problems in connectivity. For example, a high number of failures can tell you that a particular adapter has failed. Ports that are overwhelmed will show a high number of errors as well. The NetStat utility won't precisely tell you that there's an error on your network, but it provides indicators that an experienced administrator can use for diagnostic purposes. Even if there isn't an error, statistics can point out the need for an upgrade or tell you other things about your network (such as the probing of some nefarious individual). The following sections describe how to use the NetStat utility.

Display All Connections and Ports

Connectivity is the basis for network communications. Good connections let applications obtain resources from remote locations. Too many connections can provide an open door for reprehensible individuals to enter your network and cause harm. In short, you need to control the connections and ports to provide just enough connections, but no more than you actually need to make applications work. To see a list of connections and ports on your system, type **NetStat -a** and press Enter.

The output of this command will show a list of IPv4 or IPv6 addresses that include port information in most cases. For example, 192.168.0.244:139 is an IPv4 address for port 139. The output will also tell you whether the port is listening (waiting for something to use them), established (actually performing useful work), or waiting (neither listening nor performing useful work, but available). Finally, you'll discover whether the connection relies on the Transmission Control Protocol (TCP) or User Datagram Protocol (UDP). Remember that address 127.0.0.1 is the loopback (localhost) address used to connect to the local machine.

Managing the Network

PART III

In some cases, the information you see in the output won't make sense because NetStat uses a shorthand that relies on your knowledge of network addresses. You can enhance the information you receive by typing **NetStat -a -f** and pressing Enter. Now the output will contain Fully Qualified Domain Names (FQDNs) that will tell you more about the connection and possibly tell you about its source.

The output of NetStat -a can be time consuming to go through if you're in a hurry. In this case, type **NetStat -n** and press Enter to obtain just a numeric list of connections without the usual protocol information. The list only tells you the basics, which includes whether the connection is established or waiting. The output doesn't include ports that are listening. Use these steps if you want to associate the active addresses and ports with an application:

1. Type **NetStat -o** and press Enter.

   The output is the same as using the NetStat -n command, but you'll see a fifth column that contains a Process Identifier (PID).

2. Open Task Manager by right-clicking the taskbar and choosing Start Task Manager (or simply Task Manager) from the context menu.

3. Select the Processes tab.

4. Choose View ➤ Select Columns to display the Select Columns dialog box.

5. Check the PID (Process Identifier) entry and click OK.

6. Locate the PID found in the fifth column in the Task Manager display to find the application that's using the connection.

Display Application Statistics

In some cases, you need to know which applications are using a particular IP address and port. To see the application specifics, type **NetStat -b** and press Enter. The output tells you which application is using each active address and port. In addition, you see information such as the protocol in use (normally TCP or UDP).

Most of the entries will correlate directly to applications you have opened on the system such as Outlook or Firefox. You might also see applications such as MSTSC.EXE, which is used by Remote Desktop. One entry may not have an application associated with it—the microsoft-ds or Directory Services connection on port 1138. Some applications use well-known or registered port numbers as listed at http://en.wikipedia. org/wiki/List_of_TCP_and_UDP_port_numbers. Because port usage is so important, you might consider downloading and using the Microsoft Port Reporter service from http://www.microsoft.com/downloads/ details.aspx?FamilyId=69BA779B-BAE9-4243-B9D6-63E62B4BCD2E.

Display Ethernet Statistics

You use the Ethernet statistics to get a quick overview of network health. Simply type **NetStat -e** and press Enter to obtain this information. The Ethernet statistics are short and to the point. You'll see numbers for the number of packets sent, unicast packets, and non-unicast packets. However, the most interesting entries are the number of discards (packets that are malformed, which can point to a network error or unwanted outside activity), errors (normally network errors that you should fix), and unknown protocols (normally unwanted outside activity that you should investigate).

Display Protocol Information

The NetStat utility can display protocol-specific information in a number of ways. If you want to see a list of connections for a specific protocol, use the NetStat -p *Protocol* command, where *Protocol* is one of the following protocols:

- TCP
- UDP
- TCPv6
- UDPv6

For example, if you want to see all of the TCP/IPv4 connections, you'd type **NetStat -p TCP** and press Enter. You'll see essentially the same information you receive when using the NetStat -n command, except you see just the protocol you requested (see the "Display All Connections and Ports" section of the chapter for details).

If you want to see detailed protocol statistics, type **NetStat -s** and press Enter. In this case, the output contains information such as the number of packets sent and received. Using the NetStat -s command displays statistics for all of the protocols. If you combine the -s and -p

Managing the Network

PART III

command line switches, you see just the statistics for the protocol you specify. In this case, the -p command line switch can use the protocols:

- IP
- IPv6
- ICMP
- ICMPv6
- TCP
- TCPv6
- UDP
- UDPv6

For example, if you want to see the statistics for TCP/IPv4, you'd type NetStat -s -p IP and press Enter.

Set a Refresh Interval

Network connections are constantly changing. You may need to see these connections over time in order to determine the cause of a problem. In this case, you can add an automatic update interval to the NetStat command. For example, you might want to see a short list of network connections updated every 30 seconds. In this case, you type NetStat -n 30 and press Enter. The update interval appears as a number of seconds at the end of the command. To stop displaying statistics, press Ctrl+C.

Manipulate the Network Routing Tables

The Route utility tells you about routes on your network—the destinations of network connections. For example, if you have a connection from a client to a server, this utility shows it to you. The following sections tell you about the Route utility.

Print the Routing Tables

Before you can do anything with the routing tables, you need to know the current routes. To see the entire list of routes for the target system, type Route Print and press Enter. (An alternative to this command is to type **NetStat /R** and press Enter.) You'll see a list of network routes similar to the one shown in Figure 9.6. The output begins with an interface list that contains all of the adapters for the system and their respective numbers. The next section is a list of IPv4 routes, followed by a list of IPv6 routes.

Figure 9.6: The Route utility can display a list of existing destinations.

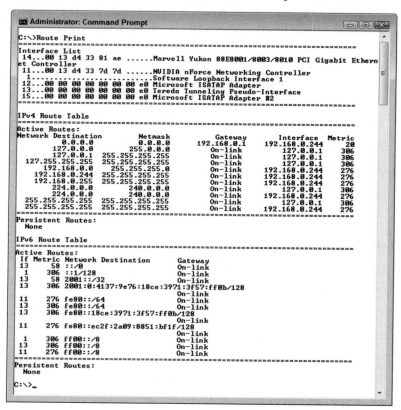

Add a New Route

In most cases, the system automatically configures routes as needed. However, you might find that you need to add a route manually when the client can't find a server.

Use the following process to add a route:

1. Type **Route Add.**

2. Provide a *Destination*, where *Destination* is an IPv4 or IPv6 address.

3. (IPv4 Only) Type **Mask**, and then provide an IPv4 mask.

4. (Optional) Provide a *Gateway* address, where *Gateway* is the IPv4 or IPv6 address of the system used as a gateway.

   If you don't provide this value, the system will use a default gateway value.

5. Type **Metric**, and then provide a metric value for the connection.

   A lower numbered metric value is faster than a higher numbered metric value. Use metric values that reflect the true speed of a new connection when compared to other connections in the routing table.

6. Type **IF**, and then provide an IPv4 or IPv6 interface address.

7. (Optional) Type **–p** to make the connection persistent.

8. (Optional) Type **–4** to force an IPv4 route or **–6** to force an IPv6 route.

9. Press Enter. The Route utility creates the new route.

Change a Route

The Route utility restricts the changes you can make to the gateway or the metric. You can't change the basic address or interface information. If you need to change more than the gateway or metric, you must delete the old route and add a new one.

Use this process to change a route:

1. Type **Route Change** *DestinationAddress*, where *DestinationAddress* is an IPv4 or IPv6 destination address that already appears in the routing table.

2. (IPv4 Only) Type **Mask** *MaskValue*, where *MaskValue* is the current mask for the destination address. You can't change the mask for a route.

3. (Optional) Type *GatewayAddress*, where *GatewayAddress* is either the existing or a new IPv4 or IPv6 gateway address.

4. Type **Metric** *MetricValue*, where *MetricValue* is either the existing or new metric value for the route.

5. Type IF *InterfaceAddress*, where *InterfaceAddress* is the existing interface address for the route. You can't change the interface address for a route.

6. Press Enter. The Route utility changes the gateway and metric information for the route as needed.

Delete a Route

You may eventually need to remove a route. In this case, all you need to do is use the Route Delete *DestinationAddress* command, where *DestinationAddress* is the destination address you want to remove. For example, if you want to remove the route for 192.168.0.244, then you'd type **Route Delete 192.168.0.244** and press Enter.

10

Creating System Connections

Managing the Network

PART III

T here are many ways to create connections between two computers. Previous chapters have concentrated on connectivity hardware, the operating system at a low level, and protocols such as TCP/IP. This chapter discusses two services used to create connections at the command line (rather than as an application): Remote Desktop and Terminal Server. In addition, you'll discover a number of utilities that help you perform remote system management.

The following sections describe how to work with these two useful services so that you can create the remote connections you need to interact with other machines, especially those servers locked in a room somewhere (hopefully they're locked up for security reasons). Of course, the techniques described in this chapter are also helpful when working with users and configuring other systems after an initial installation process completes. The point is to be able to access systems remotely when command line utilities don't provide this functionality as a built-in feature using the /S (system), /U (username), and /P (password) command line switches.

Perform Remote System Management

Remote system management involves creating a connection to a remote system, taking control of remote resources, and then using those resources to complete a task. For example, you might create a connection to a remote system for the purpose of managing the hard drive. You might need to create a partition, defragment the hard drive, or simply check it for errors. You use remote system management to improve administrator efficiency. Instead of running to each computer individually, an administrator can perform tasks from a single location. In addition, the administrator can often perform multiple tasks—while waiting for a task to complete on one system, the administrator can perform tasks on another machine. The following sections discuss several remote system management utilities.

Create Remote Connections

Remote Desktop is possibly the most useful remote system management tool that comes with Windows. Of course, there are more complete remote management tools, such as System Center Operations Manager, but these tools are complex, expensive, and definitely for the high-end professional. Anyone can use Remote Desktop, even users who simply need to access their work machine from home. The "Use the Remote Desktop Connection Application" section of Chapter 2 discusses the GUI method for working with Remote Desktop. The sections that follow describe the command line utility associated with Remote Desktop, Microsoft Terminal Services Client (MSTSC).

NOTE MSTSC is one of a few command line utilities that doesn't provide the standard textual help. When you type **MSTSC /?** and press Enter, you see a dialog box that contains the list of command line switches that are applicable for the version of MSTSC that you're using. The graphical help is perfectly normal in this case. Only a few command line utilities provide graphical help, such as the Windows Scripting engine, WScript. In most cases, Microsoft is assuming that the graphical help will prove more useful because you normally work with these utilities in a graphical environment (even though you execute them at the command line).

Edit a Connection File

The Remote Desktop application relies on Remote Desktop Protocol (RDP) files to store information about connections to remote systems. The .RDP files are actually text strings that tell the Remote Desktop application how to configure itself. If you change the extension for an .RDP file to .TXT and open it using Notepad, you'll see a list of strings like those shown in Figure 10.1. In fact, this technique is useful to know about when an .RDP file becomes corrupted.

Generally, you'll use the standard editor for changing the content of an .RDP file. To modify the content of a file, use the MSTSC /Edit *RDPFilename* command, where *RDPFilename* is the name of a connection file. For example, to change the settings of Windows Server.RDP, you'd type **MSTSC /Edit "Windows Server.RDP"** and press Enter. You'll see a Remote Desktop Connection dialog box like the one shown in Figure 10.2 where you can change the connection settings as described in the "Use the Remote Desktop Connection Application" section of Chapter 2.

Figure 10.1: .RDP files are simply a series of strings used to configure the Remote Desktop application.

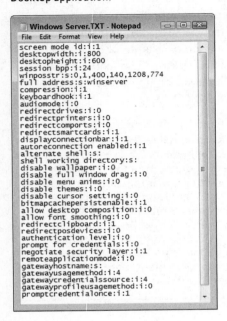

Figure 10.2: The Remote Desktop Connection dialog box lets you change the connection settings.

Connect to a Server

The MSTSC utility provides several scriptable methods of connecting to a remote system and you need to choose the best method for your particular needs. The following procedure helps you create a connection to any server:

1. Select from one of these connection techniques:

   - Type **MSTSC** *RDPFilename*, where *RDPFilename* is the name of the .RDP file you want to use. This option offers customized settings for that server but requires an initial setup process.

   - Type **MSTSC /V:***ServerName*[**:***Port*] **/Admin**, where *ServerName* is the name of the server and *Port* is an optional port number for the connection. This option relies on the default connection configuration, but offers quick connectivity to any system. It also makes it easier to add general connectivity using a batch or script file.

   - Type **MSTSC /Public**. This option displays the Remote Desktop Connection dialog box and lets the user set the connection criteria. The dialog box is automatically preconfigured with the settings found in the default configuration.

2. (Optional) Type **/F** to start Remote Desktop in full screen mode or type **/W:***Width* **/H:***Height* (where *Width* is the width of the window and *Height* is the height of the window) to open Remote Desktop using a specific window size.

3. (Optional) Type **/Span** to span multiple monitors or **/Multimon** to use multiple monitors arranged in a rectangle. Remote Desktop configures the remote desktop to match the client configuration so that you have more screen real estate when working with the remote system.

4. Press Enter. Remote Desktop opens a connection to the remote system using the connection technique and optional specifications that you supply.

Migrate an Older Connection File

You might have used earlier versions of Remote Desktop with other versions of Windows. The associated connection files might not work with the current version of Remote Desktop on your system. Fortunately, you don't have to re-create the connection files. Simply use the MSTSC /Migrate

Managing the Network

PART III

ConnectionFilename command, where *ConnectionFilename* is the name of an old connection file, to migrate the settings to a new .RDP file. For example, to migrate MyServer.RDP to a new .RDP format, type **MSTSC /Migrate MyServer.RDP** and press Enter. The MSTSC utility doesn't provide any output in this situation—you simply try the converted .RDP file to see if it works.

Set Up a Telephony Client

The Telephony Client Management Setup (TCMSetup) utility makes it possible to configure the Telephony Application Programming Interface (TAPI) for a system. TAPI is actually used for a number of connection types, including the Private Branch Exchange (PBX) connectivity required for larger organizations. The precise use of TAPI depends on the application and server that you set up, so you need to check the vendor documentation before using this utility. The following sections describe how to create and disable a connection.

Create a Connection

Before you can use TAPI for a specific purpose on a machine, you have to create a connection to a server. In order to perform this task, you use the TCMSetup /C *Server* command, where *Server* is the name of the TAPI server you want to use. For example, if you want to create a TAPI connection to WinServer, you type **TCMSetup /C WinServer** and press Enter.

The TCMSetup utility will also automatically discover any other servers on your network. In some cases, you might have multiple servers but want a client to use a specific server. In this case, add the /R command line switch to restrict discovery to the servers you specify. For example, if you want to restrict access to just WinServer, then you'd type **TCMSetup /C WinServer /R** and press Enter.

Whenever you create a connection, the TCMSetup utility displays a success message. This message appears within a dialog box, which means that someone has to dismiss it before any script containing the command can continue. Use the /Q command line switch to suppress the success message so that the command can run unattended.

Disable a Connection

At some point, you'll probably need to disable the TAPI connection you've created. To disable the TAPI connection, type **TCMSetup /C /D** and press Enter.

Perform Remote Windows Management

The Windows Remote Management (WinRM) utility helps you manage a remote system from the command line. This utility is Microsoft's implementation of the WS-Management protocol, which provides a secure method of connecting local and remote computers using a Web service. You can learn more about the WS-Management protocol at http://msdn2.microsoft.com/library/aa384470.aspx. The process for using WinRM is as follows:

1. Install Internet Information Server (IIS) support on the host system if you want to allow remote access to the machine.

2. Type **WinRM QuickConfig** and press Enter to start the Windows Remote Management (WS-Management) service, if necessary.

   You can execute commands locally or on a remote system, but the system must have the Windows Remote Management (WS-Management) running in order to respond to requests.

3. Type Y and press Enter when asked whether you want to make the changes required to use WinRM.

   When working with a remote system that isn't part of a domain, you normally have to configure IIS to support the Web service. In addition, you must enable the required firewall access.

4. Type Y and press Enter when asked whether you want to allow remote access, if you want to allow such access. Otherwise, type N and press Enter to deny remote access to the system.

5. Define the Uniform Resource Identifier (URI) that you want to access.

   The URI takes the form \\root\NAMESPACE[\NAMESPACE]\CLASS (see the "Define a URI" section of the chapter for additional details).

6. Execute a command that defines the task you want to perform. These commands take the following form:

   - G[et]: Obtains management information.

   - S[et]: Modifies the management information. You can also specify this operation as put.

   - C[reate]: Defines new instances of management resources.

   - D[elete]: Removes an instance of a management resource.

Managing the Network

PART III

- E[numerate]: Lists the instances of the specified management resource.

- I[nvoke]: Executes a method on a management resource.

- Id[entify]: Determines whether WinRM or another compatible WS-Management implementation is running on a remote machine. This command is always executed using the –Remote command line switch. For example, if you want to determine whether WinRM is running on WinServer, you'd type **WinRM Identify -Remote:WinServer** and press Enter.

7. Repeat steps 5 and 6 as needed to accomplish all required management tasks.

This process is a basic overview of what you can do. The following sections describe various tasks in greater detail.

Understanding the *WinRM* Help System

WinRM has a very odd help system when compared to other command line utilities. If you want to discover more information about a basic task, you use the WinRM *CommandName* –? command, where *CommandName* is a command such as Get or Set. For example, to learn more about the Get command, you'd type **WinRM Get –?** and press Enter.

However, if you want to discover more about a supplemental topic, such as how to create a URI, then you need to use the WinRM Help *Topic* command, where *Topic* is a topic such as URIs. Here's a list of supplemental topic commands:

- WinRM Help URIs

- WinRM Help Aliases

- WinRM Help Config

- WinRM Help CertMapping

- WinRM Help Remoting

- WinRM Help Auth

- WinRM Help Input

- WinRM Help Switches

- WinRM Help Proxy

Define a URI

Every resource controlled by WinRM has a unique URI. Using a unique URI ensures that you can access the resource whenever needed and manage it. The URIs follow a hierarchical path beginning with \\root or you can use the alias of wmi/root, which stands for Windows Management Instrumentation (WMI). There's also a schema approach that uses what looks like an HTTP address, but you really don't need to worry about three different methods of obtaining the same information. In fact, the wmi\root approach is the most reliable, so that's what you'll see used in this chapter.

The creation of a URI begins with a namespace. A namespace is simply a collection of like items. The namespace identifies the collection, and then you access resources within the namespace. Of course, Microsoft wouldn't make it easy to figure out the namespaces on your system—you need to know the secret location of the namespace listing for your machine. The following steps tell you how to locate the namespaces on your machine:

1. Open the Computer Management console found in the Administrative Tools folder of the Control Panel.

2. Open the Computer Management\Services and Applications\WMI Control folder.

3. Right-click WMI Control and choose Properties from the context menu. You'll see the WMI Control Properties dialog box.

4. Select the Security tab. You'll see the Root namespace. Click the plus sign (+) next to Root. You can drill down into the namespaces for your computer as shown in Figure 10.3.

As Figure 10.3 shows, there are many different namespaces on your machine. The most important namespace, the one you use most often, is the Common Information Model version 2 (CIMv2) namespace. This is a standardized namespace that you can read about at http://www.dmtf.org/standards/cim/. To reach the CIMv2 namespace, you'd use the wmi\root\cimv2 URI. Of course, this URI only gets you to the namespace and doesn't show you any of the resources the namespace contains.

The resource within a namespace is called a class. A full-fledged URI then is a combination of wmi/root/Namespace[/Namespace...]/Class, where Namespace is one or more hierarchical namespaces and Class is a resource within the selected namespace hierarchy. For example, if you want to discover the services on a system, then you'd use a URI for `wmi/root/cimv2/Win32_Service`. To enumerate (list) all of the services on the machine, you'd type `WinRM Enum wmi/root/cimv2/Win32_Service` and press Enter. The "Enumerate Resources" section of the chapter tells you more about enumerating resources using `WinRM`.

Figure 10.3: The Security tab shows a list of namespaces on your machine.

NOTE Many namespace names are case sensitive. When in doubt, type the namespace name precisely as you see it capitalized in the Security tab of the WMI Control Properties dialog box.

So far this section has talked about WMI. However, WMI is Microsoft specific. WMI is actually Microsoft's implementation of Web-Based Enterprise Management (WBEM). When you hear WMI, think Microsoft specific, and when you hear WBEM, think about a standard used by everyone. In fact, you can see the WBEM standard at http://www.dmtf.org/standards/wbem. The reason WBEM is so important is that you'll see a number of references to WBEM in Windows when Microsoft has tried hard to implement the standard.

One of the utilities you need to know about is `WBEMTest`. This is a GUI tool that you won't see on any menu. To start this utility, type **WBEMTest** and press Enter. Figure 10.4 shows the initial screen that you see when the utility starts.

Figure 10.4: WBEMTest is a useful utility for discovering more about WMI URIs.

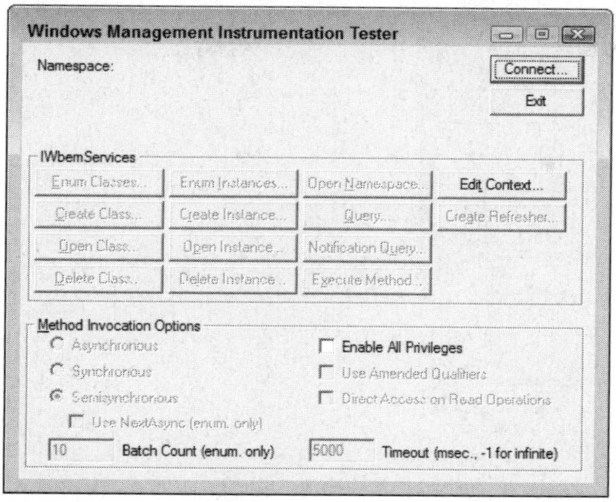

This utility has many purposes, most of which have nothing to do with this book. However, you can use the WBEMTest utility to connect to a namespace and then discover the resources it contains.

Use these steps to discover more about the wmi/root/cimv2 namespace:

1. Click Connect. You see the Connect dialog box shown in Figure 10.5.

   This dialog box has a lot of confusing-looking fields, but the only field you need to know about is Namespace. The WBEMTest utility doesn't precede the namespace with wmi, so the wmi/root/cimv2 namespace becomes simply root/cimv2.

2. Type the namespace you want to review. Click Connect.

   The buttons that were disabled in Figure 10.4 are now enabled.

3. Click Enum Classes.

   You see a Superclass Info dialog box. You could type the name of a class here, such as Win32_Service, to drill down into it, but leave the Enter Superclass Name field blank for now.

4. Click OK.

   You see a list of classes (resources) associated with the namespace you typed in step 1, as shown in Figure 10.6.

Figure 10.5: Enter a namespace in the Namespace field.

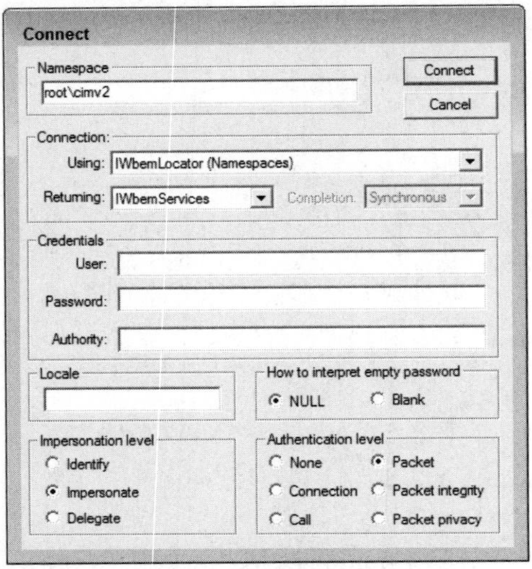

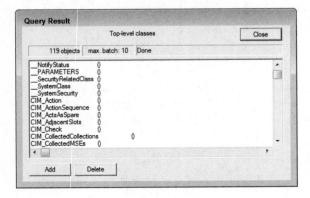

Figure 10.6: Select the resource you want to see from the list shown.

This whole process may seem error prone and difficult. The fact is that you'll very likely find a few WMI resources that you need to access and will include them in scripts, so you won't spend nearly as much time constructing URIs as you might think. However, it's a good idea to know how to construct a URI when you need it. Fortunately, Microsoft also provides a number of helpful WMI tools that you can download at http://www.microsoft.com/downloads/details.aspx?FamilyID=6430F853-1120-48DB-8CC5-F2ABDC3ED314. If you find that you need to create URIs relatively often, download these tools to ease the burden of putting them together. It's important to note that these tools require Internet Explorer because they require the use of ActiveX controls, but because the tools execute locally, using them is safe.

Enumerate Resources

Enumerating a resource means to list it. However, enumeration is a little more extensive than that. When you enumerate a resource, WinRM also examines the resource and prints out its content unless you specifically limit this output. You've already seen some simple examples of enumeration in the "Define a URI" section of the chapter. This section of the chapter begins looking at ways to get precisely the information you want as part of the enumeration.

If you looked at the list of Windows services using the WinRM utility earlier, you noticed that the list is very long and would be difficult to view even using the More utility. One way to limit the output you receive is to use the –Shallow command line switch, which displays just the basic information for each resource. In addition, you can limit the number of properties that WinRM displays by using the –BasePropertiesOnly command line switch. For example, if you type **WinRM Enum wmi/root/cimv2/ Win32_Service -BasePropertiesOnly** and press Enter you see a somewhat shorter list (even though it's still quite long).

Figure 10.7: It's easy to output a single service's data using a filter.

```
Administrator: Command Prompt

C:\>WinRM Enum wmi/root/cimv2/* -Filter:"select * from Win32_Service where Name=
\"BITS\" "
Win32_Service
    AcceptPause = false
    AcceptStop = false
    Caption = Background Intelligent Transfer Service
    CheckPoint = 0
    CreationClassName = Win32_Service
    Description = Transfers files in the background using idle network bandwidth
. If the service is disabled, then any applications that depend on BITS, such as
 Windows Update or MSN Explorer, will be unable to automatically download progra
ms and other information.
    DesktopInteract = false
    DisplayName = Background Intelligent Transfer Service
    ErrorControl = Normal
    ExitCode = 1077
    InstallDate = null
    Name = BITS
    PathName = C:\Windows\System32\svchost.exe -k netsvcs
    ProcessId = 0
    ServiceSpecificExitCode = 0
    ServiceType = Share Process
    Started = false
    StartMode = Manual
    StartName = LocalSystem
    State = Stopped
    Status = OK
    SystemCreationClassName = Win32_ComputerSystem
    SystemName = MAIN
    TagId = 0
    WaitHint = 0

C:\>_
```

Managing the Network

PART III

Filtering presents another method of reducing the size of the output. A filter can use a number of syntaxes. WMI relies on a SQL Server–like syntax. Let's say you want to find the BITS service information. In this case, you'd type **WinRM Enum wmi/root/cimv2/* -Filter:"select * from Win32_Service where Name=\"BITS\" "** and press Enter. Notice that you don't provide the name of the class, Win32_Service, as part of the URI, but you do use an asterisk (*) to specify all classes. The -Filter command line switch specifies a SQL Server-like statement that selects the BITS service from the Win32_Service class, as shown in Figure 10.7.

SQL Server statements can be difficult to put together, so WinRM provides a second, some say easier, method of creating a filter. In this case, you use the -Dialect command line switch to specify that WinRM rely on a selector syntax instead of SQL Server–like statements. To make this work, you type **WinRM Enum wmi/root/cimv2/Win32_Service -Dialect:Selector -Filter:{Name="BITS"}** and press Enter. In fact, the -Dialect command line switch lets you use all kinds of filtering methods, including exotic options such as XPath. This book assumes that you're using either the selector option or the SQL Server–like statements for filtering purposes.

It isn't always easy to create a filter that relies on a single property, such as Name. You might have to combine properties to obtain the results you want. For example, you might want to see all of the services that are set to start manually, yet are running on the host system. Because there are multiple outputs, you might want to add the More utility through a pipe so you can see the output. In this case, you'd type **WinRM Enum wmi/root/cimv2/Win32_Service -Dialect:Selector -Filter:{StartMo de="Manual";State="Running"} | More** and press Enter. If you prefer the SQL Server–like syntax, you'd type **WinRM Enum wmi/root/cimv2/* -Filter:"select * from Win32_Service where StartMode=\"Manual\" and State=\"Running\" " | More** and press Enter.

The enumeration examples to this point have shown text output. This is the output that you can read easiest at the command line. However, if you have a lot of output to process, you might decide to output it as XML, rather than as text, to make it easier to import into another application or a database. In this case, you use the -Format command line switch to change the format to one of the following options:

- XML (unformatted XML)
- Pretty (formatted XML)
- Text (the default option)

For example, you might choose to output all of the Windows service entries to an XML file. To perform this task, type **WinRM Enum wmi/root/ cimv2/Win32_Service -Format:XML > Output.XML** and press Enter. Of course, you can use any filename you want and combine this technique with any of the other enumeration command line switches discussed so far. You can now open **Output.XML** in an application such as Excel, as shown in Figure 10.8.

Figure 10.8: Converting the WinRM output to XML makes it possible to process it using Excel.

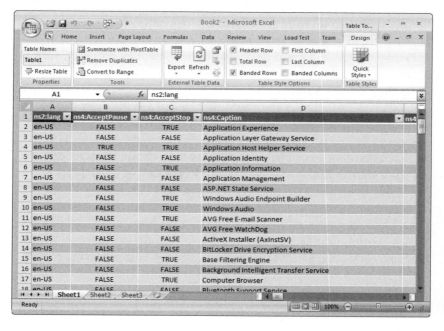

Get a Resource

Administrators often have trouble differentiating between enumerating and getting resources because the two processes seem the same. However, the two processes differ in one important aspect. Enumerating a resource means listing it. You leave the resource alone and simply look at it. Getting a resource means opening the resource in the WMI database and obtaining a copy of it, which means that you must have additional rights, but you can also do more with the data.

Managing the Network

PART III

When you get a resource, you also get a specific instance of it. In other words, you can't get all of the Windows services; you get a specific Windows service (or services) and do something with it. To make this difference clearer, you can't issue a command like this: WinRM Get wmi/root/cimv2/Win32_Service because you're looking for a nebulous number of resources. What you'd do instead is ask for a specific service, such as BITS, by typing **WinRM Get wmi/root/cimv2/Win32_Service?Name=BITS** and pressing Enter.

Notice that this syntax is much simpler than enumerating a resource because you're asking for less information. You simply type the URI as you normally would, a question mark (?), the key property that identifies the resource you want to obtain, and the value of that property. Services are identified by their name, so you use the Name property, followed by the value, such as BITS. If you use a non-key property, such as State, then you see an error message because the result would contain more than one resource.

Getting a resource is handy because you can use the output as input to scripts and batch files. The secret is to use the –Fragment command line switch, which makes it possible to obtain just a little of the output. For example, you might want to obtain the state of the BITS service. In this case, you'd type **WinRM Get wmi/root/cimv2/Win32_Service?Name=BITS -Fragment:State/text()** and press Enter. The –Fragment command line switch specifies the State property in this case. The following slash (/) and the text() function tells WinRM that you only want the value (Running, Stopped, or Paused) as output. If your machine isn't using BITS at the moment, you see Stopped as the output.

Set a Resource

Setting a resource changes the value of a property. For example, you could change the name of a service if you desired. However, setting a resource often has more of an effect than simply modifying data. For example, if you change the State property of a service, you can start, stop, pause, or continue it. Of course, changing the State property isn't the normal way to interact with a service and you won't commonly do it that way, but you could.

Let's say that you want to start the W32Time service; you'd type `WinRM Set wmi/root/cimv2/Win32_Service?Name=W32Time @{State="Running"}` and press Enter. Notice that the `Set` command begins with a URI, just like every other command so far. You access a particular resource using the same technique as you use with `Get`. To change the `State` property, you begin with the at sign (@) and enclose the property and value pair in curly braces. After you execute this command, `WinRM` displays the new property information for W32Time, which shows the new `State` property value of Start Pending. If you subsequently type `WinRM Get wmi/root/cimv2/Win32_Service?Name=W32Time` and press Enter, you'll see that the service is started. To stop the service, you type `WinRM Set wmi/root/cimv2/Win32_Service?Name=W32Time @{State="Stopped"}` and press Enter.

Figure 10.9: WinRM provides a number of configuration settings.

```
Administrator: Command Prompt

C:\>WinRM Get WinRM/Config
Config
    MaxEnvelopeSizekb = 150
    MaxTimeoutms = 60000
    MaxBatchItems = 32000
    MaxProviderRequests = 4294967295
    Client
        NetworkDelayms = 5000
        URLPrefix = wsman
        AllowUnencrypted = false
        Auth
            Basic = true
            Digest = true
            Kerberos = true
            Negotiate = true
            Certificate = true
            CredSSP = false
        DefaultPorts
            HTTP = 5985
            HTTPS = 5986
        TrustedHosts
    Service
        RootSDDL = O:NSG:BAD:P(A;;GA;;;BA)S:P(AU;FA;GA;;;WD)(AU;SA;GWGX;;;WD)
        MaxConcurrentOperations = 4294967295
        MaxConcurrentOperationsPerUser = 15
        EnumerationTimeoutms = 60000
        MaxConnections = 25
        MaxPacketRetrievalTimeSeconds = 120
        AllowUnencrypted = false
        Auth
            Basic = false
            Kerberos = true
            Negotiate = true
            Certificate = false
            CredSSP = false
            CbtHardeningLevel = Relaxed
        DefaultPorts
            HTTP = 5985
            HTTPS = 5986
        IPv4Filter = *
        IPv6Filter = *
        EnableCompatibilityHttpListener = false
        EnableCompatibilityHttpsListener = false
        CertificateThumbprint
    Winrs
        AllowRemoteShellAccess = true
        IdleTimeout = 180000
        MaxConcurrentUsers = 5
        MaxShellRunTime = 2147483647
        MaxProcessesPerShell = 15
        MaxMemoryPerShellMB = 150
        MaxShellsPerUser = 5

C:\>_
```

A more typical Set change is to configure a setting. For example, you can change the settings for WinRM to better match your use of it. To see the WinRM settings, type **WinRM Get WinRM/Config** and press Enter. You'll see the list of entries shown in Figure 10.9. Let's say you want to change the maximum number of connections that WinRM will accept from 25 to 30. The MaxConnections setting is actually part of the Service resource, so you'd use a URI of WinRM/Config/Service to reach the MaxConnection property. To accomplish this task, you'd type **WinRM Set WinRM/Config/ Service @{MaxConnections="30"}** and press Enter. When WinRM executes the command, you don't see everything shown in Figure 10.9. What you do see is the Service part of the resource.

Create a Resource

The resources you access using WMI are in a database of sorts, and as with any database, you can add new items to it. However, you'll find that unlike most databases, you'll seldom actually need to add anything to WMI. The one major exception is the listener that WinRM uses for requests. The default listener relies on HTTP, which means that the connection isn't secure. To see the current listener, type **WinRM Enum WinRM/ Config/Listener** and press Enter. Figure 10.10 shows typical output, which is the HTTP listener.

Figure 10.10: The default listener relies on HTTP.

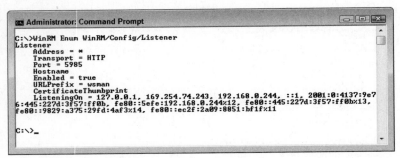

As shown in Figure 10.10, WinRM is currently listening to any client address on port 5985 using a number of local IPv4 and IPv6 addresses, including the loopback (localhost) address. As long as you only use WinRM locally and don't enable firewall access for it, the HTTP listener should be relatively safe, but administrators won't normally work locally, so it's important to add an HTTPS listener that relies on SSL to secure the communication. The easiest way to create an HTTPS listener is to use these two steps:

1. Install a server certificate when using the HTTPS transport.

    You can obtain such a certificate from a third-party source such as VeriSign. It's also possible to create a self-signed certificate using the Cert Services feature of Windows Server.

2. Type **WinRM QuickConfig -Transport:HTTPS** and press Enter.

    WinRM creates an HTTPS listener that provides access to all clients using the default client port, hostname, and local ports.

The WinRM QuickConfig command works fine if you want to use the defaults. In fact, it's the suggested approach for most situations. However, you might find that the defaults won't work for your organization, which is where the WinRM Create command comes into play. The following steps describe how to create an HTTPS listener (and also tell you how to add new entries to the WMI database):

1. Install a server certificate when using the HTTPS transport.

2. Type **WinRM Create WinRM/Config/Listener?**. This is the common part of the command.

3. Type **Address=***, where * is all addresses.

    You may substitute one or more specific addresses for * to ensure that only certain client addresses can access WinRM. For example, if you want to provide access only for the localhost address, you'd use IP:127.0.0.1 as the address.

4. Type **+Transport=*HTTPS***, where HTTPS is the transport you want to use. You may substitute HTTP if you want to use a different HTTP address.

5. (HTTPS Only) Type **@{ CertificateThumbprint="*CertNumber*"}**, where *CertNumber* is the 40-digit hexadecimal number for the certificate you installed in step 1.

NOTE It's possible to set other listener features within the @{} structure of a `WinRM Create` command. Each of these entries are a key/value pair where the key is the name of one of the entries shown in Figure 10.10 and the value is a legal value within double quotes. You can use `Hostname`, `Port`, `Enabled`, `URLPrefix`, `ListeningOn`, and `CertificateThumbprint` as key names. Therefore, if you want to set the port for an HTTP listener to 5599, you use `Port="5999"` as the key/value pair. Separate the individual entries using a semicolon. A configuration entry that sets the `Hostname` and `Port` entries would be something like this: `@{Hostname="LocalHost";Port="5999"}`.

---

6. Press Enter. `WinRM` creates the new resource for you.

Figure 10.11: Use specific addresses for improved security.

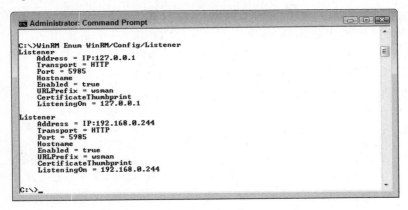

The "Delete a Resource" section of the chapter describes how to remove a resource from the WMI database. You can remove the default HTTP listener and add specific entries. For example, let's say you want to restrict access to `WinRM` to the localhost address. In this case, after you delete the original * entry, you'd type `WinRM Create `**`WinRM/Config/Listen`** **`er?Address=IP:127.0.0.1+Transport=HTTP`** and press Enter. Now, let's say you decide to add one external address—the address of the administrator machine, which is 192.168.0.244. To add this second address, you'd type **`WinRM Create WinRM/Config/Listener?Address=IP:192.168.0.244+Transp`** **`ort=HTTP`** and press Enter. Now, type **`WinRM Enum WinRM/Config/Listener`** and press Enter. You see the results shown in Figure 10.11. `WinRM` is only listening on two addresses now. Anyone else will get static. The result is improved security (the system would still be open to IP spoofing, but the perpetrator would need to know which IP address to use).

Delete a Resource

You'll likely find that you need to delete a resource at some point. It's never a good idea to delete elements from the WMI database that you aren't absolutely certain about. In fact, the WMI database will prevent you from deleting most entries. However, the one entry that you'll find a need to delete is the WinRM listener. Use the WinRM Delete WinRM/Config/ Listener?Address=*IPAddress*+Transport=*TransType* command, where *IPAddress* is either * or a legal IPv4 or IPv6 address and *TransType* is either HTTP or HTTPS. For example, to delete the default listener, you type **WinRM Delete WinRM/Config/Listener?Address=*+Transport=HTT P** and press Enter. If you wanted to delete a loopback specific listener, you'd type **WinRM Delete WinRM/Config/Listener?Address=IP:127.0.0.1+ Transport=HTTP** and press Enter.

Invoke a Method on a Resource

You probably won't use the WinRM Invoke command very often because other commands and utilities perform the task better. The WinRM Invoke command lets you execute a command locally, or when combined with the –Remote command line switch, on another system. You use the WinRM Invoke *Action ResourceURI* [–*Switch:Value*[,–*Switch:Value*...]] command, where *Action* is the action you want to perform, *ResourceURI* is the resource you want to use, –*Switch* is a switch for the resource, and *Value* is the switch value. For example, if you want to start a service such as the Bluetooth Support Service (BthServ), you'd type **WinRM Invoke StartService wmi/root/cimv2/Win32_Service?Name=BthServ** and press Enter. To stop the service, you'd type **WinRM Invoke StopService wmi/ root/cimv2/Win32_Service?Name=BthServ** and press Enter.

The WMIC utility, described in Chapter 15, is the best way to obtain a list of actions that a particular resource supports. For example, to discover the list of methods that a service supports, type **WMIC SERVICE CALL /?** and press Enter. You'll discover the services support Change, ChangeStartMode, Create, Delete, InterrogateService, PauseService, ResumeService, StartService, StopService, and UserControlService as actions.

Managing the Network

PART III

Execute Commands on a Remote System

The WinRS utility is extremely flexible. You can use it to execute any command that a remote system is capable of executing from the command line. The WinRS utility supports a host of command line switches. To see them all, type **WinRS /?** and press Enter.

In most cases, however, you use the WinRS *-r:MachineURL* *-u:Username* *-p:Password CmdString* command, where *MachineURL* is the machine name or URL you use to access the remote system, *Username* is the name of the user account, *Password* is the user's password, and *CmdString* is the command plus any required command line switches used to execute the command, to work with the remote machine. For example, let's say Sarah wants to execute Dir C:\ on a remote system named MyServer. In this case, you'd type **WinRS -r:MyServer -u:Sarah -p:Password "Dir C:\"** and press Enter.

Work with Terminal Server

Terminal Server is the support for Terminal Services, which is the basis for remote desktop connectivity in Windows. Using Terminal Server lets client systems create a remote connection to the server. For example, when you use Remote Desktop, you're relying on Terminal Server to create a remote connection for you. The following sections provide an overview of the various command line tasks you can perform with Terminal Server.

NOTE None of these utilities will work on a remote system unless you have the proper credentials. Normally, you need administrator privileges on the remote system to perform Terminal Server tasks.

Obtain Process Information

The QProcess utility makes it possible to list the processes running on the specified system. If you type **QProcess** and press Enter, you see the processes running on the local system for the current user. To see all of the processes, no matter who started them, type **QProcess** * and press Enter. You can also use the QProcess *Username* command, where *Username* is a username (including System, Network Service, and Local Service) that

you want to see. It's also possible to look for a particular program identifier or session name.

To view processes on another machine, you use the QProcess /
Server:*ServerName* command, where *ServerName* is the name of the
remote system. For example, if you want to see the processes on
MyServer, you type **QProcess /Server:MyServer** and press Enter. You
can combine the /Server command line switch with any of the other
parameters to obtain specific information. To see all of the console processes, you'd type **QProcess Console /Server:MyServer** and press Enter.

Get Session Information

Many of the Terminal Server–related commands depend on session
information to work. The QWinSta utility provides session information. To see all of the sessions on the local workstation, type **QWinSta**
and press Enter. You'll see the session name, name of the user who is
logged into the session, and a number of other pieces of information
about the session. The most important information for using other
utilities is the session name.

NOTE   It's important to remember that QWinSta is Terminal
Server–specific. You won't see other kinds of sessions on the
remote system. For example, a user who is logged in regularly
won't appear in the output. Only users who are relying on some
form of Remote Desktop or other Terminal Services support will
appear in the list.

To see the sessions on a remote system, use the QWinSta /
Sever:*ServerName* command, where *ServerName* is the name of the remote
system. For example, to see the session on MyServer, you'd type **QWinSta /
Server:MyServer** and press Enter. A session name won't match the user's
name in most cases. For example, the user Jeff might actually be logged in
as session RDP-Tcp#2. Consequently, when attempting to find a particular user, you need to look at the username first and then the session name.

It's possible to look for a session based on the username. Simply use
the QWinSta *Username* command, where *Username* is the name of the user
you want to find. For example, to locate the session associated with user
Jeff, type **QWinSta Jeff** and press Enter. The QWinSta utility provides
other command line switches that you can see by typing **QWinSta /?** and
pressing Enter.

Managing the Network

Terminate a Session

A user session might freeze or become otherwise inaccessible. Unfortunately, Windows won't release the resources used by the session until you terminate it. To terminate a session, use the Reset *SessionName* command, where *SessionName* is the name of a session. For example, to terminate session RDP-Tcp#2, you'd type **Reset RDP-Tcp#2** and press Enter. It's important to note that this command only works on the local system—you can't remotely terminate a session. To disconnect an active user, use the TSDiscon utility instead (see the "Disconnect an Active Session" section for details).

Disconnect an Active Session

An administrator might have to intervene on a user's behalf to stop an active session that has stopped working. You only want to disconnect an active session as a last resort. It's far better to try to end the errant process first using the TSKill utility (see the "End Processes" section for details). If it becomes evident that you can't salvage the session (and therefore save the user's data), use the TSDiscon *SessionName* command, where *SessionName* is the name of the session that you want to disconnect. For example, to disconnect the RDP-Tcp#2 session, you'd type **TSDiscon RDP-Tcp#2** and press Enter. (It's also possible to disconnect a session using the session ID, rather than the name, but using the name is less likely to cause errors.)

To disconnect a session on another system, use the TSDiscon *SessionName* /Server:*ServerName* command, where ServerName is the name of the server. For example, to disconnect the RDP-Tcp#2 session on MyServer, you'd type **TSDiscon RDP-Tcp#2 /Server:MyServer** and press Enter.

End Processes

The TSKill utility makes it possible to terminate applications being run under Terminal Services. You use TSKill to terminate a frozen application, rather than the entire session, when the session itself is still responsive. Use the QProcess utility described in the "Obtain Process Information" section to obtain a list of processes before you begin using TSKill. Use the TSKill *PID* command, where *PID* is a process identifier, to kill a particular process. For example, to kill process number 2232 you'd type **TSKill 2232** and press Enter. As with many of the other

Terminal Server utilities, you rely on the /Server:*ServerName* command line switch (where *ServerName* is the name of the server you want to access) to kill a process on a remote system.

Shut Down the Terminal Server

At some point, you may need to shut down the Terminal Server. In this case, you type **TSShutDn** and press Enter. This command comes with a number of additional command line switches for controlling the shutdown. For example, you can use the /Reboot command line switch to reboot the server and automatically restart it (such as after installing a patch). Type **TSShutDn /?** and press Enter to see a complete list of these command line switches. As with many of the other Terminal Server utilities, you rely on the /Server:*ServerName* command line switch (where *ServerName* is the name of the server you want to access) to perform a shutdown on a remote system.

Managing the Network

PART III

PART IV

Interacting with Active Directory

IN THIS PART ▶

Interacting with
Active Directory

PART IV

11

Configuring Directory Services

IN THIS CHAPTER, YOU WILL LEARN TO:

Interacting with
Active Directory

PART IV

Active Directory is an extremely complex database containing everything the system knows about the hardware, software, and users on a system—at least within the confines of general operating system requirements. Some software does use Active Directory for configuration storage requirements as well. There are entire books written about the content of Active Directory, so this single chapter won't try to tell you about the content of Active Directory. What this chapter does do is provide you with an overview of the various utilities that are available at the command line for managing Active Directory.

NOTE Active Directory is indeed a complex topic and you may find that you actually require more than one book to obtain all the required information. A good starting book is *Active Directory for Dummies* by Steve Clines and Marcia Loughry (For Dummies, 2008). If you want something more detailed, try *MCTS: Windows Server 2008 Active Directory Configuration Study Guide: Exam 70-640* by William Panek and James Chellis (Sybex, 2008). Another good alternative is *Active Directory: Designing, Deploying, and Running Active Directory* by Brian Desmond, Joe Richards, Robbie Allen, and Alistair G. Lowe-Norris (O'Reilly Media, 2008). Don't forget that you also have hundreds of online sources as well, such as the best practices guide provided by Microsoft at http://www.microsoft.com/downloads/details .aspx?familyid=631747a3-79e1-48fa-9730-dae7c0a1d6d3.

Manage Directory Services Using the *WMIC* NTDomain Alias

The Windows Management Interface Command line (WMIC) utility is probably the most used administrator utility because it contains so many features. You could literally perform 80 percent to 90 percent of your normal work using this one utility (one-time, maintenance, and specialized tasks still require specialized utilities). Because this utility is so huge, you'll see parts of it covered in the appropriate places in this book. The main WMIC coverage appears in Chapter 15. This chapter discusses the NTDomain alias in the sections that follow. The NTDomain alias helps you manage domain controllers and their associated workstations using the WMI database and by interacting with Active Directory.

NOTE This chapter doesn't discuss a number of WMIC features that appear in Chapter 15. For example, WMIC includes an extensive and labyrinthine help system. In addition, you can format the data in various ways and even translate it as needed for output to other tools, such as a database. Chapter 15 discusses all of these features of WMIC, so be sure to look at the "Configure the Server" section of Chapter 15 for additional information.

List the Objects

Before you can perform any other tasks, you must know what objects the domain controller supports. To obtain a list of domain objects, type **WMIC NTDomain LIST** and press Enter. In most cases, the list will be relatively long, so you'll want to pipe the data to the More utility by typing **WMIC NTDomain LIST | More** and pressing Enter. The common objects you see listed are:

- ClientSiteName
- DcSiteName
- Description
- DnsForestName
- DomainControllerAddress
- DomainControllerName
- DomainName
- Roles
- Status

List Object Properties

The NTDomain objects have properties that describe them. These properties are normally displayed in a form that's nearly impossible to read. The output begins with a listing of properties and then each object appears afterward. A better way to see the list is using a list format. To see the object properties successfully, type **WMIC NTDomain GET /Format:LIST | More** and press Enter. You'll see a list format where each object is listed separately. The property name is followed by an equals sign (=) and then the property value (if any).

Interacting with
Active Directory

PART IV

Get an Object Property

In many cases, you don't need to see every property that an object has to offer. In fact, there really is too much information for most administrators to decipher, so requesting just the properties you need clears the clutter. Use the WMIC NTDomain GET *PropertyName*[, *PropertyName*...] / Format:LIST | More command, where *PropertyName* is the name of a property you want to see, to obtain just the properties you want. For example, if you want to see just the Caption and CreationClassName properties, you'd type **WMIC NTDomain GET Caption, CreationClassName /Format: LIST | More** and press Enter.

The following list contains the properties you can request:

- Caption
- ClientSiteName
- CreationClassName
- DcSiteName
- Description
- DnsForestName
- DomainControllerAddress
- DomainControllerAddressType
- DomainControllerName
- DomainGuid
- DomainName
- DSDirectoryServiceFlag
- DSDnsControllerFlag
- DSDnsDomainFlag
- DSDnsForestFlag
- DSGlobalCatalogFlag
- DSKerberosDistributionCenterFlag
- DSPrimaryDomainControllerFlag
- DSTimeServiceFlag
- DSWritableFlag
- InstallDate

- Name

- NameFormat

- PrimaryOwnerContact

- PrimaryOwnerName

- Roles

- Status

Set an Object Property

Generally, you don't want to create or delete NTDomain entries to avoid contaminating Active Directory or causing problems with your network. However, you may want to set an object property so that it correctly reflects your network configuration. However, WMI controls what you can do even when it comes to setting a property.

Follow this procedure to properly set an object property:

1. Type **WMIC NTDomain SET /?** and press Enter.

    WMIC outputs the usual help information. In addition, at the bottom of the help listing, you see a list of properties that you can change.

2. Verify that the property you want to change appears on the list.

    If not, exit this procedure because WMIC won't let you change the property value. You must let the system change the property for you in some other way (the method depends on the property and whether the system allows changes to the property value at all).

3. Use the WMIC NTDomain SET *PropertyName=Value*[, *PropertyName=Value*] command, where *PropertyName* is the name of the property you want to change and *Value* is the value you want to assign to the property, to change the properties.

    For example, if you want to set the Roles property to Administrators, you'd type **WMIC NTDomain SET Roles=Administrators** and press Enter. Be sure to use double quotes to contain values with spaces as needed.

Query an Association

An association (or associator in Microsoft parlance) is simply an instance of a particular object class. When you query the associations

Interacting with Active Directory

PART IV

for NTDomain, you see all of the instances of this class. To see the associations for NTDomain, type **WMIC NTDomain ASSOC** and press Enter. The output shows all of the associations in HTML format (using URIs).

Manage Active Directory with the *DSQuery* Utility

While WMIC lets you interact with the WMI database (and Active Directory indirectly), Directory Services Query (DSQuery) lets you interact directly with Active Directory. You can use DSQuery to obtain information about nearly any aspect of Active Directory. In fact, there are DSQuery commands for every major Active Directory object and a special command, *, that works with any object.

The DSQuery utility is often used in combination with the DSGet utility described in Chapter 12. DSGet obtains the information set and DSQuery places a query against that information set. The following sections provide an overview of working with DSQuery to perform specific tasks.

Interact with Servers

One of the more important tasks you can perform with DSQuery is to obtain a list of servers and then interact with those servers in some way. The easiest way to obtain a list of servers without too much effort is to type **DSQuery Server** and press Enter. DSQuery will output a list of all of the servers that it can find on the network, but not necessarily a list of all of the servers. The following sections describe some additional server-level tasks you can perform.

Find the Domains

Many organizations have a large number of servers organized into a number of domains. In fact, you might not even know all of the domains that are in the organization. To obtain a list of domains in the current forest, type **DSQuery Server /Forest** and press Enter. You'll see a list of the domains that are accessible in the current forest. There isn't any way to query domains in another forest except by logging on to a machine in that forest and using DQuery on that machine.

Find a Domain

Obtaining a list of domains won't tell you much about the individual domain controllers. The following steps will help you locate a domain controller:

1. Type **DSQuery Server /Domain** *DomainName*, where *DomainName* is the name of a domain that you either know or obtained using the DSQuery Server /Forest command.
   ↳ use find domains on a server
2. Find the domain controller you want to interact with in the list.
3. Type **DSQuery Server /D** *DCName*, where *DCName* is one of the entries obtained with the DSQuery Server /Domain command.

Note the use of the /Domain command line switch the first time and the /D command line the second. The two command line switches aren't equivalent. You can add the /U *UserName* (where *UserName* is an account on the server) and /P *Password* (where *Password* is the password for the account on the remote system) command line switches to access the domain controller using a different account.

Locate a Hidden Server

If a server is hidden for some reason, you can access it by using the DSQuery Server /S *ServerName* command, where *ServerName* is the name of the server you want to find. Of course, this command assumes you have access to the server with your default account. You can add the /U *UserName* (where *UserName* is an account on the server) and /P *Password* (where *Password* is the password for the account on the remote system) command line switches to access the server using a different account.

Display a List of Hostnames

Anyone working on a large network will attest to the difficulty of remembering all of the hostnames. Even if you work on the network every day, you'll run into a server that you don't work with very often and find yourself scratching your head to remember the hostname. Rather than look up the name using a graphical utility, where you could spend more than a few minutes trying to find the hostname you need, you can obtain a quick list from Active Directory using the following script:

```
FOR /F "tokens=2 delims==," %%H IN ('DSQUERY Server') DO @
ECHO.%%H
```

The focus of this script is the DSQuery Server command, which outputs a list of all of the domain controllers. The rest of the script simply processes the output of the DSQuery Server command so that you see the hostnames. Notice how the script uses an at sign (@) in front of the Echo command so that all you see are the hostnames. It's important to include the @ as needed to keep the output of your scripts readable.

Interact with Users

Users present another common use scenario for DSQuery. In many cases, you need to obtain user information, especially on a large network where you have hundreds or thousands of users. When working with users, it's extremely common to combine DSQuery with DSGet to make the query manageable. However, you can use DSQuery directly to obtain user information. The simplest method is to type **DSQuery User** and press Enter, but such a query is nearly useless on a large network because you'd spend hours searching through the results. The following sections describe some practical ways to interact with users.

Obtain User Information Directly

It's possible to use DSQuery to obtain user information directly, even if you're not quite sure of the user's name. Use the DSQuery User /Name *UserName* command, where *UserName* is the name of the user you want to find. If you aren't quite sure of the user's name, you can rely on wildcard character combinations. For example, if you want to find all users whose names begin with J, you'd type **DSQuery User /Name J*** and press Enter.

Unfortunately, you might not know enough about the user's name to even use a wildcard. In this case, you can use a description (assuming your organization actually provides a user description, which is always a good idea). Use the DSQuery User /Desc *Description* command, where *Description* is all or part of a user description to locate, to perform this task. For example, if you want to obtain a list of all of the support personnel, you'd type **DSQuery User /Desc *Support*** and press Enter.

⎣ all users in the Support Group

Obtain a User's Logon Name

Sometimes you'll receive a help desk ticket where the user expects that you'll know their logon name, despite the fact that you have several thousand users to track. In many cases, without the logon name, you can't do much for the user. Of course, you could always track down the user and ask them for the information, but there's an easier way to obtain the information for Active Directory users. The following script displays the logon name for a user based on the last name that you pass:

```
DSQUERY USER -name %1 | DSGET USER -samid -display
```

In this case, the input you provide is the user's last name. The DSQuery User command sends the user information to the DSGet User command using a pipe (|). The DSGet utility, in turn, looks up the user's Security Accounts Manager (SAM) identifier and provides it as output on the command line. (When more than one user has the same last name, you'll see a list of all of the associated logon names, but at least the list is shorter than starting from scratch.)

Obtain a User's Full Name

Sometimes a user will provide you with their email address and a logon name and that's it. What you really want is the user's full name so that you can understand their needs better by looking up their association with the company. When this problem occurs, you can still look up the user information using Active Directory. Simply use the script shown here:

```
DSQUERY USER -samid %1 | DSGET USER -samid -display
```

In this case, the input you provide is the user's logon name. The DSQuery User command sends the user information, based on a SAM identifier search, to the DSGet User command using a pipe (|). The DSGet utility outputs the user's full name. Note that there's normally more than one way to accomplish a task. If you're using an older version of Windows or a system that doesn't have Active Directory installed, you can achieve the same results using this script:

```
NET USER %1 | FIND /I " name "
```

In this case, you pass the user's logon name to the Net utility. This utility outputs all of the information about the user to the Find utility using a pipe (|). The Find utility, in turn, locates just the name entries.

Discover User Group Membership

Many support problems revolve around security. One of the most common security problems is a lack of group membership. The user attempts to perform a task that is under the purview of a specific group and the user doesn't belong to that particular group. Unfortunately, all that the user has told you is that the task is impossible to perform and the boss really needs the task completed today. Rather than play 20 questions trying to discover the user's group membership, you can use this simple script to obtain the information from Active Directory:

```
DSQUERY USER -samid %1 | DSGET USER -memberof -expand
```

In this case, you pass the user's logon name to the DSQuery User command. The DSGet utility receives the output from DSQuery through a pipe (|). The DSGet User command then displays the group membership for the user and expands the information so you get all of the details.

Reset a User's Password

One of the tasks that administrators love least, yet perform most often, is resetting a user's password. Those users who don't keep their password recorded on a sticky note next to their monitor are prone to forgetting them. After a long weekend or a holiday, the administrator's office suddenly fills with users who have no clue as to what their password is. You could use a graphical utility to reset those passwords one at a time (wasting an entire morning as a result) or you can use this simple script to reset the password based on the user's logon name:

```
DSQUERY USER -samid %1 | DSMOD USER -pwd "newpassword"
```

In this case, the DSQuery User command obtains the user's information based on the logon name and passes it to the DSMod utility through a pipe (|). The DSMod User command uses the -pwd command line switch to change the user's password to newpassword. You could extend this script by passing a second argument to the batch file, but it really isn't necessary because the user will need to change the password anyway.

NOTE Make sure you turn off Echo when working with scripts that will reveal password information, even when this information is a default setting as shown in the examples in this book. You don't want someone peering over your shoulder to see a password that should remain private. As an alternative, you can always replace the password string with an asterisk (*). The utility will prompt you to provide a password at the appropriate time. Anything you type will appear as a series of asterisks on screen.

Interact with Computers

Many of the techniques that you use to locate and interact with users also work with computers. Of course, you could begin by getting a complete list of every computer on the system by typing **DSQuery Computer** and pressing Enter. If you're in a small company, this kind of query will work fine. However, most administrators will need something better.

For many administrators, the easiest method of finding a computer will be to search by name. In this case, you use the DSQuery Computer / Name ComputerName command, where ComputerName is the name of the computer you want to find. As with users, you can use wildcard characters to find a computer if you aren't quite sure of the computer name. It's also possible to locate a computer based on its description with the DSQuery Computer /Desc Description command, where Description is all or part of the computer's description. As with names, you can use wildcard characters to broaden your search.

In some cases, you might not actually have a complete list of all of the computers on your network or you might need to update your list. You can use DSQuery to make this process easier. Simply use the DSQuery Computer "OU=Servers,DC=MyDomain,DC=Com" /O RDN > C:\Machines.TXT command to perform the task. You must replace the OU with the organizational unit that contains the list of machines and DC=MyDomain,DC=Com with the domain you want to check. The /O RDN command line switch tells DSQuery to output the list of machines without the full name (using the Relative Distinguished Name, or RDN, instead).

Interact with Contacts

Contacts work precisely the same as users. The difference between the two kinds of entries is that a user is a member of the company and likely works in the building. A contact could be anyone who isn't a standard user, such as a customer, supplier, or consultant. In general, you obtain less information when working with contacts, but you use precisely the same techniques as you do with users to find a contact. Of course, you'll use the DSQuery Contact command instead of the DSQuery User command to locate a contact.

Interact with Groups

Groups help organize users and make it easier to perform tasks such as managing security. However, groups can also present a problem because the same group name can appear in more than one location on the network. For example, every domain controller will have an Administrators group. Unless you want to spend days searching for just the right group, you need a better way to search for groups than those you use when looking for a user (whose logon name is unique across the network).

In most cases, you already know where the group you want to find resides, so you can provide a starting node for the search. A starting node can provide a specific location, such as dc=MyCompany,dc=com, the ForestRoot, or the DomainRoot. For example, you might want to search for the Accounts user group located somewhere in the MyCompany.com domain. In this case, you'd type **DSQuery Group dc=MyCompany,dc=com / Name Accounts** and press Enter. As another example, you might want to find all management groups for administrators in the domain root of the current domain. In this case, you'd type **DSQuery DomainRoot /Name Manage* /Desc *Admin*** and press Enter.

Interact with Organizational Units

In most cases, you work with organizational units (OUs) the same way you work with groups. However, you want to find an OU to do something with it, such as cloning it. Cloning is a common administrative task. Every time you add a new office, you need to create a new OU for it. However, it's likely that you already have an entry that works fine as a template for the new office. It's possible to clone an OU by hand, but definitely time consuming. To accomplish this task, you'd need to use a script such as the one shown here:

```
DSQuery OU /Name Old | foreach-object { DSAdd OU "$($_
-replace 'Old','New')" }
```

This is one of the few cases where working with Windows Power Shell provides a decided advantage over older batch file techniques. The call to DSQuery locates the OU you want to clone. It passes this information to the foreach-object command, which processes all of the objects contained within the OU. The DSAdd call adds the cloned OU to the proper location by replacing the old OU name (Old) with the new OU name (New). Of course, you'd replace Old and New with the names of the old OU and the new OU you want to use.

Manage the Active Directory Database

The Windows NT Directory Services utility (NTDSUtil) is an interactive utility, for the most part, so you won't use it with a batch file very often. However, by entering the correct command at the command prompt, you can get to the correct area of this utility quickly. The following sections describe how to use the NTDSUtil utility.

Issue a Command

NTDSUtil is an unusual utility in that it's one of the few that eschews command line switches for the most part and also relies on multi-word commands. When you issue a command to NTDSUtil, you need to provide all of the words in its rather verbose syntax or the command will fail. Some commands place NTDSUtil in a specific mode. For example, typing the **LDAP Policies** command will place you in the LDAP Policies mode.

NOTE   Trying to cover such a robust utility in a section of a chapter is nearly impossible—it might be possible to write several chapters on the topic without exhausting it. For that reason, you'll probably want to find some additional information about NTDSUtil. You can find a wealth of tutorials online for this utility. For example, you'll find an excellent tutorial for the novice on the ComputerPerformance site at http://www.computerperformance. co.uk/w2k3/utilities/windows_ntdsutil.htm.

Now that you have a better idea of how commands work, it's time to review the NTDSUtil upper-level commands. The following list describes each of the command line arguments:

- **Authoritative restore:** Restores the Directory Information Tree (DIT) database.

- **Domain management:** Prepares the system to create a new domain.

- **Files:** Manages the NTDS database files.

- **Help:** Displays help information about the selected management function. The help you see depends on the commands you issued previously. See the **Stream** command line argument entry for details.

Interacting with Active Directory

PART IV

- **IPDeny List:** Manages the LDAP IP deny list. This list determines the machines that can access Active Directory remotely.

- **LDAP policies:** Manages the LDAP policies.

- **Metadata cleanup:** Removes old metadata from the system. This feature includes removing old objects off decommissioned servers.

- **Popups {On | Off}:** Enables or disables popups.

- **Quit:** Ends a particular command level. You must issue multiple Quit commands, one for each level. See the Stream command line argument entry for an example. Entering the Quit command at the NTDSUtil prompt always exits the application.

- **Roles:** Manages the NTDS role owner tokens.

- **Security account management:** Manages the security account database. This command line switch also searches for and removes duplicate SID entries in the security account database.

- **Semantic database analysis:** Analyzes the database looking for semantic errors.

You can start NTDSUtil with any of these commands. For example, if you want to work with the Security Accounts Management (SAM) database, then you'd type **NTDSUtil "Security account management"** and press Enter. Notice that the command is actually three words long, so you must place it within double quotes or NTDSUtil will complain that it doesn't understand the command. When working inside the interactive environment, you don't have to enclose the commands within double quotes.

Use a Stream

Even though the NTDSUtil utility is essentially an interactive environment, you can create a stream of commands to interact with it in a batch file. This stream specifies multiple commands that NTDSUtil should execute one after another as a sort of script. The commands must appear as a single string with each command separated with a space. For example, you can obtain help about the roles task by typing **NTDSUtil Roles Help Quit Quit** at the command line and pressing Enter. Here's a summary of the sequence of events that occurs with this stream:

1. The NTDSUtil prompt appears where the utility enters the Roles command. This action displays the Flexible Single Master Operations (FSMO) maintenance prompt.

2. At the FSMO Maintenance prompt, the utility enters the Help command. You see a help listing for the Roles command.

3. The utility enters the Quit command to exit the FSMO Maintenance prompt.

4. The utility enters Quit again to exit the NTDSUtil and the command prompts.

As another example, let's say you want to check for duplicate Security Identifiers (SIDs) on a server named MyServer without entering the interactive mode of NTDSUtil. In this case, you'd type **NTDSUtil "Security account management" "Connect to server MyServer" "Check Duplicate SID" Quit Quit** and press Enter. When the command completes, DupSID.LOG contains a list of any duplicate SIDs found on the target server.

Theoretically, you can create a stream of any size. If you're working with a scripting language that supports disk access, you can even place the script in another file and parse it. All this said, most administrators will probably use NTDSUtil in interactive mode.

12

Working with Directory Objects

IN THIS CHAPTER, YOU WILL LEARN TO:

Interacting with
Active Directory

PART IV

C hapter 11 concerns itself with finding information. Often, an administrator needs to find information before doing anything else. This chapter discusses the next step (or steps)—managing the information. In this chapter, you discover the utilities you can use to add, query, edit, move, and delete objects in Active Directory. In short, this chapter tells you how to perform tasks with the objects you find once you find the precise object you want to manage. It's important to understand that these utilities tend to work best with precise objects. If you haven't found precisely what you want to modify, then you need to use the techniques in Chapter 11 to find it first.

Create New Objects

The Directory Services Add (DSAdd) utility makes it possible to add new objects to Active Directory. You can add most of the objects with a GUI utility using this command line utility. The difference is that you can add the items using a script, rather than manually. The "Interact with Organizational Units" section of Chapter 11 shows one such example of adding objects—in this case, you cloned an Organizational Unit (OU). The following sections describe how to add other kinds of objects to Active Directory.

NOTE   All of the DSAdd commands work with remote systems as needed (such as when you want to configure a server). You can use the −s *Server* or −d *Domain* command line switches, where *Server* is the name of a specific server that you want the computer to use for logins and *Domain* is the name of a domain where you want the computer to log on, to log on to a particular part of the network as needed. This utility also supports the −u *Username* and −p *Password* command line switches, where *Username* is the name of an account on the server and *Password* is the account's password, to log on to the server using a different account.

Add a Computer

Normally, computers are automatically added when the system joins the domain. However, in some cases, you might have to add a computer manually or you might choose to add the computer before it joins the domain to obtain additional flexibility in how the computer is added.

The following procedure describes how to add a computer to Active Directory:

1. Type **DSAdd Computer**.

2. Type the computer's Distinguished Name (DN).

   A DN consists of the computer name, position within the organizational unit, and domain context, such as `cn=MyComputer,` `cn=Computers,dc=MyDomain,dc=com`.

3. (Optional) Type **-samid *SamName***, where *SamName* is the Security Accounts Manager (SAM) name of the computer.

   If you don't provide a SAM name, the system generates a name based on the common name provided in step 2.

4. (Optional) Type **-desc *Description***, where *Description* is a description of the computer.

5. (Optional) Type **-loc *Location***, where *Location* is the physical location of the computer.

6. (Optional) Type **-memberof *Group***, where *Group* is one or more group names separated by spaces.

   This option joins the computer to the groups that you supply.

7. Press Enter. DSAdd adds the computer to Active Directory.

Add a Contact

The server never adds contacts automatically because contacts are associated with users (or other entities) outside the organization. Unless you use the GUI to add contacts, you'll always add them using the command line utility.

The following procedure describes how to add a contact to Active Directory:

1. Type **DSAdd Contact**.

2. Type the contact's Distinguished Name (DN).

   A DN consists of the username, position within the organizational unit, and domain context, such as `cn=Joe Smith,cn=Users,dc=` `MyDomain,dc=com`.

3. Type **-fn *FirstName***, where *FirstName* is the contact's first name.

Interacting with Active Directory

PART IV

4. (Optional) Type **-mi** *Initial*, where *Initial* is the contact's middle initial.

5. Type **-ln** *LastName*, where *LastName* is the contact's last name.

6. Type **-display** *DisplayName*, where *DisplayName* is how the contact will appear to anyone accessing the account.

7. (Optional) Type **-desc** *Description*, where *Description* is a description of the contact.

8. (Optional) Type **-office** *Office*, where *Office* is the location of the contact's office.

   When the person has an office on site, you can simply provide an office number. Otherwise, you could probably provide an address.

9. (Optional) Type **-tel** *Phone#*, where *Phone#* is the contact's most commonly used telephone number.

   In times past, the telephone number would be a land line, but with many people cutting their *land* line connection, you may need to add a cellular telephone number here.

10. (Optional) Type **-email** *Email*, where *Email* is the contact's main e-mail address.

11. (Optional) Type **-hometel** *HomePhone#*, where HomePhone# is the contact's home telephone number when it differs from their main telephone number (see step 9).

12. (Optional) Type **-pager** *Pager#*, where *Pager#* is the contact's pager number, when the contact has such a device.

13. (Optional) Type **-mobile** *CellPhone#*, where *CellPhone#* is the contact's mobile telephone number (assuming that you haven't already added this number in step 9).

14. (Optional) Type **-fax** *Fax#*, where *Fax#* is the contact's facsimile number (assuming the contact relies on a separate device, rather than using e-mail).

15. (Optional) Type **-iptel** *IPPhone#*, where *IPPhone#* is the contact's Internet Protocol Phone (IPPhone) number, such as Vonage or Skype.

16. (Optional) Type **-title** *Title*, where *Title* is the contact's job title, rather than the title you use to address them.

17. (Optional) Type **-dept** *Department*, where *Department* is the contact's department within their organization.

18. (Optional) Type -**company** *Company*, where *Company* is the name of the company that the contact works for.

19. Press Enter. DSAdd adds the contact to Active Directory.

Add a Group

Groups are an essential organizational aid. They make it possible to perform tasks faster and with greater accuracy. For example, it's much easier to set the security requirements for a group one time, rather than individually for each member of the group. In addition, because you're setting security just once, there isn't any chance of giving one group member more rights than another group member. You'll usually enter groups manually, except when you rely on one of the built-in groups that comes with Windows.

The following steps describe how to add a group:

1. Type **DSAdd Group**.

2. Type the group's Distinguished Name (DN).

   A DN consists of the group name, position within the organizational unit, and domain context, such as cn=Accounting, cn=Groups,dc=MyDomain,dc=com.

3. (Optional) Type -**secgrp yes** to create a security group (one you can use for security purposes) or -**secgrp no** to add a group merely for organizational purposes.

   The default setting is to add a security group.

4. (Optional) Type -**scope** and then type one of the following scope options:

   - **l**: Defines a local group.

   - **g**: Defines a global group, which is the default option.

   - **u**: Defines a universal group. (You can't create universal groups in a mixed-mode environment, which is an environment that supports older versions of Windows, versus native mode that supports only the current version.)

5. (Optional) Type -**samid** *SAMName*, where *SAMName* is the SAM name of the group.

   If you don't provide a SAM name, the system generates a name based on the distinguished name provided in step 2.

Interacting with Active Directory

PART IV

6. (Optional) Type **-desc** *Description*, where *Description* is an explanation of the group and its purpose.

7. (Optional) Type **-memberof** *Group*, where *Group* is a space-separated listing of groups that this group belongs to.

   You must use the DN for each of the groups in the list. Make sure you enclose any DN with spaces in double quotes.

8. (Optional) Type **-members** *Member*, where *Member* is a space separated listing of groups and users that belong to this group.

   You must use the DN for each of the users and groups in the list. Make sure you enclose any DN with spaces in double quotes.

9. Press Enter. DSAdd adds the group to Active Directory.

Add an Organizational Unit

OUs help you organize entries within Active Directory to make them easier to manage. OUs don't provide any special functionality outside of Active Directory, such as groups do. To create an OU, type **DSAdd OU** *DN*, where *DN* is the OU's distinguished name. A DN consists of the OU name and domain context, such as cn=Groups,dc=MyDomain,dc=com. You can add as many levels of organization as required when creating the OU. Use the -desc Description command line switch, where Description is an explanation of the OU and its purpose, to document the entry.

Add a User

Users are part of the organization for the most part. They normally work as part of the organization, even if they work off site. In most cases, users have more rights to manage and create data than contacts. The system won't create users automatically, but there are many different ways in which to create basic user entries, such as the initial operating system configuration. No matter how you create these basic entries, they likely won't contain all of the information needed for a good user entry, so you'll need to edit them. A better choice is to manually add user entries that include complete information from the outset.

The following procedure describes how to create a user entry:

1. Type **DSAdd Contact**.

2. Type the contact's Distinguished Name (DN).

A DN consists of the username, position within the organizational unit, and domain context, such as cn=Joe Smith,cn=Users, dc=MyDomain,dc=com.

3. (Optional) Type **-samid** *SAMName*, where *SAMName* is the SAM name of the user.

   If you don't provide a SAM name, the system generates a name based on the distinguished name provided in step 2.

4. (Optional) Type **-upn** *UPN*, where *UPN* is the User Principal Name (UPN).

   The UPN provides an alternative method for logging on to a server. Instead of typing the username and domain separately, you type them together as a single entry, such as JSmith@MyDomain.com. The concept of the UPN is defined by RFC 822 (see the standard at http://www.faqs.org/rfcs/rfc822.html).

5. Type **-fn** *FirstName*, where *FirstName* is the user's first name.

6. (Optional) Type **-mi** *Initial*, where *Initial* is the user's middle initial.

7. Type **-ln** *LastName*, where *LastName* is the user's last name.

8. Type **-display** *DisplayName*, where *DisplayName* is how the user will appear to anyone accessing the account.

9. (Optional) Type **-empid** *EmployeeID*, where *EmployeeID* is the user's identifier within the organization.

10. (Optional) Type **-pwd** *Password*, where *Password* is the user's password, or **-pwd** *, to display a secure password entry screen after you create the account.

11. (Optional) Type **-desc** *Description*, where *Description* is a description of the user.

12. (Optional) Type **-memberof** *Group*, where *Group* is a space separated list of groups to which the user belongs.

    You must use the DN for each of the groups in the list. Make sure you enclose any DN with spaces in double quotes.

13. (Optional) Type **-office** *Office*, where *Office* is the location of the user's office.

14. (Optional) Type **-tel** *Phone#*, where *Phone#* is the user's telephone number within the organization (not necessarily a personal, cellular, or other telephone number).

15. (Optional) Type **-email** *Email*, where *Email* is the user's e-mail address within the organization.

16. (Optional) Type **-hometel** *HomePhone#*, where *HomePhone#* is the user's home telephone number.

17. (Optional) Type **-pager** *Pager#*, where *Pager#* is the user's pager number, when the user has such a device.

18. (Optional) Type **-mobile** *CellPhone#*, where *CellPhone#* is the user's mobile telephone number.

19. (Optional) Type **-fax** *Fax#*, where *Fax#* is the user's facsimile number (assuming the user relies on a separate device, rather than using e-mail).

20. (Optional) Type **-iptel** *IPPhone#*, where *IPPhone#* is the user's IPPhone number, such as Vonage or Skype.

21. (Optional) Type **-webpg** *WebPage*, where *WebPage* is the user's Web page within the organization.

Theoretically, you could also use this for the user's personal Web page if the organization doesn't provide an organizational Web page.

22. (Optional) Type **-title** *Title*, where *Title* is the user's job title, rather than the title you use to address them.

23. (Optional) Type **-dept** *Department*, where *Department* is the user's department within the organization.

24. (Optional) Type **-company** *Company*, where *Company* is the name of the company that the user works for.

This entry is normally left out unless the organization has more than one subsidiary.

25. (Optional) Type **-mgr** *Manager*, where *Manager* is the name of the user's manager.

26. (Optional) Type **-hmdir** *HomeDir*, where *HomeDir* is the main location of the user's data on the server.

This is the location that the system uses when the user first logs on to the system. When the path is a Universal Naming Convention (UNC) mapped path, this entry is simply a drive letter.

27. (Optional) Type **-hmdrv** *DriveLtr:*, where *DriveLtr* is the network drive the system should use to locate user data and other information.

Note that the colon after the drive letter is required.

28. (Optional) Type **-profile** *ProfilePath*, where *ProfilePath* is the location of the user's profile information.

29. (Optional) Type **-loscr** *ScriptPath*, where *ScriptPath* is the location of the user's logon script (which may not be the same location as the user's profile).

30. (Optional) Type **-mustchpwd yes** if you want the user to change their password during the next logon or **-mustchpwd no** when there isn't any need to change the password. The default setting is No.

31. (Optional) Type **-canchpwd yes** when the user is allowed to change their password or **-canchpwd no** when the user is restricted from changing their password.

The default setting is Yes.

32. (Optional) Type **-reversiblepwd yes** to store the user password using reversible encryption or **-reversiblepwd no** to use stronger, non-reversible encryption.

The default setting is No.

33. (Optional) Type **-pwdneverexpires yes** if the user can use the same password forever or **-pwdneverexpires no** when the user must change their password on a regular basis.

The default setting is No.

34. (Optional) Type **-acctexpires** *NumDays*, where *NumDays* is the number of days before the account expires.

Automatic account expiration is a helpful security feature for guest accounts to ensure that guests don't have continuous access, even when their access should end. A positive numeric value provides the number of days specified. Using 0 means that the account expires today, and a negative number indicates that the account has already expired. The default string, never, indicates that the account never expires.

35. (Optional) Type **-disabled yes** to create the account in a disabled state or **-disabled no** to make the account accessible after creation.

The default setting is No.

36. Press Enter. If you typed -pwd * in step 10, you see a password entry request—the password you type appears as a group of asterisks (*). DSAdd adds the user to Active Directory.

Get Objects

As with most databases, Active Directory provides a means for accessing the information it contains. You use the DSGet utility to perform this task. The DSGet output is unfiltered. What you see is the raw Active Directory content, which may be more information than you really want. Although the DSGet commands provide command line switches to limit the output you see, you may need to combine DSGet with DSQuery to obtain the precise output you want. For example, the "Obtain a User's Logon Name" section of Chapter 11 shows how to obtain a specific user's logon name from Active Directory. The following sections describe the various DSGet commands.

Generic *DSGET* Command Line Switches

All of the DSGet commands work with remote systems as needed (such as when you want to list elements on a server). You can use the –s *Server* or –d *Domain* command line switches, where *Server* is the name of a specific server that you want the computer to use for logons and *Domain* is the name of a domain where you want the computer to log on, to log on to a particular part of the network as needed. This utility also supports the –u *Username* and –p *Password* command line switches, where *Username* is the name of an account on the server and *Password* is the account's password, to log on to the server using a different account.

You also have a number of display options when working with the DSGet commands. The –c command line switch provides continuous operation, where DSGet continues to display output even if it encounters an error. The –L command line switch displays the output in list format (where each property appears on a single line and is followed immediately by the property value). The default option is to display the output in tabular format, which saves space, but is also harder to read. Finally, the –q command line switch executes the command without displaying any output on the standard output device.

List Computers

To obtain basic information about any computer system, type **DSGet Computer** *DN*, where *DN* is the computer's distinguished name, and press Enter. You can specify multiple computers by separating each DN with a space. The basic information isn't complete. Use the following command line switches to obtain additional information:

- -dn: Display the computer's DN.
- -samid: Display the computer's SAM identifier.
- -sid: Display the computer's Security Identifier (SID).
- -desc: Display the computer's description.
- -loc: Display the computer's location.
- -disabled: Display yes if the computer's account is disabled or no if the computer is active.

An alternative form of the DSGet Computer DN command provides access to the computer's security information. In this case, you can specify the following command line switches to obtain additional information:

- -memberof: Display the computer's group membership.
- -expand: Expand each of the groups listed using the -memberof command line switch to show the complete membership hierarchy. You must use this command line switch with the -memberof command line switch.

List Contacts

To obtain basic information about any contact, type **DSGet Contact DN**, where DN is the contact's distinguished name, and press Enter. You can specify multiple contacts by separating each DN with a space. The basic information isn't complete. Use the following command line switches to obtain additional information:

- -dn: Display the contact's DN.
- -fn: Display the contact's first name.
- -mi: Display the contact's middle initial.
- -ln: Display the contact's last name.
- -display: Display the contact's display name.
- -desc: Display the contact's description.
- -office: Display the contact's office information.
- -tel: Display the contact's main telephone number.
- -email: Display the contact's main e-mail address.

- −hometel: Display the contact's home telephone number (available when this number differs from the main telephone number).

- −pager: Display the contact's pager number (available when this number differs from the main telephone number).

- −mobile: Display the contact's mobile or cellular telephone number (available when this number differs from the main telephone number).

- −fax: Display the contact's facsimile telephone number.

- −iptel: Display the contact's IPPhone number (available when this number differs from the main telephone number).

- −title: Display the contact's job title.

- −dept: Display the department in which the contact works.

- −company: Display the contact's company name.

List Groups

To obtain basic information about any group, type **DSGet Group _DN_**, where _DN_ is the group's distinguished name, and press Enter. You can specify multiple groups by separating each DN with a space. The basic information isn't complete. Use the following command line switches to obtain additional information:

- −dn: Display the group's DN.

- −samid: Display the group's SAM identifier.

- −sid: Display the group's Security Identifier (SID).

- −desc: Display the group's description.

- −secgrp: Display yes if this is a security group or no if it's not a security group.

- −scope: Display the scope of the group: Local, Global, or Universal.

An alternative form of the DSGet Group _DN_ command provides access to the group's security information. In this case, you can specify the following command line switches to obtain additional information:

- −memberof: Display the group's group membership.

- −members: Display the groups and users that are members of this group.

- −expand: Expand each of the groups listed using the −memberof or −members command line switch to show the complete member- ship hierarchy. You must use this command line switch with the −memberof or −members command line switch.

List Organizational Units

OUs are simple Active Directory entries, so it pays to display the entire entry. Type **DSGet OU DN -Desc**, where *DN* is the OU's distinguished name, and press Enter to obtain all of the available information.

List Servers

To obtain basic information about any server, type **DSGet Server DN**, where *DN* is the server's distinguished name, and press Enter. You can specify multiple servers by separating each DN with a space. The basic information isn't complete. Use the following command line switches to obtain additional information:

- −dn: Display the server's DN.

- −desc: Display the server's description.

- −dnsname: Display the server's Domain Name System (DNS) hostname.

- −site: Display the site to which this server belongs.

- −isgc: Display yes when the server is a Global Catalog (GC) server and no when it isn't.

In some cases, you need information about the security principals that own objects on the domain controller. To obtain this information, you type **DSGet Server DN -topobjowner Display**, where *Display* is the number of objects to display, and press Enter. If you provide a value of 0, DSGet displays all of the security principals. The default number of items to dis- play is 10. The security principals are users, computers, security groups, and inetOrgPersons. The inetOrgPersons category is a special kind of Lightweight Directory Access Protocol (LDAP) user defined by RFC 2798 (http://www.faqs.org/rfcs/rfc2798.html). The output of this command is sorted in order of the security principals that own the most objects.

You may also need to know about the directory partitions on the server. In this case, you type **DSGet Server DN -part** and press Enter. The output includes all of the distinguished names of the directory parti- tions for the specified server.

Interacting with Active Directory

PART IV

List Users

To obtain basic information about any user, type **DSGet User *DN***, where *DN* is the user's distinguished name, and press Enter. You can specify multiple users by separating each DN with a space. The basic information isn't complete. Use the following command line switches to obtain additional information:

- –dn: Display the user's DN.
- –samid: Display the user's SAM identifier.
- –sid: Display the user's SID.
- –upn: Display the UPN of the user.
- –fn: Display the user's first name.
- –mi: Display the user's middle initial.
- –ln: Display the user's last name.
- –display: Display the user's display name.
- –empid: Display the user's employee identifier.
- –desc: Display the user's description.
- –office: Display the user's office location.
- –tel: Display the user's organizational telephone number.
- –email: Display the user's organizational e-mail address.
- –hometel: Display the user's home telephone number.
- –pager: Display the user's pager number.
- –mobile: Display the user's mobile or cellular telephone number.
- –fax: Display the user's facsimile number.
- –iptel: Display the user's IPPhone number.
- –webpg: Display the user's organizational or personal web page URL.
- –title: Display the user's job title.
- –dept: Display the user's department.
- –company: Display the user's company name (usually filled only when subsidiaries are involved).
- –mgr: Display the user's manager's name.

- -hmdir: Display the user's home directory. When working with a mapped UNC path, you see just a drive letter.

- -hmdrv: Display the user's home drive.

- -profile: Display the user's profile path.

- -loscr: Display the user's logon script path.

- -mustchpwd: Display yes if the user must change their password during the next logon.

- -canchpwd: Display yes if the user can change their password.

- -pwdneverexpires: Display yes if the user's password never expires.

- -disabled: Display yes if the user's account has been disabled.

- -acctexpires: Display whether the user account expires. A value of never indicates that the account never expires. Otherwise, you see a specific expiration date, even if that date is sometime in the past.

- -reversiblepwd: Display yes if the user's password relies on reversible encryption. Using reversible encryption does make the user's account more susceptible to break-in, solely for the reason that the encryption is reversible.

An alternative form of the DSGet User DN command provides access to the user's security information. In this case, you can specify the following command line switches to obtain additional information:

- -memberof: Display the user's group membership.

- -expand: Expand each of the groups listed using the -memberof command line switch to show the complete membership hierarchy. You must use this command line switch with the -memberof command line switch.

Edit Existing Objects

Sometimes you need to modify the content of an existing Active Directory entry. The DSMod utility helps you edit some, but not all, of the Active Directory objects. You can modify these object types when working with this utility:

- Computer

- Contact

Interacting with Active Directory

PART IV

- Group

- OU

- Server

- User

- Quota

- Partition

When you need to modify other object types, you must use the GUI tools. Some objects don't permit modification—at least, not directly. In these cases, you must delete the old object and then create a new one. Make sure you understand the object and its properties before you attempt to modify it.

All of the DSMod commands work essentially the same way—you provide the correct base command, the DN for the object, and then a list of property values. Any property values you provide will modify the old properties. Otherwise, the properties remain the same as before. You can't edit some properties in some objects because the property values must remain constant for the life of the object. The following sections describe how the DSMod commands work.

NOTE   All of the DSMod commands work with remote systems as needed (such as when you want to list elements on a server). You can use the –s *Server* or –d *Domain* command line switches, where *Server* is the name of a specific server that you want the computer to use for logons and *Domain* is the name of a domain where you want the computer to log on, to log on to a particular part of the network as needed. This utility also supports the –u *Username* and –p *Password* command line switches, where *Username* is the name of an account on the server and *Password* is the account's password, to log on to the server using a different account.

Modify Computer Data

To modify the data for a particular computer, type **DSMod Computer DN**, where *DN* is the computer's distinguished name, and press Enter. The following command line switches let you modify specific computer data:

- –desc: Modify the computer's description.

- `-loc`: Modify the computer's location.
- `-disabled`: Type **yes** if the computer's account is disabled or **no** if the computer is active.

In addition to modifying computer data, you can also reset the computer account. To reset the computer account, type **DSMod Computer** **DN -reset** and press Enter.

Modify Contact Data

To modify the data for a particular contact, type **DSMod Contact DN**, where *DN* is the contact's distinguished name, and press Enter. The following command line switches let you modify specific contact data:

- `-fn`: Modify the contact's first name.
- `-mi`: Modify the contact's middle initial.
- `-ln`: Modify the contact's last name.
- `-display`: Modify the contact's display name.
- `-desc`: Modify the contact's description.
- `-office`: Modify the contact's office information.
- `-tel`: Modify the contact's main telephone number.
- `-email`: Modify the contact's main e-mail address.
- `-hometel`: Modify the contact's home telephone number (available when this number differs from the main telephone number).
- `-pager`: Modify the contact's pager number (available when this number differs from the main telephone number).
- `-mobile`: Modify the contact's mobile or cellular telephone number (available when this number differs from the main telephone number).
- `-fax`: Modify the contact's facsimile telephone number.
- `-iptel`: Modify the contact's IPPhone number (available when this number differs from the main telephone number).
- `-title`: Modify the contact's job title.
- `-dept`: Modify the department in which the contact works.
- `-company`: Modify the contact's company name.

Modify Group Data

To modify the data for a particular group, type **DSMod Group** *DN*, where *DN* is the group's distinguished name, and press Enter. The following command line switches let you modify specific group data:

- −samid: Display the group's SAM identifier.

- −desc: Display the group's description.

- −secgrp: Display yes if this is a security group or no if it's not a security group.

- −scope: Display the scope of the group: Local, Global, or Universal.

In addition, you can add, remove, or change group membership. Use the following command line switches to perform this task:

- −addmbr *Member*: Adds members to the group, where *Member* is one or more distinguished names separated by spaces.

- −rmmbr *Member*: Removes members from the group, where *Member* is one or more distinguished names separated by spaces.

- −chmbr *Member*: Clears the existing members from the group and creates a new list using the supplied list, where *Member* is one or more distinguished names separated by spaces.

Modify Organizational Unit Data

OUs are simple Active Directory entries. The only information you can change is the OU description. To change the description, type **DSMod OU** *DN* **-Desc** *NewDesc*, where *DN* is the OU's distinguished name and *NewDesc* is the new description you want to use, and press Enter to make the modification.

Modify User Data

To modify the data for a particular user, type **DSMod User** *DN*, where *DN* is the user's distinguished name, and press Enter. The following command line switches let you modify specific user data:

- −upn: Modify the UPN of the user.

- −fn: Modify the user's first name.

- `-mi`: Modify the user's middle initial.
- `-ln`: Modify the user's last name.
- `-display`: Modify the user's display name.
- `-empid`: Modify the user's employee identifier.
- `-pwd`: Modify the user's password. You can either supply a password or type an asterisk (*). If you type an asterisk, DSMod will ask for the password when you press Enter.
- `-desc`: Modify the user's description.
- `-office`: Modify the user's office location.
- `-tel`: Modify the user's organizational telephone number.
- `-email`: Modify the user's organizational e-mail address.
- `-hometel`: Modify the user's home telephone number.
- `-pager`: Modify the user's pager number.
- `-mobile`: Modify the user's mobile or cellular telephone number.
- `-fax`: Modify the user's facsimile number.
- `-iptel`: Modify the user's IPPhone number.
- `-webpg`: Modify the user's organizational or personal Web page URL.
- `-title`: Modify the user's job title.
- `-dept`: Modify the user's department.
- `-company`: Modify the user's company name (usually filled only when subsidiaries are involved).
- `-mgr`: Modify the user's manager's name.
- `-hmdir`: Modify the user's home directory. When working with a mapped UNC path, you see just a drive letter.
- `-hmdrv`: Modify the user's home drive.
- `-profile`: Modify the user's profile path.
- `-loscr`: Modify the user's logon script path.
- `-mustchpwd`: Type **yes** if you want the user to change their password during the next logon.
- `-canchpwd`: Type **yes** if you want the user to be able to change their password.

- -pwdneverexpires: Type **yes** if you don't want the user's password to expire.

- -disabled: Type **yes** to disable the user's account.

- -acctexpires: Modify to change the user's account expiration date. A value of never indicates that the account never expires. Otherwise, type a positive value to set the number of days before the account expires.

- -reversiblepwd: Type **yes** to make the user's password rely on reversible encryption.

Move Existing Objects

The DSMove utility makes it possible to move Active Directory objects from one location to another. To move an object, type **DSMove DN -newparent ParentDN**, where *DN* is the object's distinguished name and *ParentDN* is the parent's distinguished name, and press Enter. Use the -newname *Name* (where *Name* is a distinguished name) command line switch to give the object a new name.

You can use the DSMove utility to work with remote systems as needed (such as when you want to move elements on a server). You can use the -s *Server* or -d *Domain* command line switches, where *Server* is the name of a specific server that you want the computer to use for logons and *Domain* is the name of a domain where you want the computer to log on, to log on to a particular part of the network as needed. This utility also supports the -u *Username* and -p *Password* command line switches, where *Username* is the name of an account on the server and *Password* is the account's password, to log on to the server using a different account.

Delete Existing Objects

It's important to delete Active Directory objects when you don't need them any longer to keep the directory from becoming clogged with old entries. To delete an object, type **DSRm DN**, where *DN* is the object's distinguished name, and press Enter.

There are a number of command line switches supplied with the DSRm utility. Type **DSRm /?** and press Enter to see a complete list of these command line switches. When working with script or batch files, use the -noprompt command line switch to delete entries without any output from the DSRm utility.

Some Active Directory objects, such as OU, are part of a tree where there are objects in the subtree. If you want to delete all of the objects within the subtree, use the -subtree command line switch. However, if you want to preserve the original object (simply eliminating the items in the subtree), use the -exclude command line switch as well.

You can use the DSRm utility to work with remote systems as needed (such as when you want to remove elements on a server). You can use the -s *Server* or -d *Domain* command line switches, where *Server* is the name of a specific server that you want the computer to use for logons and *Domain* is the name of a domain where you want the computer to log on, to log on to a particular part of the network as needed. This utility also supports the -u *Username* and -p *Password* command line switches, where *Username* is the name of an account on the server and *Password* is the account's password, to log on to the server using a different account.

PART V

Performing Diagnostics

IN THIS PART ▶

13

Monitoring System Events

IN THIS CHAPTER, YOU WILL LEARN TO:

The event log used to be a simple affair that contained a few folders or logs. The System log contained system-level events generated by the operating system, the Application log contained application-generated events, and the Security log contained security events, such as audits. Newer versions of Windows also contain these three logs, but now you have a complex affair of specialty logs for just about every purpose. An administrator could go crazy trying to figure it all out, much less monitor it using the GUI. Fortunately, the command line makes it easier to find what you need and you can automate access to specific entries using batch files or scripts. You can even use the command line to make entries. For example, you can register events generated by your batch files or scripts. The following sections tell you more about the various tasks you can perform with the event system.

Using Event Logs Effectively

Windows records all events in the event log. You can use the Event Viewer console in the Administrative Tools folder of the Control Panel to view the events. Educating yourself about the event log and understanding how to use it effectively are important. You can learn more about the event log in general on the Microsoft Web site at http://technet.microsoft.com/library/cc759538.aspx.

However, effective event log usage goes even further. As you begin writing your own applications (even batch file applications), consider adding event log entries to one of the standard logs or use a special log for the purpose. The Code Project article (http://www.codeproject.com/dotnet/evtvwr.asp) shows how to add new event logs using registry entries. You'll also want to review the MSDN "EventLog Key" article at http://msdn.microsoft.com/library/aa363648.aspx.

Create Simple System Events

It's extremely helpful to know how to create event log entries from the command line using the EventCreate utility. Doing so makes it possible to log events from batch files and other nonstandard sources. Instead of allowing the batch file to simply terminate without providing any information as to the cause of the problem, you can provide details about the failure in the event log (at least, you can provide this information when the failure isn't catastrophic).

NOTE The EventCreate utility supports the /S *Server* (where *Server* is a server name), /U *User* (where *User* is a user account on the remote system), and /P *Password* (where *Password* is the password for the remote user account) command line switches, which means that you can create event log entries on other systems. However, you should only make entries on remote systems when the entry applies to that system.

No matter what reason you might have for making an event log entry at the command line, the process is straightforward. The following steps describe how to create a simple event log entry:

1. Type **EventCreate**.

2. Type **/L Logname**, where *Logname* is the name of the log you want to use.

   The log name determines the name of the log to use for the event entry. The three standard logs found on every Windows machine are Application, Security, and System. Many machines include additional event logs installed by applications that the system uses.

3. Type **/T ERROR**, **/T WARNING**, or **/T INFORMATION** to specify the kind of event to create.

   Even though the Windows event log accepts other event types, the only three acceptable types are error, warning, and information. These three types reflect three levels of severity, with information being the least severe and error being the most severe.

4. Type **/SO Source**, where *Source* is the source of the event.

   You can use any string as the source. However, providing a meaningful application identifier is usually the best idea. Given that you'll use this feature from the command line, you might simply want to use "Command Line" as your source. When working with a batch file, use the batch filename as the source. Scripts and other forms of automation should use the script or application name.

5. Type **/ID Identifier**, where *Identifier* specifies the event identifier for the event.

The identifier is a number between 1 and 1,000. Whenever practical, provide specific numbers for specific events. For example, you might assign a value of 500 to all file errors. The event identifier lets you sort the events in a manner other than type or source, so you should also keep this in mind when you create the event identifier list for your application.

Figure 13.1: Event log entries appear just as you expect from the command line entries you provide.

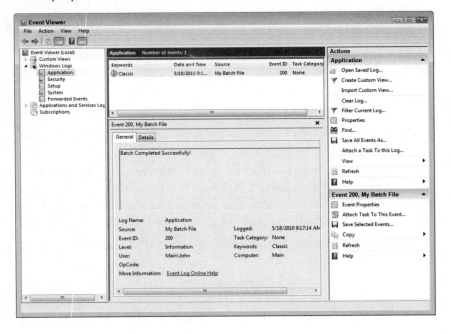

6. Type **/D** *Description*, where *Description* provides an event description.

The description should tell the viewer what happened to cause the event, the event effects, and any other pertinent information the viewer might need to resolve event problems caused by the event. Even informational events should include significant event information. For example, you might record that your application started, found no work to do, and terminated. Even though the application didn't experience an error, the information is still important to someone who expected your application to complete useful work.

7. Press Enter. EventCreate defines a new event entry in the event log that you specified.

As an example, let's say that you want to add a success message to the event log to show that your batch file completed its task successfully. In this case, you might type EventCreate /L Application /T INFORMATION / SO "My Batch File" /ID 200 /D "Batch Completed Successfully!" and press Enter. After you press Enter, you'll see a success message of "SUCCESS: An event of type 'INFORMATION' was created in the 'Application' log with 'My Batch File' as the source." When you open the Event Viewer console found in the Administrative Tools folder of the Control Panel, you'll find the success message shown in Figure 13.1 in the Windows Logs\Application folder.

NOTE The event log accepts several additional pieces of information that you can't add using the EventCreate utility. The event category requires that you register a specialized .DLL to handle the category information. Given that you probably won't add the required .DLL for a batch file application, Microsoft left this particular entry out. An event can also register data that amplifies the event description. The lack of support for this feature is regrettable because you could use it to create better event log entries. However, you can overcome this problem by providing a detailed description and possibly including the data as part of the description rather than as a separate entry.

Trigger System Events

One of the problems with the event log is that it can quickly become clogged with a lot of information—more information than many network administrators want to wade through to locate a particular event of importance. Starting with Windows XP, you can set an event trigger on the event log. When an event log entry matching the criteria you specify appears, you can tell the EventTriggers utility to perform any number of tasks—anything from sending an e-mail message to running a particular application (batch files included).

NOTE If you're using Vista or a newer version of Windows, you might notice that the EventTriggers utility isn't included by default, which is amazing because the utility first appeared in Windows XP. You can try to use this utility from your older copy of Windows. As an alternative, Microsoft also provides a GUI method for associating an event trigger with the event log that apparently doesn't have a command line alternative and therefore isn't included in this book. You can read about the GUI method at http://blogs.techrepublic.com.com/window-on-windows/?p=756.

The interesting part about using event triggers is that you can track problems occurring on any system (local or remote) with greater ease. Although you might want to look at all of those informational messages in the event log at some point, the SQL Server error message is the one that you really want to know about the second it occurs. The SQL Server message is an example of an event log entry that you want to track using an event trigger. Of course, the entry could just as easily be from any other application. For example, you might want to know when the Windows Time service fails to find an online time synchronization source.

The EventTriggers utility provides three modes of operation: Create, Delete, and Query. Each one of these modes controls a particular aspect of working with event triggers. The following sections discuss these three modes of operation and show how you use them to manage event triggers on your system.

NOTE The EventTriggers utility supports the /S *Server* (where *Server* is a server name), /U *User* (where *User* is a user account on the remote system), and /P *Password* (where *Password* is the password for the remote user account) command line switches, which means that you can create event trigger entries on other systems. In fact, you could write a batch file to obtain a list of computers on the system and place the same event triggers on every system to ensure any system encountering problems will send an e-mail or perform other tasks to handle the trigger.

Create an Event

Before you can use event triggers, you have to create them. The Create mode helps you add new event triggers. Each event trigger reacts to a separate event in the event log, so you need one event trigger for each event log entry that you want to monitor.

The following steps describe how to create an event trigger:

1. Type **EventTriggers /Create**.

2. Type **/TR** *TriggerName*, where *TriggerName* defines a human-readable name to associate with the event trigger.

   Using names such as MyTrigger probably won't work well. It's important to create a descriptive name that you'll recognize easily. Make sure you make the name unique by adding some elements for the event log entry that it monitors. For example, WinMgmtWarning63 would be a good name for an event generated by the Windows management service at the warning level for event identifier number 63.

3. Type **/TK** *TaskName*, where *TaskName* defines the name of the task to perform when the event trigger fires.

   Generally, this is the name of an application (including any required command line switches), batch file, script, or other executable entity. For example, you can tell Outlook to send you a message about the event using Outlook's command line switches to generate an e-mail.

4. (Optionally) Type **/L** *Log*, where *Log* specifies the Windows event log to monitor.

   The three common logs include Application, System, and Security. The DNS Server and Directory logs commonly appear on servers. You can also specify any custom log. You can use wildcard characters to define the log name. The default value is "*" (without the quotes), which is all of the event logs on the specified machine.

5. (Optionally) Type **/EID** *ID*, where *ID* specifies which Event ID to monitor in the event log.

   This value is application-specific, so you need to know which Event ID an application will use for a particular requirement.

6. (Optionally) Type **/T** *EventType*, where *EventType* specifies the Event Type to monitor in the event log.

   The valid values include ERROR, INFORMATION, WARNING, SUCCESSAUDIT, and FAILUREAUDIT. The SUCCESSAUDIT and FAILUREAUDIT event types only appear in Security logs.

7. (Optionally) Type **/SO *Source***, where *Source* specifies the Event Source to monitor in the event log.

   The Event Source varies by application and by entity performing a task. For example, the system can just as easily generate an event that a user can generate. Unless you want to monitor the activities of a specific entity, you should refrain from supplying this command line switch.

8. (Optionally) Type **/D *Description***, where *Description* specifies the Description to monitor in the event log.

   Using this command line switch makes the event trigger very specific. In fact, the event trigger becomes so specific that you might miss events. Use this particular command line switch with caution and only in cases where you know exactly which message you want to receive.

9. (Optionally) Type **/RU *Username***, where *Username* defines the user account to use to run the task.

   Use " " (two quotes) for the system account. The default username is the current username or the name used to access the remote system with the /U command line switch.

10. (Optionally) Type **/RP *Password***, where *Password* defines the password for the task user account.

    The EventTriggers utility ignores this value when working with the system account. Supply a value of * or None when you want the EventTriggers utility to prompt for a password.

11. Press Enter. EventTriggers defines a new event trigger using the criteria you specified.

As an example, let's say you want to create an event trigger for the custom event created in the "Create Simple System Events" section of the chapter. The event trigger will open a copy of Notepad, just so you can see something happening. You could create the event on one machine and have the command prompt appear on another. (A more practical approach would be to send an e-mail message, but the example uses this simple approach for clarity.) In this case, you'd type **EventTriggers /Create /TR MyTrigger /TK Notepad /L Application /EID 200 /T INFORMATION /SO "My Batch File"** and press Enter. EventTriggers will ask you to provide a password for running the task. Type the password and press Enter. Now, whenever the event occurs, you'll see a command prompt open with the success message.

Delete an Event

Use the Delete mode to remove any event triggers you no longer need. To delete an event trigger type **EventTriggers /Delete /TID** *ID*, where *ID* specifies the Trigger Identifier (TID) to remove from the list of event triggers. Every time you create a new event trigger, the system assigns it an identifier. You can see this identifier by using the Query mode. This command line switch accepts the * wildcard, which deletes all of the event triggers on the system.

Query an Event

The Query mode displays a list of all of the event triggers on a system. To see a complete list of all of the current event triggers, type **EventTriggers /Query** and press Enter. EventTriggers displays a list of all of the event triggers in tabular form.

You can use this list for real-time work with the event triggers. However, by changing the format, you can also use this mode to add the event triggers to a database for later reference. The following command line switches are helpful when modifying the EventTriggers / Query command output:

- **/FO {TABLE | LIST | CSV}:** Specifies the output format. The table columns define the values for output, while each row contains one event trigger entry. The CSV (comma separated value) output provides the best method for preparing the data for entry in a database. Use redirection to output the CSV data to a file and then import it to your database. The list format provides one data element per line. Each group of data elements defines one event trigger. The utility separates each event trigger by one blank line. Some people find the list format more readable when working in verbose mode since the table format requires multiple lines for each entry (the lines wrap).

- **/NH:** Specifies that the EventTriggers utility shouldn't display the column headers. You can use this option when creating pure content for reports or other needs. The EventTriggers utility accepts this command line switch only when using the table and CSV formats.

- **/V:** Outputs additional information about each event trigger. The default output includes the trigger identifier, event trigger name, and the name of the task the event trigger performs. The additional information includes the hostname, the event trigger query (the arguments used to trigger it), the description information, and the username used to run the task.

Manage Event Information

The WEvtUtil utility helps you monitor the event logs on a system. This utility replaces the other utilities provided in earlier versions of Windows (you won't find it in Windows XP or Windows 2003, but it does appear in Vista and Windows 2008). You might wonder about this change, until you begin looking at the complexity of the newer Windows event log setup, which is very complex. (The new event logs are a significant change from past versions of Windows that contained the same few logs.) The following sections describe how to perform tasks using the WEvtUtil utility.

Display a List of Publishers

In order to publish custom information in the event log as a service or application, you must become a publisher. Event publishers generally have their own log in which to place entries, so that the administrator should theoretically have an easier time finding the information. Unfortunately, to use this information successfully, you need to know the event publishers. To obtain a list of event publishers, type **WEvtUtil EP | More** and press Enter. The More utility is required because even a new Windows installation has far too many event publishers to see on a single screen. As an alternative, you can send the list to a file by typing **WEvtUtil EP > EventPublishers.TXT** and pressing Enter. What you'll see in the output is a list of publisher names, such as Application Error, but no additional information.

Get a Publisher

Simply having a name doesn't tell you much about a publisher. In order to obtain any useful information, you must get the publisher from WEvtUtil. The easiest way to perform this task is to use the WEvtUtil GP *PublisherName* command, where *PublisherName* is the name of a publisher such as Application Error. For example, to learn more about the Application Error publisher, type **WEvtUtil GP "Application Error"** and press Enter. You'll see publisher details like those shown in Figure 13.2.

Two special command line switches provide additional information. If you want to see the actual message that a publisher produces, use the /GM command line switch. Some publishers also output specific events. You can obtain this information using the /GE command line switch.

Figure 13.2: Detailed publisher information is helpful in learning about the publisher.

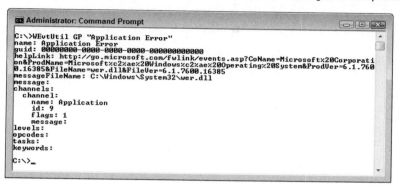

```
Administrator: Command Prompt

C:\>WEvtUtil GP "Application Error"
name: Application Error
guid: 00000000-0000-0000-0000-000000000000
helpLink: http://go.microsoft.com/fwlink/events.asp?CoName=Microsoft%20Corporati
on&ProdName=Microsoft%c2%ae%20Windows%c2%ae%20Operating%20System&ProdVer=6.1.760
0.16385&FileName=wer.dll&FileVer=6.1.7600.16385
messageFileName: C:\Windows\System32\wer.dll
message:
channels:
  channel:
    name: Application
    id: 9
    flags: 1
    message:
levels:
opcodes:
tasks:
keywords:

C:\>_
```

If you plan to work with the output of this command in another application or simply want an easier way to view it in a browser, you can use the /F:XML command line switch. The output is in XML format. For example, if you type WEvtUtil GP "Application Error" /GM / GE /F:XML > ApplicationError.XML and press Enter, you receive an XML file that contains detailed publisher information in a form that you could use in another application.

Enumerate the Logs

The new version of the event log has a host of logs in it. You still have access to the same three logs of the past: Application, Security, and System, but the new event log has many others. Besides having more logs to deal with, the machines on your network might not even have all the same logs because many logs are application- or service-specific. Consequently, before you can assume anything about the logs on a system, you must enumerate them by typing WEvtUtil EL | More and pressing Enter.

Unfortunately, just enumerating the logs probably won't answer the question of whether a particular log exists with any ease. In this case, use the WEvtUtil EL | Find /I "SearchTerm" command, where SearchTerm is one or more words for the log that you want to find. For example, you might want to see what media-related logs appear on the system. In this case, you'd type WEvtUtil EL | Find /I "Media" and press Enter.

Query Log Events

The WEvtUtil QE command outputs event information from a log or
log file. The path argument normally contains the name of the log.
For example, if you want to read all of the events in the Application
log in text format (rather than an unreadable form of XML), you type
WEvtUtil QE Application /F:XML and press Enter. However, if you use
the /lf option, then you must provide the physical path to the event log
file. This argument also supports the following options (the long names
appear in parentheses after the option):

- **/lf:{True | False} (logfile):** Specifies that the path argument
  contains a physical path to a log file, rather than a log filename.

- **/sq:{True | False} (structuredquery):** Specifies that the path
  argument contains a path to a file that contains a structure query.

- **/q:*Value* (query):** Provides an XPath query to filter the events read
  from the log. The utility returns all of the events when you don't
  provide this option. You can't use this option with the /sq option.

- **/bm:*Value* (bookmark):** Specifies a path to a file that contains a
  bookmark from a previous query. Using a bookmark lets you continue a previous query.

- **/sbm:*Value* (savebookmark):** Specifies a path to a file that the utility
  uses to store a bookmark for the current query. The bookmark file
  extension should be XML.

- **/rd:{True | False} (reversedirection):** Defines the direction in
  which the utility reads events. The default setting of True returns
  the most current events first.

- **/f:{XML | Text} (format):** Determines the output format of the
  data. The default setting is Text. When you use XML, the output
  appears as an XML file that you can view using any XML viewer
  (making the output considerably easier to understand).

- **/l:*LCID* (locale):** Provides a locale string that defines the locale
  used to output text information. This option is only available when
  you use the /f option to print events in text format.

- **/c:*Number* (count):** Defines the maximum number of events to
  read. If you combine this switch with the bookmark feature, you
  can read a segment of the event log at a time.

- **/e:*RootElementName* (element):** Defines a root element name to use
  to produce well-formed XML.

Unfortunately, displaying every event in the Application log is going to be time consuming. You'll want to query the event log in some way, but most people are daunted by technical terms like XPath. Fortunately, there's an easy way to build a query for WEvtUtil. Just follow these steps:

1. Open the Event Viewer.

2. Right-click the log you want to work with and choose Filter Current Log from the context menu.

   The example works with the System log, but you can use any log you want. You see the Filter Current Log dialog box shown in Figure 13.3.

Figure 13.3: The Filter Current Log dialog box makes it easy to create XPath queries.

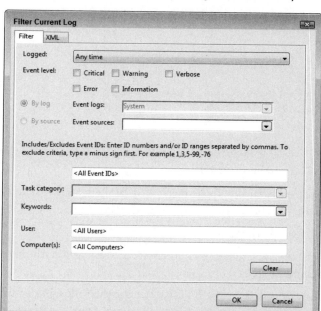

3. Configure the filter as you normally would.

   The example sets the filter to find all Information entries from the Service Control Manager.

4. Select the XML tab. You see the XML version of the filter shown in Figure 13.4.

Figure 13.4: The XML tab of the Filter Current Log dialog box contains the XPath you need.

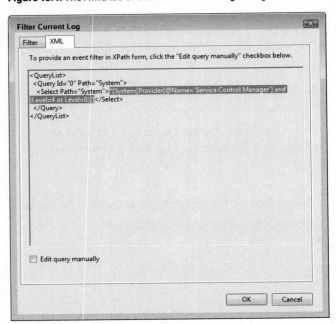

5. Select the XPath statement from the Path attribute of the <Select> element as shown in Figure 13.4.

   To do this, place the cursor at the beginning of the statement, and then press Shift+Right Arrow to highlight the remaining text.

6. Press Ctrl+C to copy the text to the clipboard.

7. Use the XPath text you just copied to create a command with the /Q command line switch.

   The previous example uses the XPath to create the following command that finds just the Information level entries from the Service Control Manager. (Even though the command occupies multiple lines in the book, you should type it as a single line command.)

```
WEvtUtil QE System /F:Text /Q:"*[System[Provider[@
Name='Service Control Manager'] and (Level=4 or
Level=0)]]"
```

Get a Log

It's helpful to know the current configuration of a log when looking for places you can make changes in the event log system. Use the WEvtUtil GL *LogName* command, where *LogName* is the name of the log you want to view, to perform this task. For example, if you want to get the configuration of the Application log, you type **WEvtUtil GL Application** and press Enter.

Get Log Status Information

All of the event logs maintain status information. To obtain the current statistics about any log, use the WEvtUtil GLI *LogName* command, where *LogName* is the name of the log you want to view, to perform this task. For example, if you want to determine the status of the Application log, you type **WEvtUtil GLI Application** and press Enter. The statistics are:

- creationTime
- lastAccessTime
- lastWriteTime
- fileSize
- attributes
- numberOfLogRecords
- oldestRecordNumber

Set a Log

Setting or configuring a log means changing individual log values. For example, you can enable or disable the log. You use the WEvtUtil SL *LogName* command, where *LogName* is the name of the log you want to change, to perform this task. You follow the basic command by any of the following command line switches to configure specific log elements:

- **/e:{True | False} (enabled):** Enables or disables the log. The default value is True to enable the log.

- **/i:{System | Application | Custom} (isolation):** Defines the log isolation mode: system, application, or custom. In addition, the mode identifies the other logs with which the log shares a session, which means these other logs have write permission for the target log. Use the System mode when a log affects that system as a whole. The resulting log shares a session with the System log. The Application mode is the option to use with general applications. Logs in this class share a session with the Application log. The Custom mode is for private logs that you don't want to share a session with any other log. You must use the /ca option to define security for custom logs.

- **/lfn:*Value* (logfilename):** Provides the full path to the physical location of the log on the hard drive.

- **/rt:{True | False} (retention):** Determines whether the log retains existing entries when the log becomes full. When you set the log retention mode to True, the log retains earlier entries when the log becomes full and discards all new entries. The default value of False discards older entries in favor of new ones.

- **/ab:{True | False} (autobackup):** Performs an automatic backup of the log when it reaches maximum size. You must set the retention value to True using the /rt option when using this feature.

- **/ms:*Value* (maxsize):** Specifies the maximum log size in bytes. Log files are always multiples of 64 KB, so Windows rounds any value you provide to a multiple of 64 KB.

- **/l:*Value* (level):** Defines the log level filter (normally critical, error, warning, information, or verbose). You may use any valid level value. This feature is only applicable to logs with a dedicated session (which means that the isolation mode is normally custom). You can remove a level filter by setting the value to 0.

- **/k:*Value* (keywords):** Defines the log keyword filter (common keywords include Audit Failure, Audit Success, Classic, Correlation Hint, Software Quality Monitoring [SQM], Windows Diagnostics Infrastructure [WDI] Context, and WDI Diag). The value can include any valid 64-bit keyword mask. This feature is only applicable to logs with a dedicated session (which means that the isolation mode is normally custom).

- **/ca:*Value* (channelaccess):** Defines the access permission for an event log. You must provide a valid security descriptor defined using the Security Descriptor Definition Language (SDDL). You can learn more about SDDL at http://msdn2.microsoft.com/en-us/library/aa379567.aspx.

- **/c:*Value* (config):** Defines a path to a configuration file. The configuration file contains log file settings in the form of an XML file. When using this feature, you must not specify the logname command line argument because this value is already part of the configuration file. Here's a typical example of a configuration file:

```
<?xml version="1.0" encoding="UTF-8"?>
<channel name="Application" isolation="Application"
        xmlns="http://schemas.microsoft.com/
win/2004/08/events">
  <logging>
    <retention>true</retention>
    <autoBackup>true</autoBackup>
    <maxSize>9000000</maxSize>
  </logging>
  <publishing>
  </publishing>
</channel>
```

Notice that the <channel> element includes the log filename as Application and an isolation level (/i) of Application. The logging options appear as part of the <logging> element. Each child element name is the long name for an option. For example, the <retention> element corresponds to the /rt command line argument. You can add other configuration options to the log, such as the publishing options.

As an example of how to use this command, let's say you want to change the maximum size of the application log to 1,048,576 bytes. In this case, you'd type **WEvtUtil SL Application /MS:1048576** and press Enter.

Export a Log

You can choose to export all or part of a log at any time to make a backup copy of it using the WEvtUtil EPL *LogName BackupName* command, where *LogName* is the name of the log you want to export and *BackupName* is the name of the file you want to use for export purposes. For example, to make a backup copy of the Application log, you type **WEvtUtil EPL Application /BU:ApplicationOld.EVTX** and press Enter. This command also supports the following command line switches:

- **/lf:{True | False} (logfile):** Specifies that the path argument contains a physical path to a log file, rather than a log filename.

- **/sq:{True | False} (structuredquery):** Specifies that the path argument contains a path to a file that contains a structure query.

- **/q:*Value* (query):** Provides an XPath query to filter the events read from the log. The utility returns all of the events when you don't provide this option. You can't use this option with the /sq option. See the "Query Log Events" section of the chapter for an example of using XPath to query the event logs.

Archive a Log

Archiving a log is different from exporting it in that the archive is a self-contained format designed solely for backup purposes. The WEvtUtil utility creates the log in a specific folder based on the current locale or a locale you provide using the /L:*Locale* (where *Locale* is the number of the locale you want to use) command line switch. For example, to archive the Application log, you type **WEvtUtil AL Application** and press Enter. Notice that you don't provide a backup filename when using this command.

Clear a Log

From time to time you need to clear the event logs or they become quite large and consume a large amount of hard drive space (not to mention being hard to use). Use the WEvtUtil CL *LogName* command, where *LogName* is the name of the log you want to clear to perform this task. For example, if you want to clear the Application log, you type **WEvtUtil CL Application** and press Enter.

Depending on company policy, you may need to create a backup of the event log before you clear it. In this case, you rely on the /BU:*BackupName* command line switch, where *BackupName* is the name of the backup file. For example, if you want to clear the Application log and back it up to ApplicationOld.EVTX, you'd type **WEvtUtil CL Application /BU:ApplicationOld.EVTX** and press Enter.

14

Monitoring System Performance

N o matter what you do with your system, at some point you'll want to know how it's performing. Performance data generally takes two forms. The static variety acts as a long-term record of the performance of your system as a whole. You can use it to track the performance of your system over time. The dynamic variety shows the current performance of your system. You can use it to check for changes in system status, look for positive gains after optimization, and even use it to troubleshoot your system (such as when a network card fails to deliver the throughput you anticipated).

Unlike many of the utilities discussed in this chapter, you can perform setups using the command line utilities, but actual monitoring usually occurs using the Performance console found in the Administrative Tools folder of the Control Panel. This chapter focuses on the command line tasks—those parts of performance monitoring that other books tend to ignore. However, you'll need to augment this information with a usage guide for the Performance console. This book won't tell you how to use the graphical interface. The following sections describe the command line interface in detail.

Add Performance Counters

Performance monitoring relies on the existence of counters. A counter is a special piece of code that counts something. The count might reflect the number of times a user accesses a file or makes a network request. No matter what the counter monitors, it provides output that the various performance monitoring applications can use to report performance data. In many cases, the performance counters appear as part of the application, so they're available from the moment you install the application. However, you can also obtain external counters. The LodCtr utility loads a counter into the system so that you can access it from performance monitoring software.

Load a Performance Counter

To load a new performance counter, you use the LodCtr *Filename* command, where *Filename* defines the name of a file with an .INI extension that contains the initialization data for a counter. The .INI file normally contains the name of the .DLL with the counter code, counter definitions (such as the human-readable name and any required help text), and the explanation text for an extensible counter .DLL. For example, to load counters from an .INI file named MyCounter.INI, you'd type **LodCtr MyCounter.INI** and press Enter.

Save Performance Counter Settings

You can save all of the current performance counter settings in the registry to a file. The resulting .INI file makes it easier to set up the counters on a system after you reconfigure it or move counters to a new system. To save the current performance counter settings, you use the LodCtr /S:*Filename* command, where *Filename* defines the name of an initialization file that contains counter registration information. The registration strings generally include the First Counter, First Help, Last Counter, and Last Help information for each of the counters. You'll also see a [PerfStrings_009] section that includes a list of all the performance counter strings by number. For example, to save all of the current settings to a file named MyCounters.INI, you'd type **LodCtr /S:MyCounters.INI** and press Enter.

NOTE Even though the documentation for this utility seems to say that the utility produces a .REG (registry) file, the file isn't a registry script. If you try to install the file using the RegEdit utility, the RegEdit utility displays an error. In fact, the file does appear in the .INI file format and you should probably give it an .INI file extension, rather than the .REG file extension Microsoft recommends.

Restore Performance Counter Settings

If you have an .INI file that contains a list of counter settings, you can restore those settings to any machine that has the counters installed. To restore counter settings, you use the LodCtr /R:*Filename* command, where *Filename* defines the name of an initialization file that contains counter registration information. For example, to restore all of the settings found in a file named MyCounters.INI, you'd type **LodCtr /R:MyCounters.INI** and press Enter.

Manage Performance Logs and Alerts

The Windows performance monitoring software includes the capability of creating performance logs and of creating alerts. The logs act as a historical record of the data the performance monitoring software collects. The alerts can perform tasks based on the current system performance. For example, if a system is low on memory or other resources, you can use an alert to send a message to the administrator to fix the problem. To perform this task, you use the LogMan *Verb CollectionName* command, where *Verb* is an action term and *CollectionName* is the name of the counter you want to interact with. The following sections describe each of the tasks you can perform using the LogMan utility.

Create a Performance Log

You can use the LogMan Create command to create four different kinds of performance data collectors: Counter, Trace, Alert, and configuration (abbreviated as Cfg). As a minimum, you must supply a collector name using the –N *Name* command line switch, where *Name* is the name of the data collector. For example, if you want to create a Counter data collector named MyCounter, you'd type **LogMan Create Counter -N MyCounter** and press Enter. This command creates a blank collector that won't do anyone much good, but LogMan accepts it.

To create a useful data collector, you need to add one or more counters. The –C command line switch helps you perform this task. Let's say you want to collect data for % Processor Time, % Idle Time, and % User Time for all of the processors. To create this data collector, you'd type **LogMan Create Counter -N MyCounter -C "\Processor(_Total)\% Processor Time" "\Processor(_Total)\% Idle Time" "\Processor (_Total)\% UserTime"** and press Enter. LogMan creates a usable data collector, but it isn't started yet. You can either start the data collector manually or use one of the following command line switches to augment or start it.

- –m [start] [stop]: Modifies the collection to use a manual start or stop, rather than relying on a scheduled beginning or ending time.

- –rf [[hh:]mm:]ss: Runs the collection for the specified time.

- –b M/d/yyyy h:mm:ss[{ AM | PM }]: Defines the starting time for the collection. Collection continues until the specified ending time (see the –e command line switch) or you manually end the collection process using the stop verb. The default setting uses the current day and time. You can input times using a 24-hour clock. When specifying a time based on a 12-hour clock, add the ~a.m. or ~p.m. option.

- **–e** *M/d/yyyy h:mm:ss*[{ *AM* | *PM* }]: Defines the ending time for the collection. The default setting uses the current day and time. You can input times using a 24-hour clock. When specifying a time based on a 12-hour clock, add the ~a.m. or ~p.m. option.

- **–o** { *Filename* | DSN!Log }: Specifies the output information for the collection. You can use an output file by specifying a path and filename. As an alternative, you can specify a SQL database (for any vendor that supports SQL) by including the Open Database Connectivity (ODBC) DSN and the log set name within the SQL database. The default setting is to use a file with the same name as the performance collection and a .BLG extension for counters or an .ETL extension for traces.

- **–[–]r:** Repeats the collection daily at the specified begin and end time when used with a single dash. This command is only valid for begin and end times specified on the same day, month, and year.

NOTE   Any entry with an optional dash has both an on and off state. Using a single dash turns on the feature and using a double dash turns off the feature. For example, –r repeats the collection daily, but ––r turns off this feature (removes the daily collection feature).

- **–[–]a:** Appends data to the existing log file when used with a single dash. Overwrites the existing log file when used with a double dash. The default setting is to overwrite the existing log file.

- **–[–]ow:** Overwrites any existing file with the same name.

- **–[–]v [** *nnnnnn* | *mmddhhmm* **]:** Attaches versioning information (either a number or the current date) to the end of the log filename when used with a single dash. Removes the versioning information when used with a double dash.

- **–[–]rc** *Filename*: Runs a command after the system closes the log when used with a single dash. Disables running a command when used with a double dash. The commands always run in the foreground (so the user can see them).

- **-[-]max Size:** Defines the maximum log file size in megabytes when used with a single dash. When the log file exceeds the maximum size, the system stops collecting data even if other command line arguments specify a longer collection time. This command line switch specifies the number of records when used with a SQL output. Removes the log file size restriction when used with a double dash.

- **-[-]cnf [[[hh:]mm:]ss]:** Creates a new file when the specified time elapses or the file reaches the maximum file size when used with a single dash. Removes the collection time restriction when used with a double dash.

- **-y:** Answers yes to all questions without prompting. This feature lets you set up counters and traces within a batch file without worrying about interruptions.

- **-ets:** Sends commands to event trace sessions without saving or scheduling.

> **NOTE** Some of these command line switches, such as –ets, affect other LogMan commands. Type **LogMan** *Verb* **/?** (where *Verb* is an action such as Create) and press Enter to see additional help about any particular LogMan verb.

Start Collecting Data

Unless you set a specified time for data collection to begin, you must start it manually. To perform this task, use the LogMan Start CollectorName command, where CollectorName is the name of a data collector. For example, if you want to start a data collector named MyCounter, type **LogMan Start MyCounter** and press Enter.

Stop Collecting Data

Once you collect enough data, you can stop any data collector manually. To perform this task, use the LogMan Stop CollectorName command, where CollectorName is the name of a data collector. For example, if you want to stop a data collector named MyCounter, type **LogMan Stop MyCounter** and press Enter.

Query a Collection

LogMan provides two levels of query. The first level is to obtain a list of data collectors. Simply type **LogMan Query** and press Enter to see the list.

After you have a list of data collectors, the second level is where you can obtain more detailed information using the LogMan Query *DataCollector* command, where *DataCollector* is the name of the data collector (also called a provider) that you want to see. For example, if you want to see the specifics about MyCounter, you'd type **LogMan Query MyCounter** and press Enter. Figure 14.1 shows typical output from a query.

Figure 14.1: LogMan can provide details about the data collectors you create.

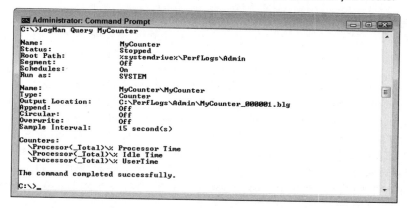

Update a Collection

The LogMan Update command works like the LogMan Create command discussed in the "Create a Performance Log" section of the chapter. In fact, you use the same techniques. The difference is that you update (modify) an existing data collector, rather than create a new one, so you only provide the information you want to change.

It's important to realize that the LogMan Update command erases the old content of a setting. For example, if you want to add a counter, then you must include all of the old counters, plus the new one. For example, to update MyCounter to include the % Privileged Time counter, you'd type **LogMan Update MyCounter -C "\Processor(_Total)\% Processor Time" "\Processor(_Total)\% Idle Time" "\Processor(_Total)\% UserTime" "\Processor(_Total)\% Privileged Time"** and press Enter.

Delete a Collection

When you no longer need a data collector, you should delete it, if for no other reason than to preserve system resources. Use the `LogMan Delete CollectorName` command, where `CollectorName` is the name of any data collector, to perform this task. For example, to delete `MyCounter`, you'd type **LogMan Delete MyCounter** and press Enter.

Create New Performance Logs from Existing Logs

The `ReLog` utility lets you create new performance logs from existing performance logs. The new logs can use a different sample rate. In addition, you can use this utility to convert a log from one format to another. For example, you can use this utility to convert older logs, including those from Windows NT 4.0 (such as the compressed log format) to newer formats.

To perform a basic conversion, use the `ReLog InputFile -F Format -O OutputFile` command, where `InputFile` is the name of the original performance log, `Format` is an output format, and `OutputFile` is the name of an output file. For example, to convert a binary file named `MyData.BLG` to CSV format, you'd type **ReLog MyData.BLG -F CSV -O MyData.CSV** and press Enter. The acceptable formats are:

- binary (Bin)
- circular binary (Bincirc)
- Comma Separated Value (CSV)
- Tab Separated Value (TSV)
- SLQ Database (SQL)

When you perform the conversion, you'll see statistics for the input and output files like those shown in Figure 14.2. It's important to view these statistics to ensure the information you think you're supposed to get in the output file is actually there. The use of the wrong command line switches can make a big difference in the output. Figure 14.3 shows an Excel view of the resulting output file.

Figure 14.2: Make sure you check the input and output log statistics from the conversion.

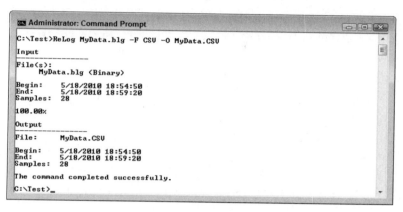

Figure 14.3: Excel can easily read the resulting CSV performance log file.

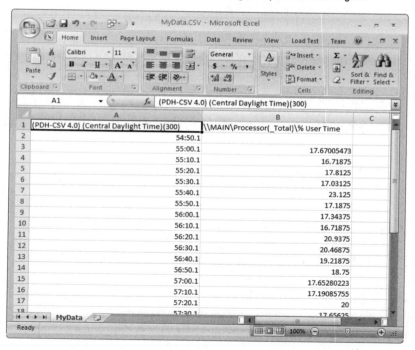

As with many utilities, you can go beyond the basics by adding more command line switches. The following list contains command line switches you can use to augment a conversion:

- **−c** *CounterPath* **[***CounterPath* **...]**: Defines one or more counters to filter from the input log. The output log contains the remaining counters. Each performance counter has a path that begins with the counter object, specific counter, and finally the instance. Consequently, the \Process(_Total)\% Processor Time counter path would collect the _Total instance of the % Processor Time counter found in the Processor object. Make sure you place each counter path in double quotes. The counter path can include wildcard characters. Here's a list of acceptable counter path formats:

  - \\machine\object(parent/instance#index)\counter

  - \\machine\object(parent/instance)\counter

  - \\machine\object(instance#index)\counter

  - \\machine\object(instance)\counter

  - \\machine\object\counter

  - \object(parent/instance#index)\counter

  - \object(parent/instance)\counter

  - \object(instance#index)\counter

  - \object(instance)\counter

  - \object\counter

- **−cf** *Filename*: Specifies a file containing a list of performance counters to collect. Each counter path must appear on a separate line.

- **−t** **value**: Changes the sampling rate by writing every nth record into the output file. For example, if the original file contains one record for each second, specifying a value of two would change the sampling rate to one every other second. The default setting writes every record into the output.

- **−b** *M/d/yyyy h:mm:ss*[{ *AM | PM* }]: Defines the starting time for the collection. Collection continues until the specified ending time (see the -e command line switch) or you manually end the collection process using the stop verb. The default setting uses the current day and time. You can input times using a 24-hour clock. When specifying a time based on a 12-hour clock, add the ~a.m. or ~p.m. option.

- **-e** *M/d/yyyy h:mm:ss*[{ *AM* | *PM* }]: Defines the ending time for the collection. The default setting uses the current day and time. You can input times using a 24-hour clock. When specifying a time based on a 12-hour clock, add the ~a.m. or ~p.m. option.

- **-config** *Filename*: Specifies a configuration filename that contains all of the command line options.

- **-q**: Lists all of the performance counters found in the input file. You can use this list to create input for the -c or -cf command line switches.

- **-y**: Answers yes to all questions without prompting. This feature lets you set up counters and traces within a batch file without worrying about interruptions.

Remove Performance Counters

The UnlodCtr utility unloads counters from memory. You won't generally need this utility unless you loaded a custom counter. To use this utility, type **UnlodCtr** *CounterName*, where *CounterName* is the name of the counter that you want to remove, and press Enter.

Convert Event Trace Logs

The TraceRpt utility converts the binary data in the Event Trace Logs (ETL) for the system into a format that you can use for permanent database storage or other needs. These .ETL files appear all over the hard drive and they're used by a variety of applications. Therefore, you need to know something about the .ETL file to make any sense of the content, even after you perform the conversion.

The TraceRpt utility supports a number of conversion types. The most common type uses the TraceRpt *InputFile* -F Format -O *OutputFile* or TraceRpt *InputFile* -OF *Format* -O *OutputFile* command, where *InputFile* is the name of the original .ETL file, *Format* is an output format, and *OutputFile* is the name of an output file. The main difference between the -F and -OF command line switches is that -F supports XML and HTML as output, while -OF supports CSV, Event Extended

(EVTX), and XML as output. For example, to create an Excel-viewable CSV file from MyTrace.ETL, you'd type **TraceRpt MyTrace.ETL -OF CSV -O MyTrace.CSV** and press Enter.

It's also possible to create two different reports. The –summary command line switch produces a simple text report named Summary.TXT. The –report command line switch produces a more detailed report in XML format named Workload.XML. You can add a filename to either command line switch to change the output filename. The TraceRpt utility provides a number of other interesting command line switches to modify the output. Type **TraceRprt /?** and press Enter to see a complete list of these switches.

PART VI

Performing Maintenance

N THIS PART ▶

Performing Maintenance

PART VI

15

Performing Basic Maintenance

Performing Maintenance

PART VI

The command line offers an amazing array of maintenance-related commands. In fact, there are far too many of them to discuss in a chapter. You could possibly write an entire book on just this aspect of the command line. Of course, you use some commands far more often than others. Although it's important to know how to use the Boot Configuration Data Store Editor (BCDEdit) to control the boot configuration, you'll probably use it once or twice during the entire lifetime of a particular system. (However, every machine will likely require that you use it at least once, so you can't forget about BCDEdit either.) On the other hand, the Windows Management Interface Command (WMIC) utility contains so much functionality that you may very well find yourself using it every day. With this in mind, this chapter discusses those utilities that are both important and will require at least occasional use.

Configure the Server

You may wonder what Windows Management Instrumentation (WMI) is all about, and it's important to know a little about it. In 1996, BMC Software, Cisco Systems, Compaq Computer, Intel, and Microsoft sponsored the Web-Based Enterprise Management (WBEM) initiative. The whole purpose of WBEM was to make it possible to manage systems across a network even if those systems weren't normally compatible. For example, using WBEM, you could manage Linux and Windows servers from the same location with equal ease—at least, that's the theory. For the most part, the theory does work and many companies have adopted WBEM as a basis for performing management tasks without platform considerations. In fact, the Distributed Management Task Force (DMTF) has a number of standards for WBEM and you can see them at http://www.dmtf.org/standards/wbem/.

NOTE This book does provide enough information about WMIC to help you perform most common tasks. It doesn't document WMI or WMIC completely because the application is large and complex enough to warrant a book of its own. If you find that you need additional information about WMI, check out *Understanding WMI Scripting* by Alain Lissoir (Digital Press, 2003). This book contains 579 pages on the topic of WMI scripting, including the use of WMIC.

WMI is Microsoft's next step for WBEM. Even though this is still supposedly an open standard, WMI builds on WBEM and implements it at a lower level. The instrumentation takes place through device drivers, services, and other software, making the entire structure of a system appear more as a hierarchical database than a collection of statistics that someone could use for management tasks. As a result, WMI lets you do more than WBEM, but the added functionality also makes WMI considerably more complex. The point is that WMI looks like a hierarchical database of any system you want to manage that supports WMI. You can learn more about WMI at `http://www.microsoft.com/whdc/system/pnppwr/wmi/wmi-acpi.mspx`.

`WMIC` is an extremely powerful utility that you'll see demonstrated throughout the book. This utility is the command line interface for WMI. You'll probably need to spend some time working with `WMIC` before you can make it do everything you want. Because WMI reflects the setup of your machine and not mine, it's impossible to provide detailed particulars of every element of `WMIC` in this book. However, `WMIC` does work well for many common tasks where you know that most machines will have essentially the same configuration. The following sections describe `WMIC` in detail.

Understand the SQL Syntax of *WMIC*

The basic usage technique for `WMIC` isn't hard. You have access to a number of global command line arguments, some aliases for particular parts of the system, and alias-specific command line switches. The difficulty comes when you begin using the `WMIC` command for real work. In most cases, you'll need to use a SQL Server–like syntax that tells `WMIC` precisely what element of your system to work with. Given that `WMIC` makes your system look like a hierarchical database, the use of a SQL Server–like syntax works well. The actual name for this syntax is WMI Query Language (WQL) and you can find detailed information about it at `http://msdn.microsoft.com/library/aa394552.aspx`. As an example of WQl at work, the `WMIC ComputerSystem Where Name="%COMPUTERNAME%" Call Rename Name="`*NewName*`"` command, where *NewName* is the name you want to assign to your computer, defines a new name for your computer. The rest of this section takes this command apart.

The term `ComputerSystem` is an alias. It references the computer system elements of WMI. You need an alias to locate the particular branch of the database that contains the element that you want to work with.

The Where clause tells WMIC which property to access within the alias. In this case, the name of the property must match the %COMPUTERNAME% expansion variable. This system environment variable appears with every copy of Windows and it always contains the name of the local system. Consequently, you can create commands that will run on any system simply by referencing the expansion variable. The ComputerSystem alias supports a number of properties including (to see this list for yourself, type **WMIC ComputerSystem** and press Enter):

AdminPasswordStatus	AutomaticReset-BootOption	AutomaticReset-Capability
BootOptionOnLimit	BootOptionOnWatchDog	BootROMSupported
BootupState	Caption	ChassisBootupState
CreationClassName	CurrentTimeZone	DaylightInEffect
Description	Domain	DomainRole
EnableDaylight-SavingsTime	FrontPanelReset-Status	InfraredSupported
InitialLoadInfo	InstallDate	KeyboardPassword-Status
LastLoadInfo	Manufacturer	Model
Name	NameFormat	NetworkServer-ModeEnabled
NumberOfProcessors	OEMLogoBitmap	OEMStringArray
PartOfDomain	PauseAfterReset	PowerManagement-Capabilities
PowerManagement-Supported	PowerOnPassword-Status	PowerState
PowerSupplyState	PrimaryOwnerContact	PrimaryOwnerName
ResetCapability	ResetCount	ResetLimit
Roles	Status	SupportContact-Description
SystemStartupDelay	SystemStartupOptions	SystemStartupSetting
SystemType	ThermalState	TotalPhysicalMemory
UserName	WakeUpType	Workgroup

Every WMIC command can perform an action. The number of actions depends on the alias that you're working with. You can see a list of actions for a particular alias by typing **WMIC** *Alias* **/?** (where *Alias* is a WMIC alias that you want to learn about) and pressing Enter. If you want to learn more about a particular action, type **WMIC Alias Action /?** and press Enter. The ComputerSystem alias provides the following actions (these actions are typical):

- **ASSOC:** Displays a list of the associators of the current alias. Think again about the hierarchical nature of the WMI database. An *associator* would be a WMI element that appears as a child of the current node in the database.

- **CALL:** Calls the specified method with the arguments you provide. Every alias provides special methods for configuration tasks. In the case of the example, the command calls on the Rename method. The ComputerSystem alias also provides the JoinDomainOrWorkgroup and the UnJoinDomainOrWorkgroup methods. To see the list of calls for a particular alias, type **WMIC Alias Call /?** and press Enter. The methods normally include input and output arguments. The help listing tells you about each of these arguments, but you don't necessarily need to use all of them. For example, the example call only uses the Name argument, but it also includes the UserName and Password arguments when you work on a remote system. To use an argument, provide its name, followed by an equals sign, followed by the value of that argument in double quotes as shown in the example.

- **CREATE:** Creates a new instance of a particular element. You must provide the arguments required to create the element. The element also has optional arguments that you don't have to provide. If you don't supply enough arguments, then WMIC displays an error message that normally tells you what arguments are missing.

- **DELETE:** Removes an existing element. Make sure you use a Where clause that defines the element completely. Otherwise, you might delete something you really wanted to keep.

- **GET:** Obtains all of the details for a particular alias. However, the true power of this action is retrieving individual property values. For example, if you want to determine the current startup delay for your system, you'd type **WMIC ComputerSystem Where Name="%COMPUTERNAME%" GET SystemStartupDelay** and press Enter. In this case, SystemStartupDelay is one of the properties that the ComputerSystem alias supports.

Performing Maintenance

PART VI

- **LIST:** Obtains all of the details for a particular alias. You can specify how much information to provide using the Brief and Full settings. For example, if you type **WMIC ComputerSystem LIST Brief** and press Enter, WMIC only provides the Domain, Manufacturer, Model, Name, PrimaryOwnerName, and TotalPhysicalMemory properties as output. You can combine the LIST command with the Where filter to obtain specific results. For example, let's say you need to know about the Microsoft Help Viewer 1.0. In this case, you'd type **WMIC Product Where Name="Microsoft Help Viewer 1.0" List** and press Enter to see the information for the Microsoft Help Viewer 1.0, rather than all of the applications on the machine.

- **SET:** Sets the value of a property directly. You must include a Where clause that specifies which element to change. For example, if you want to change the system startup delay (at the boot manager) to 35 sections, you'd type **WMIC ComputerSystem Where Name="%COMPUTERNAME%" SET SystemStartupDelay=35** and press Enter. Type **WMIC Alias SET /?** and press Enter to see a list of properties you can change. The ComputerSystem alias includes the following writeable properties:

  - AutomaticResetBootOption

  - CurrentTimeZone

  - EnableDaylightSavingsTime

  - Roles

  - SystemStartupDelay

  - SystemStartupOptions

  - SystemStartupSetting

  - Workgroup

Use Aliases in *WMIC*

As mentioned in the "Understand the SQL Syntax of WMIC" section of the chapter, much of your work with WMIC involves using aliases. Using an alias means that you don't have to worry about the physical structure of WMI—you can access the information you need quickly and easily (or at least more easily than if you also had to worry about the path to a particular WMI element). The following list tells you about the aliases that WMIC supports:

- **Alias:** Provides access to a list of all of the aliases available on the local system.

- **Baseboard:** Provides access to features on the motherboard (system board). For example, if you type **WMIC Baseboard GET Manufacturer** and press Enter, you'll see the name of the manufacturer of your motherboard.

- **BIOS:** Provides access to the Basic Input/Output System (BIOS) management features. For example, if you type **WMIC BIOS GET BIOSVersion** and press Enter, you'll see the version of the BIOS installed in the system. This isn't the same as the firmware update. To obtain the firmware version, type **WMIC BIOS GET SMBIOSBIOSVersion** and press Enter.

- **BootConfig:** Provides access to boot configuration information. Microsoft may not support this feature with newer versions of Windows—always use the BCDEdit utility instead for making changes to the boot configuration.

- **CDROM:** Provides access to all of the CD and DVD devices on the system. For example, if you want to obtain the name and volume of each of your CD or DVD devices, you would type **WMIC CDROM GET Name, VolumeName** and press Enter (notice that you must separate the individual properties with commas).

- **ComputerSystem:** Manages the computer system configuration.

- **CPU:** Provides access to the CPU. You'll see one entry for each CPU. If the CPU is dual (or more) processing, the output displays one entry for each processor in the CPU. One of the more important properties is the status indicator, which provides a simple indication of whether the CPU is currently operating within designed parameters (the output is a simple OK when the CPU is functioning properly). Type **WMIC CPU GET Status** and press Enter to obtain the status information.

- **CSProduct:** Provides access to the computer system product information. For example, you'd use this alias to determine the system's Universally Unique Identifier (UUID), which is actually better than a serial number because it's unique across all systems.

- **Datafile:** Manages information about data files on the system. This alias locks up the machine if you don't use it correctly. You must provide specific data file criteria in order to achieve good results. For example, if you want to locate all of the executable files in the Windows directory, type `WMIC DataFile Where "Path='\\ Windows\\' and Extension='exe'"` and press Enter. Notice the use of double quotes to encompass the search criteria and single quotes to encompass values. In addition, notice the use of double back-slashes in the path variable. You can't use expansion variables in this case.

- **DCOMApp:** Manages the Distributed Component Object Model (DCOM) applications on the system. You can use this feature to start, stop, install, and remove DCOM applications as needed using a simple batch file. Because DCOM applications can become quite complex, make sure you understand how to configure DCOM applications using the Component Services console first.

- **Desktop:** Manages the user's desktop. Unfortunately, this alias assumes that the user's desktop includes a GUI. Consequently, this alias doesn't work well with Windows Server 2008 Server Core, but it works fine with all other versions of Windows. You can obtain information such as the screen saver that the user is employing and what the desktop has for a background image.

- **DesktopMonitor:** Provides access to statistics about the configuration of the desktop on the specified system.

- **DeviceMemoryAddress:** Provides access to the memory ranges used by physical devices installed on the system. You'll see one entry for each memory range used by a device. The output of this alias is somewhat useless because it doesn't provide names for each of the devices, but you can still use it to detect a specific memory range.

- **DiskDrive:** Provides access to hard drives and hard drive–like devices, such as USB flash drives. The output includes formatting, status, and other statistics that are helpful for managing the hard drive. For example, if you want to quickly determine drive status, type `WMIC DiskDrive GET Name, Caption, NeedsCleaning, Status` and press Enter.

- **DiskQuota:** Manages disk space usage on Windows NTFS volumes. You must have the disk quota feature enabled to use this alias. Otherwise, when you type `WMIC DiskQuota` and press Enter, you'll see a list of the partitions on the current drive, but none of the drives will show that they have any space used. Setting a disk quota is somewhat complex, partly because you have to provide so much information to do it. A disk quota is a combination of a user account and a disk, so you normally specify both. For example, you may want to set a disk quota for a user named John on the C drive of 600,000,000 bytes. In this case, you'd type `WMIC DiskQuota Where (User="Win32_Account.Domain='MAINXP',Name='John'" And QuotaVolume="Win32_LogicalDisk.DeviceID='C:'") SET WarningLimit=600000000` and press Enter. As you can see, the `Where` clause is complex. The `User` property includes both a domain and a name value. The `QuotaVolume` property must reflect the actual C drive entry, which includes all of the additional text shown. Once you know how to select the user and drive, you use the `SET` verb to change the `WarningLimit` property as shown. The best way to learn how to form this particular command is to spend time selecting users and drives first, and then using what you learn to set the property values.

- **DMAChannel:** Provides access to Direct Memory Access (DMA) channel information on the system. You'll see one entry for each DMA channel. The output of this alias is somewhat useless because it doesn't really tell you anything about DMA channel usage.

- **Environment:** Manages environment variable information. This alias provides extensive information about the environment variables and makes it easy to query them from a remote system. For example, you'd type `WMIC Environment Where Name="Path" GET VariableValue` and press Enter to determine the path for a system.

- **FSDir:** Provides specifics about a particular directory or file on a hard drive. This alias locks up the machine if you don't use it correctly. You must provide double backslashes for the path. For example, if you want to determine the statistics for the Windows directory on the D drive, then you would type `WMIC FSDir Where Name="D:\\Windows"` and press Enter. You can't use expansion variables in this case.

- **Group:** Manages groups on the specified system. Make sure you differentiate between the `Caption` and `Name` properties. The `Caption` property requires that you provide a realm or domain with the group name. To see the difference between the two, type `WMIC Group LIST Brief` and press Enter.

- **IDEController:** Provides access to information about the Integrated Device Electronics (IDE) controllers on the system.

- **IRQ:** Provides access to information about the Interrupt Request (IRQ) lines on the system. You'll see one entry for each IRQ line. The output of this alias is somewhat useless because it doesn't really tell you anything about IRQ usage.

- **Job:** Manages jobs on the system through the Task Manager.

- **LoadOrder:** Manages the order in which system services load. Normally, you won't want to change these entries because a change in order could prevent a service from starting. However, this feature is helpful when you suspect a service isn't starting as anticipated (make sure you create a copy of the order when the system is in a known good working state). To create a copy of the current load order, type **WMIC LoadOrder > LoadOrder.TXT** and press Enter. The load order will appear in LoadOrder.TXT.

- **LogicalDisk:** Provides access to information about the logical disks on the system. The information includes only local drives.

- **Logon:** Provides access to information about the current logon sessions. Unfortunately, the output isn't very useful because it doesn't contain logon names—it provides logon identifiers instead, so you need to perform additional processing.

- **MemCache:** Provides access to the cache memory information for a system. To check the status of the Static Random Access Memory (SRAM) on a system, type **WMIC MemCache GET Purpose, InstalledSize, Status** and press Enter.

- **MemoryChip:** Provides information about memory chips installed on the system. Most systems don't support this alias.

- **MemPhysical:** Provides information about the physical memory installed on a system.

- **NetClient:** Provides information about Terminal Services and the Remote Desktop functionality the service provides.

- **NetLogin:** Provides information about logons for the specified system. This alias requires a little extra work to use because you must provide a more complex WQI statement. To obtain information about any particular user, type **WMIC NetLogin Where (Name Like "%UserName")** and press Enter. Once you get past the initial requirement to provide additional information, you can use the standard actions to obtain specific data.

- **NetProtocol:** Manages the network protocols used on the current system. When working with this protocol to obtain information, use the `Caption` property instead of the `Name` property to access particular protocols. For example, the `Caption` property may display `NetBIOS`, while the `Name` property displays `MSAFD NetBIOS [\Device\ NetBT_Tcpip_{2CFD1858-4741-4AD2-AD9B-E00D23BF8ED9}] DATAGRAM 2`. Use the `Name` property when you want to modify a specific protocol to ensure you change the correct protocol.

- **NetUse:** Manages network connectivity information on the specified system. For example, you would use this alias to discover mapped network drives. In this case, you'd type **WMIC NetUse Where ResourceType="Disk" GET LocalName, RemoteName** and press Enter.

- **NIC:** Provides access to information about the Network Interface Controllers (NICs) installed on the specified system.

- **NICConfig:** Manages the NIC setup. Unlike most of the aliases, this alias doesn't include a `Name` property, so you must use the `Caption` property. To obtain a list of NICs on the target system, type **WMIC NICConfig GET Caption** and press Enter.

- **NTDomain:** Manages Windows domain information, including several useful Active Directory settings.

- **NTEvent:** Displays the entries in the Windows event log. This alias locks up the machine if you don't use it correctly (even if you do use it correctly, the required search can require several minutes). For example, if you want to discover any System event log entries with a type greater than 4, type **WMIC NTEvent Where "LogFile='system' and Type>'4'"** and press Enter. You can't use this alias to add new event entries to the log.

- **NTEventLog:** Manages the Windows event logs. Unlike the `NTEvent` alias, which helps you manage the actual event log entries, this alias controls the actual logs. For example, you can use this alias to manage the event log size. This is also the alias you use to clear the event log. To clear the System event log, you'd type **WMIC NTEventLog Where LogFileName="System" CALL ClearEventLog** and press Enter. If you choose to save the log before clearing it, add the `ArchiveFileName` argument.

- **OnBoardDevice:** Provides access to adapter devices built onto the motherboard. At least, it should provide this access. Testing on several systems shows that support for this feature is sketchy at best. You'll generally manage adapters on the motherboard using the same techniques that you use to manage stand-alone adapters.

- **OS:** Provides access to statistics about the current operating system. For example, to obtain the operating system name and build, you'd type **WMIC OS GET Caption, BuildNumber** and press Enter.

- **Pagefile:** Provides information about the Windows page file. You can't use this alias to control the page file size.

- **PageFileSet:** Manages the Windows page file. However, instead of using a method to set the page file, you use properties. For example, to set the page file on drive C to an initial size of 2 GB and a maximum size of 2 GB, you'd type **WMIC PageFileSet Where Name="C:\\ PageFile.SYS" SET InitialSize=2048,MaximumSize=2048** and press Enter. Notice that you separate the SET arguments with commas and that you have to use a double backslash for the page file entry, even though the Name property displays with a single backslash.

- **Partition:** Provides statistics about the partitions on the hard drive. You can't use this alias to change the partition sizes.

- **Port:** Provides information about the I/O ports on the system. For example, if you wanted to detect any failed ports, you could type **WMIC Port Where(NOT Status="OK") GET Caption, Description** and press Enter. Notice the use of the word NOT to indicate that the ports aren't OK. You'll see one entry for each port. The output of this alias is somewhat useless because it doesn't tell you the name of each port; you must correlate the address range to the actual port.

- **PortConnector:** Provides access to the physical ports on the system. You can use this feature to find the physical port names (such as LPT1), their connection type, and port type. The listing includes both internal and external connectors. It even includes the motherboard ports, such as fan connectors. To obtain a listing of the most commonly used port information, type **WMIC PortConnector GET ConnectorType, InternalReferenceDesignator, PortType** and press Enter.

- **Printer:** Manages the logical printer characteristics for the system. The list of printers includes any mapped printer connections. Use the CALL verb to access any of these management methods: AddPrinterConnection, CancelAllJobs, Pause, PrintTestPage,

RenamePrinter, Reset, Resume, SetDefaultPrinter, and SetPowerState. For example, if you wanted to resume printing on a networked printer named HP LaserJet 5 located on WinServer, you'd type **WMIC Printer Where Caption="\\\\WinServer\\HP LaserJet 5" CALL Resume** and press Enter. Notice that you must use four backslashes to begin the UNC location of the printer.

- **PrinterConfig:** Provides information about the physical characteristics of both local and networked printers. The statistics include the printer resolution, any driver information, and whether the printer prints in color (along with other useful information).

- **PrintJob:** Manages individual print jobs for the local machine. You can also use methods to pause and resume individual jobs.

- **Process:** Manages processes on the local machine. You can obtain a wealth of information about each process, including memory statistics. The methods associated with this alias let you attach a debugger to a process, create a new process, obtain process owner information, set the process priority, and even terminate the process. Normally, you'll want to perform all tasks using the ProcessID property. To obtain a list of Process Identifiers (PIDs) and their associated application names, type **WMIC Process GET Name,ProcessID** and press Enter. Once you have the ProcessID, you can perform tasks such as terminating the process. To terminate a process with a PID of 688, you'd type **WMIC Process Where ProcessID=688 CALL Terminate** and press Enter.

- **Product:** Manages products on the local machine. This alias provides the equivalent of all of the information you'd find in the Add/Remove Programs applet (Programs and Features in Vista and above) in the Control Panel, so it's an essential aid on Windows Server 2008 Server Core (because it lacks the GUI required to access the Add/Remove Programs applet). In addition to the product name and vendor support information, you can also find the product uninstall information, which helps you perform the uninstall at the command line, rather than use the GUI as normal. Special methods let you configure, install, uninstall, reinstall, or upgrade application packages as needed.

For example, after you get a product installed, you can use WMIC to manage it. If you need to change the application configuration, type **WMIC Product Where Name="*ProductName*" Call Configure** and press Enter, where *ProductName* is the name of the product you

Performing Maintenance

PART VI

want to work with. Likewise, you can remove a product that you no longer need by typing **WMIC Product Where Name="ProductName" Call Uninstall** and pressing Enter. Only the methods that the setup program supports will work. You can also use the WMIC Install method when you want to install an advertised product—one that was previously advertised using the Advertise method.

- **QFE:** Provides a listing of all of the Quick Fix Engineering (QFE) patches for the Windows system. This alias only lists the fixes and you can't use it to manage them in any way.

- **QuotaSetting:** Manages the quota settings on the local hard drive. You must use the SET verb to change the settings. For example, if you want to configure the C drive default quota limit to 1 GB, you would type **WMIC QuotaSetting Where Caption="C:" SET DefaultLimit=1073741824** and press Enter. To enable the quota you just set, type **WMIC QuotaSetting Where Caption="C:" SET State=1** and press Enter. If you also want to deny disk space to users who exceed their quota, you can set the State to 2. Combine this alias with the DiskQuota alias to create a complete disk quota solution.

- **RDAccount:** Manages the accounts that can access a server using Remote Desktop. This alias assumes that the Remote Desktop Listener is active (see the RDToggle alias for details). You need not add users to the account listing to see that some users have access by default. Type **WMIC RDAccount GET AccountName**, press Enter, and you'll see this list of standard users:

  - BUILTIN\Administrators

  - NT AUTHORITY\LOCAL SERVICE

  - NT AUTHORITY\NETWORK SERVICE

  - NT AUTHORITY\SYSTEM

  - BUILTIN\Remote Desktop Users

  Remote access actually depends on two features, the account name and the terminal name (console or Remote Desktop Protocol-Transmission Control Protocol, RDP-TCP, in most cases). To remove a user from the list, you must include both the account name and the terminal name to ensure you delete the right account. To remove the administrator's account from console access, type **WMIC RDAccount where "TerminalName='console' and AccountName like '%Administrators%'" CALL Delete** and press Enter.

Interestingly enough, you can't add new accounts using the RDAccount alias; you must use the RDPermissions alias to do it.

- **RDNIC:** Manages the NIC associated with the Remote Desktop connection. You can configure items such as the number of connections allowed.

- **RDPermissions:** Manages permissions for Remote Desktop connections. To add a user to the console terminal, type **WMIC RDPermissions Where TerminalName="Console" CALL AddAccount "Domain\UserName",2** and press Enter. You must provide a domain and a username as shown. The second value is the permission preset. It uses the following values:

    - 0: Guest access—the user can only log on to the system.

    - 1: User access—the user has the following permissions: Logon, Query Information, Send Message, and Connect.

    - 2: Full access—the user has full system access.

- **RDToggle:** Manages the Remote Desktop listener settings.

- **RecoverOS:** Manages the system recovery options, including the memory dump feature.

- **Registry:** Provides access to the physical features of the registry such as size and location. You can also provide a proposed registry size.

- **SCSIController:** Provides information about any Small Computer System Interface (SCSI) devices on the selected computer. In addition, this alias provides information about Redundant Array of Inexpensive Disk (RAID) controllers. You can use calls to set the power state and to reset the controller.

- **Server:** Provides statistics about the server such as the logon errors and number of bytes received.

- **Service:** Manages the services running on the target system. You can use calls to start, stop, pause, continue, and perform other tasks with services. To determine the status of the services, type **WMIC Service GET Name,State** and press Enter. To start a particular service, type **WMIC Service Where Name="ServiceName" CALL StartService** and press Enter.

- **ShadowCopy:** Provides information about volumes with shadow copy management. You can also use this alias to add shadow copy management to a volume.

- **ShadowStorage:** Provides information about the shadow copy storage areas for the target system. This alias lets you set the maximum storage area size through a property and create new storage areas using a method.

- **Share:** Shares the specified resource on the target system.

NOTE   The Microsoft documentation provides entries for the SoftwareElement and SoftwareFeature aliases. However, these aliases don't appear to provide any functionality. In fact, during testing they output an error code of 0x80041010. You should probably avoid using these aliases until Microsoft makes them functional and provides better documentation for them.

- **SoundDev:** Provides statistics about any sound devices on your system. You can't use this alias to change any sound system features.

- **Startup:** Provides information about the applications and services that run automatically when the computer starts. This feature works similarly to the Startup tab of the System Configuration Utility (MSConfig.EXE), except that you can't make any changes to the setup.

- **SysAccount:** Provides a list of the system accounts that includes account statistics such as their global SIDs.

- **SysDriver:** Provides a list of the system drivers. The methods provided with this alias let you pause and resume the service. You can also interrogate the service for additional information.

- **SystemEnclosure:** Provides statistics about the system enclosure, such as whether it provides a hot-swappable disk feature.

- **SystemSlot:** Provides information about the system slot configuration of the motherboard. Theoretically, this alias also provides information about other motherboard connections such as port, peripheral, and proprietary connection points, but normally you won't actually see this information provided.

- **TapeDrive:** Provides information about any tape drives installed on the target system.

- **Temperature:** Provides information about any temperature sensors installed on the system. Unfortunately, this feature doesn't work at all on older systems and may not work on newer systems either. When this alias does work, you obtain a considerable amount of information about the sensor—everything you could ever want except the temperature. The `CurrentReading` property should contain the current temperature, but it often doesn't.

- **TimeZone:** Provides complete information about the time zone settings on the target machine. However, you can't use this alias to change any of the settings.

- **UPS:** Provides complete statistics about the Uninterruptible Power Supply (UPS) attached to the target system. The statistics you receive depend, in part, on the capabilities of the UPS. Newer UPSs tend to provide more information than older setups. In some cases, you can even detect the operating temperature of the UPS. The UPS must rely on the UPS service in Windows for this feature to work. You can't change any of the UPS feature settings using this alias.

- **UserAccount:** Manages user account information. You can add, delete, or modify user entries as needed. The modifications include the ability to rename the user account, disable the account, and set account password requirements. For example, if you want to set the user's full name, type **WMIC UserAccount Where Name="UserName" SET FullName="FullName"** and press Enter.

- **Voltage:** Provides information about any voltage sensors installed on the system. Unfortunately, this feature doesn't work at all on older systems and may not work on newer systems either. When this alias does work, you obtain a considerable amount of information about the sensor—everything you could ever want except the power supply voltages. The `CurrentReading` property should contain the current voltage readings, but it often doesn't.

- **Volume:** Manages the volumes on the target system. You obtain detailed statistics about the volume in question. In addition, you can use methods to add a mount point, start `ChkDsk`, defragment the drive (or exclude it from defragmentation), obtain a fragmentation analysis, mount and dismount the drive, and format the drive. The properties let you change the volume letter, the volume label, or enable or disable indexing for the volume.

- **VolumeQuotaSetting:** Associates a disk quota setting with the specified volume. See the `QuotaSetting` alias for additional details.

- **VolumeUserQuota:** Associates a per-user storage setting with the specified volume. See the `DiskQuota` alias for additional information.

Performing Maintenance

PART VI

- **WMISet:** Manages the WMI settings for the target system. You'll use properties to change the writable settings. For example, if you wanted to change the maximum log file size to 64 KB, type **WMIC WMISet SET MaxLogFileSize=65536** and press Enter.

Get Help in *WMIC*

WMIC is a huge utility—perhaps the largest utility you'll find in Windows. It's also an incredibly important utility with extreme flexibility. Authors have written entire books on this utility and still not covered everything WMIC has to provide (check out books such as *Microsoft Windows Scripting with WMI: Self-Paced Learning Guide* by Ed Wilson, Microsoft Press, 2005). The point is that you are unlikely to find every answer you need in a book of any sort. It simply isn't possible for an author to anticipate your every question and provide an answer that fits every need. What you really need is an understanding of the WMIC help system so that you can take the canned answers that you do have and create your own specific answers.

To get an overview of WMIC, type **WMIC /?** and press Enter. Unlike most utilities, you see several pages of help screens like the one shown in Figure 15.1. The help screens begin with global switches that control things such as the privileges that WMIC should use when making a request of the WMI database. The second page of help shows the aliases you can access. It isn't until the sixth page of help that you see some additional command line switches that determine how you enter commands. For example, you can choose to use the full class or path when specifying a WMI object rather than the shorter aliases that WMIC normally uses.

Figure 15.1: The WMIC basic help isn't all that basic and consists of multiple screens.

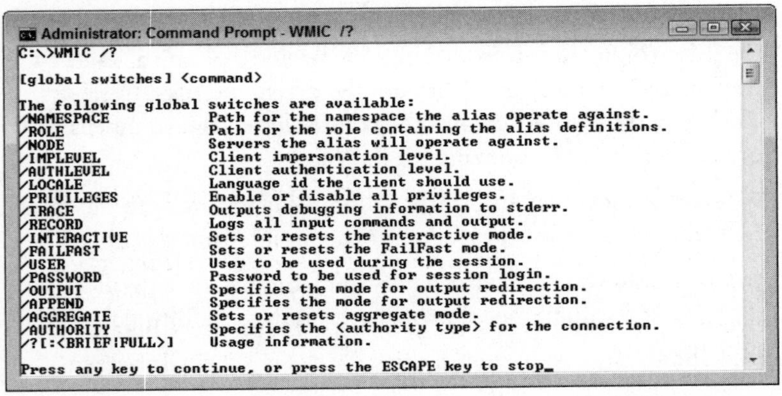

Even when it comes to something simple like an overview, WMIC holds some surprises. Microsoft didn't want to bore you with too many details, so the help screen shown in Figure 15.1 uses the brief format. To display the full format, type **WMIC /?:Full** and press Enter. Figure 15.2 shows the difference in the amount of information you receive. As you can see, there's more information. The basic help information goes on for eleven screens now, instead of the original six.

Figure 15.2: Full help provides additional useful information but at the cost of additional screens.

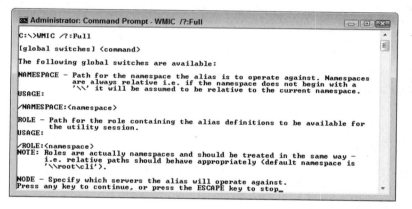

Every one of the entries shown in Figure 15.1 and Figure 15.2 can provide additional help. For example, if you want to learn more about an alias such as CPU, you'd type **WMIC CPU /?** and press Enter. (The "Use Aliases in WMIC" section of the chapter provides a full list of the aliases that WMIC supports.) You see an overview like the one shown in Figure 15.3. This help screen doesn't look very useful at first, but it shows the verbs you can use with a particular alias. The CPU alias supports the ASSOC, CREATE, DELETE, GET, and LIST verbs. Notice that the CPU alias doesn't support the SET verb, so you can't use the SET verb to modify anything about the CPU (which makes sense because there's nothing you can change about the CPU in your system). You can find a list of these verbs and their meaning in the "Understand the SQL Syntax of WMIC" section of the chapter.

You can continue drilling down into help as needed to learn more about WMIC usage. For example, let's say you want to learn about the List verb. In this case, type **WMIC CPU LIST /?** and press Enter. Figure 15.4 shows the first screen of this help entry. The help screens begin with a listing of the output formats that the List verb supports. Each output format provides you with a different number of properties, so the format you select is important. The next screen describes the /Format and /Translate command line switches for this verb (see the "Format Data in WMIC" and "Translate Data in WMIC" sections of the chapter for details).

Figure 15.3: Before you use an alias, determine which verbs it supports.

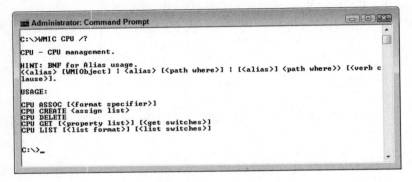

Figure 15.4: Verb-specific information tells you all of the adjectives you can use with the verb.

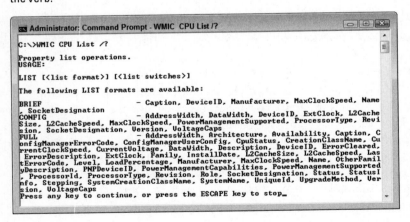

If you think that the help screens are over at this point, you're wrong. You can drill down even further. If you want to learn more about the Brief output format, you type **WMIC CPU LIST Brief /?** and press Enter. Figure 15.5 shows this additional level of detail.

Figure 15.5: Every verb entry includes subentries for each of the adjectives and command line switches the verb supports.

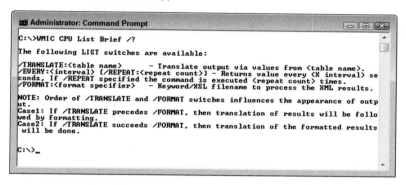

Not satisfied yet? You can go even deeper. Type **WMIC CPU LIST Brief /Format /?** and press Enter to see the kinds of formatting you can perform when working with the Brief adjective. Figure 15.6 shows the help for this level.

Figure 15.6: Discover the kinds of formatting you can use with a particular adjective.

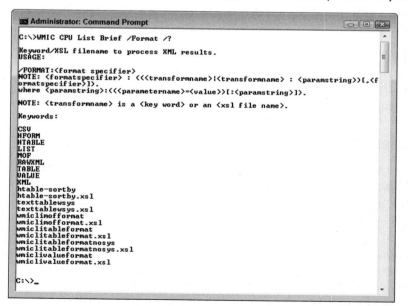

If you haven't noticed yet, this section has built a relatively complex command using the help system. The sad thing is that most administrators don't get down to this level of help—they have no clue that it exists because it doesn't exist for most command line utilities. If you have a question about creating a WMIC command, simply try to drill down to whatever level you need using help.

Now that you've followed the WMIC CPU List command to this level, let's try one of those formats. Type **WMIC CPU LIST Brief /Format:LIST** and press Enter. You'll see CPU details such as those shown in Figure 15.7. Of course, your details will match the specifics of your system.

Figure 15.7: Create a command you want to use with help and then try it out.

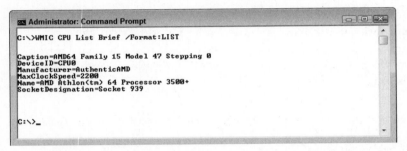

The point of this section is that help can assist you in creating any command. The reason you need canned commands is to avoid wasting hours trying dead-ends in help. Canned commands get you to almost the right place quickly and then you fine-tune your commands using help.

Format Data in *WMIC*

Formatting doesn't change the content of the information you obtain from WMIC. If you type **WMIC CPU LIST** and press Enter, you'll receive a certain amount of information, no matter what /Format command line switch option you use. However, the default tabular format shown in Figure 15.8 is a little hard to read and it gets harder when you request additional information.

The information in Figure 15.8 is definitely usable, but you wouldn't want to try to find anything specific. Try typing **WMIC CPU List /Format:List** and pressing Enter. Even though the output shown in Figure 15.9 is significantly larger, it's also easier to read. (Figure 15.9 doesn't show all of the information—it shows only about half of it.)

Figure 15.8: WMIC defaults to a tabular format, which can be hard to read.

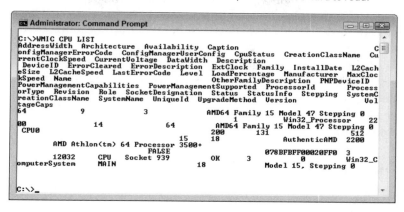

Figure 15.9: The List format is significantly easier to read than the Table format.

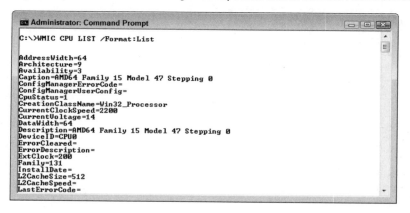

Humans often need data in formats other than those that are easily read at the command line. Try typing **WMIC CPU LIST /Format:HForm > MyCPU.HTML** and pressing Enter. When you open this file up in a browser, you see a nicely formatted web page suitable for just about any need, as shown in Figure 15.10. If you prefer a tabular format for complex data, type **WMIC CPU LIST /Format:HTable > MyCPU2.HTML** and press Enter instead (in fact, try this second command now and compare the two outputs to see the difference). To see a better use of the HTable format, type **WMIC IRQ LIST /Format:HTable > IRQ.HTML** and press Enter to see a list of IRQs. In short, you don't have to view WMIC output at the command line to use it. There are situations where you want to save complex data in HTML or other formats that make it possible to view the data using the GUI.

The output that WMIC provides appears in whatever order it appears in the WMI database, which may not be the order you want. Fortunately, you can transform the outputted data as you format it. Transformation means adding a condition as part of the formatting criteria. For example, you can tell WMIC to sort the information by a certain field using the sortby keyword (the keywords are case sensitive, as are the field names). You might decide to sort the IRQ list by the IRQNumber field to make it easier to find a particular IRQ by typing **WMIC IRQ LIST /Format:HTable :"sortby=IRQNumber" > IRQ.HTML** and pressing Enter.

Figure 15.10: Use the HForm format to create an HTML file suitable for your browser.

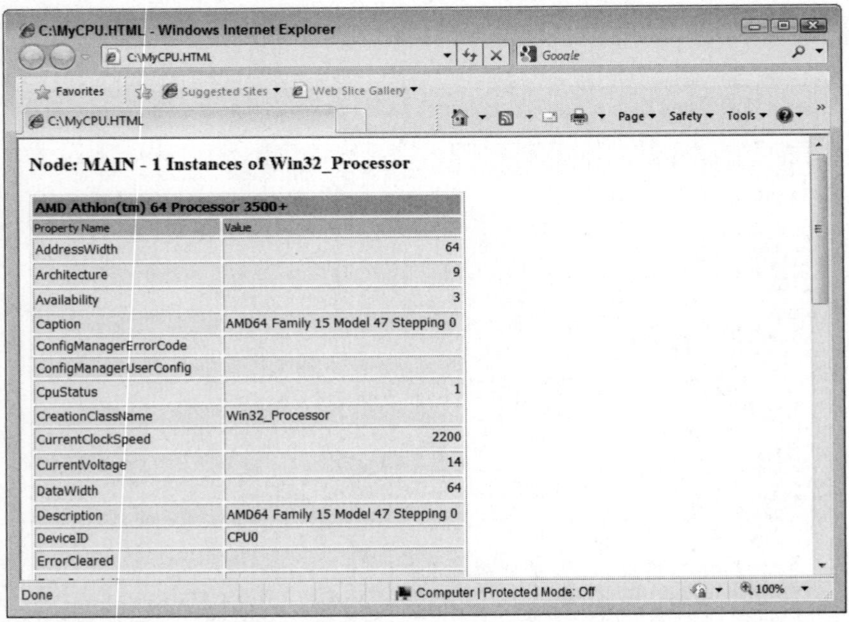

All sorting occurs using a text sort, so the output from the sortby keyword alone might not be sufficient. The previous example does sort the information, but not in a way that really works with IRQs. In this case, you can precede the sortby keyword with the datatype keyword and tell WMIC what data type to use. For example, type **WMIC IRQ LIST / Format:HTable:"datatype=number":"sortby=IRQNumber" > IRQ.HTML** and press Enter to obtain the results shown in Figure 15.11. Notice that the IRQs now appear in the order that you probably anticipated earlier. Notice that you must separate each of the entries with a colon.

Another level of sorting is to tell WMIC to sort in descending, rather than ascending order. In this case, you'd type **WMIC IRQ LIST /Format:HTable:"datatype=number":"orderby=descending":"sortby=IRQNumber" > IRQ.HTML** and press Enter. Notice the addition of the orderby keyword. Again, you separate each of the formatting criteria using a colon. It's possible to sort by any number of fields and each field set can have different criteria. The rule is to place the criteria (orderby or datatype) before the sortby keyword because WMIC processes each instruction in order.

Figure 15.11: Sorting makes it easier to use some types of output.

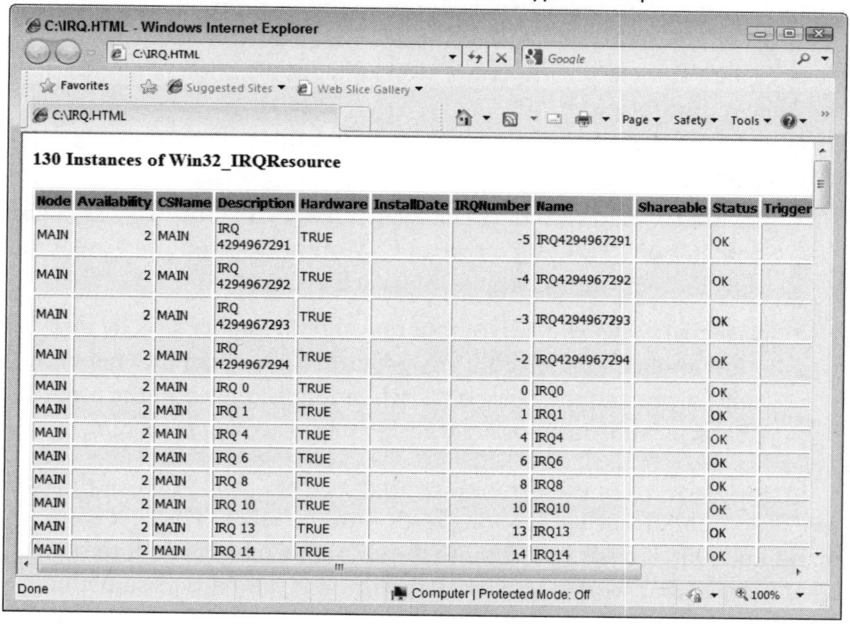

130 Instances of Win32_IRQResource

Node	Availability	CSName	Description	Hardware	InstallDate	IRQNumber	Name	Shareable	Status	Trigger
MAIN	2	MAIN	IRQ 4294967291	TRUE		-5	IRQ4294967291		OK	
MAIN	2	MAIN	IRQ 4294967292	TRUE		-4	IRQ4294967292		OK	
MAIN	2	MAIN	IRQ 4294967293	TRUE		-3	IRQ4294967293		OK	
MAIN	2	MAIN	IRQ 4294967294	TRUE		-2	IRQ4294967294		OK	
MAIN	2	MAIN	IRQ 0	TRUE		0	IRQ0		OK	
MAIN	2	MAIN	IRQ 1	TRUE		1	IRQ1		OK	
MAIN	2	MAIN	IRQ 4	TRUE		4	IRQ4		OK	
MAIN	2	MAIN	IRQ 6	TRUE		6	IRQ6		OK	
MAIN	2	MAIN	IRQ 8	TRUE		8	IRQ8		OK	
MAIN	2	MAIN	IRQ 10	TRUE		10	IRQ10		OK	
MAIN	2	MAIN	IRQ 13	TRUE		13	IRQ13		OK	
MAIN	2	MAIN	IRQ 14	TRUE		14	IRQ14		OK	

You may also want to give the output a specific title. In this case, you use the title keyword. For example, if you want to give the output the title of My Output, type **WMIC IRQ LIST /Format:HTable:"datatype=number":"sortby=IRQNumber":"title=My Output" > IRQ.HTML** and press Enter.

Administrators often need to import data from WMIC into a database. Computers have different data interpretation needs from humans. The /Format command line switch offers two computer-friendly choices. To obtain CSV output, type **WMIC CPU LIST /Format:CSV > MyCPU.CSV** and press Enter. Most databases will import CSV data without problem. Sometimes you need data in XML format. In this case, type **WMIC CPU**

LIST /Format:RawXML > MyCPU.XML. The result is a full XML page, not a partial page or a fragment. Unfortunately, the CSV and XML formats produced by /Format aren't always accepted by applications because the output doesn't conform to standards. In most cases, you want to translate, rather than format data for import into an application using the techniques described in the next section.

Translate Data in *WMIC*

Formatting changes the appearance of the data but doesn't modify the content. Translation is an actual change to the structure of the data to make it work better with applications. Consequently, if you want to transfer data from WMIC to a database or other application, you typically translate it, not format it.

Most of the WMIC aliases support two translations. The following list describes each of these translation types:

- **NoComma:** Creates a fixed field length table that works well for database import. This isn't a type of CSV output, so you can't use it for direct import into an application such as Excel.

- **BasicXml:** Creates XML output that should import directly into most applications without any problems. The difference between this output and the /Format switch output is that all of the usual character substitutions are translated into actual characters.

In most cases, you use /Translate after /Format. The order of the two switches is important because one feeds into the other. The first command line switch feeds its data into the second. Consequently, to obtain XML output that works with most applications, you'd type something like WMIC CPU LIST /Format:RawXML /Translate:BasicXml > MyCPU.XML and press Enter.

NOTE This book doesn't cover some specialty utilities and scripts found only on Windows Server 2008 Server Core. If you want Server Core–specific information, you should refer to *Administering Windows Server 2008 Server Core* by John Mueller (Sybex, 2008).

Activate Windows

The Windows Software License Manager (SLMGR) tool is one of those tools that you'll use a few times, but you must use it at least once to activate your copy of Windows. Otherwise, you'll find that your copy becomes useless at some point. You can also use this tool to install a product key, display the activation information (in case a support person needs it), and reset the licensing status of the system. This tool isn't available with older versions of Windows such as Windows Server 2003 and Windows XP. The following sections describe some important uses for this tool.

> **NOTE** Like many utilities, you can perform tasks on a remote machine by supplying a machine name, username, and password as the first three arguments to the SLMGR.VBS script. There aren't any special command line switches associated with this information.

Perform an Activation

You must activate your copy of Windows at least once or it'll stop working. To activate your copy of Windows, type **CScript %SYSTEMROOT%\System32\SLMGR.VBS /ato** and press Enter to activate the local machine. In most cases, if you attempt to use this command more than once, the script will display an error message telling you that the system is already activated. Newer versions of Windows, such as Windows 7, simply keep telling you that the product has been activated.

The /ato command line switch assumes that you have an Internet connection for activation purposes. You might not have such a connection available. In this case, you'd call Microsoft to activate your copy of Windows and receive an activation code in return. Once you have the activation code, you can type **CScript %SYSTEMROOT%\System32\SLMGR.VBS /atp ConfirmationID** and press Enter, where *ConfirmationID* is the code you receive from Microsoft.

Display the Activation Information

At some point, you might need to obtain the activation information for your machine. To obtain this information, type **CScript %SYSTEMROOT%\ System32\SLMGR.VBS /dli** and press Enter. The script will output the licensed status of your system, a partial product key, and the precise version of Windows that you're using.

In some cases, you need more information about the activation status of your system than the /dli command line switch provides. To obtain additional information, type **CScript %SYSTEMROOT%\System32\SLMGR.VBS /dlv** and press Enter.

Change the Product Key

If you didn't provide an appropriate product key during the installation process, you need to supply one before you activate Windows. To provide a new product key for your installation, use the CScript %SYSTEMROOT%\System32\SLMGR.VBS /ipk *Key* command, where *Key* is the product key for your Windows installation.

Manage the System Time

Not having the correct time on your system might seem merely inconvenient. However, having the wrong time can have serious implications. For one thing, Kerberos authentication relies on the two authenticating systems to have the right time. A difference of five minutes between the systems can mean the difference between Kerberos working and not working. All sorts of applications are time dependent now too. A time error could prevent something as simple as automatic updates from working properly. The W32Tm utility is the best method for working with time on your system. With this in mind, the following sections discuss a few time setting–specific tasks.

NOTE You may have used the Net Time command in the past to manage time on a system. Microsoft is slowly phasing out this command and has made some features, such as querying the time servers, unavailable in newer versions of Windows. It's a good idea to update any scripts or batch files you might have now that rely on Net Time to use W32Tm instead.

Update the Time

Ensuring that your system has the correct time means getting the time from a Reliable Time Source (RTS). The reliability of a time source depends on who is using it and for what purpose. Synchronizing all of the systems on your network to a single server could work just fine, but most organizations really need to synchronize to an external source such as time.nist.gov. Many organizations will have one or two servers synchronize to the remote source and then have every other system synchronize to the servers. No matter what technique you use, you need an RTS to ensure the time on your system is accurate. To update the time on any system, type **W32Tm /Resync** and press Enter. However, let's say you want to use a domain time source instead. In this case, you use the following procedure:

1. Type **W32Tm /Config /SyncFromFlags:DomHier /Update** and press Enter. This command sets the system to rely on the domain hierarchy.

2. Type **Net Stop W32Time** and press Enter.

3. Type **Net Start W32Time** and press Enter. The stopping and starting of the service makes the change to the service settings so that a resynchronization will use the domain hierarchy in place of an Internet source.

4. Type **W32Tm /Resync /Rediscover** and press Enter. This command resynchronizes the computer to the domain source after rediscovering those sources.

Configure a Time Source

If you're using a centralized time source, but it isn't in a domain setting, then you need to create a manual time source. In other words, you override the default time sources that Windows would normally use. The easiest way to perform this task is to use the following steps:

1. Type **W32Tm /Config /ManualPeerList:*Server* / SyncFromFlags:Manual /Update** and press Enter, where *Server* is the address of a server you want to use for synchronization. If you want to use multiple servers, create a space-delimited list of server names.

2. Type **Net Stop W32Time** and press Enter.

3. Type **Net Start W32Time** and press Enter. The stopping and starting of the service makes the change to the service settings so that a resynchronization will use the manual time source in place of an Internet source.

4. Type **W32Tm /Resync /Rediscover** and press Enter. This command resynchronizes the computer to the manual time source after rediscovering those sources.

Obtain Time Settings Information

It pays to know how the W32Time service is configured. Configuration errors cause all kinds of problems on networks. You can use the W32Tm /Query command to obtain four different kinds of W32Time service information using the following command line switches:

- **/Source:** Displays the time source for the local computer.

- **/Configuration:** Displays the W32Time service configuration information. For example, you'll discover the current time source. When you add the /Verbose command line switch, you also see any undefined or unused W32Time service settings.

- **/Peers:** Displays one or more peers used for time updates. If you're using an Internet time source, the list contains only the currently selected source, rather than all of the sources that Windows normally uses.

- **/Status:** Displays the W32Time service status information, including the time and date of the last synchronization.

For example, if you want to obtain the current W32Time service status, you type **W32Tm /Query /Status** and press Enter. You'll see a number of interesting statistics, including the time and date of the last synchronization and the source of that synchronization.

In addition to the W32Tm /Query command, you can use the W32Tm /TZ command to obtain current time zone information. When you type **W32Tm /TZ** and press Enter, you obtain the currently selected time zone, its standard time bias (time change from Greenwich Mean Time), and its daylight savings time bias (if any).

Manage the Boot Configuration

You won't change the boot configuration of a system very often. In fact, you might not need to ever change the boot configuration of a system unless something goes wrong or the system has more than one boot partition on it (such as a system used for testing). Even so, you need to know how to use the Boot Configuration Data Store Editor (BCDEdit) utility to make changes to the boot configurations when they do become necessary.

> **WARNING**   Using BCDEdit incorrectly can cause significant problems, including making your system unbootable. Make changes carefully and one at a time to ensure you don't cause yourself problems. Before you make any changes, type **BCDEdit /Export BCDBackup** and press Enter. This command creates a backup of your configuration. If you make a mistake, type **BCDEdit /Import BCDBackup** and press Enter to correct it.

Enumerate the Configurations

Before you can do any work with BCDEdit, you need to know the current boot configuration. To obtain this information, type **BCDEdit /Enum** and press Enter. Figure 15.12 shows one possible configuration that includes Windows 7 and Windows XP on the same system.

The configuration shown in Figure 15.12 has three sections. The first section is the boot manager, which is the application that displays the boot selections when you first start the machine. The boot manager also loads the correct operating system based on your selection. Notice the identifier entry in the list—the identifier entry always tells you what type of configuration entry you're viewing. The interesting pieces of information for the boot manager are the device (which tells you where the boot information is stored), the default entry (which tells you the default boot selection), the displayorder entry (which determines how each of the boot selections appears on the boot menu), and the timeout (which determines how long the system waits for you to make a boot selection).

Figure 15.12: Enumerate the current configuration before you make any changes.

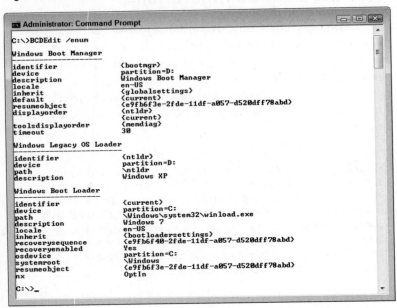

The next section is for a legacy operating system. In this case, you're looking at a Windows XP configuration. The device and path entries combine to describe the location of the boot files. The description is what the user sees during the boot process.

The third section contrasts with the legacy section. In this case, you're looking at the kinds of entries that you'll find for a Vista or Windows 7 boot configuration. The device, path, and description entries are the same as for a legacy entry. The osdevice and systemroot entries tell the location of Windows for the boot partition. The recoveryenabled entry determines whether the boot manager boots into the recovery screen should it detect a problem with your Windows configuration.

Get *BCDEdit* Help

BCDEdit is a relatively complex utility that provides somewhat convoluted help options. If you type **BCDEdit /?** and press Enter, you see an overview of the BCDEdit utility. As with the WMIC utility, you can drill down when working with BCDEdit. For example, if you want to learn more about the /Enum command line switch, type **BCDEdit /Enum /?** and press Enter.

However, there's additional help that you need to know about. For example, the IDs that you see in Figure 15.12 are consistent across installations. To learn more about those IDs, you type **BCDEdit /? ID** and press Enter. For example, you'll discover that {memdiag} is an entry for memory diagnostics. The following list describes special help entries that BCDEdit supports:

- **TOPICS:** Displays a list of detailed help topics, which includes the commands, standard identifiers, data types, and other command line options.

- **ID:** Displays a list of well-known identifiers for the operating system. For example, the {bootmgr} entry refers to the Windows Boot Manager entry.

- **TYPES [{BOOTAPP | BOOTMGR | BOOTSECTOR | CUSTOMTYPES | FWBOOTMGR | MEMDIAG | NTLDR | OSLOADER | RESUME}]:** Displays help information about configuration entry types. Using TYPES alone displays a list of the available types. Using TYPES with a specific entry, such as TYPES BOOTAPP, displays the type information for that entry. For example, if you want to learn more about {ntldr} types, you'd type **BCDEdit /? TYPES NTLDR** and press Enter.

- **FORMATS:** Displays information about the type information formatting rules.

Edit an Existing Boot Setting

In general, it's dangerous to create or delete boot settings. The installation software makes all of the boot settings you normally need unless you're working with something extremely esoteric. However, you'll have plenty of opportunity to change boot settings. For example, both the Vista and Windows 7 installation disks insist on assigning a generic, non-useful name, to any legacy boot partition on your system. Let's say you have Windows XP installed on your machine. If you want the boot entry to actually read Windows XP, you need to modify its description. To perform this task, you type **BCDEdit /Set {ntldr} Description "Windows XP"** and press Enter.

Every BCDEdit /Set command follows the same basic format. You begin by providing the ID of the section you want to change, which is {ntldr} in this case. Next, you provide the name of the property you want to change, which is Description in this case. Finally, you provide the value you want to assign to the property, which is "Windows XP" in this case.

Change the Boot Sequence

One of the things that you'll want to change relatively often is the boot sequence. The option you use most often may not appear at the top of the list when you start the system. Look at Figure 15.12 again and notice that the {ntldr} entry appears first and then the {current} entry. If you want to change the order of these entries, you type **BCDEdit /Set {bootmgr} displayorder {current} {ntldr}** and press Enter. Because the displayorder property requires two entries, you provide both entries and use a space to delimit them.

Set the Default Boot Item

If you're working with a multi-boot setup, you might want to configure the system to automatically boot a particular partition. Look at Figure 15.12. The {current} partition is the default boot partition. Let's say you want to make {ntldr} the default partition. In this case, you type **BCDEdit /Set {bootmgr} default {ntldr}** and press Enter.

16

Managing System Users

Performing Maintenance

PART VI

The command line is helpful for automating common user management tasks. For example, configuring the auditing policies for a group of users is extremely easy at the command line. On the other hand, the command line can't easily perform some user management tasks. If you want to see the overall statistics of user productivity on a computer, that's best left to the GUI because seeing that kind of data is easier using charts and graphs. In short, the command line and GUI environments each have their particular uses. This chapter focuses on common tasks that you could probably automate to some extent.

NOTE As with many command line tasks, the tasks in this chapter usually require administrator privileges. However, because of the nature of the tasks performed in this chapter, the requests for administrator-level elevation become quite annoying after a while when working on Vista or Windows 7 systems. To avoid this problem, right-click the Command Prompt shortcut and choose Run as Administrator from the context menu. User Account Control will ask you whether you want to run the command processor as an administrator. Click Yes. You can now accomplish all of the required tasks without continuous interference from Windows.

Audit User Access

Auditing system activity is a necessary process in many situations. Of course, there's the obvious use of ensuring the system remains secure by thwarting any misguided user activity. However, auditing can help you do more than just check security. For example, careful auditing can often alert you to potentially damaging system activities or help you better understand why a system doesn't perform as well as it could. Checking object access can help you better define how a user interacts with a system so that you can make the system more efficient. A user's privilege use can help you locate security holes that occur when a user has too many rights, some of which aren't even used. The following sections discuss the AuditPol utility, the command line interface for auditing needs.

List the Policies

Before you can use audit policies, you need to know which policies are available and whom they affect. Windows applies categories of auditing policies to specific users, so you actually have two concerns when discovering the current auditing configuration. The AuditPol /List command makes it possible to check users, auditing categories, and auditing subcategories as described in the following sections.

List Audit Users

To discover which users are audited, type **AuditPol /List /User** and press Enter. The output of this command provides a list of which users are audited, but not how they're being audited. To discover how the user is being audited, you type **AuditPol /Get /User:UserName /Category:*** and press Enter, where *UserName* is the user's name (see the "Get a Policy" section of the chapter for additional information). If you also want to know the user's Security Identifier (SID), type **AuditPol /List /User /V** and press Enter. The SID comes in useful for a number of purposes and ensures that you can uniquely identify the user to the system.

List Audit Categories

Many of the AuditPol commands require that you know a category. If you want information for all categories, you simply use the asterisk (*), but often the wildcard search returns far too much information to be useful unless you limit the output in some other way. Consequently, knowing the precise category you want is important in many situations. To obtain a basic category listing, type **AuditPol /List / Category** and press Enter. In most cases, the basic listing is all you need. However, if you plan to work with the category at a detailed level or want to search for its entry in the registry, you need a Globally Unique Identifier (GUID) that precisely identifies the category to the system. To obtain this information, type **AuditPol /List /Category /V** and press Enter.

List Audit Subcategories

Categories are divided into subcategories. For example, the Object Access category contains a subcategory of File System (among other subcategories). You can choose to audit a user's access to the file system, without monitoring other kinds of Object Access, by specifying a subcategory. To obtain the subcategories of a specific category, type AuditPol /List /Subcategory:"*CategoryName*" and press Enter, where *CategoryName* is the name of any category you want to see.

If you want to see multiple categories, simply create a list separated by commas of category names. For example, to see the subcategories of the Account Logon and Account Management categories, you'd type AuditPol /List /Subcategory:"Account Logon","Account Management" and press Enter. To see all of the subcategories for every category, type AuditPol /List /Subcategory:* and press Enter. As with categories, subcategories have GUIDs. To see the GUIDs for the subcategories, add the /V command line switch.

Get a Policy

Listing a policy simply tells you that the policy exists but doesn't tell you the policy setting. Getting a policy won't tell you that the policy exists—you must already know that the policy exists. However, it does tell you how the policy is configured. Even though listing and getting may sound a lot alike, the two are completely different. The AuditPol / Get command is all about discovering the system settings.

It's also important to understand that audit policies are configured at two levels. First, you can configure an audit policy at the system level, which means that the policy affects everyone. Second, you can configure an audit policy for a specific user, which means that the policy affects only that user. The AuditPol /Get /User command tells you about specific user settings, while the AuditPol /Get /Category and AuditPol /Get /Subcategory commands tell you about system-level settings.

A special setting level affects the system directly when an audit event occurs. For example, the CrashOnAuditFail option causes the system to crash when the auditing system fails for some reason. This is a safety feature because it ensures that no one can turn off auditing and then continue to use the system unless they use the standard methods to do so and have the proper rights. The following sections describe all of these AuditPol /Get command scenarios.

Get Audit Users

The AuditPol /Get /User command obtains information about a specific user. In most cases, you want to know a user's full rights, so you'll type **AuditPol /Get /User:*UserName* /Category:***, where *UserName* is the name of the user, and press Enter. However, you can specify a particular category to discover information about just that category or you can use the /Subcategory command line switch to be even more selective and discover information about just one setting. The output you see contains three columns: the name of the category or subcategory, the inclusive setting, and the exclusive setting.

NOTE   When you set a user audit policy, it's either inclusive or exclusive. An inclusive policy is one that adds to the system-level settings. For example, if you audit the user's failure to log on to the system, it's an inclusive policy because it's in addition to any system-level settings. However, if the system normally monitors logon failures, but you don't want to check a particular user, then you'd create an exclusive policy. Even though everyone else is monitored, this particular user is excluded from the policy. It's unusual to create exclusive policies—inclusive policies are far more common.

You may need to output the user settings in a form that you can import into a database. In this case, you'd add the /R command line switch to create Comma Separated Value (CSV) output. For example, if you need to retrieve the settings for user Jamal and put them in a CSV file, you'd type **AuditPol /Get /User:Jamal /Category:* /R > AuditPol .CSV** and press Enter.

Get Audit Categories

The AuditPol /Get /Category command obtains the system-wide settings for both categories and subcategories. For example, if you type **AuditPol /Get /Category:*** and press Enter, you see output similar to that shown in Figure 16.1 (which shows only a partial listing of the categories and subcategories). Of course, you can choose to obtain a specific category by using the category name in place of *. For example, to obtain the Logon/Logoff category, you type **AuditPol /Get /Category:"Logon/ Logoff"** and press Enter. As with the user information, you can output the categories to CSV format using the /R command line switch.

Figure 16.1: Getting the categories also obtains the subcategory information.

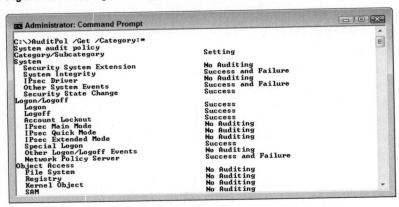

Get Audit Subcategories

Use the `AuditPol /Get /Subcategory` command when you need to obtain the system-wide setting for a single subcategory. For example, to retrieve the status of the Logon subcategory, you'd type **AuditPol /Get / Subcategory:"Logon"** and press Enter. Unlike the /Category command line switch, you can't use * with the /Subcategory command line switch.

Get Audit Options

The `AuditPol /Get /Option` command retrieves audit policy settings that affect the system as a whole when certain audit policy events occur. The following list describes each of these options:

- **CrashOnAuditFail:** When you enable this setting, it forces the system to crash should the auditing system become unable to log events. The advantage to this setting is that it forces everyone to use the auditing policies you set. However, the disadvantage is that an outsider could use this option to force the server to crash and cause an apparent Distributed Denial of Service (DDoS) attack. You need to use this setting with care. After this event occurs, only administrators can log on to the system. The administrator must fix whatever caused the crash before the system will allow anyone to log back on. This setting is generally useful on client systems, but not recommended for servers.

- **FullPrivilegeAuditing:** When you tell the system to audit privileges, it normally does so for most privileges, but it leaves out a few commonly used privileges to keep the event log from quickly over-flowing, such as the following privileges:

- Generate security audit (SeAuditPrivilege)

- Bypass traverse checking (SeChangeNotifyPrivilege) debug programs (SeDebugPrivilege)

- Create a token object (SeCreateTokenPrivilege)

- Replace process-level token (SeAssignPrimaryTokenPrivilege)

- Generate security audits (SeAuditPrivilege)

- Back up files and directories (SeBackupPrivilege)

- Restore files and directories (SeRestorePrivilege)

  Enabling this setting forces the system to audit all privilege changes except SeAuditPrivilege. You can't audit the SeAuditPrivilege because it would cause an endless loop—every access to the audit system generates this privilege and therefore every entry to the log would generate another SeAuditPrivilege event.

- **AuditBaseObjects** and **AuditBaseDirectories:** Kernel objects come in two forms: container objects and base objects. The **AuditBaseObjects** policy affects base objects, those that can't contain object objects such as semaphores and mutexes. The **AuditBaseDirectories** policy affects container objects, those that can contain other objects, such as directories. Many kernel objects are unnamed and rely only on a handle that's accessible to just the process that created the object for access. Unnamed kernel objects are secure, but they don't allow interprocess communication, which is often necessary in applications. Named kernel objects do allow interprocess communication, but they present security risks because another process (other than those that should use the named process) can interact with the kernel object should it discover the object's name. Setting either of these options forces the operating system to assign a System Access Control List (SACL) to the named objects so that the auditing system can monitor them. The normal use for these settings is to detect and thwart squatting attacks (see the article at http://en.wikipedia.org/wiki/Squatting_attack for details). A problem with these settings is that you normally must reboot the system before the changes you make take effect.

You use these options individually. For example, to obtain the status of the `CrashOnAuditFail`, you type `AuditPol /Get /Option:CrashOnAuditFail` and press Enter. Unlike other audit policy settings, options are either enabled or disabled.

Set a Policy

Setting a policy is the act of creating a new entry for the system or a particular user. These settings work as stated in the "Get a Policy" section of the chapter. When you create a new policy, the user or the system as a whole is monitored for the success or failure of certain actions. You can also enable or disable audit options that perform a task based on an audit event (such as crashing the system when someone tries to override the audit system). The following sections describe how to set an audit policy.

Set Audit Users

The `AuditPol /Set /User` command controls settings made to a specific user. When working with users, you must remember that you can create inclusive settings that add to the system-level settings or exclusive settings that remove auditing from the system-level settings. Audits can affect failures and successes. You can also enable or disable a setting. For example, to set a user account to add (inclusive) failure auditing to the `Object Access` category, you'd type `AuditPol /Set /User:Username /Category:"Object Access" /Include /Failure:Enable`, where *Username* is the name of the user, and press Enter.

All user-level settings follow this same pattern. You provide the username, a category or subcategory, whether the setting is inclusive or exclusive, whether the auditing is for a success or failure, and whether the setting is enabled or disabled. As another example, let's say you want to create an exclusion for a user for Logon subcategory auditing for both success and failure. In this case, you'd type `AuditPol /Set /User:Username /Subcategory:"Logon" /Exclude /Failure:Enable /Success:Enable` and press Enter.

Set Audit Categories

The `AuditPol /Set /Category` command controls settings made to the system as a whole. Unlike user-level settings, you simply set the policy to monitor success or failure. There isn't any concept of inclusion or exclusion. For example, to audit Account Logon failures, you'd type `AuditPol /Set /Category:"Account Logon" /Failure:Enable` and press Enter. `AuditPol` sets all of the subcategories for the entire `Account Logon` category to audit failures.

Set Audit Subcategories

The `AuditPol /Set /Subcategory` command controls settings made to the system as a whole, just like the category-level command. However, this command lets you set the individual subcategory entries, rather than an entire category. For example, you might want to failure audit the `Credential Validation` subcategory of the `Account Logon` category. To perform this task, you type `AuditPol /Set /Subcategory:"Credential Validation" /Failure:Enable` and press Enter.

Set Audit Options

The `AuditPol /Set /Option` command controls the audit policy options described in the "Get Audit Options" section of the chapter. You either enable or disable these options. For example, to enable the `CrashOnAuditFail` option, you type `AuditPol /Set /Option:CrashOnAuditFail /Value:Enable` and press Enter.

Perform a Backup

If you have a complex audit policy setup, you'll want to create a backup of it occasionally to ensure you don't lose the settings and have to make them all over again. You can also create a backup so that you can move the settings to another machine. No matter what reason you have for making the backup, type `AuditPol /Backup /File:Filename`, where *Filename* is the name of the backup file you want to use, and press Enter to create the backup.

Perform a Restore

Restoring a backup will overwrite all of the current settings for the target system. It's important to understand that restoring a backup is the same as making all the settings changes by hand. To perform this task, type `AuditPol /Restore /File:Filename`, where *Filename* is the name of the backup file you want to use, and press Enter.

Clear an Audit Policy

You made a mistake. In fact, you made a really big mistake and the audit logs are filling up faster than you can clear them. The system is completely messed up and you don't know what to do about it. To correct this problem, type `AuditPol /Clear` and press Enter. This command essentially resets all of the audit policies to the state they were in when you installed Windows. Of course, you'll lose any good changes you made, but you'll also get rid of any incorrect settings you made as well.

Remove an Audit Policy

There are times when you simply want to remove the existing audit policies for a user or for all users on a system. A new company policy may define system-level settings that everyone should use, rather than rely on special settings for individual users. Alternatively, you might have monitored a particular user for a while, but decided the monitoring is no longer necessary and want to remove all of the auditing with one command. No matter what reason you have to make the change, you can type `AuditPol /Remove /User:Username`, where `Username` is a particular user's name, and press Enter to remove the audit policies for a specific user. To remove the audit policies for all users, type `AuditPol /Remove /AllUsers` and press Enter.

Work with Group Policies

Group policies make it possible to create security and usage configurations for users without having to set every user's configuration individually. Setting the group policy is one task, working with it is another. The following sections describe how to work with group policies from the user's perspective.

Obtain Group Policy Results

Use the `GPResult` command to obtain the Resultant Set of Policy (RSoP) for a particular user on a system. This command considers all of the security settings for both the computer and the user and creates a resultant policy—the policy that actually affects the user's security setup on the system. The `GPResult` command is one of the few commands where

typing **GPResult** and pressing Enter displays the help information. If
you want to see the RSoP for the user and computer, type **GPResult /R**
and press Enter. This report can be a little long, so GPResult makes it
possible to create an HTML report out of the information. Simply type
GPResult /H MyReport.HTML and press Enter. Figure 16.2 shows typical output from this command. You can likewise use the /X *Filename*
command line switch (where *Filename* is the name of the file you want
to use) to output the report in XML format suitable for import into a
database.

Figure 16.2: GPResult makes it possible to create a report from the RSoP
information.

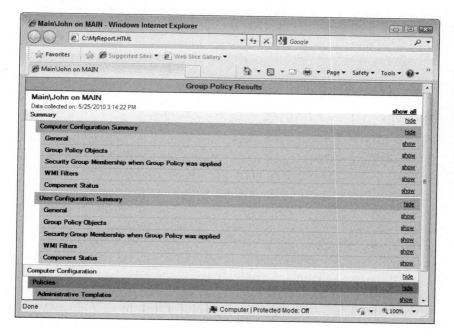

Performing Maintenance

PART VI

NOTE   Microsoft provides a wealth of articles on RSoP. For
example, you can see how RSoP affects Internet Protocol
Security (IPSec) assignments at http://technet2.microsoft.
com/windowsserver/en/library/35675107-c728-47cd-8ad9-bfd-
2d5e7fe0a1033.mspx. You'll also find an excellent article on plan-
ning and logging RSoP at http://www.windowsnetworking.com/
articles_tutorials/Resultant-Set-Policy-Planning-Logging
.html.

You may decide you need something other than the default output. For example, if you need just the computer or the user information, you can type **GPResult /R /Scope:Computer** or **GPResult /R /Scope:User** and press Enter. Use the /H command line switch in place of the /R command line switch when you need an HTML report in place of the on-screen report. If you want even more information than the default report supplies, use the /V command line switch. For example, type **GPResult /R /V /Scope:Computer** if you want to discover detailed information about the computer. The /Z command line switch provides even more information for those who need it.

The GPResult utility works with the current user by default. However, you can use the /User command line switch to obtain information about other users. For example, if you want to find information about user Samantha, you'd type **GPResult /R /User Samantha** and press Enter. As with many command line utilities and commands, you can use the /S Server, /U Username, and /P Password command line switches to access information on remote systems.

Manage Group Policies

The Group Policy Update (GPUpdate) utility lets you update the group policies on a computer. Use this utility as a replacement for the now obsolete /refreshpolicy command line switch for the SecEdit utility. Using this utility ensures that essential group policy changes appear on a computer, especially systems that are on 24 hours per day. To ensure that the host system is updated after you make group policy changes, type **GPUpdate** and press Enter. If you want to apply only the computer changes, type **GPUpdate /Computer** and press Enter. Likewise, if you want to apply only the user changes, type **GPUpdate /User** and press Enter.

Foreground policy changes won't actually affect the user immediately in most cases. For example, if you give the user additional rights, the user won't actually see the change until the user logs back on to the system after a reboot or a logoff. To ensure foreground changes actually take effect, type **GPUpdate /Boot** or **GPUpdate /Logoff** and press Enter. Using the /Logoff command line switch is fine for all soft settings, such as security changes. However, if the policy update affects the hardware in some way, it's normally better to use the /Boot command line switch to force a reset of the hardware.

Obtain Session Status Information

The Query utility helps you see how users are employing resources on the current machine. You can learn about the processes users have started, the sessions that the machine is supporting, information about the users themselves, and basic Terminal Server information as well. The following sections describe this utility in more detail.

Get Process Information

Windows provides a number of ways to display the active processes. (A process isn't necessarily just an application—services also create processes.) For example, if you want to use the GUI approach, you can rely on Task Manager. The Query Process command provides a quick way of obtaining a list of running processes from the command line. If you want to discover the processes started by the current user, type **Query Process** and press Enter.

In some cases, you need to know more than the current user. To see all of the processes started by anyone, type **Query Process** * and press Enter. If you want to see the processes started by a specific user, but not the current user, type **Query Process** *Username* and press Enter, where *Username* is the name of the user that started the process. For example, if you want to see all of the system processes, type **Query Process System** and press Enter. It's also possible to see processes based on a session type. For example, administrators often need to know which services are running. To see this information, type **Query Process Services** and press Enter.

Get Session Information

The Query Session command helps you discover information about Remote Desktop sessions on the current machine. Actually, the utility also shows information about the user that's currently logged on to the machine and the services session (session 0 on most systems) as well. To see the basic session information, type **Query Session** and press Enter. If you want session statistics (such as the number of sessions the machine has created), type **Query Session /Counter** and press Enter.

Get User Information

The Query User command displays information about users logged on to the machine. To see all of the users logged on to the system, type **Query User** and press Enter. If you want to see a specific user's information, type **Query User** *Username* and press Enter, where *Username* is the name of the user you want to see. You can also type the session name to see all of the users logged on under a particular session or the session identifier. No matter how you request the information, you see the username, session name, session ID, state, idle time, and logon time as output.

Get Terminal Server Information

The Query TermServer command locates any Remote Desktop Session Host servers on the domain. It's important to stress domain in this case because the command doesn't appear to work with workgroups. You have to have Active Directory set up and the whole domain configured for this command to work (as is the case for a few other commands). To obtain a list of all of the Remote Desktop Session Host servers on the network, type **Query TermServer** and press Enter. If you want to locate a particular server, type **Query TermServer** *ServerName*, where *ServerName* is the name of the server you want to locate, and press Enter.

Get the User's Identity

Batch and script files often require that you know the user's identity in order to perform certain tasks. For example, a user might not have the rights required to perform the entire task, so you can modify the batch or script file execution to take this issue into account. Knowing the user's name (which is part of their identity, along with the user's security identifier and other elements) can also help make the batch file or script friendlier because you can use the user's name in prompts. Finally, you sometimes need to know the user's name to accomplish the task, such as when you need to set user-level auditing. The following sections describe two ways you can use to detect the user's identity.

Obtain User Logon Information

The QUser utility is a very simple way to find the user's identity. If you type **QUser** and press Enter, you see the username, session name, session ID, state, idle time, and logon time for every user logged on to the system. In fact, you see all of these statistics whenever you use the QUser utility, but you can ask for a single user's information.

If you're interested in a particular user, then you can use the QUser Name command, where Name is the user's name. You might be interested in a particular kind of session, such as a console session. In this case, you use the QUser SessionName command, where SessionName is the name of the session. You'll see every user logged on using that session type. Finally, you can see which user is logged on by a session identifier. For example, if you want to see which user is logged on session 1, then you'd type **QUser 1** and press Enter. The first session, session 1, is normally the local user.

Discover User Identity

The WhoAmI utility is a utility that you used to download as part of the Windows Resource Kit (see http://www.microsoft.com/downloads/details .aspx?FamilyID=3e89879d-6c0b-4f92-96c4-1016c187d429). However, starting with Windows XP Professional and Windows 2003, you started getting this utility as part of the operating system. When you type **WhoAmI** and press Enter, you see just the logon name of the user. The logon name consists of the domain name/username. If the user isn't part of a domain, then you see machine name/username instead.

Sometimes you need more than just the user's logon name. To obtain the user's User Principal Name (UPN), type **WhoAmI /UPN** and press Enter. Likewise, to obtain the user's Fully Qualified Domain Name (FQDN), type **WhoAmI /FQDN** and press Enter. There are a few situations where you need the user's logon identifier. Type **WhoAmI /LoginID** and press Enter to obtain this information. Don't confuse the logon identifier with the user's Security Identifier (SID).

You can use WhoAmI to obtain more information about the user. For example, if you want to find the user's SID, type **WhoAmI /User** and press Enter. If you need to know the user's group affiliations, type **WhoAmI /Groups** and press Enter. Acquire the user's privileges by typing **WhoAmI /Priv** and press Enter. Finally, if you need everything that WhoAmI can tell you about the user, type **WhoAmI /All** and press Enter.

17

Securing the System

Security is an extremely complex topic and this chapter doesn't seek to tell you everything there is to know about security. However, it does help you understand how to enhance security using command line tools—an often missed opportunity in other books and articles. Command line tools can help you automate security to an extent. You can't use command line tools to eliminate manual security measures, but some tasks can easily be automated. For example, there really isn't a good reason to manually scan the drivers on every system on a network. You can easily automate this task and then review a report afterward to determine remedial actions that you normally perform manually. Automation can also help you detect viruses and set consistent policies on a network. This chapter explores these topics to help you enhance your overall network security.

Setting Basic Security

Other chapters in this book have already helped you start the security process. For example, Chapter 1 begins the process by telling you how to work with services. Holes created by services that you don't actually need can cause problems, so proper service management is essential (Chapter 8 provides additional information on managing services).

Chapter 7 describes how to secure your data using Cipher, ICACLS, OpenFiles, and TakeOwn. The simple act of restricting data access makes a big difference in network security because many companies leave data open to anyone to access. Use the information in Chapter 13 to monitor system events, because these event entries often point out potential security problems by helping you see any unusual entry patterns.

Monitoring the user is also important. Chapter 16 shows how to audit user activities, so that you can detect unusual user activity. Of course, WMIC is the utility of choice for configuring user accounts locally and you use the DS* utilities in Chapter 11 and Chapter 12 for domain configuration. All of these utilities, taken in combination, help you create a basic security screen for your system.

Add Virus and External Intrusion Protection

Virus and external intrusion protection takes several forms. First, you can erect a wall around your network in the form of firewalls and anti-virus software. The following sections help partially with this form of protection. Second, you can detect and eliminate viruses and intrusions after the fact. The following sections are more focused on this goal than on actual prevention. Third, you can educate users not to leave the door open to virus and intrusions in the first place. The following sections won't help with this goal at all. Fourth, you can plug any existing holes in the operating system, services, drivers, and applications. The following sections also help in this goal a little by helping you verify the drivers on your system. In short, the following sections help but won't be a complete solution for your virus and external intrusion protection.

NOTE   There are many levels of threats to a computer system. Of course, there are threats to the network as a whole, servers, and individual machines. A threat can be internal from users, incorrect configurations, loose security, or external from nefarious individuals who are intent on harming your organization. A threat can be personal, such as an individual user downloading a virus, or corporate, such as someone trying to steal the latest intellectual property from your network. Threats can be directed at your company personally or the result of a shotgun blast from a script kiddie picking low-hanging fruit. The point is that you have many threats to deal with and erecting walls will only solve a few of them. You must combine preventative and detection software with training, policies, and other elements to create an effective defense against all these threats. Most importantly, the smart administrator is constantly thinking outside the box because the enemy certainly is.

Performing Maintenance

PART VI

Remove Viruses

The Blast Clean (BlastCln) utility, supplied with some versions of Windows such as Windows XP, helps you locate and remove two common viruses on your system, Blaster and Nachi. Microsoft updates the BlastCln utility monthly through the Windows Update service. In fact, you've probably run this utility every time you visited Windows Update without really knowing it because this utility appears on the list every month. However, you might want to check your machine more often than once a month to ensure it remains clean. In addition, running the utility as part of Windows Update doesn't provide you with a detailed report of any potential infestations on your system. You can learn a little more about this utility from the Knowledge Base article at http://support.microsoft.com/?kbid=833330. To perform a detailed manual check of your system, type **BlastCln /V** and press Enter.

If you want to use BlastCln from within a batch file or script, type **BlastCln /Q** and press Enter so that the utility runs without alerting the user. If you do want detailed information, but don't want to be bothered with BlastCln requests as it runs as part of the batch file or script, type **BlastCln /V /U** and press Enter.

Detect and Remove Malicious Software

The Malicious software Removal Tool (MRT) helps you remove common malicious software from your system. You can find a description of this utility in the Knowledge Base article at http://support.microsoft. com/?id=890830. It's important to review this Knowledge Base article relatively often because Microsoft updates it each month with the list of viruses that MRT can detect. If you're an administrator, make sure you check the deployment instructions in the Knowledge Base article at http://support.microsoft.com/kb/891716. To use the wizard-based GUI of MRT shown in Figure 17.1, type **MRT** and press Enter.

Figure 17.1: MRT supports both a GUI and command line interface.

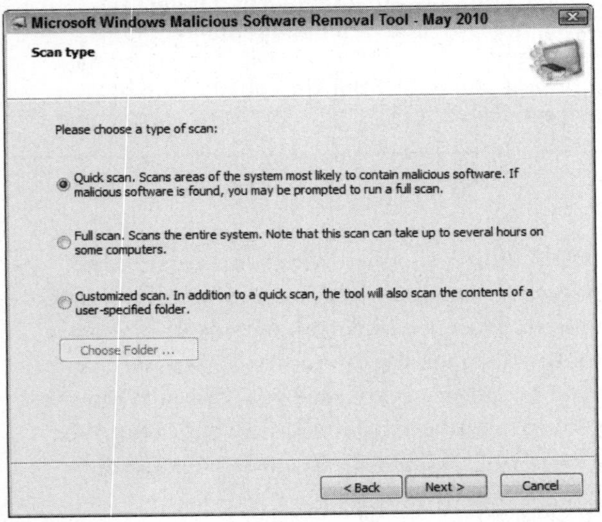

A more common way to use MRT from the command line is to type **MRT /Q** and press Enter. This command performs a quick scan of the system and automatically cleans any infections that the scanner finds. If you want to perform an extended scan to locate even the most stubborn malicious software that MRT can find, type **MRT /F:Y** and press Enter. Some administrators may not feel comfortable letting MRT work on its own. If you simply want to detect the malicious software and then manually clean it up, type **MRT /N** and press Enter.

Verify System Files

The System File Scan (SFC) utility can help you keep viruses at bay by ensuring you have the correct version of the system files on your system. Viruses often replace system files with patched versions that contain the virus code. Hitchhiking on an existing system file makes it less likely that someone will remove the virus and ensures that the virus gets a chance to run, so virus writers are motivated to use system files whenever they think they can. The following sections describe how to perform basic tasks with SFC.

Performing Maintenance

> **NOTE** The syntax of the SFC utility presented in this chapter is specific to Windows 7, Vista, Windows Server 2008 Full version, and Server Core. The syntax is completely different from older versions of SFC that you find in products such as Windows XP. The older Windows products use a command line that looks like this: SFC [/SCANNOW] [/SCANONCE] [/SCANBOOT] [/REVERT] [/PURGECACHE] [/CACHESIZE=x]. If you need this and other older versions of the command line for Windows administration, get *Windows Administration at the Command Line* (Sybex, 2007).

Perform a Scan

To scan all of the protected system files immediately and repair any damage found, type **SFC /ScanNow** and press Enter. The utility normally relies on the content of the \WINDOWS\system32\dllcache folder to make repairs to the system files. However, it can also use the Windows DVD, the content of service pack folders, or even online sources when necessary.

In many cases, you'll want to know what repairs SFC is going to make before you let SFC make them. In this case, type **SFC /VerifyOnly** and press Enter. You'll see SFC perform a verification process, as shown in Figure 17.2.

Figure 17.2: The verification process shows any corrupted or compromised files.

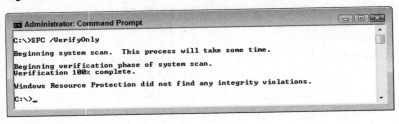

Scan a File

The SFC scanning process can require an extended time to complete (up to 15 minutes on many systems). You probably won't want to wait all that time if you suspect only one file is corrupted or tainted in some way. In this case, type **SFC /ScanFile=**_Filename_ and press Enter, where _Filename_ is the name of the file you want to scan. Unless the file is in the current directory, you need to supply the full path to the file. SFC scans the file and replaces it with a good copy should it find that the file is incorrect in some way.

Verify a File

It's also possible to verify a file, rather than scan it. Verifying the file saves time in some cases. SFC simply tells you whether or not the file is corrupt and then you can replace it using whatever technique works best. You might want to use this approach when scanning multiple machines in a batch process. To verify a file, type **SFC /VerifyFile=**_Filename_ and press Enter, where _Filename_ is the name of the file you want to scan. Unless the file is in the current directory, you need to supply the full path to the file.

Verify Drivers

The Verifier utility performs general driver verification on your system through the Driver Verifier. Driver vendors are supposed to use this utility to ensure their drivers don't make illegal system calls or cause system corruption. You can use Verifier to ensure you do have good drivers loaded on your system and that a virus hasn't modified the driver files on your machine. Most of the drivers on your machine appear in the

\WINDOWS\system32\drivers folder and have a .SYS file extension. If you want to use the GUI version of the Verifier wizard, type **Verifier** and press Enter. The following sections describe common tasks you can perform with the Verifier utility at the command line.

Perform a Query

None of the drivers are verified on a new system. However, as the machine configuration changes and you do verify older drivers, you end up with a number of drivers that aren't checked. To obtain a list of drivers that have been verified, type **Verifier /Query** and press Enter. A new system will tell you that none of the drivers are verified.

Query the Verifier Settings

When you use Verifier, you can either choose to use the standard settings for checking drivers or create special settings. The standard check includes the Special Memory Pool, Forcing Interrupt Request Level (IRQL) Checking, Memory Pool Tracking, I/O Verification (but not the enhanced version), Deadlock Detection, and DMA Verification checks. Technically, every driver on your machine should be able to pass a standard check. The driver vendor should provide you with information about any drivers that won't pass the Verifier checks. To see the settings, type **Verifier /QuerySettings** and press Enter. You'll see a list of settings like the ones shown in Figure 17.3.

Figure 17.3: Verifier shows the tests that it runs when you check the drivers.

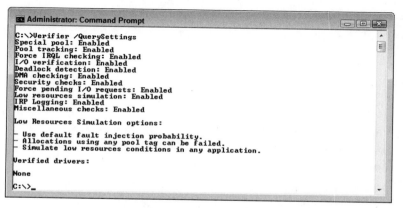

Change the *Verifier* Settings

Verifier settings come in two forms: volatile (temporary) and permanent. Volatile settings take effect immediately and last until you reboot the system. You can only perform the Special Memory Pool, Forcing IRQL Checking, and Low Resources Simulation checks when using volatile settings on older versions of Windows. Windows 7 allows you to use volatile settings to perform any test.

Permanent settings don't take effect immediately. You make the change to the settings and then reboot the system for these changes to take effect.

To create a volatile setting, you use the /Volatile /Flags *FlagNumber* command line switch combination, where *FlagNumber* is a number that you create based on the tests you want to run. To create a permanent setting, you use the /Flags FlagNumber command line switch. The FlagNumber is based on the following bit values (older versions of Windows only support Bit 0 through Bit 7):

- Bit 0: Special Pool Checking
- Bit 1: Force IRQL Checking
- Bit 2: Low Resources Simulation
- Bit 3: Pool Tracking
- Bit 4: I/O Verification
- Bit 5: Deadlock Detection
- Bit 6: Enhanced I/O Verification (Unused in Windows 7)
- Bit 7: DMA Verification
- Bit 8: Security Checks
- Bit 9: Force Pending I/O Requests
- Bit 10: IRP Logging
- Bit 11: Miscellaneous Checks

The bit numbers can be a little confusing, but you can use the Calculator application to make things easier. Use these steps to create the *FlagNumber*:

1. Open the Calculator to Scientific view in older versions of Windows or Programmer view in Windows 7.

2. Set the Calculator to Binary mode.

3. Beginning with Bit 11, type a **1** if you want to run a test or **0** if you don't want to run it. Keep typing 0s and 1s until you finish all 12 bits (8 bits when working with older versions of Windows because these older versions start at Bit 7 instead of Bit 11).

4. Set the Calculator to Decimal mode. You see the number you need to type. For example, if you want to run just Special Pool Checking and Low Resources Simulation, you get a value of 5 (000000000101 in binary mode). To run all 12 tests in Windows 7, you use a value of 4,095.

To set `Verifier` to temporarily run all tests, type **`Verifier / Volatile /Flags 4095`** and press Enter. Likewise, to set `Verifier` to run all tests permanently, type **`Verifier /Flags 4095`**, press Enter, and reboot the machine.

Clear the Verifier Settings

If you don't want `Verifier` to perform any tests, you need to clear the settings. You can do that using the technique found in the "Change the Verifier Settings" section of the chapter, or you can type **`Verifier /Reset`** and press Enter.

Check the Drivers

`Verifier` won't perform any checks immediately because the drivers are in use. In order to verify the drivers, you must reboot the system after telling `Verifier` what to check. Because of the reboot requirement, the easiest check in most cases is to verify all of the drivers. To perform this task, type **`Verifier /Standard /All`** (to perform the standard checks) or **`Verifier /All`** (to perform custom checks) and press Enter. `Verifier` displays a summary screen that shows which checks it will perform and on which drivers (all of them).

It's possible to check individual drivers. In this case, you type **`Verifier /Standard /Driver DriverName`** or **`Verifier /Driver DriverName`** and press Enter, where *DriverName* is the name of the driver you want to check. As with the all driver checks, you see a summary screen telling you what `Verifier` will do during the next reboot.

Configure Local Security Policies

Local security policies are those that exist on the local machine rather than on the domain. When working with workgroups, local security policies are all you have. The Security Edit (SecEdit) utility helps you analyze and manage local security policies on your system. In some cases, you can also merge local and domain security policies to create a single policy.

Security policies appear within Security Database (SDB) files. Unfortunately, Microsoft has used the .SDB file extension for more than security databases—you'll find them cropping up all over your machine (for example, many applications use Setup.SDB to hold their setup instructions). In general, the security database that you want to work with appears in the \Windows\security\database directory of the target machine.

To obtain help when using the SecEdit utility, type **SecEdit /?** and press Enter. However, to get command-specific help, type **SecEdit /Command**, where *Command* is the command you want to know about, and press Enter (without the ?). For example, to get help on the SecEdit /Analyze command, you type **SecEdit /Analyze** and press Enter. The following sections describe how to work with the local security database on any system.

WARNING   Always make a copy of the security database before you do anything with it. Otherwise, you might find that you need to re-create the security policies from scratch.

Perform an Analysis

You can spend hours looking for security problems on a system or you can compare the system to a known good database of settings. Use the SecEdit /Analyze command to compare the settings on the target system to the settings contained within a database file of known good settings. For example, if your baseline security database is named SecCheck.SDB, you type **SecEdit /Analyze /DB SecCheck.SDB** and press Enter to perform a check of the current system against the baseline. The results from the check normally appear in \Windows\security\logs\scesrv.LOG, but you can override this destination using the \Log *LogName* command line switch, where *LogName* is the name of the log you want to use.

Performing Maintenance

PART VI

> **NOTE**   Microsoft may supply standard security templates
> somewhere, but they apparently aren't for download. You should
> find a security template on your system with the Windows
> default security settings as described in the Knowledge Base
> article at http://support.microsoft.com/kb/313222. However, to
> obtain a database you can use for work with your system, you
> need to configure a system as you want it to appear, and then
> use the \Windows\security\database\SecEdit.SDB file (renamed)
> from that system for SecEdit tasks.

Configure Security Policies

The SecEdit /Configure command makes it possible to configure a system based on the content of the .SDB file you provide. For example, if
you want to configure your system based on the content of SecBasic
.SDB, you type **SecEdit /Configure /DB SecBasic.SDB** and press Enter.

If you use the basic command, SecEdit replaces the entire target
computer configuration with the configuration you supply. However, in
some cases, you might only want to replace specific areas. In this case,
you use the /Areas *Area1 Area2* ... command line switch, where *Area1*
and *Area2* are areas that you want replaced. You can specify multiple
areas by separating each area with a space. The following list contains
the valid security areas:

- **SECURITYPOLICY:** Defines the user security policy, which includes
  account policies, audit policies, event log settings, and security
  options.

- **GROUP_MGMT:** Defines the restricted group settings.

- **USER_RIGHTS:** Defines the user rights assignments to system objects.

- **REGKEYS:** Defines the registry permissions.

- **FILESTORE:** Defines the file system permissions.

- **SERVICES:** Defines the system service settings.

Export Policies

At some point you'll want to make a backup of your security policies.
The SecEdit /Export command makes it possible to create a backup of
the security policies on the target system. To use the basic form of this
command, type **SecEdit /Export /Cfg Cfg.TXT** and press Enter. The /Cfg
command line switch is required.

In some cases, you might want to merge the existing database with a baseline database. Use the /DB command line switch. For example, if you want to merge the local settings with SecCheck.SDB, type **SecEdit /Export /Cfg Cfg.TXT /DB SecCheck.SDB** and press Enter. It's also possible to merge the local and domain security settings into a single backup file. In this case, type **SecEdit /Export /Cfg Cfg.TXT /MergedPolicy** and press Enter.

As with configuration, you don't have to export all of the settings into a configuration file. You can use the /Areas command line switch to limit the number of settings that SecEdit saves. See the "Configure Security Policies" section of the chapter for details about the /Areas command line switch.

Import Policies

When you need to import settings into an .SDB, you use the SecEdit /Import command. For example, you might need to import settings into your basic template used to configure other machines. Unlike configuration, this command doesn't necessarily work with the target machine—you can use it on an arbitrary database. If your database is named SecEdit.SDB and the configuration file is named CFG.TXT, then type **SecEdit /Import /DB SecEdit.SDB /Cfg CFG.TXT** and press Enter to import the settings from CFG.TXT into SecEdit.SDB.

SecEdit normally tries to mesh the .SDB with the configuration file. When there's a conflict, the configuration file (template) always wins. However, you can change this behavior using the /Overwrite command line switch. In this case, SecEdit clears the .SDB file first, and then adds the settings from the configuration file to it, even if the configuration file isn't complete.

As with configuration, you don't have to import all of the settings into the local security policy. You can use the /Areas command line switch to limit the number of settings that SecEdit imports. See the "Configure Security Policies" section of the chapter for details about the /Areas command line switch.

Validate a Policy File

You have a configuration (template) file, but you don't know whether the template file is accurate. Use the SecEdit /Validate command to ensure the accuracy of the configuration file before you use it.

To validate the content of CFG.TXT against SecEdit.SDB, type **SecEdit /Validate SecEdit.SDB /Cfg CFG.TXT** and press Enter. You see a simple message that tells when the validation completed successfully as output.

Work with General Applications

The TaskKill and TaskList utilities make it possible to control and monitor applications running on the system. You can see every utility that's running and then terminate anything that shouldn't be running. Of course, you always use TaskList first to see which applications are running and rely on TaskKill only after you determine that the application really shouldn't be running.

> **WARNING** Terminating an application using TaskKill can cause data loss because the application ends without saving any data it's working with at the time. Use TaskKill as a last resort, rather than the first option when working with errant applications. Of course, you can always use TaskKill to stop known Trojans, viruses, and adware.

Use *TaskKill* and *TaskList* Filters

Sometimes utilities output too much information for the administrator to use, as is the case with the TaskKill and TaskList utilities. Both the TaskKill and TaskList utilities support a /FI command line switch that lets you filter their output. The filters can become complex, so it's best to put the filters together one piece at a time until you obtain the results you want.

Table 17.1 describes the filter criteria. Filters are essential in some cases, especially when working with the /V command line switch. For example, if you want verbose information about the applications you're using, you can type **TaskList /V /FO LIST /FI "USERNAME eq** *AUserName*" **| More** and press Enter, where *AUserName* is the name of the user you want to see. Notice that you must enclose the filter criteria in quotes. In this case, you're telling the system to filter by username where the username equals the username you select (System in Figure 17.4). Of course, you'll use your name when trying out this command line on your machine. Figure 17.4 shows typical output from this command.

Figure 17.4: Use filters with TaskList and TaskKill to keep the amount of output under control.

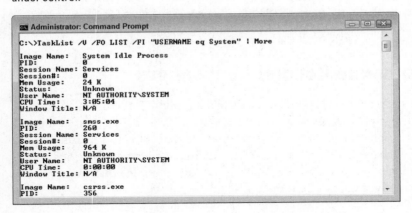

Table 17.1: An Overview of TaskKill and TaskList Filters

Filter	Description	Comparison Operators	Valid Values
STATUS	Use this filter to locate any applications that are no longer responding so that you can manually end them.	eq, ne	Running or Not Responding
IMAGENAME	Use this filter to locate a particular application in the list based on its filename.	eq, ne	The executable filename
PID	Use this filter to locate a particular instance of an application when there's more than one copy of the application running.	eq, ne, gt, lt, ge, le	Process Identifier
SESSION	Unless you're using a sharing application such as Terminal Services, this filter is useless because every application running is for the current session.	eq, ne, gt, lt, ge, le	The session number
SESSIONNAME	Unless you're using a sharing application such as Terminal Services, this filter is useless because every application running is for the current session.	eq, ne	The name of the session

Table 17.1: An Overview of TaskKill and TaskList Filters *(continued)*

Filter	Description	Comparison Operators	Valid Values
CPUTIME	Use this filter to locate applications that have just started or have been running a long time. For example, you might notice a sudden drop in system performance and can use this filter to locate applications that have just started to help determine which application might have caused the performance problem.	eq, ne, gt, lt, ge, le	The amount of time that the application has used the CPU in hours, minutes, and seconds since the session has started
MEMUSAGE	Sometimes you have more applications loaded than the system can comfortably support. Use this filter to locate applications that you can end or possible candidates for removal from the system.	eq, ne, gt, lt, ge, le	The amount of memory the application uses in kilobytes
USERNAME	Use this filter to separate applications that the user starts from those the system starts.	eq, ne	The name of the user who started the application
SERVICES	Use this filter to locate the application hosting a particular service on the system.	eq, ne	A service name
WINDOWTITLE	Use this filter to locate a particular application based on the name it displays to the user.	eq, ne	The name the application displays to the user on the title bar
MODULES	Use this filter to locate applications based on the modules they use. You can use this filter to help locate a variety of problems, including .DLL conflicts (when two applications use the same .DLL, but they each need a different .DLL version).	eq, ne	The filenames of any modules that an application uses

Performing Maintenance

PART VI

In some cases, you must combine multiple filters to get manageable results. For example, simply looking for processes created by a particular individual might not be enough to limit the list to a reasonable size. So, you might decide to add another filtering criterion, such as CPUTIME. For example, if you type **TaskList /V /FO LIST /FI** "USERNAME **eq System**" **/FI** "CPUTIME **eq 0:00:00**" and press Enter, you see all of the processes created by the system and haven't used any CPU time.

Terminate Tasks

Terminating applications using TaskKill is always the option of last resort. However, sometimes an application crashes and you have to end it using TaskKill. To end an application using TaskKill, type **TaskKill /IM** *ImageName* **/T** and press Enter, where *ImageName* is the application's executable name. For example, Microsoft Word's image name is actually WinWord.EXE. The /T command line switch ensures that the entire application is killed, rather than just the main executable. You can obtain the image name of an application using the TaskList utility.

There are times when you have multiple copies of the same application running on a system. For example, you can start multiple copies of Notepad. If you use the image name to kill the application, TaskKill will terminate every copy of Notepad, not just the one you want terminated. In this case, you must use the Program Identifier (PID) to terminate the application. The PID uniquely identifies every process. Use the TaskList utility to obtain a list of PIDs. To terminate an application using a PID, type **TaskKill /PID** *ID* **/T** and press Enter, where ID is the PID of the process you want to end. To further ensure you locate the right application, combine the TaskKill utility with a filter as described in the "Use TaskKill and TaskList Filters" section of the chapter.

List Applications

Use the TaskList utility to list applications running on a system. To see all of the applications running on a system, type **TaskList** and press Enter. You see the image name, PID, session name, session number, and memory usage for each application.

When you need to see all of the statistics for the applications running on a system, type **TaskList /V** and press Enter. The output will now display the image name, PID, session name, session number, memory usage, status, user name, CPU time, and window title for each application. In most cases, the output is going to be overwhelming, so you'll want to use a filter. See Table 17.1, "An Overview of TaskKill and TaskList Filters", for information on using filters.

In some cases, the default tabular format of the TaskList output doesn't work well. Trying to see verbose output using tabular format is difficult because the entries span several lines on a typical console window. To make the output more readable, use the /FO *Format* command line switch, where *Format* is one of the supported formats: Table, List, or Comma Separated Value (CSV). For example, if you want to create a verbose list of applications in a form suitable for import into a database, you'd type **TaskList /V /FO CSV > Applications.CSV** and press Enter.

List Services

The basic TaskList utility commands don't show services, which are special applications that run in the background. In order to see services, you must type **TaskList /SVC** and press Enter. The output includes the image name, PID, and services supplied by the process. You can't use the /SVC command line switch with the /V or /M command line switches, so you can't obtain verbose information about services. Unfortunately, the output of this command includes all of the applications in addition to the services.

You have a number of ways to get around the problem of seeing processes with the services. One technique is to rely on the fact that SvcHost.EXE is the image name of the application that runs most (but not all) of the services. To find the low-level services (those not associated with applications) running on your system, you type **TaskList /SVC /FI "ImageName eq SvcHost.EXE"** and press Enter.

Another way to find services is to rely on the fact that processes display N/A in the Services column of the output. You can pipe the output of the TaskList utility to the Find utility to obtain a list of all of the services by typing **TaskList /SVC | Find "N/A" /V** and pressing Enter. This section approach finds both low-level services and those associated with applications.

18

Interacting with the Registry

Performing Maintenance

PART VI

The registry affects every part of the Windows experience. It contains settings for everything from services to applications. Some settings are personal and others affect the system as a whole. In fact, the registry is an extremely complex database that Windows won't run without. Any damage to the registry can cause catastrophic results. Most administrators will face some type of registry damage on user systems on a regular basis. The causes are many—everything from errant applications to viruses and external intrusions. Microsoft has tried many times over the years to replace the registry with something else, but it has so far failed because the registry truly is an essential component of Windows. The following sections provide insights into working with the registry from the command line.

WARNING   Any change you make to the registry is potentially dangerous and could result in data loss, an unbootable system, or other problems. Always create a backup of your registry before you make any changes. The "Save the Registry" section of the chapter describes how to create such a backup. You could also use the material found in the "Export Registry Entries" section to create a backup. Whatever technique you use, always create a backup and make sure it will be accessible should registry damage occur after a change.

Perform Basic Registry Tasks

You'll commonly use the Registry Editor (RegEdit.EXE) utility in GUI mode. To start this utility in GUI mode, simply type **RegEdit** and press Enter. You'll see an initial display like the one shown in Figure 18.1. The left pane shows hives and keys, while the right pane shows values associated with the hives and keys that you select in the left pane. Anyone who's worked with the registry already knows about hives, keys, and values.

Figure 18.1: RegEdit provides the means for viewing, creating, deleting, and modifying registry settings.

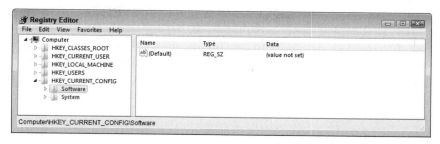

> **NOTE** A hive is a major data storage unit—think of it as an equivalent of a table within a database because the purpose is the same. Keys are entries within the hive—you can view them as individual records within the database. Values contain the actual registry information—you can view them as fields. If you don't already know these three terms, then you don't have enough knowledge to begin working with the registry and should probably not use the information in this chapter until you do have a good working knowledge of the registry. Making changes to the registry without the required registry knowledge will almost certainly damage the database at some point and could even cause Windows to stop working.

One of the more interesting command line switches is /V. Type **RegEdit** /V and press Enter to see the advanced (verbose) mode. If you're familiar with the standard registry appearance, you'll suddenly notice some registry keys that RegEdit didn't display before. Use this option with care; all of the registry settings are editable if you have the proper permissions and the new settings tend to have dramatic system results.

If you want to edit a registry on another machine, you must configure that machine to allow remote edits by starting the Remote Registry service. In addition, you must right-click the HKEY_LOCAL_MACHINE\ SYSTEM\CurrentControlSet\Control\SecurePipeServers\winreg key in the Registry Editor and choose Permissions from the context menu. Ensure that the Administrators group has full access to this key (and therefore the remote registry). To remotely edit the system-wide settings such as the HKEY_LOCAL_MACHINE hive found in System.DAT, type **RegEdit /L:*Path*** and press Enter, where *Path* is the location of the System.DAT file on the remote system. To remotely edit the user database that appears in the individual user directories in User.DAT and contains the HKEY_CURRENT_USER hive, type **RegEdit /R:*Path*** and press Enter, where *Path* is the location of the User. DAT file on the remote system. The following sections describe other tasks you can perform using RegEdit.

RegEdit as an Undocumented Utility

The RegEdit utility is extremely powerful, yet it's one of the most undocumented utilities available on your machine. The Microsoft-recommended command line switches for the RegEdit utility appear in the Knowledge Base article at http://support.microsoft.com/kb/q82821/. The Knowledge Base article limits you to the /V and /S command line switches.

Even Windows won't help much when using this utility. The RegEdit utility itself doesn't display any helpful information when you type **RegEdit /?** and press Enter. The Windows help file just barely discusses using the utility in GUI mode. In short, not only is this utility extremely powerful, you also won't get much help from Microsoft in using it. Because RegEdit is so undocumented, your ability to continue using the command line switches described in the sections that follow will depend on Microsoft continuing to support them in an undocumented state. In short, there's no guarantee that you'll have continued access to these features.

Export a Registry Key

The registry contains a lot of potentially valuable information that's incredibly time consuming to retrieve if you don't use a batch file or script. You can use the /E command line switch within a batch file to save user settings prior to a system change. For example, typing **RegEdit /E Test.REG "HKEY_CURRENT_USER\Software\Nico Mak Computing"** and pressing Enter at the command prompt saves the WinZIP application settings to a file named Test.REG (registry files normally use the .REG extension).

As a more practical example, if you want to save all of the startup applications found in the Run key, you type **RegEdit /E HKLM_Run.REG** **"HKEY_LOCAL_MACHINE\Software\Microsoft\Windows\CurrentVersion\Run"** and press Enter. Notice that you must enclose keys with spaces in the name in double quotes to ensure the RegEdit utility interprets them correctly. In addition, you must use an uppercase /E when working with newer versions of Windows.

When you specify a particular key, you get the entire tree. For example, if you type **RegEdit /E HKCU_Software.REG "HKEY_CURRENT_USER** **Software"** and press Enter, you get the entire Software key and associated subkeys. If you want only specific subkeys, then you must export the subkeys one at a time.

Import a Registry Key

At some point, you'll need to import the registry files you've been collecting. To perform a standard import, type **RegEdit *RegFilename*** and press Enter, where *RegFilename* is the name of the file that contains the registry information. However, using this technique displays a warning message to the user, which would be annoying if you have a lot of files to import.

A second method to import registry files is to type **RegEdit /S** ***RegFilename*** and press Enter. The /S command line switch tells RegEdit to perform tasks silently. The advantage of using this command line switch is that your batch file or script can proceed without bothering the user. Of course, the disadvantage is that the silent mode leaves the registry open to potential abuse. Fortunately, newer versions of Windows require a permission escalation before any registry change can take place, so the user will be aware of the change, but will only have to allow it once.

Delete a Registry Key

Sometimes you need to remove a registry key. Use the /D command line switch to perform this task. Simply type **RegEdit /D *Key*** and press Enter, where ***Key*** is the registry key (and its associated subkeys) that you want to delete. This switch appears to work fine on Windows 9*x* systems, but doesn't always work with Windows NT and above. If you need to delete a registry key using a newer version of Windows, use the Reg utility described in the "Manage the Registry" section of this chapter.

Save the Registry

It isn't possible to back up the registry using a standard backup program because the registry files are normally in use when Windows is running. Of course, you can always boot from the installation DVD and make a copy of System.DAT and each of the User.DAT files, but that's time consuming and error prone at best. A better method is to export the entire registry and save the exported file. To export the entire registry, type **RegEdit /E RegBackup.REG** and press Enter. The resulting RegBackup.REG file contains the entire registry for the user who's currently logged on to the system.

Restore the Registry

Windows always has a registry or it won't boot. Consequently, to restore the registry, you must somehow restore the settings while Windows is running, which seems like a disaster waiting to happen unless you perform the task carefully. Simply typing **RegEdit *RegBackup.REG*** and pressing Enter won't do the trick (be sure your replace *RegBackup.REG* with the name of your backup file). Yes, any settings in RegBackup.REG will overwrite the settings in the current registry, assuming you have the correct permissions. However, you can't guarantee that the new registry will precisely match the old registry. In some cases, Windows won't even boot after the update. To ensure that you get a precise duplicate, you must first clear the existing registry and then add the new values. To perform this task, type **RegEdit /C RegBackup.REG** and press Enter. The /C command line switch completely clears the old registry settings and replaces the registry with the settings you provide. This process is one way and destructive—there's no undo button, so make sure you use the correct registry file.

Use the SCRegEdit Script

Microsoft has begun using a new scripting file format called the Windows Scripting File (WSF). The SCRegEdit.WSF file on your system is just one of many .WSF files you should expect to see at some point. (Not all versions of Windows include this script, but the script works fine in all versions of Windows.) The purpose of this script is to make it easier to perform certain types of registry edits. The following sections detail the kinds of registry edits you can perform and the command line switches you use to perform the tasks.

NOTE The "Use the Windows Scripting File" section of Chapter 22 tells you more about .WSF files. You can't execute .WSF scripts on older versions of Windows because the WScript and CScript utilities aren't set up to support them.

Set Automatic Updates

This feature of the SCRegEdit script lets you set the automatic update feature for Windows without relying on the GUI. To see the current automatic updates setting, type **CScript %WinDir%\System32\SCRegEdit .WSF /AU /V** and press Enter. To change the setting, type **CScript %WinDir%\System32\SCRegEdit.WSF /AU *Value*** and press Enter, where *Value* is one of the values shown in the following list:

- 1: Disable Automatic Updates
- 4: Enable Automatic Updates

For example, if you want to configure automatic updates so that they always occur, type **CScript %WinDir%\System32\SCRegEdit.WSF /AU 4** and press Enter. Note that you don't use a slash with the 4 (this is the most common mistake people make when using SCRegEdit).

NOTE The SCRegEdit script only supports values 1 and 4. If you want to use another setting, such as 2 for checking updates, but allowing the user to decide whether to download and install them, you must use some other method.

Enable Terminal Services

It's often helpful to use Remote Desktop to administer any Windows system. Using this approach lets you combine the benefits of both the command line and the GUI to get work done faster.

There are two forms of this particular script feature. The first form is for newer versions such as Vista. This form provides additional security not provided with previous versions of Windows, so it's more secure, but also limits connectivity. To see this form of Terminal Services setting, type **CScript %WinDir%\System32\SCRegEdit.WSF /AR /V** and press Enter. If you want to enable the newer form of Terminal Services connectivity, type **CScript %WinDir%\System32\SCRegEdit.WSF /AR 0** and press Enter. Likewise, to disable the newer form of Terminal Services connectivity, type **CScript %WinDir%\System32\SCRegEdit.WSF /AR 1** and press Enter.

The second form of Terminal Services connectivity lets older versions of Windows make a connection to the local system. Except for the amount of security provided, this form works just like the other form of this feature. When working in secure mode, Terminal Services relies on the Credential Security Support Provider (CredSSP) to provide security. Read more about CredSSP at http://blogs.msdn.com/windowsvista-security/archive/2006/08/25/724271.aspx. You may also want to review the group policy settings for this feature at https://msdn2.microsoft.com/en-us/library/bb204773.aspx. To see this form of Terminal Services setting, type **CScript %WinDir%\System32\SCRegEdit.WSF /CS /V** and press Enter. If you want to enable the older form of Terminal Services connectivity, type **CScript %WinDir%\System32\SCRegEdit.WSF /CS 0** and press Enter. Likewise, to disable the older form of Terminal Services connectivity, type **CScript %WinDir%\System32\SCRegEdit.WSF /CS 1** and press Enter.

Configure the IP Security (IPSec) Monitor

You may need to provide remote management capability for the IPSec feature of Windows. Use this script feature to modify the remote management capability as needed. To see the IPSec Monitor setting, type **CScript %WinDir%\System32\SCRegEdit.WSF /IM /V** and press Enter. If you want to allow IPSec monitoring, type **CScript %WinDir%\System32\SCRegEdit.WSF /IM 1** and press Enter. Likewise, to disallow IPSec monitoring, type **CScript %WinDir%\System32\SCRegEdit.WSF /CS 0** and press Enter.

NOTE The Internet Engineering Task Force (IETF) created the Internet Protocol (IP) Security Protocol Working Group to look at the problems of IP security, such as the inability to encrypt data at the protocol level. It's currently working on a wide range of specifications that will ultimately result in more secure IP transactions. For example, IPSec is used in a variety of object-based group policy schemes. Windows currently uses IPSec for network-level authentication, data integrity checking, and encryption.

Manage the DNS Service Priority and Weight

The Domain Name System (DNS) service is one of the more important features of Windows because it helps set the addresses for each node on the network. In fact, the services provided are standardized across all operating systems as part of RFC 2782 (see http://www.faqs.org/rfcs/rfc2782.html for details). You'll normally use this script feature on domain controllers only. The DNS Service (SRV) records have both a priority and a weight. The priority affects the LdapSrvPriority registry setting (see http://www.microsoft.com/technet/prodtechnol/windows2000serv/reskit/regentry/55945.mspx for details).

When two DNS servers have the same priority setting, Windows relies on the weight setting to determine which server to use. You set the priority using the /DP command line switch. To see the DNS Service Priority and Weight setting, type **CScript %WinDir%\System32\SCRegEdit.WSF /DP /V** and press Enter. To change the setting, type **CScript %WinDir%\System32\SCRegEdit.WSF /DP Value** and press Enter, where *Value* is a number between 0 and 65,535 that defines the server priority. Microsoft recommends a value of 200.

Use the Command Line Reference

The SCRegEdit script also includes a command line reference for performing some common command line tasks. When you type **CScript %WinDir%\System32\SCRegEdit.WSF /CLI** and press Enter, you'll see a display similar to the one shown in Figure 18.2.

Figure 18.2: The /CLI command line switch is useful because it provides information on performing common tasks.

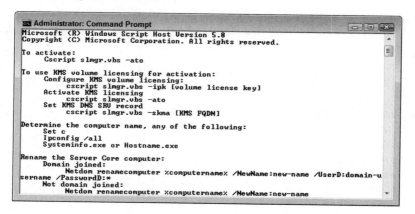

The command line information tells you how to perform common tasks using the current version of the server. Since Microsoft will likely keep this file updated as it provides revisions, you should refer to this information when it appears that an update has made an older configuration technique incomplete. Unfortunately, the information only tells you how to perform the most basic tasks and not in any particular order.

Manage the Registry

The Reg utility makes it possible to perform registry edits from the command line. In fact, this one utility makes it possible to script just about any registry editing requirement without much effort. To see the basic list of tasks you can perform, type **Reg /?** and press Enter. You can obtain specific information by adding an operation name. For example, type **Reg Query /?** and press Enter to learn more about the Query operation. The following sections describe the Reg utility in more detail.

Understand the Registry Settings

Before you make registry changes from the command line, it's important to know about the data values you use to perform the task. Table 18.1 shows all of the common registry data types and their value type equivalents, and provides a description of how that value type is used.

Table 18.1: Common Registry Value Types

Data Type	Value Type	Description
String Value	REG_SZ	Contains a simple string value. Sometimes the string looks like other kinds of data, but it's always in string format. Make sure you type any string in the correct format. For example, the individual numbers in a color tuple should have a single space separating them.
Binary Value	REG_BINARY	Contains binary data that can include both computer and human-readable numeric data. You type the input as numbers. However, the editor translates any numbers into human-readable form when possible. For example, type **34** and you'll see the number 4 displayed in the human-readable area.

Table 18.1: Common Registry Value Types *(continued)*

Data Type	Value Type	Description
DWORD (32-bit) Value	REG_DWORD	Contains a 32-bit numeric value.
QWORD (64-bit) Value	REG_QWORD	Contains a 64-bit numeric value.
Multi-String Value	REG_MULTI_SZ	Contains multiple strings separated by a carriage return/line feed combination. The strings appear in a single line in the Registry Editor value pane. Double-click the entry to see the individual strings.
Expandable String Value	REG_EXPAND_SZ	Contains a string that includes expansion variables, such as **%SYSTEMROOT%**, that translate into specific computer data such as a directory location.
Custom Value	N/A	Custom values are uncommon, but you'll see them. Whenever you encounter a custom value, refer to the vendor data to determine how to set the value. In some cases, you'll be able to use an existing entry as a pattern for setting your own value.

It's also important to know about the abbreviations used for each of the registry hives. The following list defines each of the abbreviations used with the Reg utility:

- HKLM: HKEY_LOCAL_MACHINE
- HKCU: HKEY_CURRENT_USER
- HKCR: HKEY_CLASSES_ROOT
- HKU: HKEY_USERS
- HKCC: HKEY_CURRENT_CONFIG

Query a Registry Entry

The Query operation makes it possible to discover existing registry entries. To perform a basic query, use the Reg Query *Key* command, where *Key* is the registry key you want to find. For example, if you want to see the current desktop colors, you type **Reg Query "HKCU\Control Panel\Colors"** and press Enter. If you want to see a specific registry value, add the /V *ValueName* command line switch, where *ValueName* is the name of the value you want to see. For example, to see the ActiveTitle color, you type **Reg Query "HKCU\Control Panel\Colors" /V ActiveTitle** and press Enter. To see the default value, use the /VE command line switch instead.

Of course, you might not know what you need to find. For example, you might not know where the ActiveTitle color is located in the registry. In this case, you use the Reg Query *KeyRoot* /F *SearchTerm* command, where *KeyRoot* is a key abbreviation and *SearchTerm* is the term you want to find. In most cases, you also need to add the /S command line switch to search the entire key hierarchy. Consequently, to find ActiveTitle, you type **Reg Query HKCU /F ActiveTitle /S** and press Enter. You can also add the /K command line switch to search within keys only, the /D command line switch to search within data only, the /C command line switch to perform case sensitive searches, and the /E command line switch to perform exact searches. It's even possible to search for specific data types by using the /T *Type* command line switch, where *Type* is one of the following types: REG_SZ, REG_MULTI_SZ, REG_EXPAND_SZ, REG_DWORD, REG_QWORD, REG_BINARY, or REG_NONE.

Add a Registry Entry

Registry entries are actually comprised of three parts. First, there's the key that holds the data. Second, there's the data name—the name of a data element within the key. Third, there's the data value. In some cases, all you really need is the key. In this case, you can use the Reg Add *KeyName* command, where *KeyName* is the name of the key you want to add. For example, to add a key named MyData to the HKEY_CURRENT_USER\ Software branch, you type **Reg Add HKCU\Software\MyData** and press Enter.

Values come in two forms. You can add a default value or a named value. To add a default value, use the Reg Add *KeyName* /D *Value* command, where *Value* is the value you want to add. For example, to add a default value of Hello to the HKEY_CURRENT_USER\Software\MyData key, you type **Reg Add HKCU\Software\MyData /D Hello** and press Enter.

Most values are named. When working with a named value, you use the Reg Add *KeyName* /V *Name* /D *Value* command, where *Name* is the name of the value. For example, to add a named value of TheData with a value of Hello to the HKEY_CURRENT_USER\Software\MyData key, you type **Reg Add HKCU\Software\MyData /V TheData /D Hello** and press Enter.

All added values have a default type of REG_SZ. Of course, not all registry values are strings. In fact, registry values can include these types: REG_SZ, REG_MULTI_SZ, REG_EXPAND_SZ, REG_DWORD, REG_QWORD, REG_BINARY, and REG_NONE (the Reg utility doesn't support custom types). To add a named value of a specific type, you use the Reg Add KeyName /V Name /T Type /D Value command, where Type is one of the type keywords. For example, to add a DWORD value of 42 to a named value of TheData in the HKEY_CURRENT_USER\Software\MyData key, you type **Reg Add HKCU\ Software\MyData /V TheData /T REG_DWORD /D 42** and press Enter.

Delete a Registry Entry

The Reg utility provides quite a bit of flexibility for deleting registry entries. You can delete an entire key, the default value, a single named value, or all of the values. To delete an entire key, use the Reg Delete KeyName command, where KeyName is the name of the key you want to delete. For example, to delete the HKEY_CURRENT_USER\Software\MyData key, you type **Reg Delete HKCU\Software\MyData** and press Enter. The Reg utility asks whether you really want to delete the key. Type **Y** and press Enter to complete the task. Of course, you can avoid answering the question by using the /F command line switch. Simply type **Reg Delete HKCU\Software\MyData /F** and press Enter to delete the key without any additional input.

Although you won't do it very often because most values are named, it pays to know how to delete the default value. In this case, use the Reg Delete KeyName /VE command. For example, to delete the default value for the HKEY_CURRENT_USER\Software\MyData key, you type **Reg Delete HKCU\Software\MyData /VE** and press Enter.

Named values require that you provide the value name using the Reg Delete KeyName /V ValueName command, where *ValueName* is the name of the value you want to delete. For example, if you want to delete the TheData value in the HKEY_CURRENT_USER\Software\MyData key, you type **Reg Delete HKCU\Software\MyData /V TheData** and press Enter.

Finally, you might want to simply clear all of the values for a particular registry key. To perform this task, use the Reg Delete KeyName /VA command. For example, to delete all of the values for the HKEY_CURRENT_USER\ Software\MyData key, you type **Reg Delete HKCU\Software\MyData /VA** and press Enter.

Copy a Registry Entry

Administrators sometimes use an existing registry key as the basis for creating a new registry key. Copying the existing registry key saves time when the two registry keys are nearly the same. The Reg utility only allows you to copy keys—you can't copy values. In most cases, you want to copy the entire registry key hierarchy, so you include the /S command line switch. To perform this task, use the Reg Copy *SourceKey TargetKey* /S command, where *SourceKey* is the path of the existing key and *TargetKey* is the path of the key you want to create. For example, to copy the HKEY_CURRENT_USER\Software\MyData key to MyData2, you type **Reg Copy HKCU\Software\MyData HKCU\Software\MyData2 /S** and press Enter. Notice that you must provide the full path for both the source and destination keys.

Compare Registry Entries

The registry can contain repeat entries. For example, two users might rely on the same application. The application would generate the same set of registry entries for each user. By comparing the registry entries, you can see differences in the way the users configure their applications. The Reg utility makes it possible to perform comparisons using the Reg Compare *Key1 Key2* command, where *Key1* is the first key and *Key2* is the second key. For example, if you want to compare MyData with MyData2, type **Reg Compare HKCU\Software\MyData HKCU\Software\MyData2** and press Enter (notice that you must provide the full path for both keys). Use the /S command line switch if you also want to compare subkeys of both keys.

The standard output of the comparison only tells you whether the two entries compare. However, you sometimes require more information. A series of special command line switches tells Reg about the additional information you require as shown in the following list.

- **/OA:** Output all of differences and matches
- **/OD:** Output only differences
- **/OS:** Output only matches
- **/ON:** No output

You don't have to compare entire keys. It's possible to compare individual values. Use the /VE command line switch to compare the default values of the keys you provide. For example, to compare the default values of MyData and MyData2, you type **Reg Compare HKCU\Software\ MyData HKCU\Software\MyData2 /VE** and press Enter. To compare named values, use the **/V** *ValueName* command line switch, where *ValueName* is the name of the value you want to compare. For example, to compare the TheData named value for each of the previous keys, you type **Reg Compare HKCU\Software\MyData HKCU\Software\MyData2 /V TheData** and press Enter.

Export Registry Entries

The Reg utility makes it possible to create a backup of individual keys or entire hives (but not individual values). To perform this task, use the Reg Export *KeyName Filename* command, where *KeyName* is the name of a hive or key that you want to export and *Filename* is a .REG file you want to use to store the information. For example, to export the HKEY_CURRENT_USER\ Software\MyData key to MyDataBackup.REG, you type **Reg Export HKCU\ Software\MyData MyDataBackup.REG** and press Enter.

You can use the /Y command line switch to overwrite an existing .REG file without prompting. For example, to overwrite the MyDataBackup.REG file containing the HKEY_CURRENT_USER\Software\ MyData key without prompting, you type **Reg Export HKCU\Software\ MyData MyDataBackup.REG /Y** and press Enter.

NOTE   The Reg Save command syntax is precisely the same as the Reg Export command. The difference is that the Reg Save command produces a different file format than the Reg Export command, so the outputs aren't interchangeable. However, the Reg Restore command syntax is different from the Reg Import command. These two commands aren't the same and you should use the appropriate command in your batch files or scripts. To make your batch files and scripts look more consistent, use the Reg Save and Reg Restore commands together and the Reg Export and Reg Import commands together.

Import Registry Entries

You can also use the Reg utility to import .REG files using the Reg Import *Filename* command, where *Filename* is the name of a .REG file. For example, to import MyDataBackup.REG, you type **Reg Import MyDataBackup.REG** and press Enter. The one big difference between using Reg and RegEdit is that the Reg utility never asks whether you're sure that you want to import the registry entries.

Restore Registry Entries

Importing registry entries implies placing the registry entries precisely where you exported them. The HKEY_CURRENT_USER\Software\MyData key doesn't suddenly appear in another part of the registry when you import it. The Restore operation can place a registry entry in a new location using the Reg Restore *RestoreLocation Filename* command, where *RestoreLocation* is the path to a hive or key that receives the restored data and *Filename* is the name of a .REG or .HIV (hive) file. For example, to restore MyDataBackup.REG to the HKEY_LOCAL_MACHINE\ Software\MyData key, you type **Reg Restore HKLM\Software\MyData MyDataBackup.REG** and press Enter.

PART VII

Creating Batch Files

N THIS PART ▶

Creating Batch Files

PART VII

19

Changing the Batch File Environment

Creating Batch Files

PART VII

B atch files are an old technology—they appeared long before Windows was even a glint in Bill Gates's eyes. However, even as old as batch files are, they're still incredibly useful and represent one of the simplest automation methods available. Like anything, a batch file can become complex, but many batch files are a simple list of commands that you need to run. In many cases, the author of a batch file has little or no programming skills. Amazingly, Microsoft's attempts to replace the simple batch file haven't met with much success yet simply because batch files are so simple to use.

One of the more important aspects of using batch files is to ensure they have the correct environment in which to operate. In many cases, this simply means ensuring you use the Set command to provide the correct environment variables (see the "Set the Environment" section of Chapter 1 for details). However, you need to consider a number of other environmental concerns when creating a batch file and this chapter discusses them.

Use the CMD Switches

The command interpreter, CMD.EXE, is the most important part of the command line because it affects everything you do at the command line. A small change in the command interpreter can make a significant change in the way your applications run. The default command prompt setup assumes that you don't want to use any of the command line switches and that you want to start in your home directory.

Whenever you want to start a new command processor, you type CMD and press Enter. To close the command processor, type Exit and press Enter.

It's also possible to execute commands automatically when you start the command processor. If you use the CMD /C *String* command, where *String* contains one or more commands that you want to execute, the command processor performs the task specified by String and then terminates the command interpreter session. Generally, you won't get to see any application output using this technique unless the application provides graphical output or you use redirection to save the results in a file. For example, if you type CMD /C "Dir *.* > Output.txt" and press Enter, the system opens a new command processor, executes the Dir command, and places the output in Output.txt. Verify that the command created Output.txt by typing Dir Output.txt and pressing Enter. To see the result, type **Notepad Output.txt** and press Enter. You'll see the result of the Dir*.* command as part of the content of Output.txt in Notepad.

Old Versus New Command Line

Some batch files really are quite old and amazingly, they still work in many cases. However, it's dangerous to assume that a batch file will continue to run no matter how old it is. If you used the Disk Operating System (DOS) at some point, it's important to remember that the command line switches that Windows supplies for the CMD.EXE command interpreter in no way match what you used in the past. Microsoft does make some command line switches available for compatibility purposes. For example, the /X command line switch is the same as /E:ON, /Y is the same as /E:OFF, and /R is the same as /C. The command interpreter ignores all other old switches; you need to use the command line switches described in this chapter instead.

You might also remember a few convenience features from the days of DOS that no longer appear as part of Windows. For example, at one time you could create a setup menu by using the [MENU] entry in Config.SYS. The Config.NT file doesn't support this setup. The only alternative is to create multiple Config.NT files and assign them to applications as needed. In short, even though the command interpreter does many of the same things that the DOS version does, this command interpreter is different and you need to proceed with caution about any assumptions you want to make.

Using the CMD /K *String* command performs the command specified by String. The command window remains after execution ends so that you can see the application results. For example, if you type **CMD /K "Dir *.*"** and press Enter, you see the results of the Dir command on screen. To exit the new command processor session, you must type **Exit** and press Enter.

NOTE When using either the /C or /K command line switches, you can specify multiple commands by creating a single string that contains all of the commands. Separate each command using a double ampersand (&&). You must enclose the entire string in double quotes. For example, "Dir *.DOC&&Dir *.TXT" would perform two Dir commands. The first would search for any file with a .DOC extension, while the second would search for any file with a .TXT extension.

There are many reasons to start a new command processor—most of which revolve around creating a special environment. For example, you might normally run batch files with echo on so that you can see the commands as they execute. However, one command might not work well with echo. In this case, you start a new command processor with the /Q command line switch, which turns off echo, so that the single command can execute properly.

Another reason to start a separate command processor is to enable command extensions using the /E:On command line switch. The command extensions provide added functionality for these commands: Assoc, Call, ChDir (CD), Color, Del (Erase), EndLocal, For, FType, GoTo, If, MkDir (MD), PopD, Prompt, PushD, Set, SetLocal, Shift, and Start (also includes changes to external command processes). The "Use Command Extensions" section of the chapter tells you how the command extensions affect these commands.

Use the /F:On command line switch to enable file and directory name completion characters. File and directory completion allow speed typing at the command line. For example, if you want to type **Dir Temp**, using directory or file completion, you could type **Dir T**, and then press Ctrl+D (for a directory) or Ctrl+F (for a directory or file). The command interpreter automatically completes the directory or filename for you. If you type in a partition string that doesn't match any entries, the command interpreter beeps to signify that the entry is incorrect. When the command interpreter sees multiple entries that could match the entry you provide, it displays the first entry in the list. You cycle through the entries by pressing Ctrl+D or Ctrl+F again. Use the Shift+Ctrl+D and Shift+Ctrl+F control key combinations to move backward through the list of choices. You can change the control characters that this feature uses by changing the associated registry entry. You must enclose any file or directory names that begin with special characters in quotes. These characters include <space> & ( ) [ ] { } ^ = ; ! ' + , ` ~.

In some cases, you even start another command processor for the sake of the user interface. Use the /T:FG command line switch to set the foreground (F) and background (G) colors. You must place the values together, without any space between. The following list tells you which colors you can use at the command prompt, along with their associated hexadecimal color number:

- 0: Black
- 1: Blue

- **2:** Green
- **3:** Aqua
- **4:** Red
- **5:** Purple
- **6:** Yellow
- **7:** White
- **8:** Gray
- **9:** Light blue
- **A:** Light green
- **B:** Light aqua
- **C:** Light red
- **D:** Light purple
- **E:** Light yellow
- **F:** Bright white

Configure the Command Interpreter in the Registry

Many of the command line behaviors depend on registry settings. The following steps help you configure the registry to use the command interpreter with greater efficiency:

1. Type `RegEdit` and press Enter. You see the Registry Editor.

2. Locate the settings found in the `HKEY_CURRENT_USER\Software\Microsoft\Command Processor` key for the local user or the `HKEY_LOCAL_MACHINE\SOFTWARE\Microsoft\Command Processor` for everyone using the same machine. Figure 19.1 shows the `HKEY_LOCAL_MACHINE` setting.

   The command interpreter looks for these registry settings when you don't provide an appropriate command line switch. If you don't see the registry entry, then the command interpreter uses a default setting. Local user settings always override the machine settings, and command line switches always override the registry settings. Here are the registry settings and their meanings.

Creating Batch Files

PART VII

Figure 19.1: The command interpreter receives many settings from the registry.

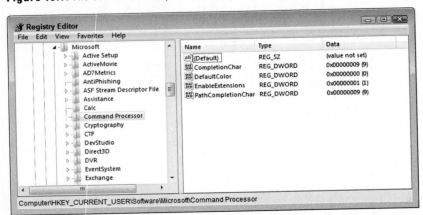

NOTE If the Command Processor key lacks the appropriate value, right-click the key and choose one of the value entries from the New menu. The Registry Editor will create a new value of the specified type for you. Type the value name and press Enter. Double-click the new value and type the value data in the editor dialog box. Click OK to complete the action.

---

3. (Optional) Double-click the AutoRun value and type the command you want to run automatically each time the command processor runs. Click OK to complete the entry.

    AutoRun defines the command that you want the command interpreter to run every time you open a command prompt. This value is of type REG_SZ or REG_EXPAND_SZ. Simply provide the executable name along with any command line switches that the executable may require. As with the string for the /C and /K command line switches, you can separate multiple commands using a double ampersand (&&).

4. (Optional) Double-click the EnableExtensions value and type a value of 1 to enable extensions or 0 to disable extensions. Click OK to complete the entry.

    EnableExtensions specifies whether the command interpreter has extensions enabled. See the /E:ON command line switch description for a list of the applications that this entry affects. This value is of type REG_DWORD.

5. (Optional) Double-click the CompletionChar value and type a hexa-decimal value for the completion character. Click OK to complete the entry.

    CompletionChar defines the file completion character (see the /F:ON command line switch for details). The default character is Ctrl+F (0x06). Use a value of a space (0x20) to disable this feature since the space isn't a valid control character. This value is of type REG_DWORD.

6. (Optional) Double-click the PathCompletionChar value and type a hexadecimal value for the path completion character. Click OK to complete the entry.

    PathCompletionChar defines the directory completion character (see the /F:ON command line switch for details). The default char-acter is Ctrl+D (0x04). Use a value of a space (0x20) to disable this feature since the space isn't a valid control character. This value is of type REG_DWORD.

7. (Optional) Double-click the DelayedExpansion value and type **1** to enable delayed expansion or **0** to disable delayed expansion. Click OK to complete the entry.

    DelayedExpansion specifies whether the command interpreter uses delayed variable expansion. See the /V:ON command line switch de-scription for additional information. This value is of type REG_DWORD.

8. Close the Registry Editor.

9. Close any open copies of the command interpreter and open a new command interpreter to see the results of changes that you've made.

Use Command Extensions

Command extensions (see the "Use the CMD Switches" section of the chapter for a list of command line switches to use to enable features such as command extensions) are additional processing that the com-mand interpreter provides for certain commands. The effects vary by command, but generally the commands receive additional functionality. In some cases, such as the del (erase) command, the extensions simply change the way the command works. The following list describes the command extension changes to each of the affected commands:

- **Assoc:** Microsoft hasn't documented how command extensions change the Assoc command. Even though Microsoft lists it as one of the commands that changes with command extensions, there isn't any obvious difference at the command line.

- **Call:** Accepts a label as the target for a call (rather than a filename as normal). This feature means that you can transfer control from one portion of a batch file to another. Using extensions means that you can call the label using call :Label Arguments. Notice that you must precede the label with a colon.

- **Chdir (CD):** Displays the directory names precisely as they appear on your hard drive. For example, if a directory name has a space, you'll see the space when you change directories. Capitalization is also the same. A directory name that appears with an initial capital letter in Windows Explorer also appears that way at the command prompt. In addition, when you turn off the command extensions, the command doesn't treat spaces as delimiters. Consequently, you don't need to surround directory names with spaces or with quotes in order to obtain the correct results from this command.

- **Color:** Microsoft hasn't documented how command extensions change the Color command. Even though Microsoft lists it as one of the commands that changes with command extensions, there isn't any obvious difference at the command line.

- **Del (Erase):** Changes the way the /S command line switch works. The command shows you just the files that it deletes, rather than showing you all of the files, including those that it couldn't find.

- **EndLocal:** Restores the command extension settings to their state before calling the SetLocal command. Normally, the SetLocal command doesn't save the state of the command extensions.

- **For:** Implements an expanded number of For command options. When working with directories, you process directories, rather than a list of files within a directory, using this call: for /D {%% | %}Variable in (Set) do Command [CommandLineOptions]. You can also perform recursive processing of a directory tree. Using this feature means that a single command can process an entire tree, rather than using individual commands to process a branch. Use the `for /R [[Drive:]Path] {%% | %}Variable in (Set) do Command [CommandLineOptions]` command line syntax to perform recursion. It's also possible to iterate through a range of values, similar to the functionality of the `For` loop used in higher level languages, using this command syntax: `for /L {%% | %}Variable in (Start#,Step#,End#) do Command [CommandLineOptions]`. Variable substitution is another useful feature that using command extensions provide. Finally, you can perform complex file parsing and iteration with the command extension in place.

- **FType:** Microsoft hasn't documented how command extensions change the FType command. Even though Microsoft lists it as one of the commands that changes with command extensions, there isn't any obvious difference at the command line.

- **Goto:** Defines a special label called `:EOF`. If you define a `Goto` command in a batch file with the `:EOF` label, the system transfers control to the end of the current batch file and exits. You don't need to define the label in the batch file to make this feature work.

- **If:** Defines additional comparison syntax that makes the `If` command considerably more flexible. See the "Employ the If Command" section of Chapter 21 for details.

- **MkDir (MD):** Lets you create intermediate directories with a single command. For example, you could define an entire subdirectory structure using `MD MyDir/MySub1/MySub2`. If `MyDir` doesn't exist, the system creates it first, then `MySub1`, and, finally, `MySub2`. Normally, you'd need to create each directory separately and use the CD command to move to each lower level to create the next subdirectory.

- **PopD:** Removes any drive letter assignment made by the `PushD` command.

- **Prompt:** Supports additional prompt characters. The `$+` character adds one or more plus signs (+) to the command prompt for every level of the `PushD` command. Using this feature lets you know how many levels of redirection the `PushD` command has saved on the stack and how many more times you can use the `PopD` command to extract them. The `$m` character adds the remote name associated with a drive to the command prompt. The command prompt doesn't display any additional information for local drives.

- **PushD:** Allows you to push network paths onto the stack as well as local drive letters and path information.

- **Set:** Displays all currently defined environment variables when you use the Set command alone. Displays the specified environment variable when you supply an environment variable name, but not an associated value. If you supply only a partial variable name, the Set command displays all of the variables that could match that name.

- **SetLocal:** Allows the SetLocal command to enable or disable command extensions as needed to meet specific language requirements.

- **Shift:** Supports the /N command line option, which lets the Shift command shift variables starting with the *n*th variable. For example, if you use Shift /2 at the command line, then variables %0 and %1 are unaffected by the shift, but variables %3 through %9 receive new variable input.

- **Start:** Microsoft hasn't documented how command extensions change the Start command. Even though Microsoft lists it as one of the commands that changes with command extensions, there isn't any obvious difference at the command line.

Modify *Config.NT*

The Config.NT file contains a number of entries that affect how the system works at the command prompt. At one time, the configuration file contained a wealth of device drivers and statements that defined how the command prompt used files and buffers. However, the Config.NT file rarely contains device drivers and these driver entries are normally defined by third-party software for you. Even so, Config.NT still contains settings that modify how the command interpreter works and therefore has an effect over your session. The following sections describe common additions you can make to the Config.NT file.

Config.NT and *AutoExec.NT* **Considerations**

Some people may remember Config.SYS, the file that DOS uses to perform the same configuration that Windows performs with Config.NT. In fact, some people try to move Config.SYS to the Windows environment. Fortunately, the 32-bit version of Windows accepts many older DOS commands even when it doesn't use them. For example, the FastOpen utility provides a caching feature in DOS to make directory searches faster. Even though Windows provides this file too, it doesn't actually use the functionality and FastOpen doesn't actually perform any task. Once you move to the 64-bit versions of Windows, much of this functionality is missing completely. For example, you can't create a Config.NT file that contains a reference to the FastOpen utility.

More than a few people are complaining that Windows 7 lacks the Config.NT and AutoExec.NT files. Microsoft has been moving away from supporting these two files and you may find that they're completely missing in your copy of Windows. The main reason for this change is to improve Windows security by eliminating the need to write files to the %WinDir%\System32 directory. However, you can add the files for any application that needs them to your %WinDir%\System32 directory. Some applications will display a dialog box saying the two files are missing, while others will simply fail to start (see the vendor documentation for clues as to whether the missing files are the source of your problem). Windows 7 may not actually process the commands in these files, but the commands will be there for applications that require them. If your application absolutely requires full Config.NT and AutoExec.NT file support, try using Windows XP Mode (download the required support from http://www.microsoft.com/windows/virtual-pc/download.aspx and learn more about Windows XP Mode at http://www.microsoft.com/windows/virtual-pc/).

One version of Windows that requires special handling when it comes to Config.NT is Windows Server 2008 Server Core. Given that Server Core lacks the functionality required for an application server (which means providing complex server-based applications such as a database-based application), you may never see a driver entry in Config.NT. However, because ANSI.SYS affects the command line directly, it's one of the few device driver entries that you could see when working with Server Core.

Use *ANSI.SYS* to Control the Environment

The ANSI.SYS device driver provides added functionality for applications at the command prompt. By using special escape codes, you can create a character-based user interface for your batch files. You can find a good listing of ANSI escape codes at http://www.evergreen.edu/biophysics/technotes/program/ansi_esc.htm and on the Microsoft Web site at http://www.microsoft.com/technet/archive/msdos/comm1.mspx?mfr=true. To add ANSI.SYS to Config.NT, use the Device=*Path*/ANSI.SYS command, where *Path* is the full path to ANSI.SYS on the host system.

If you're working with systems for those with special needs, use the /R command line switch to change the line scrolling functionality to improve readability when working with screen reader programs. A screen reader program interprets the screen content and presents it using some other form of output. Normally, screen reader applications say what's on screen to help those with special sight needs understand the content.

Set the Command Interpreter Location

Some command line applications require a large amount of what is termed as conventional memory—the memory below the 640 KB boundary that you see when you type **Mem** and press Enter (the Mem utility isn't available on 64-bit systems). This setting affects only 32-bit systems and normally you don't need it when working with modern systems and newer applications. None of the utilities discussed in this book require this setting. Check the conventional memory requirements for your utility before you change this setting.

To load part of the command processor into the High Memory Area (HMA) use the DOS=HIGH command. The HMA is a memory area between the 640 KB boundary and the 1 MB limit normally used by the command line. The default setting is DOS=LOW (which means that the command processor loads entirely in the 640 KB area). Generally, you want to load the command environment into high memory to preserve more conventional memory for applications.

Use the DOS=HIGH, UMB or DOS=LOW, UMB command to tell the command environment that it should manage the Upper Memory Blocks (UMBs) created by a UMB provider. Windows provides a UMB provider as a default. DOS users used to rely on a special program named EMM386.EXE to perform this task. The UMB argument tells the command environment to manage the UMBs, which frees additional memory for loading applications in areas other than conventional memory. The default setting is DOS=LOW, NOUMB.

Run Character Mode Applications Only

You can execute any kind of application you want from the command prompt. If you want to start Notepad, simply type **Notepad** and press Enter. However, mixing Windows and older DOS applications can sometimes cause problems. Developers wrote DOS applications with the expectation that these applications controlled the entire machine, which can cause myriad problems with Windows applications. If you have one of these older applications (and they're quite rare), you can help the DOS application execute properly by adding the NTCMDPROMPT entry to Config.NT. This entry tells the operating system to disallow Windows application execution at the command prompt, which means that the DOS application continues to feel that it owns the machine. Of course, you can start your Windows applications from another command prompt or by using any of the usual techniques, such as the Start menu.

Display the *Config.NT* Commands

Normally, you won't see any information about the commands that execute before the command window opens; all you see is a command prompt. Adding an ECHOCONFIG to the Config.NT file displays each of the commands as they execute. Using this feature can help you diagnose problems with the Config.NT file contents.

Control the Expanded Memory EMM Entry

Older applications, especially character mode (DOS) games, rely on the Expanded Memory Specification (EMS) memory to overcome command prompt memory limitations. It's important to remember that the command line effectively limits the amount of memory available to DOS applications to 640 KB minus any memory that the operating system uses. Normally, you set the amount of this memory as part of the application's Program Information File (PIF). However, the PIF doesn't let you control the Expanded Memory Manager (EMM), which is the application that actually makes the memory accessible. The EMM entry lets you change how the EMM works. The following steps help you configure EMM support:

1. Type EMM= to start the EMM entry.

2. (Optional) Type A=*AltRegSets*, where *AltRegSets* is a number between 1 and 255, to define how many alternative mapping

register sets the EMM has available for mapping memory between extended memory and conventional memory.

The default setting of 8 works fine in most cases. Check your application documentation for additional requirements.

3. (Optional) Type B=*BaseSegment*, where *BaseSegment* is a hexadecimal address that defines the base segment, the location where the EMM places code within the DOS conventional memory area from extended memory as needed.

   Generally, any setting you choose works fine. However, some applications use specific segments for their use. Using the same memory segment for two purposes causes memory corruption and can cause the application to fail. The application documentation should tell you about any requirements. You can set the base segment to any hexadecimal value between 0x1000 and 0x4000. The default setting is 0x4000.

4. (Optional) Type RAM to specify that the EMM should only use 64 KB of address space from the UMB area for the EMM page.

   Normally, the EMM uses the entire UMB for the EMM page to improve EMM performance. However, your application may require more conventional memory than this practice allows. Using the RAM option reduces the EMM page size, which makes it easier for the command environment to load more applications in upper memory—freeing conventional memory for application use.

Set the Number of Accessible Files

The Files setting may not seem very important, but every file handle you provide to the command environment uses conventional memory. Remember that conventional memory is already quite small and many older applications barely load in the space provided. The default Files=40 setting usually provides a good compromise. This setting means that the command environment can open 40 files, which is more than sufficient for most older applications. You can increase the number to as many as 255 when your application complains that it's out of file handles or decrease the number to as little as 8 when the application complains about a lack of memory.

Control Extended Memory with *HIMEM.SYS*

The HIMEM.SYS driver provides extended memory support at the command prompt. (You won't find this driver supplied with 64-bit versions of Windows and the old driver won't work in these newer operating systems.) The eXtended Memory Specification (XMS) is a method that applications use to overcome the DOS memory limitations. You set the amount of available XMS using the PIF for the application. However, you can further refine XMS functionality by using the following procedure:

1. Type **device=***Path***/HIMEM.SYS**, where *Path* is the location of HIMEM. SYS on the host system.

2. (Optional) Type **/HMAMIN=***m*, where *m* specifies how many KB of HMA memory an application must request in order for HIMEM.SYS to fulfill the request.

    Some applications ask for small pieces of the HMA, which fragments an already small memory area and makes it unavailable for other applications. It becomes a question of efficient memory use. An application that can use a larger piece of the HMA will likely free more conventional memory for use by other applications. You can specify any value between 0 and 63. The default value is 0. Setting this command line switch to 0 or omitting it from the command line lets HIMEM.SYS allocate the HMA memory to the first application that requests it, regardless of how much HMA memory that application will use.

3. (Optional) Type **/INT15=***xxxx*, where *xxxx* specifies the amount of extended memory in kilobytes that HIMEM.SYS should reserve for the Interrupt 15h interface.

    You may wonder what the Interrupt 15h interface is all about; it's the method that applications use to interact with XMS. The only time you need to use this command line switch is if you have an older DOS application, very likely a game or graphics application, which relies on XMS memory. The application will very likely display a nebulous error message that specifically mentions the Interrupt 15h interface. Make sure you set the amount of XMS memory to 64 KB larger than the amount required by the application. You can specify any value from 64 KB to 65,535 KB. However, you can't specify more memory than your system has installed.

Creating Batch Files

PART VII

When you specify a value less than 64, HIMEM.SYS sets the value to 0. The default value is 0.

4. (Optional) Type **/NUMHANDLES=**_n_, where _n_ specifies the maximum number of Extended Memory Block (EMB) handles that the system can use simultaneously.

   Every time an application requests more memory, it needs a handle to access that memory. Generally, you don't need to provide this command line switch unless you have an older graphics-intensive application. You can specify a value from 1 to 128. The default setting is 32, which is more than enough for most applications. Changing the number of handles uses more memory for housekeeping chores, so you'll want to use this command line switch with care.

5. (Optional) Type **/TESTMEM:ON** to perform a memory check when you open the command prompt.

   Most people don't actually know whether the memory they're using is good, so checking it from time to time is a way to reduce unwelcome surprises. However, running the test takes time. You'll see a noticeable delay in displaying the command prompt when you use this command line switch. In most cases, it's far better to test your memory using a third-party diagnostic program that works outside of Windows's influence. Otherwise, you can't be sure that you're testing all of the memory and won't know which surprises Windows has hidden from view. The HIMEM.SYS test is more thorough than the test that runs when you start your computer, so you can use it when you don't have any other means of testing available.

6. Type **/VERBOSE** to display additional status and error messages while HIMEM.SYS is loading.

   The system normally doesn't display any messages unless it encounters a problem loading or initializing HIMEM.SYS. Adding this command line switch can point out potential problems in your system setup and aid in diagnosing application problems that you wouldn't normally detect. You can abbreviate this command line switch as /V. Unfortunately, despite the documentation for HIMEM.

SYS online, you can't display the verbose messages by pressing the Alt key as the system loads HIMEM.SYS into memory; you must use the /VERBOSE command line switch to see the extended messages.

Modify *AutoExec.NT*

Although Config.NT offers some interesting low-level methods of changing the command line environment, the AutoExec.NT file provides far more opportunities. Any application that you can access from the command line is also a candidate for inclusion in the AutoExec.NT file. Adding applications that you always use can set up the command line from the outset, so you see what you need without entering any commands at all. You can also program the AutoExec.NT file as you would any other batch file.

The sections that follow describe some utilities that you'll use most often from within the AutoExec.NT file. These utilities tend to configure the command environment, in some way, to make your computing experience better. However, don't limit yourself to these selections—any command or utility described in the book is a candidate for inclusion.

Set the Code Page Number with the *CHCP* Utility

A code page defines language support at the command prompt. In the days of DOS, you needed to provide a code page to obtain proper language support at the command prompt, but Windows doesn't usually require you to set a code page. You might need to set a code page for older character-mode applications. Only the OEM font you installed as part of Windows displays properly when you use a raster font in a windowed command prompt. However, you can use any of the supported code pages in full screen mode or with a TrueType font. To add code page support, use the CHCP *nnn* command, where *nnn* defines the code page to use. The standard code page numbers appear in Table 19.1. Code pages 874 through 1258 are both OEM and ANSI implementations that are only available in Windows. You can install additional code pages as needed. The Web site at http://www.i18nguy .com/unicode/codepages.html#msftdos shows how these code pages appear.

Table 19.1: Standard OEM and OEM/ANSI Code Pages

Code Page	Country or Language
437	United States
850	Multilingual (Latin I)
852	Slavic (Latin II)
855	Cyrillic (Russian)
857	Turkish
860	Portuguese
861	Icelandic
863	Canadian-French
865	Nordic
866	Russian
869	Modern Greek
874	Thai
932	Japanese Shift-JIS
936	Simplified Chinese GBK
949	Korean
950	Traditional Chinese Big5
1258	Vietnam

Add DPMI Support Using the *DosX* Utility

The DOS Protected Mode Interface (DPMI) is one method for a DOS application to access more than the 640 KB that DOS (the command line) typically allows. In addition, this interface provides protected memory access, so the DOS application doesn't interfere with Windows operation. You can read about DPMI at http://whatis.techtarget.com/

definition/0,,sid9_gci213913,00.html. To use this interface, an application developer needs to provide special support in the application; usually as part of a third-party add-on library. All you need to know is whether the application (typically a game) supports DPMI to use this feature. To include DPMI support, add the DOSX command to AutoExec.NT.

Enable Graphics Character Support with the *GrafTabl* Utility

Normally, the system displays any extended characters your application needs to display as plain text. In some cases, this means the extended characters won't display correctly because your system may lack the capability required to display the extended characters properly. The GrafTabl utility helps Windows display extended characters as graphics, which means they always display correctly as long as you have the proper code page support loaded. The GrafTabl utility only affects extended character display; you need to use the Mode or CHCP utilities to change the console input. To include this support, add the GrafTabl *xxxx* command, where *xxxx* is a code page number (see Table 19.1 for examples), to AutoExec.NT. To see the current GrafTabl status, type **GrafTabl /Status** and press Enter.

Save Memory Using the *LH* Command

The Load High (LH) command attempts to load a utility into high memory, instead of using application memory. Loading the utility high saves memory that memory-hungry applications can use to load. Generally, you should try to load high all of the utilities that you can, including DosX and ReDir. Windows 64-bit editions don't support this command. To load a command high, type **LH *Command***, where *Command* is the command you want to load. For example, if you want to load DosX high, you add LH DosX to AutoExec.NT.

Install the Network Redirector Using the *ReDir* Utility

Use this utility to load the VDM Virtual Device Driver (VDD) redirector. The redirector provides virtual device access from the command prompt. Essentially, it provides network access. To use this command, add the ReDir command to AutoExec.NT.

20

Working at the Command Prompt

Creating Batch Files

PART VII

Chapter 19 discusses ways in which you can make the command line more useful from outside the command line—through the registry, Config.NT, AutoExec.NT, or other means. You can also type commands at the command line to improve your efficiency at certain tasks, which is the topic of this chapter. For example, the simple act of giving your command line a useful title can make it easier to select the correct command line from a number of command line entries on the taskbar. Changing the screen colors can make text easier to see. You can also redirect the clipboard to make it more useful. The following sections describe these, and other, techniques you can use to make working at the command line easier.

Redirect Command Line Output to the Clipboard

Anyone who's used redirection knows the benefits of sending output data to another location, such as a file, or getting input from another location, such as the COM port. The Clip utility lets you perform redirection using the Windows Clipboard. You use redirection or the pipe command as you normally do. For example, the Dir | Clip command sends the output for the directory command to the clipboard. Fortunately, you don't have to do anything special to use this command—simply type **Clip** as part of a pipe.

You don't need to supply any command line switches when using this command. It works much like the More command. For example, if you want to place the output of the Dir command on the clipboard, you would type **Dir | Clip** and press Enter. At this point, you can type **Notepad** and press Enter to start the Notepad utility. Select Edit ➤ Paste and you'll see the output of the Dir command in Notepad, where you can edit the information to suit your needs.

It's also possible to use Clip with redirection. For example, you might want to place the content of a file on the clipboard. Let's say the name of the file is MyDir.TXT. In this case, you type **Clip < MyDir.TXT** and press Enter. The content of MyDir.TXT will appear on the clipboard where you can paste it into a Windows application.

Manage Usernames and Passwords

The CmdKey utility helps you manage username and passwords. Using this utility, you can display, create, and delete credentials as needed. However, this utility only works with the current user. In other words, the credentials you manage are for the current user, not for another user on the same system. To work with other users, you must first log on as that user. Consequently, this command works well with logon batch files that perform tasks on the user's behalf, but not necessarily as a good tool for administering users at the command line.

A system can have two kinds of passwords managed by CmdKey. The first is generic passwords that you can use anywhere. For example, you might create a username and password to access a remote system using a Virtual Private Network (VPN). The second is domain passwords that you use to access a domain server. These password types appear in the Type field output when you list credentials for your system. The following sections describe tasks you can perform using the CmdKey utility.

Display Usernames

The /List command line switch lets you list all of the credentials associated with the current account. To display all of the credentials for the current user, type **CmdKey /List** and press Enter. Figure 20.1 shows typical output from this command (the output on your system will reflect your credentials).

Figure 20.1: The /List command line switch shows the credentials stored for the current user.

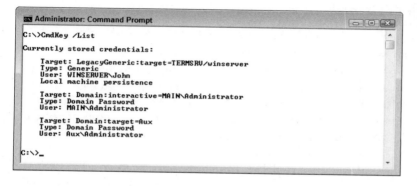

```
C:\>CmdKey /List

Currently stored credentials:

    Target: LegacyGeneric:target=TERMSRV/winserver
    Type: Generic
    User: WINSERVER\John
    Local machine persistence

    Target: Domain:interactive=MAIN\Administrator
    Type: Domain Password
    User: MAIN\Administrator

    Target: Domain:target=Aux
    Type: Domain Password
    User: Aux\Administrator

C:\>_
```

If you prefer to see the credentials for a specific target, use the CmdKey / List:*TargetName* command, where *TargetName* is the name of a specific target (such as a client machine or server). Using Figure 20.1 as a source, if you wanted to see the credentials for Aux, you'd type **CmdKey /List:Aux** and press Enter.

Create Users

The CmdKey utility automatically adds credentials as you supply them when accessing another system. However, you might want to add a credential before you need to use it. In this case, you use the CmdKey / Add:*TargetName* /User:*Username* /Pass:*Password* command, where *TargetName* is the name of the system you want to access, *Username* is the account you want to use on the remote system, and *Password* is the password for that system. The /Pass command line switch is optional, but if you don't supply it, Windows will still need to ask for the password before you can access the remote system. For example, if you want to add a machine named MyServer for an account named Stan with a password of MyPassword, you type **CmdKey /Add:MyServer /Username:Stan / Pass:MyPassword** and press Enter.

CmdKey also supports smartcards. In this case, you use the CmdKey / Add:*TargetName* /Smartcard command. The CmdKey utility will obtain the required credentials from the smartcard and store them for you.

If you want to create generic credentials instead of domain credentials, you use the /Generic command line switch in place of the /Add command line switch. The technique is precisely the same and you can still use a smartcard to add the credentials if desired.

Delete Users

At some point, you might have credentials that you really don't need on your system. Removing unneeded credentials helps keep things fast because Windows doesn't have to search through unneeded credentials each time another system asks for verification, which happens far more often than you might think. In addition, removing these credentials closes a potential security hole because unused accounts are often used by outsiders to gain access to your network. Use the CmdKey / Delete:*TargetName* command, where *TargetName* is the machine name of the credential you want to delete, to remove old credentials. For example, if you previously created a credential for a system named Aux, you'd type **CmdKey /Delete:Aux** to remove the credential.

Credentials for Remote Access Server (RAS) require special handling. In this case, you type `CmdKey /Delete /RAS` and press Enter to delete the credential.

Change Screen Colors

Color is an important issue for most people. It's not necessarily a touchy-feely issue (although that's part of it), but a matter of being able to see content (legibility and accessibility). The light gray on black combination that the command line sports by default doesn't necessarily work for many people, especially if you have trouble seeing darker color combinations, so a change in color can make you a lot more efficient. The `Color` command changes the foreground (text) and background colors of the command window.

To change the command line color, use the `Color` *FG* command, where *F* is the foreground color and *G* is the background color. You must place the values together, without any space between. For example, to change the foreground color to black and the background color to white, you type `Color 0F` and press Enter. If you use the `Color` command without specifying color values, the command changes the colors to the default values used when you opened the command window. The following list tells you which colors you can use at the command prompt, along with their associated color number:

- **0:** Black
- **1:** Blue
- **2:** Green
- **3:** Aqua
- **4:** Red
- **5:** Purple
- **6:** Yellow
- **7:** White
- **8:** Gray
- **9:** Light blue
- **A:** Light green
- **B:** Light aqua

- C: Light red
- D: Light purple
- E: Light yellow
- F: Bright white

Configure the System Date

The Date command displays or sets the system date. To see the current date, type **Date /T** and press Enter. You can use redirection to place the date in a file and then use the file within scripts and batch files as needed. Using the /T command line switch lets you obtain the date without Windows prompting you for a new date.

NOTE   The output of the Time and Date commands appears unaffected by the settings you use to display time and date within Windows. Consequently, you always see the date in a MM/DD/YYYY format and the time in a 12-hour HH:MM AM/PM format.

Normally, you don't need to set the system date at the command line because the system date automatically reflects the hardware clock of the host system. However, there are rare situations when you're working with a command that requires a date change or the date is incorrect during a repair. During these times, you can manually set the date so that it's correct. To set the date, use the Date *NewDate* command, where *NewDate* is the new date in MM/DD/YYYY format. For example, to set the current date to 7 June 2010, type **Date 06/07/2010** and press Enter.

Configure the System Time

The Time command displays or sets the system time. To see the current time, type **Time /T** and press Enter. You can use redirection to place the time in a file and then use the file within scripts and batch files as needed. Using the /T command line switch lets you obtain the time without Windows prompting you for a new time.

Normally, you don't need to set the system time at the command line because the system time automatically reflects the hardware clock of the host system. However, there are rare situations when you're working with a command that requires a time change or the time is incorrect during a repair. Time is especially critical when working with security because Kerberos has strict time constraints for the difference in time between client and server systems. During these times, you can manually set the time so that it's correct. To set the time, use the Time *NewTime* command, where *NewTime* is the new time in HH:MM:SS.SS AM/PM format. Setting the seconds and partial seconds is optional. For example, to set the current time to 12:01 p.m., type **Time 12:01 PM** and press Enter.

NOTE You can use 24-hour time when setting the time. For example, Time 2:00 PM and Time 14:00 are both the same command.

Change the Command Window Title

The Title command makes it easy to change the title of any command prompt window you create. The title that a command window displays might not seem important at first, but it can be important for two reasons:

1. If you have multiple command windows open, using a descriptive title can make it easier to locate the correct command window on the Windows taskbar.

2. It's important to remember that Windows associates settings changes you make with the command window title.

Changing the title affects how Windows stores the settings changes you make. The Title command can change the title of a command window. To change the title, use the Title *"New Title"* command, where *New Title* is a string that describes the new window. For example, to change the title to My Command Window, you type **Title "My Command Window"** and press Enter. Notice that you must enclose the title in double quotes.

NOTE You may find that you can type `Title My Command Window` and press Enter to change the command prompt title on your machine. Newer versions of the `Title` command are smart enough to know that all of the words following the command are part of the new title. However, typing the command without double quotes can lead to problematic habits when working with other commands and utilities. Even though some commands will work on some systems without the double quotes, it's always best to use the double quotes when you have content with spaces in it to ensure the command interpreter knows that the content should be treated as a single entity, rather than multiple entities. Otherwise, you could end up damaging your system when the command or utility treats your unquoted entries as individual elements.

21

Creating and Testing Batch Files

IN THIS CHAPTER, YOU WILL LEARN TO:

B atch files have been around since the days of DOS. They're reliable, easy to write, exceptionally easy to understand for the most part, and there's a large base of batch file code you can download from the Internet. For these reasons, and many more, you really need to know how to write batch files—at least, simple batch files. Automating tasks using batch files makes you far more efficient and frees time that you need to perform tasks that you really must perform manually. This chapter can't provide you with every piece of information about writing batch files. In fact, you can easily find a dozen books whose whole purpose is to tell you how to write batch files. The purpose of this chapter is to introduce you to the batch file commands and demonstrate some simple tasks you can perform using them.

Use Batch File Commands

Batch files are a type of simple programming that can help you store a series of commands that you want to execute more than once. The batch file normally appears within a file with a .BAT extension. In most cases, you won't need to perform any programming to create a batch file; simply create a file that contains the commands you want to execute one after the other.

NOTE Windows doesn't support the Break command found in many older batch files. The original purpose of the Break command was to provide control over the Ctrl+Break key. Setting Break ON would let someone press Ctrl+Break to stop execution of a batch file. Windows ignores this command line switch. In addition, some versions of Windows, such as Windows Server 2008 Server Core, change support for some batch commands from previous versions of Windows and add new commands. Consequently, batch files that worked fine in Windows XP may suddenly stop working in Server Core. (If you've already updated your batch files to work in Vista (or newer versions of Windows), they should also work fine in Server Core.)

Even with the limitations of a batch file, however, you might be surprised at the number of ways that people use them. For example, if you find that you're constantly forgetting how to perform tasks at the command line, create a menu system with your favorite commands. That way, you only have to look up the command information one time. The following sections describe the programming features of batch files and provide you with some sample batch files.

Finding Code Online

It's beneficial to become a code hound—someone who digs around online and in books looking for useful pieces of code. If you can find working code that does almost what you want to do, all you need to do is make some modifications to that code, rather than start writing it from scratch. Creating code from scratch is often harder than using code that's already tested and used for some other task.

This chapter contains batch file examples that help you understand basic principles and perform some essential tasks at the command line. However, if you're like me, you'll want more; you'll want examples that show you how to perform more tasks than I could ever include in a single book. You can find a wealth of batch files for performing administrative or other essential tasks at the Rob van der Woude Web site at http:// www.robvanderwoude.com/batchfiles.php. In fact, you can find an entire page of batch file resources at http://www.windows-networking.com/kbase/WindowsTips/WindowsNT/AdminTips/Miscellaneous/Batchfileprogrammingresources.html.

Employ the *Call* Command

You use the Call command to call another location within the current batch file or to start another batch file. When you want to call another location in the same batch file, you use the label formatting shown here:

```
Call :MyLabel
```

Calling another batch file is similar. You provide the drive, path, and filename of the batch file. In addition, you can provide command line arguments for the external batch file as shown here:

```
Call C:\MyBatchFiles\MyBatch.BAT CommandArg1
```

A call is different from going to another location. When a call completes, the batch file returns to the calling location and executes the next instruction. In contrast, when you use the GoTo command, the batch file actually transfers control to the new location. The return feature of the

Creating Batch Files

PART VII

Call command lets you create an advanced programming construct called recursion. Recursion occurs when a batch file calls itself. You must provide an exit strategy, however, or the batch file will enter an endless loop.

The easiest way to see the effect of the Call command is to create two batch files named Batch1.BAT and Batch2.BAT. Here's the content for Batch1.BAT:

```
@ECHO OFF
Call Batch2.BAT
Call Batch2.BAT Passed %1 %PATH%
ECHO In Batch 1
GOTO :EOF
ECHO Goodbye
```

Here's the content for Batch2.BAT:

```
ECHO In Batch 2, Goodbye
IF NOT [%1]==[] ECHO String: %1
IF NOT [%2]==[] ECHO Batch 1 Input: %2
IF NOT [%3]==[] ECHO Environment Variable: %3
```

Looking at the Batch1.BAT content, the example begins by turning off echo. You'll normally add this code to your batch files so the user doesn't see a lot of confusing text that has nothing to do with the current task. Preceding the ECHO command with the @ sign tells the system not to display the ECHO command either. The first call to Batch2.BAT doesn't pass any information, so Batch2.BAT only displays the message "In Batch 2, Goodbye." The second call to Batch2.BAT passes the three kinds of information you can include with a batch file:

- A string
- A local variable (argument)
- A global variable

The code then proceeds to display "In Batch 1" and exits. The GOTO :EOF statement is special; it tells the batch file to end now. You don't have to define a label, in this case, because EOF is built into the command process. (See the "Employ the *GoTo* Command" section of this chapter for details.)

The Batch2.BAT file always echoes "In Batch 2, Goodbye." In this case the IF statements verify that the caller has passed information to the batch file. When the caller doesn't pass the required variables, then the batch file doesn't display any information for that input. The

[%1]==[] construct is one way to check for an empty input. Figure 21.1 shows the output from this application. Notice the sequence of events. The first batch file calls the second batch file. When the second batch file is finished, execution continues with the next statement in the first batch file.

Figure 21.1: Calls provide a means of performing subtasks in a batch file and then continuing with the main task.

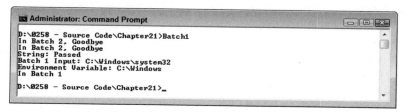

Windows provides enhanced methods of working with variables in batch files. These enhanced expansions help you pass specific variable information to a callee from your batch files. See the "Utilize Variable Substitution" section of the chapter for details on using this technique.

Employ the *Choice* Command

The Choice command lets you add interactive processing to batch files. Whether you use this option depends on the kind of automation you want to add to your processing tasks. Most of the automation you create for optimization tasks won't require any kind of interactivity because you already know how you want the task performed based on experience you obtained performing the task manually. However, sometimes you do need to add some interactivity. For example, you might run the command one way on Friday and a different way the rest of the week. The Choice command can also help you add safeguards that ensure the user understands the ramifications of performing a certain task before they actually do it. Vista and newer versions of Windows change the Choice command significantly, breaking many batch files. This newer form of the Choice command differs not in arguments, but in how you combine those arguments at the command line. Here's the command line for Vista and above:

```
CHOICE [/C choices] [/N] [/CS] [/T timeout /D choice]
[/M text]
```

The changes make the command clearer, but they break existing batch files in a way that you can't easily fix. The new /CS command line switch lets you make choices case sensitive, so you can have 26 additional menu choices (for a total of 52 letter combinations). However, notice that /T no longer takes both a default option and a timeout value. The new form requires that you provide a choice using the /D command line switch instead. You must also provide the /M command line switch to specify optional text. The following sample code performs the same task, but the first form works in Windows XP and earlier, while the second form works in Vista and newer versions of Windows:

```
Old Choice Command Form
CHOICE /C:N /N /T:N,15
Vista and Server Core Choice Command Form
CHOICE /C N /N /T 15 /D N
```

NOTE Vista and newer versions of Windows provide alternatives for the Choice command. The TimeOut utility provides a specific timeout value without requiring the user to make a choice. You can learn more about this utility in the "Employ the TimeOut Utility" section of the chapter. The WaitFor utility lets you use signaling between systems or applications on the same system. One application sends a signal and another reacts when it receives the signal.

When you use Choice by itself, it displays a simple [Y,N] prompt that doesn't accomplish much unless you also provide an Echo command to describe what the user should say yes or no to. Normally, you'll combine the Choice command with one or more arguments. Listing 21.1 shows a simple example of the Choice command at work.

Listing 21.1: Using the *Choice* Command

```
Echo Off

REM Keep repeating until the user enters E.
:Repeat

REM Display the choices.
Choice /C DCE /N /T 15 /D E /M "Choose an option (D)isplay,
(C)opy,~CA
    or (E)nd."
REM Act on the user choice.
```

```
If ErrorLevel 3 GoTo End
If ErrorLevel 2 GoTo Copy
If ErrorLevel 1 GoTo Display

REM Copy the file.
:Copy
Echo You chose to copy the file.
GoTo Repeat

REM Display the file.
:Display
Echo You chose to display the file.
GoTo Repeat

REM End the batch processing.
:End
Echo Goodbye
Echo On
```

The code begins by creating a repeat label so the batch file continues working until the user specifically stops it. Next, the code uses the Choice command to display the choices to the user. The /C switch tells Choice that the valid options are D, C, or E instead of the default Y or N. Because the text specifically defines the characters that the batch file expects, the batch file uses the /N switch to suppress displaying the valid key choices on the command line. The /T command line switch tells Choice to automatically choose E after 10 seconds. The /D command line switch provides the default choice of E. Finally, the /M command line switch provides the message displayed to the user.

Although this batch file doesn't actually do anything with a file, it shows how you'd set up the batch file to process the user choice. Notice that the batch file uses the ErrorLevel clause of the If statement to detect the user choice. The ErrorLevel clause detects every choice lower than the user selection, so you must place the values in reverse order, as shown. In addition, you must specifically set the batch file to go to another location because it will process all other statements after the current error level.

The processing code simply displays a string telling you what choice the user made. Normally, you'd add tasks that the batch file should perform based on the user's selection. Notice that the copy and display selections tell the batch file to go back to the Repeat label. This is the most common technique for creating a menu loop in a batch file. The batch file ends by telling the user goodbye and turning echo back on.

Employ the *Echo* Command

The command line uses the term *echo* to describe the process where the system echoes (repeats) every command in a batch file to the command line. Echo provides a means of seeing which command the system is processing. However, echo can become confusing for users who aren't aware of or don't care about the commands that are executing. In addition, echo can disrupt visual effects, such as menu systems, that you create. To turn echo on, type **Echo On** and press Enter. Likewise, to turn echo off, type **Echo Off** and press Enter. Type **Echo** and press Enter to display the current echo status.

You can precede the Echo command with the @ sign so it doesn't appear as one of the commands. If you type **@Echo Off** and press Enter, the command processor would turn off echo without displaying the Echo command at the command prompt.

Use the ECHO *Message* command, where *Message* is the text you want to display. Simply type the text you want to see after the Echo command. In this case, the system won't display the Echo command, just the message you want to display. For example, if you want to display Hello at the command line, you type **Echo Hello** and press Enter. Don't use the @ sign with this form of the Echo command or the user won't see the message.

Employ the *Exit* Command

Most people associate the Exit command with closing the current command window. Using Exit alone will close the command window. However, you can also use this command within a batch file to exit the batch file.

To perform a basic exit, type **Exit /B** and press enter. This command specifies that you want to exit a batch file, rather than the current command line session. If you don't specify this command line switch, the command window closes, even when you issue the Exit command from a batch file.

It's also possible to provide an exit code with your batch file. The default exit code of 0 tells the caller that the batch file didn't experience any errors, but you can provide other exit codes to denote errors. Use the Exit *ExitCode* command, where *ExitCode* is a numeric value, to provide an exit code as output. For example, if you type **Exit 5** and press

Enter, the batch file exits with an exit code of 5. You can use exit codes to alert the caller to errors or special conditions. The exit codes aren't defined by the system, so you can define any set of exit codes that you deem necessary for your application.

Employ the *ForFiles* Utility

The ForFiles utility provides a means of looping through a list of files and performing actions on those files one at a time. For example, you might want to process all files that someone has changed since a certain date. In most respects, this loop method works precisely the same as the For command described in the "Employ the *For* Command" section of the chapter. Use the following steps to create a ForFiles command:

1. Type **ForFiles** to start the command.

2. (Optional) Type **/P *Pathname***, where *Pathname* specifies the starting point for a search.

   The path is the starting folder in the search. The default setting uses the current directory as the starting point.

3. (Optional) Type **/M *SearchMask***, where *SearchMask* defines a search mask for the files.

   You can use the asterisk (*) and question mark (?) as wildcard characters, just as you would when using the Directory command. The default setting searches for all files in the target directory.

4. (Optional) Type **/S**.

   Use the /S command line switch to search all of the subdirectories of the specified directory.

5. (Optional) Type **/C *Command***, where *Command* specifies the command you want to execute for each file.

   Always wrap the command in double quotes to ensure it isn't interpreted as part of the ForFile command. The default command is "CMD /C Echo @File". Always precede internal command processor commands with CMD /C. The "Use the CMD Switches" section of Chapter 19 tells you about other CMD utility switches that might be helpful when creating your command. The following list describes the ForFiles variables that you can use as part of the command:

   - **@File:** Returns the name of the file, including the file extension.

   - **@FName:** Returns the name of the file without the extension.

- **@Ext:** Returns only the file extension.

- **@Path:** Returns the full path of the file. This information includes the drive as well as the actual path.

- **@RelPath:** Returns the relative path of the file. The relative path begins at the starting folder.

- **@IsDir:** Specifies whether the file type is a directory. True indicates a directory entry.

- **@FSize:** Indicates the size of the file in bytes.

- **@FDate:** Indicates the date that someone last modified the file.

- **@FTime:** Indicates the time that someone last modified the file.

NOTE   You can include special characters in a command by using the 0x*HH* format where *HH* is a hexadecimal number. For example, you can specify a tab by typing **0x09**.

---

6. (Optional) Type **/D *Date***, where *Date* selects files that have a last modified date within the specified range.

    You specify a specific date using the month/day/year (mm/dd/yyyy) format. Add a plus sign (+) if you want files after the specified date or a minus sign (–) if you want files before the specified date. For example, /D -01/01/2008 would select all files modified before January 1, 2008. You can also specify a relative date by providing a positive or negative number. For example, /D -7 would select all files modified within the last seven days. The /D command line switch accepts any number between 0 and –32,768.

7. Press Enter.

If you type **ForFiles** and press Enter, you see a list of the files within the current directory. You could redirect this output to a file for further processing if desired. To see just the filenames without the extensions, you'd type **ForFiles /C "CMD /C Echo @FName"** and press Enter. An extension of this command might look for just the batch files in the current directory. In this case, you type **ForFiles /M *.BAT /C "CMD /C Echo @FName"** and press Enter. You might want to look for the batch files in subdirectories too, so you'd need to type **ForFiles /S /M *.BAT /C "CMD /C Echo @FName"** and press Enter. To filter the information even more, you might look for all of the batch files in the current directory and its children that have been modified in the last seven days by typing `ForFiles /S /M *.BAT /D -7 /C "CMD /C Echo @FName"` and pressing Enter. Of course, you can make the command for working with the file as complex as desired or even call on another batch file or script to perform the processing.

Employ the *For* Command

The `For` command fulfills a special niche in batch file programming. In many cases, you can make complex file selections for utilities using wildcard characters. Unfortunately, using wildcard characters won't always work. Sometimes you need to know the name of the file. A command line utility might not support wildcard characters or the file argument doesn't easily fit within the wildcard method of description. That's where the `For` statement comes into play for batch files. This command takes the form:

```
FOR %%variable IN (set) DO command [command-parameters]
```

You can also use this command at the command prompt to process files manually. Instead of using a single percent (%) symbol, you use two in front of the variable. Here's a sample of how you can use this command in a batch file:

```
Echo Off
For %%F In (*.BAT *.TXT) Do Dir %%F /B
Echo On
```

In this case the `For` command processes all of the files that have a .BAT or .TXT extension in the current directory. The command processes the files in the order in which they appear in the directory and you have no guarantee what the order is. The `%%F` variable contains the name of an individual file. The `Dir` command is called once for each file with the `%%F` variable as an input. In this case, the command outputs the filenames using the bare format, so you could use this batch file to create a text file containing a list of files that match the criteria. Additional processing could archive the files or do anything else that you might like.

It's important to remember that you can normally achieve the same output using multiple methods. For example, try typing `For %%F In (*.BAT *.TXT) Do Echo %%F` instead and you see the same output. It's also quite easy to combine commands using pipes. For example, type `For %%F In (*.BAT *.TXT) Do Dir %%F /B | Find "For"` to find all of the batch and text files that begin with the word For. Of course, you could do the same thing by typing **For %%F In (For*.BAT For*.TXT) Do Dir %%F /B.**

Every For command consists of at least three, and normally four, components. You always include these elements in the order shown:

1. **{%Variable | %%Variable}:** Specifies a replaceable parameter; the argument that will receive the individual members of a set. The replaceable parameter takes two forms. Use the %Variable form when you want to use the replaceable parameter as input to another command or utility. Use the %%Variable form when you want to use the replaceable parameter for activities within the batch file. The variable names are case sensitive, so %f isn't the same as %F. In addition, you must use an alphabetical variable name, such as %A, %B, or %C.

2. **(Set):** Defines the set to process. The set can include one or more files, directories, range of values, or text strings that you want to process with the specified command. For example, you can use environment variables as the set. The command For %%P In (%PATH%) Do ECHO %%P would display the members of the PATH environment variable as individual strings.

3. *Command:* Specifies the command you want to perform for each entry in the set.

4. **(Optional)** CommandLineOptions: Defines the command line options for the command that you want to perform for each entry in the set. The command line options are command or utility specific; see the other entries in this book for details.

Perform Complex File Iteration

You can use the For command to process command output, strings, and the content of files. In this case the For command begins by breaking the input into individual lines of content and discarding any blank lines. It then breaks whatever input you provide into specific tokens based on the rules you specify. A token can be a control character, a special word, or anything else you can define as part of the simple syntax for this command. The For command passes the token to a command you specify as input. Here's the command line syntax for this form of the For command:

```
for /F ["ParsingKeywords"] {%% | %}Variable in (FileNameSet)
do Command
    [CommandLineOptions]
for /F ["ParsingKeywords"] {%% | %}Variable in
("LiteralString") do
```

```
Command [CommandLineOptions]
for /F ["ParsingKeywords"] {%% | %}Variable in ('Command')
do Command
    [CommandLineOptions]
```

Notice that you need to use a different command line syntax for each kind of input. A filename appears without quotes, while a string appears in double quotes and a command appears in single quotes. The small differences in command format determines how the For command views the input.

The ParsingKeywords input is a quoted string that specifies the rules for parsing the input into tokens. These keywords always appear in double quotes, as shown. The following list describes the keywords you can use:

- **eol=c:** Specifies an end of line character. The For command only allows you to specify one character.

- **skip=N:** Specifies the number of lines to skip at the beginning of the file.

- **delims=xxx:** Specifies a delimiter set. The delimiter set defines which characters the For command views as elements between tokens. The default setting relies on the space and tab. Consequently, the For command produces a new token every time it sees a space or tab within the input.

- **tokens=X,Y,M-N:** Defines which tokens to retrieve from each line of text to pass to the For command body for each iteration. The For command allocates one variable for each of the tokens. The M-N format defines a range of tokens to use as input. Whenever the last character in a processed string is an asterisk (*), the For command creates an additional variable to receive the additional text on the line after the For command parses the last token.

- **usebackq:** Specifies that you can use quotation marks to quote filenames in FileNameSet, a back quoted string is executed as a command, and a single quoted string is a literal string command.

You need to use a slightly different command line syntax with the For command when you rely on the usebackq keyword. Here are the three command lines using this syntax:

```
for /F ["usebackqParsingKeywords"] {%% | %}Variable in
("FileNameSet")
    do Command [CommandLineOptions]
for /F ["usebackqParsingKeywords"] {%% | %}Variable in
```

```
('LiteralString') do Command [CommandLineOptions]
for /F ["usebackqParsingKeywords"] {%% | %}Variable in
('Command') do
    Command [CommandLineOptions]
```

This special parsing form of the For command has a lot of practical purposes. For example, you could use it to tear a batch file apart into its constituent parts by typing **For /F "tokens=1,*" %%A IN (For1.BAT) DO Echo Command: %%A Arguments: %%B**. In this case the For command looks into the For1.BAT batch file and processes it one line at a time. The first word in each line of the batch file is normally a command; the remainder of the line is its arguments. So the For command separates the batch file commands from the arguments by using the tokens=1,* parsing keyword. Figure 21.2 shows the output. Notice how tokens=1,* actually creates two variables—%%A contains the first word and %%B contains the rest of the string.

Figure 21.2: Using parsing techniques to take output from commands, files, and variables apart.

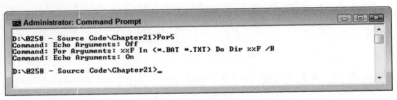

As previously mentioned, the usebackq form requires a little extra thought. Let's say you want to obtain a directory listing of just the filenames and not the extensions. Yet another way to obtain this listing is to parse the output of the Dir *.BAT /B command by typing **FOR /F "usebackq delims=." %%i IN (`Dir *.BAT /B`) DO @echo %%i**. In this case, the output of the Dir *.BAT /B command is processed, but only the filename part appears in the output due to the use of usebackq and delims with a period as the delimiter.

Utilize Variable Substitution

Variable substitution is the act of exchanging a variable name for the content of that variable. However, unlike expansion, you don't necessarily use all of the variable content. For example, instead of using the entire path for a file, you might just use the drive letter, the path, or the filename. The following list describes the basic forms of variable substitution available with the For command. (The list assumes that you're using a variable named I, which translates into %I at the command line.)

- **%~I:** Removes any surrounding quotation marks from the variable content.

- **%~fI:** Expands %I to a fully qualified pathname.

- **%~dI:** Expands %I to a drive letter only.

- **%~pI:** Expands %I to a path only.

- **%~nI:** Expands %I to a filename only.

- **%~xI:** Expands %I to a file extension only.

- **%~sI:** Creates a path variable and then changes any long directory names into their short name equivalents.

- **%~aI:** Obtains the file attributes of the input file.

- **%~tI:** Obtains the date and time of the input file.

- **%~zI:** Obtains the size of the input file.

- **%~$PATH:I:** Searches the directories listed in the PATH environment variable for the file specified by I. The system then expands the first match that it finds to a fully qualified filename, which includes the drive, path, and filename. This variable substitution returns an empty string when the PATH environment variable is undefined or if the system can't find a match for the filename.

Use these variable substitutions to obtain specialized output from your batch file. For example, you might want to see the full path to the batch files in the current directory, along with the file attributes. In this case, you type **For %%I In (*.BAT) Do Echo %%~fI %%~aI**. Figure 21.3 shows typical output from this command.

Figure 21.3: Variable substitution can help you obtain specialized output.

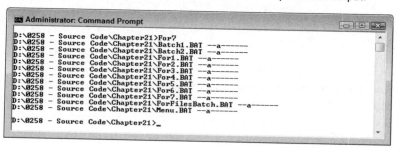

Creating Batch Files

PART VII

You can use these variable substitutions in combination to produce specific results. For example, you might want to create a directory-like listing of files. The following list provides some ideas on how to use the variable substitution arguments in combination:

- **%~dpI:** Outputs just the drive letter and path of a file, without including the filename.

- **%~nxI:** Outputs the filename and extension but leaves out the drive letter and path.

- **%~fsI:** Outputs the file information using the short name (8.3 format) form only.

- **%~dp$PATH:I:** Locates the file using the PATH environment variable. The system outputs just the drive letter and path of the first match found.

- **%´zaI:** Creates the same output as the Dir command. However, the output is different from the Dir command because the file listing could span multiple directories. The focus of the listing is different.

Employ the *GoTo* Command

The GoTo command transfers control from one part of a batch file to another. You can't use the GoTo command to transfer control to other batch files. For this task, you use the Call command described in the "Employ the *Call* Command" section of the chapter. The GoTo command takes a simple form: GoTo Label, where Label is a keyword used to define the transfer point in the batch file. Labels are always preceded by a colon, such as :MyLabel. Listing 21.1 and Listing 21.2 show the GoTo command in action.

Employ the *If* Command

To write any reasonably complex batch file, you need to perform flow control—the active selection of code to run based on current conditions. For example, you might want to know that the previous task succeeded before you begin the next task. In some cases, you'll look for a specific file or act on user input to the batch file. You can also verify that the user provided a certain input string. The point is that you can exercise some control over how the batch files react to system and environmental conditions. Batch files don't provide extensive decision-making support, but you can use these three forms of the If statement to increase the flexibility of your batch files:

```
If [Not] ErrorLevel number command
If [Not] string1==string2 command
If [Not] Exist filename command
```

In all three cases, you can add the word "Not" to perform the reverse of the check. For example, you can perform a task when a given file doesn't exist, rather than when it does exist. By combining both versions of the If statement, you can create the equivalent of an If...Else statement found in most programming languages.

The ErrorLevel argument requires special consideration. Whenever you run an application, batch file, or script, the system provides a numeric error level as output. By convention, an error level of 0 always represents success. Other numbers represent an error or special condition. A special condition isn't always an error; it's simply not complete success. In fact, you might expect an application, batch file, or script to exit with a special condition. For an example of a command that exits with special conditions, review the Choice command in the "Employ the *Choice* Command" section of the chapter. Error conditions can represent a user, system, or application failure. For example, consider the XCopy error levels shown in Table 21.1.

Table 21.1: XCopy Error Levels

Error Level	Meaning
0	Success, no error occurred.
1	The system didn't find any files to copy.
2	The user stopped XCopy by pressing Ctrl+C.
4	The application experienced an initialization error. The system doesn't have enough memory or disk space. You may have entered an invalid drive name or used invalid syntax at the command line.
5	The system experienced a disk write error.

As you can see, the cause of an error varies greatly depending on conditions. In all cases, you could rightfully say that the application has experienced an error. However, notice that error level 2 could actually

Creating Batch Files

PART VII

occur by design. The user recognizes an error and presses Ctrl+C to stop the copying process before it completes. In this case, you have to consider whether the error level defines a special condition or an error by prompting the user and handle it appropriately. Listing 21.2 shows examples of the various If statement forms at work.

Listing 21.2: Using the If Statement in Batch Files

```
Echo Off

REM Verify the user has provided an action.
If %1Err==Err GoTo ProcessError

REM Simulate an error when the file doesn't exist.
Copy MyFile.TXT MyFile2.TXT
If Not ErrorLevel 1 GoTo CheckFile
    Echo The File doesn't exist so the batch file can't copy
it.

REM Check for a specific file and process it when it does
exist.
:CheckFile
If Exist MyFile.TXT GoTo ProcessFile

REM If the file doesn't exist then create it. Display a
message with
REM instructions and then let the user type the text.
Echo Type some text for the test file. Press Ctrl+Z when you
finish.
Pause
Copy CON MyFile.TXT

REM This is a label for processing the file.
:ProcessFile

REM Determine whether the user wants to display the file.
If Not %1==Display GoTo Process2
    Echo MyFile.TXT Contains:
    Type MyFile.TXT
    GoTo TheEnd
```

```
REM Determine whether the user wants to delete the file.
:Process2
If Not %1==Delete GoTo ProcessError
    Erase MyFile.TXT
    Echo Deleted MyFile.TXT
    GoTo TheEnd


REM The user didn't define a processing action.
:ProcessError
Echo You didn't tell the batch file what to do!
Echo Type UseIf Display to display the file or
Echo UseIf Delete to delete the file.

:TheEnd
Echo On
```

The first line of this example demonstrates a principle that you should always use in batch files that you expect someone else will use—check for errors within the limits of the batch file to do so. In this case, the batch file expects the user to type **UseIf Display** or UseIf Delete and press Enter. When the user doesn't provide any input value, then the first input value, %1, is blank so the string Err equals Err and the code goes to a label named ProcessError. Batch files can work with up to nine input values at a time using %1 through %9 as variables. The GoTo statement always tells the code to go to a label within the batch file. You define a label by preceding the label name with a colon such as :ProcessError.

The next segment of code attempts to copy a temporary file to another file. The operation results in an error that you can trap using the ErrorLevel statement when the file doesn't exist. When the ErrorLevel value matches the value you provide, then the If statement executes the command. In this case, because the code uses the Not clause, the reverse is true: the If statement only executes the GoTo command when the error level is not 1. Notice that, in this case, the code uses the Echo command to display an error message to the user—Echo works not only for turning messages on or off but for displaying custom messages to the user that the Echo setting doesn't hide as well.

Once the code performs these initial steps, it determines whether the MyFile.TXT file does exist using the Exit clause of the If statement. When the file exists, the code immediately begins processing it. Otherwise, the code displays a message prompting the user to type information for such a file. Notice the Pause command, which pauses the batch file execution until the user presses a key. The Copy command sends whatever the user types at the console (CON) to the MyFile.TXT file until it detects an end of file character, which the user creates by pressing Ctrl+Z.

Now that you know the file exists, the batch file can process it. This batch file provides two options: displaying the file and deleting it. The problem with batch files is that they use case-sensitive string comparisons—the word Delete is different from the word delete so error trapping can cause false problems. Some developers resolve this problem by using single character command line switches for batch files. That way, all you need to do is perform two checks, one for uppercase and another for lowercase. The example uses a full word for the purpose of demonstration. To see how this works, type **UseIf delete** and press Enter at the command line instead of UseIf Delete—the code displays a failure message. When the user does type **UseIf Delete**, the batch file erases the file and displays a success message. Likewise, when the user types **UseIf Display** and presses Enter, the code sends the content of MyFile.TXT to the display. In both cases, the code goes to TheEnd where the batch file turns Echo back on.

Employ the *Pause* Command

The Pause command stops batch file execution to give the user time to react to a particular need. For example, if you need the user to change media to complete the batch file, you could use the Echo command to tell the user about the need and then use the Pause command to tell the user to press any key when the media exchange is complete. To use the Pause command, type **Pause** and press Enter.

Employ the *Prompt* Command

The Prompt command changes the command line prompt. For example, instead of the usual drive letter, directory, and greater than (>) sign, you could use the time and date as a prompt. In fact, the prompt can contain any text you want. Use the Prompt *Descriptor* command to change the prompt, where *Descriptor* is one or more special letters as shown in Table 21.2. For example, if you want to display the current date and a greater than sign, you type **Prompt DG** and press Enter.

Table 21.2: Prompt Letter Combinations

Combination	Description
$A	& (Ampersand)
$B	| (Pipe)
$C	((Left parenthesis)
$D	Current date
$E	Escape code (ASCII code 27)
$F	) (Right parenthesis)
$G	> (Greater than sign)
$H	Backspace (erases previous character)
$L	< (Less than sign)
$N	Current drive
$P	Current drive and path
$Q	= (Equals sign)
$S	(Space)
$T	Current time
$V	Windows version number
$_	Carriage return and linefeed
$$	$ (Dollar sign)
$+	Displays zero or more plus sign characters depending on the depth of the PushD utility directory stack. The display shows one character for each level you've pushed onto the stack. Requires that you have command extensions enabled.
$M	Displays the remote name associated with the current drive letter. If this is a local drive, then the system displays an empty string. Requires that you have command extensions enabled.

Employ the *Rem* Command

The Rem (Remark) command lets you add comments to your batch files. Given that batch files often use difficult to read coding sequences and that you'll probably want to modify them at some point, lots of comments are advisable. In fact, you'll want to add at least one comment for each complex line of code in your batch file. Many people have lost the use of interesting and helpful batch files because they contain complex code that becomes unreadable after the initial writer forgets what the code means. Listing 21.1 and Listing 21.2 show how to use the Rem command.

Employ the *TimeOut* Utility

The TimeOut utility provides a unique feature in that you can tell it to wait for a specified time period no matter what the user does. Consequently, unlike the Choice command, when you tell TimeOut to wait 30 seconds, it waits the entire time period even if the user presses a key. In addition, the TimeOut utility doesn't display a message for the timeout, so you can use this utility where silence is necessary (such as a background task).

To create a pause in your batch file, use the TimeOut /T *Value* command, where *Value* specifies the timeout value. You may specify any value from −1 to 99999 seconds. A value of −1 means that the utility waits indefinitely for a key press. The utility won't allow you to combine a value of −1 with the /NOBREAK command line switch since that would effectively lock the system. For example, if you want to pause your application for 10 seconds, you type **TimeOut /T 10**.

If you want to prevent TimeOut from recognizing key presses, add the /NoBreak command line switch. The TimeOut utility waits for the specified time period before it exits. For example, to keep the user waiting for 10 seconds, type **TimeOut /T 10 /NoBreak**.

Test Batch Files

It's important to remember the place that batch files occupy in the hierarchy of automation. A batch represents a fast and simple way of executing a series of tasks using applications, commands, and utilities. The batch file possesses basic programming structures and you can perform amazing tasks at times with those structures, but in the end, batch files are somewhat limited. Something as simple as a disk being full or a lack of rights to create a file in a specific location can cause the batch file to fail. Error trapping in such cases is difficult because you have to check for error levels from the errant application, command, or utility and not every one of them supports output error levels. The following sections describe some batch file techniques you should consider using, especially when working with large systems.

Add Debug Information to Batch Files

Developers of most applications know how to add debugging statements to their code. The debugging statements aren't for general use; they simply make it easier to check the application for flaws. In addition, the debugging statements make it possible to track program flow and generally help the developer understand the application better. A batch file can also include debugging information, even though there aren't specific statements to perform the task. The following code shows one method you can use:

```
@IF NOT DEFINED DEBUG @ECHO OFF
ECHO
@ECHO ON
```

In this case, the debug trigger is an environment variable named DEBUG. You can set this environment variable to any value desired by using the Set command. Type **Set DEBUG=** and press Enter to turn off debugging. The purpose of this debugging statement is to keep echo on when you're debugging the batch file. During the debugging cycle, you want to see all of the statements, so you display them by keeping the echo on. When the batch file runs normally, the user won't have an environment variable named DEBUG, and the batch file turns off echo so the user doesn't see all of the intervening commands. Using the ECHO command by itself displays the current echo state so you can easily test this technique for yourself.

Notice that the batch file doesn't include anything special for the @ECHO ON statement. It's bad practice to use conditional statements with commands that set the system back to a default state. In this case, you can set echo on without considering the current echo state because having echo on is the default setting.

You can extend debugging to other activities. For example, you might want to know the current value of a variable within the batch file. Because you don't have a debugging environment that you can rely on to perform such tasks, you'll need to use other methods with a batch file. Listing 21.3 shows one technique you can use to extend a batch file to output debugging information about an internal variable (note that this example also uses the DEBUG environment variable).

Listing 21.3: Adding Simple Debugging to a Batch File

```
@ECHO OFF

REM Locate all of the temporary files on your hard drive.
@ECHO Locating temporary files to delete.
FOR /F %%F IN (DelFiles.TXT) DO CALL :GetFile %%F
GOTO :NextStep

REM This is the actual code for handling the temporary file
REM processing.
:GetFile
IF DEFINED DEBUG @ECHO Adding %1 to the list.
Dir %1 /B /S >> DeleteMe.TXT
GOTO :EOF

REM You would normally place the next step of the processing
REM task here.
:NextStep

@ECHO ON
```

This is actually a batch file within a batch file. The code begins by displaying information to the user that it's collecting a list of temporary files. At this point, the user normally waits while the batch file does its job in complete silence. However, as a developer, you really need to know what's going on within the batch file. To make this work, you need to execute multiple commands. Consequently, the batch file calls a label named :GetFile and passes it the %%F argument.

Now, look at the :GetFile label and you'll see two statements. The first displays the current %%F value when you create an environment variable named DEBUG. However, notice that it's called %1 here, not %%F. Whenever you employ a Call command to pass control to a label within a batch file, you create a new batch file context. As far as the :GetFile label is concerned, it exists in a different batch file from the original that called it. The first batch file passes %%F as an input value, so it appears as %1 to the :GetFile label code. The second statement in :GetFile is the Dir command that locates the files you want to delete based on the file specification.

Notice that the :GetFile section ends with GOTO :EOF, which should end the batch file. It does, in fact, end the :GetFile batch file and returns control to the FOR command that called it. Now the FOR command can process the next file extension in the list. Figure 21.4 gives you a better idea of how this batch file works with and without DEBUG defined. Notice the batch file doesn't display the file extensions the first time because DEBUG isn't defined yet.

Figure 21.4: Batch files can output as little or as much debugging information as needed.

The examples in this section have only shown a single level of debugging so far. However, you can create as many levels of debugging as you want by adding some additional code. Listing 21.4 shows the example in Listing 21.3 with a second level of debugging added.

Listing 21.4: A Batch File with Multiple Debug Levels Defined

```
IF NOT DEFINED DEBUG2 @ECHO OFF

REM Set the second level of debugging.
IF DEFINED DEBUG2 SET DEBUG=TRUE

REM Locate all of the temporary files on your hard drive.
@ECHO Locating temporary files to delete.
FOR /F %%F IN (DelFiles.TXT) DO CALL :GetFile %%F
GOTO :NextStep

REM This is the actual code for handling the temporary file
REM processing.
:GetFile
IF DEFINED DEBUG @ECHO Adding %1 to the list.
Dir %1 /B /S >> DeleteMe.TXT
GoTo :EOF
```

```
REM You would normally place the next step of the processing
REM task here.
:NextStep

REM Always remember to remove additional debugging levels.
IF DEFINED DEBUG2 SET DEBUG=

@ECHO ON
```

The two levels of debugging for this example are `DEBUG` and `DEBUG2`. When you define the `DEBUG2` level, the batch file automatically defines `DEBUG` for you and then removes the `DEBUG` definition when the batch file ends. As shown in the code, the `DEBUG2` level displays all of the batch code as it executes. Although this display can be handy, as shown in Figure 21.5, it can also become quite messy. You don't always need it to locate a problem in your batch file. In fact, displaying the code can sometimes hide problems in plain sight.

Figure 21.5: Display code statements in batch files with care to avoid overwhelming yourself with too much content.

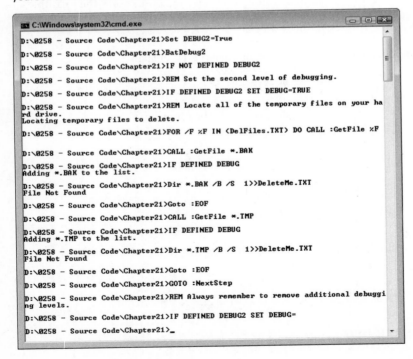

Many people claim that batch files don't offer any form of debugging. Admittedly, batch files don't provide the robust debugging features that full-fledged programming languages do, but batch files don't require these advanced levels of debugging either since they normally perform simple tasks. Using the techniques found in this section, you can provide at least a modicum of debugging functionality for your batch files.

Identify Batch Files and Their Actions

If you work on a large system, you know that automation isn't just a nicety; it's a requirement if you want to stay on top of maintenance actions. However, automation brings with it all kinds of problems. One of the more critical problems is identifying which machine produced a particular data file. After all, if a machine encounters an error, you want to know which machine to fix. The same concept holds true for other kinds of data. No matter what data you collect, data without an attached context is worthless. With this in mind, you can use code as shown in Listing 21.5 to create a descriptive data file.

Listing 21.5: Creating a Descriptive Data File Header

```
@ECHO OFF

REM Add identifying information.
@ECHO Computer: %COMPUTERNAME% > Temps.TXT
@ECHO User: %USERNAME% >> Temps.TXT

REM Add the date and time.
Date /T >> Temps.TXT
Time /T >> Temps.TXT

REM Create a header for the data.
@ECHO. >> Temps.TXT
@ECHO Temporary Files: >> Temps.TXT
@ECHO. >> Temps.TXT

REM Locate all of the temporary files on your hard drive.
@ECHO Locating temporary files to delete.
FOR /F %%F IN (DelFiles.TXT) DO Dir %%F /B /S >> Temps.TXT

@ECHO ON
```

This example uses several techniques to output descriptive data. First, it combines standard text with environmental variable expansion. Every Windows machine will include the %COMPUTERNAME% and %USERNAME% environment variables (or you can define them in the unlikely event that they don't exist). Notice the first output contains just a single redirection (>) symbol, so this first line always erases any existing file.

Second, the example uses the Date and Time utilities to output the date and the time. Notice the use of the /T command line switch to prevent these utilities from prompting the user for the date or time. It's a common error not to include the /T command line switch, so you should watch for the error in your own code.

Third, the example creates a header for the data. Notice the use of the special ECHO. command to create a blank space in the output. The addition of the period prevents echo from displaying its status. Because there isn't any other data to display, the ECHO command simply displays a blank line. The remainder of this example outputs a temporary file listing.

Adding the identifying information to the data file is fine when you don't want to maintain backups of previous data and when the data resides on the original machine. Of course, things change when you want to create a historical view of the data or store the information in a centralized location. In this second instance, you need a unique filename for every submission. Listing 21.6 shows how to add the information to the filename, rather than the data file.

Listing 21.6: Adding Descriptive Information to a Data File

```
@ECHO OFF

REM Create a new environment variable with the identifying
REM information for this file. Start with the computer and
REM user name.
SET DataStore=%COMPUTERNAME%
SET DataStore=%DataStore%_%USERNAME%

REM Add the date.
SET DataStore=%DataStore%_%DATE:~4,2%
SET DataStore=%DataStore%_%DATE:~7,2%
SET DataStore=%DataStore%_%DATE:~10,4%
```

```
REM Add the time.
SET DataStore=%DataStore%_%TIME:~0,2%
SET DataStore=%DataStore%_%TIME:~3,2%
SET DataStore=%DataStore%_%TIME:~6,2%

REM Add the file extension.
:SetExtension
SET DataStore=%DataStore%.TXT

REM Locate all of the temporary files on your hard drive.
@ECHO Locating temporary files to delete.
@ECHO Saving files to "%DataStore%".
FOR /F %%F IN (DelFiles.TXT) DO Dir %%F /B /S >>
"%DataStore%"


@ECHO ON
```

In this example, the batch files build up an environment variable named DataStore that contains the computer and usernames, along with the date and time. Obtaining the computer and usernames are simply a matter of using the existing %COMPUTERNAME% and %USERNAME% environment variables. However, the date and time prove more interesting.

Even though the Set command doesn't show them, Windows dynamically generates several environment variables each time you request them, including %DATE% and %TIME%. When working at DOS, you had to generate these environment variables yourself, which is a time-consuming and error-prone process (see the examples at http://www.robvanderwoude.com/datetime.php for details). Unfortunately, these environment variables contain characters that you can use for a filename including the slash (/) and colon (:). Consequently, you can't use the variables directly. The solution is to extract the numbers you need. For example, to extract the first two numbers of the time, you use %TIME:~0,2%, where the first number is the starting point in the string and the second number defines the number of characters to use. Strings in batch files always rely on a 0-based starting point.

The %DATE% environment variable requires a little more manipulation than %TIME%. In this case, the string contains the day of the week, so you must extract that information from the string as well. Consequently, the month always appears at position 4, rather than 0.

Now that the batch file has built a unique filename based on the machine name, username, date, and time, it adds a file extension of .TXT to it. The result appears in place of the standard filename in the FOR command for this example. Notice that you must enclose the filename with quotes because it could contain a space.

Use a Centralized Data Store

One problem that none of the examples in the book has addressed so far is the use of a centralized data store. Overcoming this problem with scripts is relatively easy because you have access to standard database objects. With the proper code, you can simply send the data from a client machine to a server and never have to worry about it again except for analysis purposes. However, batch files don't support database objects and the individual machine records discussed so far in the book are ill suited for import into a database. If you have a large network, it's unlikely that you'll want to view every one of those individual records.

You have options at your disposal when working with individual commands. For example, many commands and utilities support the Comma Separated Value (CSV) format. When working with one of these utilities, you simply specify that you don't want headers and that the system should use the CSV format. Unfortunately, these utilities won't address special needs, such as error reports or a listing of interesting files on a machine (perhaps an unacceptable or unsupported application, temporary files, viruses, adware, or spyware). For all of these needs and many more, you must create the output in a form that lends itself to use with a database. Fortunately, creating your own CSV output (a data form commonly accepted by databases) isn't difficult. Listing 21.7 shows one way to do it with a list of temporary files.

Listing 21.7: Creating Output for a Database

```
@ECHO OFF

REM Clean up any existing output file.
IF EXIST Output.CSV Del Output.CSV

REM Create a new environment variable to hold the static
REM data for this session.
SET DataEntry="%COMPUTERNAME%"
```

```
SET DataEntry=%DataEntry%, "%USERNAME%"
SET DataEntry=%DataEntry%, "%DATE%"
SET DataEntry=%DataEntry%, "%TIME%"

REM Locate all of the temporary files on your hard drive.
@ECHO Locating temporary files to delete.
FOR /F %%F IN (DelFiles.TXT) DO CALL :AddValue %%F
GOTO :Finished


REM Work with the individual directory entries as a set
REM and process them as part of a FOR command.
:AddValue
@ECHO Adding database values for %1.
FOR /F "delims==" %%E IN ('Dir %1 /B /S') DO @ECHO
%DataEntry%, "%%E" >> Output.CSV
GOTO :EOF


:Finished
@ECHO ON
```

The idea behind CSV is that you encapsulate the individual data values in quotes and separate them with commas. This example works as most batch files that create CSV will work. You begin by creating one or more static data values that provide a snapshot of this particular session. When you combine this data with other snapshots, the static information provides the means for separating the individual data entries.

The example requires two FOR loops in this case. The first FOR command parses the file specifications located in the DelFiles.TXT file and passes them to a secondary routine.

The secondary FOR loop processes the individual file entries returned by the Dir command. Notice the two additions to the FOR command. First, you must provide the "delims==" option so that the FOR loop doesn't cut off the paths at the first space. Second, notice that this FOR loop doesn't process the data as a file; it uses the command representation instead. Remember that single quotes are for commands and double quotes are for strings. The resulting Output.CSV file contains a pure string representation that you could open in Notepad if desired. However, the power of this particular routine is that you can also open it as a database in a database application or even in Excel. Figure 21.6 shows typical output presented in Excel.

Creating Batch Files

PART VII

Figure 21.6: CSV files make it very easy to move data to a spreadsheet or database.

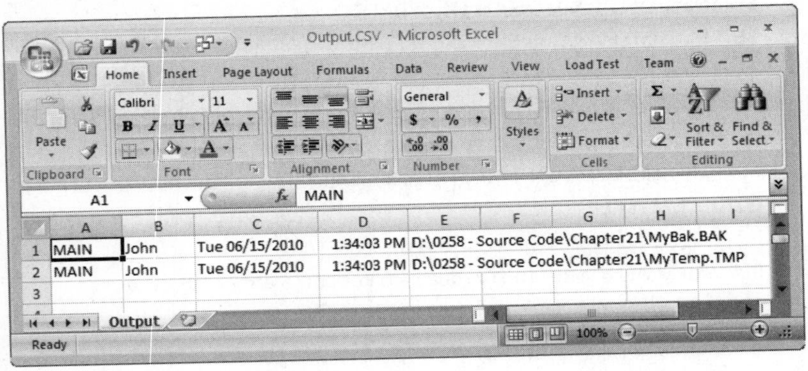

Store and Retrieve Directories with the *PushD* and *PopD* Commands

Windows maintains a directory stack that you can use to store locations that you visit. You use this stack to store directory information and then retrieve it as needed. The PushD and PopD commands provide access to the directory stack and help you move around your hard drive more efficiently.

NOTE Think about a stack as you would a stack of pancakes. Fry a pancake and you can add it to the top of the stack. Get hungry and you can remove a pancake from the top of the stack to eat it. The first (bottom) pancake on the stack is always the last pancake off. When the pancakes are all gone, the stack is empty.

If you move around your hard drive a lot, using the PushD and PopD commands can save you considerable typing time. However, most people use these commands to simplify batch files. No matter which way you use them, the directory stack is a handy way for tracking your movement.

To save the current location on the stack, type **PushD** and press Enter. If you want to save a specific location, use the PushD *Path* command, where *Path* is a location that you want to store on the stack. For example, to save C:\ on the stack, type **PushD C:** and press Enter. To restore a directory location, type **PopD** and press Enter. The command processor will return you to the location on the top of the stack.

The PushD and PopD commands can also use command extensions to change to a network drive. When you use PushD in this manner, Windows automatically maps a drive to the network path for you. The PopD command treats the networked drive as it would any other mapped drive for your system. You can also specify the next directory as the parent directory by using the .. syntax with the PushD command.

PART VIII

Creating Scripts

IN THIS PART ▶

22

Discovering Scripting Basics

IN THIS CHAPTER, YOU WILL LEARN TO:

▶ **USE SCRIPTING LANGUAGES** (Pages 436–441)

- Learn the Basics of JavaScript (Page 436)
- Learn the Basics of VBScript (Page 438)
- Use the Windows Scripting File (Page 439)

▶ **EXECUTE SCRIPTS** (Pages 442–445)

- Run Scripts with the *CScript* and *WScript* Utilities (Page 442)
- Configure the Host and Property Page Options (Page 444)

Creating Scripts

PART VIII

S cripts represent a step up from batch files. They provide additional flexibility and help you perform more tasks. However, along with these positives, you also have to face a little longer learning curve to use scripts. Even so, scripting isn't as difficult as working with many programming languages. If you know how to work with batch files, scripting becomes significantly easier. In sum, scripting represents the next step up for administrators who need something more than batch files can provide in the way of automation. The following sections provide some information you can use to get started with scripting. Of course, there are entire books written about scripting, so these sections are only an overview.

Use Scripting Languages

There are many scripting languages on the market today. Space won't allow me to discuss them all, even if I knew them all. The following sections discuss JavaScript and VBScript for one reason—they're the languages that Windows supports out of the box so you don't need to install anything special to use them. Of the two, JavaScript enjoys greater popularity and you can use it on more than one platform. Consequently, the scripting examples in the book mainly rely on JavaScript.

NOTE   You'll find that JavaScript comes in several slightly different forms and names. Besides JavaScript, you'll see this language as LiveScript, JScript, and ECMAScript. You can find an interesting language history at http://www.webmasterworld.com/ forum91/68.htm (may require a log on).

Learn the Basics of JavaScript

This chapter doesn't provide a nuts and bolts discussion of JavaScript—it assumes that you have some experience using this language. Because this language is used in so many ways, you can find great JavaScript resources online. Many sites include tutorials, a reference, and sample code. If you want to be sure your code runs in as many environments as possible, make sure you download a copy of European Computer Manufacturer's Association (ECMA) standard 262 from http://www.ecma-international. org/publications/standards/Ecma-262.htm, which is the standard for JavaScript. Here are some steps to follow to discover JavaScript.

1. Get an introduction to JavaScript at `http://www.w3schools.com/js/js_intro.asp`.

2. Start learning JavaScript using a good tutorial such as those found at:
   - `http://www.w3schools.com/js/default.asp`
     An excellent structured tutorial for first-time users.
   - `http://www.cs.brown.edu/courses/bridge/1998/res/javascript/javascript-tutorial.html`
     An extremely simple and quick tutorial.
   - `http://www.echoecho.com/javascript.htm`
     A comprehensive, but less structured tutorial.

3. Get a JavaScript reference from one of the following locations:
   - `http://developer.mozilla.org/en/docs/JavaScript_Language_Resources`
     A good standards-based reference.
   - `http://www.microsoft.com/downloads/details.aspx?FamilyId=01592C48-207D-4BE1-8A76-1C4099D7BBB9`
     The Microsoft perspective of JavaScript.

4. Discover additional JavaScript resources from places such as `http://msdn.microsoft.com/en-us/library/ms950396.aspx`.

Verifying Your JavaScript Setup

You may run into a problem where the scripts in this book don't work. Double-clicking the script file doesn't work and it appears that you can't do anything else with the file either. In fact, Windows might not know anything about the file at all. Although it does happen with VBScript, most people have problems getting their JavaScript (JS) files to run correctly after they install certain kinds of software or perform actions with virus detection software. If you double-click on a JS file and nothing happens, the problem might be in the registry. For whatever reason (and I wasn't able to verify a single specific reason), sometimes people find Windows or another external application removes their JavaScript settings.

The main problem is that the registry lacks entries for the `.JS` extension handler. Use these steps to repair your JavaScript Setup.

(continued)

Creating Scripts

PART VIII

Verifying Your JavaScript Setup *(continued)*

1. Verify that you have the handler installed by viewing the `HKEY_CLASSES_ROOT\.JS` key first. This key should say JSFile as the (Default) value.

2. Look at the `HKEY_CLASSES_ROOT\JSFile` entry. It should have JScript Script File as the (Default) value and `@%SystemRoot%\System32\wshext.dll,-4804` as the FriendlyTypeName value.

3. Verify the JScript verbs. You should see two open verbs.

    The first is at `HKEY_CLASSES_ROOT\JSFile\Shell\Open\Command` and should have a (Default) value of `%SystemRoot%\System32\WScript.exe "%1" %*`.

    The second is at `HKEY_CLASSES_ROOT\JSFile\Shell\Open2\Command` and should have a (Default) value of `%SystemRoot%\System32\CScript.exe "%1" %*`.

4. If you're not seeing these entries, it means that something has gone awry with your registry. When this problem occurs, you can usually restore your JavaScript and VBScript settings by typing **RegSvr32 WSHExt.DLL** in the `\Windows\System32` folder and pressing Enter.

Learn the Basics of VBScript

This chapter doesn't provide a VBScript tutorial. Unfortunately, VBScript is also less popular than JavaScript, so you won't find as many resources online for using it. However, a few developers still use VBScript for their application needs. The following steps can help you discover VBScript:

1. Get a VBScript overview from one of the following places:

    -   `http://msdn.microsoft.com/en-us/library/t0aew7h6.aspx`
        Includes a VBScript user's guide and language reference.

    -   `http://www.w3schools.com/vbscript/vbscript_ref_functions.asp`
        Provides an overview of the VBScript functions with a short description of each.

2. Start learning VBScript using a good tutorial such as those found at:

    -   `http://www.w3schools.com/vbscript/vbscript_intro.asp`
        An excellent structured tutorial for first-time users.

- `http://www.w3schools.com/vbscript/vbscript_examples.asp`
  Provides basic examples you can use to learn how VBScript works.

- `http://www.intranetjournal.com/corner/wrox/progref/vbt/`
  An extremely simple and quick tutorial.

- `http://www.intranetjournal.com/corner/aitken/vbs-1.shtml`
  A detailed article that provides VBScript basics.

- `http://www.tizag.com/vbscriptTutorial/`
  A tutorial focused on browser programming that also works well for basic learning purposes.

3. Get a VBScript reference from one of the following locations:

- `http://msdn.microsoft.com/library/d1wf56tt.aspx`
  The essential Microsoft perspective of the topic.

- `http://www.w3schools.com/vbscript/vbscript_ref_functions.asp`
  An online reference where clicking a function name displays details about that function.

4. Discover additional VBScript resources from places such as:

- `http://www.visualbasicscript.com/`
  Provides a forum for asking questions about VBScript.

- `http://www.cetus-links.org/oo_vbscript.html`
  A centralized list of VBScript links.

- `http://searchvb.techtarget.com/generic/0,295582,sid8_gci1158017,00.html?track=NL-283&ad=539962`
  Additional VBScript resource links.

Use the Windows Scripting File

The Windows Scripting File (WSF) isn't a new scripting language. Instead, it's a new way to package your scripts. Current script technology doesn't make it easy to create certain kinds of scripts. For example, if you have code written in VBScript that you want to combine with code written in JavaScript, you can't do it. The WSF technology provides a significant number of advantages to the script developer including:

- Using `Include` statements to add external code to your script.

- Using more than a single language per scripting file (of course, you must have all of the required scripting engines installed on your system).

- Adding type libraries to your script, which means you have access to type library features such as constants.

- Adding XML components to your code by using an XML editor to create the file.

- Including multiple applications in a single file.

Microsoft has only recently begun using the WSF. In fact, you can't execute WSF files in older versions of Windows such as Windows XP—you need Vista or newer versions of Windows to use this technology.

NOTE You can find a wealth of information about Windows scripting technologies online. However, one of the more interesting places to look is the Batch Scripts for Windows site at http://www.wilsonmar.com/1wsh.htm. If you want to learn about WSF files in a hurry, you may want to obtain the video found at http://www.onscript.com/training-videos/titles/windows-script-files-unmasked.asp.

The best way to edit a WSF file is to use an editor designed for the purpose. You may find the combination of XML and scripting code a little disorienting at first and a good editor can help you overcome that problem. One of the better editors is Script Editor 2.1 from Brinesoft (http://script-editor.brinesoft.qarchive.org/).

A WSF file begins with a <job> element. The <job> element can contain an id attribute that you can use later to execute a specific job within a file. For example, if the source code file contains the following <job> element:

```
<job id="MyJob">
```

and the name of the file is MyScript.WSF, you can execute it by typing **CScript //Job:MyJob MyScript.WSF** and pressing Enter. Of course, as with any good XML, you must include the ending </job> element.

Having the <job> element isn't enough to create a script, however. You must also include the <script> element. The <script> element defines the beginning of a scripting area and a job can include more than one scripting area. Each scripting area can include a single language.

Consequently, the <script> element normally has the language attribute. When you want to execute a VBScript, you set the language attribute to VBScript. The <script> element can also include the scr attribute, which defines the location of external code. Consequently, if your script is in VBScript and it relies on the MyExternal.VBS file, the <script> element would include both entries like this:

```
<script language="VBScript" src="MyExternal.VBS">
```

The final essential WSF element is the <reference> element. You use it to reference external code. The type library must appear in the registry before you can use it. To register a type library, type **RegSvr32** *TypeLibraryName* and press Enter, where *TypeLibraryName* is the full name of the type library. Normally, you perform this task in the %SYSTEMROOT%\ System32 directory, but you can perform it in any directory in which the type library file appears. The <reference> element accesses the external code using its progid attribute. The actual usage of the external code looks similar to how you might have worked with it in earlier versions of Visual Basic. Here's an example of external code access in a WSF file:

```
<job id="ExternalCodeAccess">
    <reference progid="MyComponent.MyClass">
    <script language="VBScript">
        Dim ObjRef
        Set ObjRef = CreateObject("MyComponent.MyClass")
        Result = ObjRef.MyMethod
        If Result = 0 then
            WScript.Echo "An Error Occurred"
        End If
    </script>
</job>
```

The <reference> element makes it possible to load the external code contained in the MyComponent file. You access a particular class, MyClass, within that object and instantiate by setting ObjRef equal to the output of CreateObject(). Now that the code has an object to use, it can call the MyMethod() method. The output of this call appears in Result. When Result contains an unexpected value, the code can display an error message to the user. Although this feature is very simple, it does provide you with access to a wealth of additional resources and makes your scripts considerably more flexible.

Creating Scripts

PART VIII

Execute Scripts

All you need to create a standard script is a text editor, such as
Notepad, and a little time. (If you want to create a WSF, then you really
should use an editor designed for the purpose.) You can also use script-
specific tools such as the Visual Basic Editor or Microsoft Script Editor
provided with Microsoft Office. A number of third parties also produce
products that can help you create and even compile your script.

No matter what you do to create your script, however, it's useless
unless you can run it. Windows provides two interpreters—applications
that run scripts—for you to use. The first, CScript, works at the command line and the second, WScript, works from within Windows. The
following sections describe both options.

Run Scripts with the *CScript* and *WScript* Utilities

Windows supports two methods of starting scripts. The CScript application works at the command prompt, while the WScript application
works from within the graphical user environment. Both applications
accomplish the same task—they provide a means for interpreting a
script file you create.

CScript and WScript use the same command line. You must provide
a script name as the first command line argument. Most scripts have a
.VBE or .JS file extension, but any extension is acceptable. For example,
you can still use .VBS files with Windows Script Host (WSH), but the
icon won't look right, in some cases, and you can't double-click it to
start the execution with newer Windows products. The .VBS extension
is the right choice for older versions of Windows. The icon is yellow for
.VBE files and blue for .JS and WSF files. The following sections describe
how to perform scripting tasks.

Obtain *CScript* and *WScript* Help

As with most utilities, you use the /? command line switch to obtain
help. To obtain help type **CScript /?** or **WScript /?** and press Enter.
When working with CScript you see the help information at the command line. WScript displays help in a dialog box.

Execute a Script

To execute a script, you use the CScript *ScriptName* or WScript *ScriptName* command, where *ScriptName* is the name of the script you want to execute. For example, to execute Test.JS using CScript, you type **CScript Test.JS** and press Enter.

If you want to ensure that the script executes without user intervention, use the //B command line switch (notice the double slash used for CScript and WScript command line switches). For example, if you want to execute Test.JS in batch mode using CScript, you'd type **CScript //B Test.JS** and press Enter.

On the other hand, you might need to provide full interactivity when working with a script. In this case, you use the //I command line switch. To execute Test.JS with full interactivity using CScript, you'd type **CSript //I Test.JS**.

In some cases, you want your script to execute silently. To help accomplish this task, you need to execute the script without displaying a logo using the //NoLogo command line switch. You normally execute such scripts in batch mode as well. For example, if you want to execute Test.JS quietly using CScript, you'd type **CScript //B //NoLogo Test.JS** and press Enter.

Debug a Script

One of the advantages of scripts over batch files is that you gain access to a debugger—a special program you can use to step through your script one command at a time to see how it works. There are actually two debugger switches associated with CScript and WScript. The //D switch enables Active Debugging, which is a setup that shows any debugging statements within your code. Debugging statements don't normally execute—they only execute when you're actually debugging your code. To access the debugging statements within Test.JS using CScript, type **CScript //D Test.JS** and press Enter.

The //X command line switch actually opens a debugger and loads your code into it so that you can debug your code even if you don't have debugging statements added to it. This is the mode where you can single step through your application to see how it works. To debug Test.JS in the debugger using CScript, type **CScript //X Test.JS** and press Enter.

Errant scripts can cause problems for your system. If you're debugging your script, it means that the script might end up in an endless

Creating Scripts

PART VIII

loop or freeze in other ways. Fortunately, you can tell the script to stop running at a certain point using the //T:*TimeLimit* command line switch where *TimeLimit* is the amount of time the script can run in seconds. For example, to give Test.JS ten seconds to run using CScript, you type **CScript //T:10 Test.JS** and press Enter.

Change the Default Application

If you double-click a script file in Windows Explorer or type its name at the command line, the command processor looks up the default script application and uses it to execute the script. Consequently, the choice of default application is important when you want to obtain specific results from your script. To change the default application, use the //H:CScript command line switch to select CScript and the //H:WScript command line switch to select WScript. For example, to select CScript as the default application using CScript, you type **CScript //H:CScript** and press Enter.

Configure the Host and Property Page Options

You don't have to rely exclusively on command line switches to configure WSH; you can configure two WSH options from the Windows Script Host Settings dialog box shown in Figure 22.1. Type **WScript** and press Enter. You'll see the Windows Script Host Settings dialog box.

Figure 22.1: Configure WSH to meet specific needs.

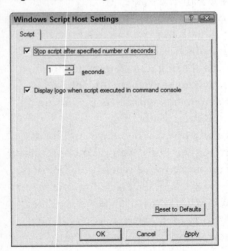

The Stop Script after Specified Number of Seconds check box tells WSH to stop executing a script after a certain time interval has elapsed. The edit box below it contains the number of seconds to wait. Setting this option is like adding the //T command line switch to every script that you run.

The Display Logo When Script Executed in Command Console check box determines whether WSH displays WSH logo when running scripts from the DOS prompt. Normally, Windows checks this option, which is the same as adding the //Logo command line switch to every script that you run. Clearing this option tells WSH that you don't want to display the logo, which is the same as using the //NoLogo command line switch.

You can also display the Windows Script Host Settings dialog box for individual scripts. Simply right-click the script file and select Properties from the context menu. Select the Script tab to see the options. These settings only affect the individual script file; the options for WSH in general remain the same.

23

Using the Scripting Objects

I f you had to try to create all of the supporting code used to write a script by hand, you'd be working quite hard and for a long time. Fortunately, someone has already written a considerable amount of code for you. This code appears within objects, which you can think of as boxes that hold code and data. You really don't need to know much more about the objects than the fact that they make it easier to write scripts. You use the contents of these objects just as you do commands at the command line to perform tasks. Unlike commands and utilities, however, these objects are available for use directly within the scripting environment; you don't even have to know where they physically reside on the hard drive.

Understanding Properties and Methods

A programming object models real-world objects in several ways. When working with WSH objects, you have access to properties and methods. A property or method helps define the object and tells you what you can do with the object. It helps to think of the abstract elements, both properties and methods, in ways that you would think of their real-world equivalents.

A property describes the object in some way. For example, when you look at an object such as an apple, you see that it has a color, perhaps red. The color is a property of the apple. In this case, the color property has a value of red. Just as apples have all kinds of properties, such as the number of seeds in the core, WSH objects also have a number of properties that you use to discover more about the WSH object.

Real-world objects can also perform tasks. A car can move forward or backward. You press the gas pedal, a method, to move the car forward or backward. Even though you press the gas pedal in both cases, you must set the gear shift in a different position to accomplish the task. Likewise, WSH objects have methods that you use to perform tasks. Settings in properties often affect how these tasks are performed. Just as pressing the gas pedal is a car method that's affected by the gear shift position property, WSH objects have methods that respond differently depending on how you set the properties.

All of these objects are packaged together to make them easy to access and use. Think about them as being in a special box called the Windows Scripting Host (WSH) (or sometimes Windows Script Host). You'll see WSH mentioned quite often in this chapter because it provides the environment in which your scripts execute. Think of WSH as a sort of house with rooms for each of the objects it supports. Your code moves from room to room using the objects that it needs to perform tasks. The following sections tell you more about the objects that come with WSH.

Use the *WScript* Object

The WScript object is the main object for WSH. You'll access every other object through this one.

Use the *WScript* Properties

The WScript properties tell you something about your script as a whole, including such necessary items as the arguments the user passes to your script at the command line. The following sections tell you about the properties that the WScript object supports.

Understand the *Application* Property

The Application property provides you with access to a low-level interface for WScript. An *interface* is a pointer to a list of functions that you can call for a particular object. Only advanced programmers need this property because WSH exposes all of the basic functions for you.

Use the *Arguments* Property

The Arguments property provides a complete list of the arguments for this script. Applications pass arguments on the command line. WSH passes the argument list as an array. You create a variable to hold the argument list and then access the individual arguments as you would any array. The Arguments.Count property contains the total number of array elements. The following code shows a typical use for this property:

```
// Display the number of arguments.
WScript.Echo("The number of arguments is: " + WScript.
Arguments.Count());

// If there are arguments, display them on screen.
if (WScript.Arguments.Count() > 0)
{
    // Get the list of arguments.
    objArgs = WScript.Arguments;
```

```
// Display each argument in turn.
for (i=0; i<objArgs.length; i++)
{
    WScript.Echo("Argument " + i + " is: " + objArgs(i))
}
}
```

Use the *FullName* Property

The FullName property contains the full name of the scripting engine along with the fully qualified path to it. For example, if you were using CScript, you might get C:\Windows\System32\CScript.EXE as a return value. The following code shows a typical use for this property:

```
// Display the full name of the scripting engine.
WScript.Echo(WScript.FullName);
```

Use the *Interactive* Property

The Interactive property returns true if the script is in interactive mode (the user can interact with the script to perform tasks). The following code shows a typical use for this property:

```
// Determine whether the script is in interactive mode.
if (WScript.Interactive)
{
    WScript.Echo("The script is in interactive mode.");
}
```

Use the *Name* Property

The Name property returns the friendly name for WScript. In most cases, this is Windows Scripting Host. The following code shows a typical use for this property:

```
// Show the friendly name for the scripting host.
WScript.Echo("The friendly name is: " + WScript.Name);
```

Use the *Path* Property

The Path property provides just the path information for the host executable. For example, if you were using CScript, you may get a return value of: C:\Windows\System32\. The following code shows a typical use for this property:

```
// Provide the full path to the scripting engine.
WScript.Echo("The scripting host path is: " + WScript.Path);
```

Use the *ScriptFullName* Property

The ScriptFullName property contains the full name and path of the script that's running. The following code shows a typical use for this property:

```
// Show the full name of the script that is executing.
WScript.Echo("The script name and path are: " + WScript.
ScriptFullName);
```

Use the *ScriptName* Property

The ScriptName property provides just the script name. The following code shows a typical use for this property:

```
// Show the short name of the script that is executing.
WScript.Echo("The script name is: " + WScript.ScriptName);
```

Use the *Version* Property

The Version property returns the WSH Version number. The following code shows a typical use for this property:

```
// Display the version number of WSH.
WScript.Echo("The WSH version number is: " + WScript.
Version);
```

Use the *WScript* Methods

Remember that all of these properties tell you about the WScript object. You can also use methods to perform tasks with the WScript object. The following sections provide a brief overview of the more important methods you'll use with the WScript object. Note that most of these methods require you pass one or more parameters as input. A *parameter* is a piece of data the method uses to perform a task.

Creating Scripts

PART VIII

Use the CreateObject Method

The CreateObject(*strProgID*) method creates the object specified by strProgID. This object could be WSH specific, such as "WScript.Network" or application specific, such as "Excel.Application". The following code shows a typical use for this method:

```
// Create a WSH object.
WshShell = WScript.CreateObject("WScript.Shell");

// Use the object to display a popup.
WshShell.Popup("Hello World!");
```

Use the *GetObject* Method

The GetObject(*strPathname* [, *strProgID*]) method retrieves the requested object. strPathname contains the filename for the object you want to retrieve. In most cases, this is going to be a data file, but you can retrieve other kinds of objects as well. As soon as you execute this command, WSH starts the application associated with that object. For example, if you specified C:\MyText.TXT as the strPathname, then WSH may open Notepad to display it. The optional strProgID argument allows you to override the default processing of the object. For example, you may want to open the text file with Word instead of Notepad. The following code shows a typical use for this method:

```
// Obtain access to the file system object.
FSO = new ActiveXObject("Scripting.FileSystemObject");

// Get the current directory.
ScriptPath = FSO.GetFile(WScript.ScriptFullName).
ParentFolder;

// Create the text file path.
TextPath = ScriptPath + "\\Hello.TXT";

// Open the text file in Notepad.
WScript.Echo("Opening " + TextPath);
WScript.GetObject(TextPath);
```

Working with Objects

Scripts have a definite advantage over batch files because you can use objects in scripts. An object can be anything. For example, you can create an object that contains an Excel worksheet and use the functionality of Excel to perform tasks at the command line. A worksheet could hold a directory listing, and you can use the database features of Excel to perform a customized sort. All you need to do is create the object using the `WScript.CreateObject()` method or new `ActiveXObject()` constructor. If you already have a data file available to use for your application, then use the `WScript.GetObject()` method to open the data file directly. In most cases, you don't even need to worry about which application to use because the system uses the correct application by default.

Applications are an obvious kind of object. Your machine contains literally thousands of objects, all of which are available for use. For example, you can load an XML document by using the `Msxml2.DOMDocument.5.0` object. Once you create this object, you can load the XML document using the `Load()` method and then process it using the various methods that the object provides. For example, use the `TransformNode()` method to use XML Stylesheet Language Transformation (XSLT) to transform the XML document from one presentation to another.

Make sure you spend time looking at all of the objects described in the script resource Web pages and coding examples provided in this chapter. You might be surprised at how much work a script can perform with only a modicum of work on your part. Even though the `WScript` objects described in this section are your most important resource, don't neglect the other resources at your fingertips.

Use the *Echo* Method

The `Echo(AnyArg)` method displays text in a window (`WScript`) or to the console screen (`CScript`). AnyArg can contain any type of valid output value. This can include both strings and numbers. Using `Echo` without any arguments displays a blank line. The following code shows a typical use for this method:

```
// Display a simple message.
WScript.Echo("Hello World!");
```

Creating Scripts

PART VIII

Use the *GetScriptEngine* Method

The GetScriptEngine(*strEngineID*) method registers an alternative script engine such as PerlScript (see the PerlScript site at http://www.xav.com/perl/Components/Windows/PerlScript.html or the Windows Script Host Resources site at http://labmice.techtarget.com/scripting/WSH.htm for details on this alternative). strEngineID contains the identifier for the script engine that you want to retrieve. You'll need to register the engine using the GetScriptEngine.Register() method before you can actually use it. A script engine also requires you to provide a default extension. A description of how to work with alternative script engines is outside the scope of this book.

Use the *Quit* Method

The Quit(*intErrorCode*) method exits the script prematurely. The optional intErrorCode argument returns an error code if necessary. You can test for this value using the ErrorLevel clause in batch files. The following code shows a typical use for this method:

```
// Exit prematurely with an exit code of 42.
WScript.Quit(42);
```

Use the *WScript.WshArguments* Object

Whenever you start a script, you have the option of passing one or more arguments to it on the command line. That's where the WshArguments object comes into play. It helps you determine the number of arguments and then retrieves them as needed. You'll always use the WScript.Arguments property to access this object; it's not directly accessible. The following list describes the properties for this object:

- **Item(intIndex):** Retrieves a specific command line argument. intIndex contains the index of the argument that you want to retrieve. The array used to hold the arguments is 0 based, so the first argument number is 0.

- **Count():** Returns the number of command line arguments.

- **Length():** Returns the number of command line arguments. WSH provides this property for JScript compatibility purposes.

Here's an example that shows how to use this object:

```
// Display the number of arguments.
WScript.Echo("The number of arguments is: " + WScript.
Arguments.Count());

// If there are arguments, display them on screen.
if (WScript.Arguments.Count() > 0)
{
   // Get the list of arguments.
   objArgs = WScript.Arguments;

   // Display each argument in turn.
   for (i=0; i<objArgs.length; i++)
   {
      WScript.Echo("Argument " + i + " is: " + objArgs(i))
   }
}
```

Use the *WScript.WshShell* Object

You'll use the WScript.WshShell object to access the Windows shell (the part of Windows that interacts with applications and creates the user interface) in a variety of ways. For example, you can use this object to read the registry or to create a new shortcut on the desktop. This is an exposed WSH object, which means you can access it directly. However, you need to access it through the WScript object like this: WScript.WshShell. The "Script the Command Line and System Environment," "Script the Registry," and "Create .*LNK* Files" sections of the chapter provide examples of how to use this object. The WScript.WshShell doesn't include any properties. The following list describes the WshShell methods:

- **CreateShortcut(*strPathname*):** Creates a WSH shortcut object. *strPathname* contains the location of the shortcut, which will be the desktop in most cases.

- **DeleteEnvironmentVariable(*strName[, strType]*):** Deletes the environment variable specified by *strName*. The optional *strType* argument defines the type of environment variable to delete. Typical values for *strType* include System, User, Volatile, and Process. The default environment variable type is System.

- **GetEnvironmentVariable(*strName*[, *strType*])**: Retrieves the environment variable specified by *strName*. Default environment variables include NUMBER_OF_PROCESSORS, OS, COMSPEC, HOMEDRIVE, HOMEPATH, PATH, PATHEXT, PROMPT, SYSTEMDRIVE, SYSTEMROOT, WINDIR, TEMP, and TMP. The optional *strType* argument defines the type of environment variable to delete. Typical values for *strType* include System, User, Volatile, and Process. The default environment variable type is System.

- **Popup(*strText*[, *intSeconds*][, *strTitle*] [,*intType*])**: Displays a message dialog box. The return value is an integer defining which button the user selected including the following values: OK (1), Cancel (2), Abort (3), Retry (4), Ignore (5), Yes (6), No (7), Close (8), and Help (9). *strText* contains the text that you want to display in the dialog box. *intSeconds* determines how long WSH displays the dialog box before it closes the dialog box and returns a value of –1. *strTitle* contains the title bar text. The *intType* argument can contain values that determine the type of dialog box you'll create. The first *intType* argument determines button type. You have a choice of OK (0), OK and Cancel (1), Abort, Retry, and Ignore (2), Yes, No, and Cancel (3), Yes and No (4), and Retry and Cancel (5). The second *intType* argument determines which icon Windows displays in the dialog box. You have a choice of the following values: Stop (16), Question (32), Exclamation (48), and Information (64). Combine the *intType* argument values to obtain different dialog box effects.

- **RegDelete(*strName*)**: Removes the value or key specified by strName from the registry. If *strName* ends in a backslash, then RegDelete removes a key. You must provide a fully qualified path to the key or value that you want to delete. In addition, *strName* must begin with one of these values: HKEY_CURRENT_USER, HKEY_LOCAL_MACHINE, HKEY_CLASSES_ROOT, HKEY_USERS, HKEY_CURRENT_CONFIG, or HKEY_DYN_DATA.

- **RegRead(*strName*)**: Reads the value or key specified by strName from the registry. If *strName* ends in a backslash, then RegRead reads a key. You must provide a fully qualified path to the key or value that you want to read. In addition, *strName* must begin with one of these values: HKEY_CURRENT_USER, HKEY_LOCAL_MACHINE, HKEY_CLASSES_ROOT, HKEY_USERS, HKEY_CURRENT_CONFIG, or HKEY_DYN_DATA. RegRead can only read specific data types including REG_SZ, REG_EXPAND_SZ, REG_DWORD, REG_BINARY, and REG_MULTI_SZ. Any other data types will return an error.

- **RegWrite(*strName*, *anyValue*[, *strType*])**: Writes the data specified by anyValue to a value or key specified by *strName* to the registry. If *strName* ends in a backslash, then RegWrite writes a key. You
  must provide a fully qualified path to the key or value that you
  want to write. In addition, *strName* must begin with one of these
  values: HKEY_CURRENT_USER, HKEY_LOCAL_MACHINE, HKEY_CLASSES_
  ROOT, HKEY_USERS, HKEY_CURRENT_CONFIG, or HKEY_DYN_DATA. RegRead
  can only write specific data types including REG_SZ, REG_EXPAND_SZ,
  REG_DWORD, and REG_BINARY. Any other data types will return an
  error.

- **Run(*strCommand*[, *intWinType*][, *lWait*])**: Runs the command or
  application specified by strCommand. You can include command
  line arguments and switches with the command string. *intWin-*
  Type determines the type of window that the application starts in.
  You can force the script to wait for the application to complete by
  setting *lWait* to True; otherwise, the script begins the next line of
  execution immediately.

- **SetEnvironmentVariable(*strName*, *strValue*[, *strType*])**: Sets
  the environment variable named *strName* to the value specified
  by *strValue*. The optional *strType* argument defines the type of
  environment variable to create. Typical values for *strType* include
  System, User, Volatile, and Process. The default environment variable type is System.

Use the *WScript.WshNetwork* Object

The WshNetwork object works with network objects such as drives and
printers that the client machine can access. This is an exposed WSH
object, which means you can access it directly using the WScript
.WshNetwork object. The following sections describe the properties and
methods you use when working with the WScript.WshNetwork object.

Use the *WScript.WshNetwork* Properties

The WScript.WshNetwork object provides identification information for
the network. The following sections describe properties associated with
this object.

Use the *ComputerName* Property

The ComputerName property returns a string containing the client computer name. The following code shows a typical use for this property:

```
// Create the WshNetwork object.
WshNetwork = WScript.CreateObject("WScript.Network")

// Show the computer name.
WScript.Echo(WshNetwork.ComputerName);
```

Use the *UserDomain* Property

The UserDomain property returns a string containing the name of the domain that the user has logged into. The following code shows a typical use for this property:

```
// Create the WshNetwork object.
WshNetwork = WScript.CreateObject("WScript.Network")

// Show the domain name.
WScript.Echo(WshNetwork.UserDomain);
```

Use the *UserName* Property

The UserName property returns a string containing the name that the user used to log on to the network. The following code shows a typical use for this property:

```
// Create the WshNetwork object.
WshNetwork = WScript.CreateObject("WScript.Network")

// Show the username.
WScript.Echo(WshNetwork.UserName);
```

Use the *WScript.WshNetwork* Methods

As with any other WSH object, the WshNetwork object uses methods to work with network resources. The following sections describe the methods associated with this object.

Use the *AddPrinterConnection* Method

The AddPrinterConnection(*strLocal*, strRemote [, *1Update*]
[, strUser] [, *strPassword*]) method creates a new printer connection for the local machine. strLocal contains the local name for
the printer specified by strRemote. The strRemote value must contain
a locatable resource (normally a network printer, but it can be any
locatable resource used for printing) and usually uses a UNC format
such as \\Remote\Printer. Setting 1Update to True adds the new connection to the user profile, which means Windows makes the connection
available each time the user boots their machine. strUser and strPassword
contain optional username and password values required to log on to the
remote machine and create the connection. The following code shows a
typical use for this method:

```
// Create the WshNetwork object.
WshNetwork = WScript.CreateObject("WScript.Network")

// Add a remote printer connection.
// !!! You must change this code to match your system!!!
WshNetwork.AddPrinterConnection("LPT1", "\\\\MyServer\\
Printer");
```

Use the *EnumNetworkDrives* Method

The EnumNetworkDrives()method returns a WshCollection object containing the list of local and remote drives currently mapped from the client
machine. A WshCollection object is essentially a 0-based array of strings.
The following code shows a typical use for this method:

```
// Create the WshNetwork object.
WshNetwork = WScript.CreateObject("WScript.Network")

// Get the drive list.
DriveList = WshNetwork.EnumNetworkDrives();

// Enumerate the drives.
for (i=0; i<DriveList.length; i+=2)
{
    // The local drive letter is first and then the UNC
location.
```

Creating Scripts

PART VIII

```
        WScript.Echo("Drive: " + DriveList.Item(i) + " is: " +
    DriveList.Item(i+1));
    }
```

Use the *EnumPrinterConnections* Method

The EnumPrinterConnections() method returns a WshCollection object containing the list of local and remote printers currently mapped from the client machine. A WshCollection object is essentially a 0-based array of strings. The following code shows a typical use for this method:

```
    // Create the WshNetwork object.
    WshNetwork = WScript.CreateObject("WScript.Network")

    // Get the printer list.
    PrintList = WshNetwork.EnumPrinterConnections();

    // Enumerate the drives.
    for (i=0; i<PrintList.length; i+=2)
    {
        // The local drive letter is first and then the UNC
    location.
        WScript.Echo("Printer: " + PrintList.Item(i) + " is: " +
    PrintList.Item(i+1));
    }
```

Use the *MapNetworkDrive* Method

The MapNetworkDrive(*strLocal*, strRemote [, *lUpdate*] [, strUser] [, *strPassword*]) method creates a new drive connection for the local machine. strLocal contains the local name for the drive specified by strRemote. The strRemote value must contain a locatable resource and usually uses a UNC format such as \\Remote\Drive_C. Setting lUpdate to True adds the new connection to the user profile, which means Windows makes the connection available each time the user boots their machine. strUser and strPassword contain optional username and password values required to log on to the remote machine and create the connection. The following code shows a typical use for this method:

```
    // Create the WshNetwork object.
    WshNetwork = WScript.CreateObject("WScript.Network")
```

```
// Map a network drive.
// !!! You must change this code to match your system!!!
WshNetwork.MapNetworkDrive("Z", "\\\\MyServer\\
ASharedDrive");
```

Use the *RemoveNetworkDrive* Method

The RemoveNetworkDrive(*strName* [, 1Force] [, 1Update]) method deletes a previous network drive mapping. If strName contains a local name, Windows only cancels that connection. If strName contains a remote name, then Windows cancels all resources associated with that remote name. Set 1Force to True if you want to disconnect from a resource whether or not that resource is in use. Setting 1Update to True removes the connection from the user profile so that it doesn't appear the next time that the user logs on to the machine. The following code shows a typical use for this method:

```
// Create the WshNetwork object.
WshNetwork = WScript.CreateObject("WScript.Network")


// Remove the network drive.
// !!! You must change this code to match your system!!!
WshNetwork.RemoveNetworkDrive("Z");
```

Use the *RemovePrinterConnection* Method

The RemovePrinterConnection(*strName* [, 1Force] [, 1Update]) method deletes a previous network printer connection. If strName contains a local name, Windows only cancels that connection. If strName contains a remote name, then Windows cancels all resources associated with that remote name. Set 1Force to True if you want to disconnect from a resource, whether or not that resource is in use. Setting 1Update to True removes the connection from the user profile so that it doesn't appear the next time that the user logs on to the machine. The following code shows a typical use for this method:

```
// Create the WshNetwork object.
WshNetwork = WScript.CreateObject("WScript.Network")


// Remove the printer connection.
// !!! You must change this code to match your system!!!
WshNetwork.RemovePrinterConnection("LPT1");
```

Creating Scripts

PART VIII

Create a Basic Script

Scripts can make the command line significantly easier to automate and can improve the reliability of command line tasks by helping you perform tasks in the same sequence every time. This section shows how to create basic scripts in both VBScript and JavaScript so you can see the differences between the two languages. You'll also see how to use some of the objects described in the scripting object-specific sections of the chapter. The following code shows a basic example in VBScript:

```vbscript
' Test1.VBS shows how to use functions and subprocedures
' within a WSH script.

WScript.Echo("The value returned was: " +
CStr(MyFunction(1)))

function MyFunction(nSomeValue)
    WScript.Echo("Function received value of: " +
CStr(nSomeValue))
    Call MySubprocedure(nSomeValue + 1)
    MyFunction = nSomeValue + 1
end function

sub MySubprocedure(nSomeValue)
    WScript.Echo("Subprocedure received value of: " +
CStr(nSomeValue))
end sub
```

As you can see, the sample code uses the WScript object to send information to the screen. The WScript object is always available at the command line, even though you've probably never used it as part of a browser application. As shown in the example, it's important to know how to use both functions and subs, the two building blocks of VBScript. The following code shows a similar example for JavaScript:

```javascript
// Test1.JS shows how to use functions within a WSH script.

WScript.Echo("The value returned was: " + MyFunction(1));

function MyFunction(nSomeValue)
{
```

```
    WScript.Echo("The value received was: " + nSomeValue);
    return nSomeValue + 1;
}
```

JavaScript only provides functions, so that's all this example demonstrates. It's also important to notice that VBScript requires you to convert numeric values to a string, while JavaScript performs the conversion automatically. The following sections show how to perform certain command line–oriented tasks using scripting.

Script the Command Line and System Environment

Many of your scripts require access to the command line. The command line is where you type switches to modify the behavior of the script, as many of the utilities described in this book do. The system environment contains user, application, and operating system values, such as the user's name or the version of the operating system. The JavaScript code in Listing 23.1 retrieves information from the command line. It also retrieves information about the application environment.

Listing 23.1: Working with the Command Line and System Environment

```
// ProgInfo.JS determines the specifics about your program
and then
// displays this information on screen.

// Create some constants for display purposes (buttons and
icons).
var intOK = 0;
var intOKCancel = 1;
var intAbortRetryIgnore = 2;
var intYesNoCancel = 3;
var intYesNo = 4;
var intRetryCancel = 5;
var intStop = 16;
var intQuestion = 32;
var intExclamation = 48;
var intInformation = 64;

// Create some popup return values.
var intOK = 1;
var intCancel = 2;
```

```javascript
var intAbort = 3;
var intRetry = 4;
var intIgnore = 5;
var intYes = 6;
var intNo = 7;
var intClose = 8;
var intHelp = 9;

// Create a popup display object.
var WshShell = WScript.CreateObject("WScript.Shell");

// Create a variable for holding a popup return value.
var intReturn;

// Get the program information and display it.
WshShell.Popup("Full Name:\t" + WScript.Fullname +
        "\r\nInteractive:\t" + WScript.Interactive +
        "\r\nName:\t\t" + WScript.Name +
        "\r\nPath:\t\t" + WScript.Path +
        "\r\nScript Full Name:\t" + WScript.ScriptFullName +
        "\r\nScript Name:\t" + WScript.ScriptName +
        "\r\nVersion:\t\t" + WScript.Version,
        0,
        "Program Information Demonstration",
        intOK + intInformation);

// Ask if the user wants to display the argument list.
intReturn = WshShell.Popup("Do you want to display the
argument list?",
            0,
            "Argument List Display",
            intYesNo + intQuestion);

// Determine if the user wants to display the argument list
and
// display an appropriate message.
if (intReturn == intYes)

    // See if there are any arguments to display.
    DisplayArguments();
else
```

```
    WScript.Echo("Goodbye");

function DisplayArguments()
{

    // Create some variables.
    var strArguments = "Arguments:\r\n\t";     // Argument
list.
    var intCount = 0;                    // Loop counter.

    // See if there are any arguments, if not, display an
    // appropriate message.
    if (WScript.Arguments.Length == 0)
       WshShell.Popup("There are no arguments to display.",
           0,
           "Argument List Display",
           intOK + intInformation);

    // If there are arguments to display, then create a list
    // first and display them all at once.
    else
    {
        for (intCount = 0;
             intCount < WScript.Arguments.Length;
             intCount++)

            strArguments = strArguments +
                         WScript.Arguments.Item(intCount)
 + "\r\n\t";

        WshShell.Popup(strArguments,
                     0,
                     "Argument List Display",
                     intOK + intInformation);
    }
}
```

When you run this script, you'll see a dialog box containing all of the information about the script engine. When you click OK, the program asks if you want to display the command line arguments. If you say yes, then you'll see anything you typed at the command line. Otherwise, the script displays a Goodbye message.

Creating Scripts

PART VIII

You should notice a few things about this example. First, the code creates a WshShell object. You need access to the WshShell object for many of the tasks you'll perform with scripts. The code also shows how to use the Popup() method to obtain information from the user. Finally, the code uses the Arguments object to access the command line information. Notice the object hierarchy used in this example.

Script the Registry

Many of the utilities described in this book rely on the registry to store and retrieve data about the machine, the operating system, the user, and the application itself. Knowing how to access the registry from your script is important because you also need to access these values in order to discover how a particular utility will react or how the user had configured the system. You can also use the registry to store and retrieve values for your script. The example in Listing 23.2 shows how to use VBScript to access information in the registry. You don't want to change information unless you have to, but seeing what's available in the registry is a good way to build your knowledge of both scripting and the registry. Note that this example uses the command line argument to determine which file extension to look for in the registry. The example uses the .TXT file extension when you don't supply one.

Listing 23.2: Working with the Registry

```
' RegRead.VBE will display the application extension
information
' contained in the registry.

' Create an icon and button variable for Popup().
intOK = 0
intInformation = 64

' Create a popup display object.
set WshShell = WScript.CreateObject("WScript.Shell")

' Create variables to hold the information.
strExtension = ""     ' File extension that we're looking
for.
strFileType = ""      ' Holds the main file type.
strFileOpen = ""      ' File open command.
```

```
    strFilePrint = ""      ' File print command.
    strDefaultIcon = ""  ' Default icon for file type.

    ' See if the user provided a file extension to look for.
    ' If not, assign strExtension a default file extension.
    if (WScript.Arguments.Length > 0) then
        strExtension = WScript.Arguments.Item(0)
    else
        strExtension = ".txt"
    end if

    ' Get the file type.
    strFileType = WshShell.RegRead("HKEY_CLASSES_ROOT\" +_
                     strExtension + "\")

    ' Use the file type to get the file open and file print
    ' commands, along with the default icon.
    strFileOpen = WshShell.RegRead("HKEY_CLASSES_ROOT\" +_
                     strFileType +_
                     "\shell\open\command\")
    strFilePrint = WshShell.RegRead("HKEY_CLASSES_ROOT\" +_
                     strFileType +_
                     "\shell\print\command\")
    strDefaultIcon = WshShell.RegRead("HKEY_CLASSES_ROOT\" +_
                     strFileType +_
                     "\DefaultIcon\")

    ' Display the results.
    WshShell.Popup "File Type:" + vbTab + vbTab + vbTab +
    strFileType +_
          vbCrLf + "File Open Command:" + vbTab + strFileOpen +_
          vbCrLf + "File Print Command:" + vbTab + vbTab +
    strFilePrint +_
          vbCrLf + "Default Icon:" + vbTab + vbTab +
    strDefaultIcon,_
          0,_
          "RegRead Results",_
          intOK + intInformation
```

When you run this script, it reads the command line. If you haven't supplied a value, the script assigns a default extension of .TXT. The script uses the extension to locate information in the registry such as the file open and print commands. Finally, the script uses the Popup() method to display the output.

You should notice several differences between this example and the JavaScript example in Listing 23.1. First, the method for creating an object requires the use of a set—you can't simply assign the object to a variable. You'll also notice that VBScript has access to all of the standard Visual Basic constants such as vbTab and vbCrLf. Finally, VBScript handles many of the method calls as subs, not as functions. You need to exercise care when working in a mixed environment.

Create *.LNK* Files

Up until now, you may have taken .LNK (link) files for granted in Windows because they're exceptionally easy to create. However, sometimes you want to automate the process of creating links on the user's machine, so it's good to know how to create them using a script as well. You'll find a ton of references to an elusive Shortcut utility for Windows online, but you won't find the actual executable on your hard drive, which may leave you puzzling for a long time. It's possible to create .LNK files using scripts. Listing 23.3 shows a script that places a .LNK file on your desktop for Notepad. Now you can double-click this .LNK file and open a copy of Notepad (menu not required).

NOTE Windows Server 2008 Server Core may not display links on the desktop. In this case, you can still place links in a common folder, such as %USERPROFILE%, which points to your user folder. You can still type the .LNK filename and press Enter to use the link file from the command line. In short, .LNK files are still useful, even if you can't see their physical manifestation in the form of an icon.

Listing 23.3: Creating a New *.LNK* File

```
' Create the shell object.
Set WshShell = WScript.CreateObject("WScript.Shell")


' Define the location of the LNK file.
LinkFilename = WshShell.ExpandEnvironmentStrings("%USERPROF
ILE%")
LinkFilename = LinkFilename + "\Desktop\Notepad.LNK"
```

```
' Create the LNK file object.
Set LNKFile = WshShell.CreateShortcut(LinkFilename)

' Set the LNK file contents.
LNKFile.TargetPath = "%SYSTEMROOT%\System32\Notepad.EXE"
LNKFile.Arguments = ""
LNKFile.Description = "Open Notepad"
LNKFile.HotKey = ""
LNKFile.IconLocation = "%SYSTEMROOT%\System32\Notepad.EXE,
1"
LNKFile.WindowStyle = "1"
LNKFile.WorkingDirectory = "C:\"

' Save the LNK file to disk.
LNKFile.Save
```

The code begins by creating a Windows Script shell. This shell provides access to features such as environment strings and the function for creating a shortcut. The next step creates a location name based on the user's profile—the \Users\UserName folder for the user. You may use any of the environment variables that Windows supports to obtain information for your scripts. It then adds the actual .LNK file location to the path.

Now that the code has a path to use for creating the .LNK file, it uses the CreateShortcut() function to create it. At this point, the script sets the various .LNK file contents. Any field you can change in a .LNK file, you can also change using a script. Finally, the script saves the results to the hard drive. It's essential to perform this final step or the .LNK file won't work. Simply type the .LNK filename and press Enter to execute it at the command line. For example, in this case you would type **Notepad.LNK** and press Enter at the command line to start a copy of Notepad.

NOTE   You can find a downloadable version of the Shortcut command at http://www.optimumx.com/download. The Shortcut command provides the means to create a .LNK file without resorting to using a script. In addition, you can use it to create an .INI file that contains all of the .LNK file configuration information. The ReadMe.TXT file that comes with the Shortcut command tells you about all of the command line parameters you need to use it.

24

Creating Advanced Scripting Examples

IN THIS CHAPTER, YOU WILL LEARN TO:

Creating Scripts

PART VIII

C hapters 22 and 23 provide you with some scripting basics and information sources you can use to learn more about scripting. This chapter takes things one step further. In this chapter, you find some advanced scripting techniques you can use to make your scripting experience better. Even if you skip this chapter for now, you can come back to it later and use it as a reference for scripting techniques as the need arises.

Script Registry Entries

The RegIni utility lets you perform registry manipulations that involve security or other configurations. You can also use it to perform a list of registry modifications as a script, rather than individually using RegEdit. The most common use of this utility is to modify the security settings for the registry as explained by the Knowledge Base article at http://support.microsoft.com/?kbid=245031. The Knowledge Base article at http://support.microsoft.com/?kbid=237607 has additional information on using this utility for security purposes. You can find a more complete discussion of how to use RegIni, including creating scripts using a number of techniques, on the Windows IT Library site at http://www.windowsitlibrary.com/Content/237/2.html.

To use this utility, you type **RegIni *Scriptname*** and press Enter, where *Scriptname* is the name of a file that contains the instructions you want RegIni to perform. If you want to use this utility to perform tasks on another system, you include the –m *ComputerName* command line switch where *ComputerName* is the name of another system using the UNC format. For example, if you want to execute a script called MyScript.RegIni on MyServer, you type **RegIni –m \\MyServer MyScript.RegIni** and press Enter.

Newer versions of RegIni, such as those found in Windows 7, have additional rules that older versions of RegIni don't follow, such as the requirement to use quoted strings. Because of the new requirements, old scripts won't run when using newer versions of RegIni unless you use the –b command line switch to relax the script requirements. When using an older script with a newer version of RegIni, type **RegIni -b Scriptname** and press Enter. Newer versions of RegIni also include some usage enhancements that you can see by typing **RegIni /?** and pressing Enter.

Script Networking Solutions

Many of the utilities discussed in this book are mini-command processors. For example, the WMIC utility actually opens into a separate environment in which you can execute commands—the command line interface almost ends up being a scripting environment. The Network Command Shell (NetSH) utility extends this idea by providing an extensible command processor. You access the functionality that this utility provides by loading a helper Dynamic Link Library (DLL). Each helper DLL places the NetSH utility into a different context. The use of helper DLLs theoretically makes it possible for third-party vendors to add NetSH functionality as part of their network product installation. The following sections describe the NetSH utility in more detail.

Discover the *NetSH* Helper List

To discover the NetSH helper list, type **NetSH Show Helper** and press Enter. This command displays a list of helper DLLs installed on your machine, which may differ from the list shown in Figure 24.1 based on the operating system features you have installed.

Notice the hierarchy of contexts displayed in Figure 24.1. To access the IPv4 context at the command line, you must type **NetSH Interface IPv4** and then the command you want to use. Likewise, if you want to access the 6To4 context, you must type **NetSH Interface IPv6 6To4** at the command line.

Figure 24.1: Obtain a list of helper DLLs for your setup using the NetSH Show Helper command.

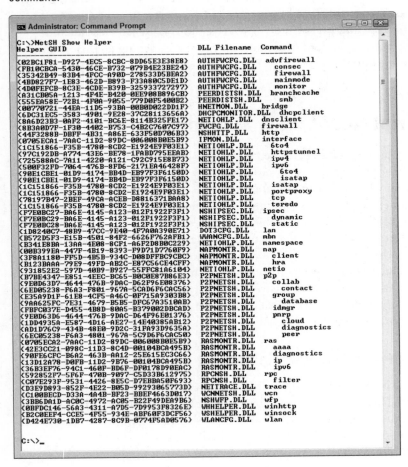

Get *NetSH* Help

Like many of the complex utilities that Microsoft provides, such as WMIC, NetSH uses a hierarchical help structure. Typing any context by itself (or followed by a question mark (?) or Help) displays the list of commands for that context. For example, to see help for IPv4, you type **NetSH Interface IPv4 /?** and press Enter.

Type a command to see the list of subcommands or the instructions for using that command. Type a subcommand to see the instructions for using that subcommand. For example, to discover how to add a new

IP address, type **NetSH Interface IP Add Address** /? at the command prompt and press Enter. You'll see a help display explaining the command, as shown in Figure 24.2.

Figure 24.2: The multilevel command structure provided by NetSH provides you with help at each step.

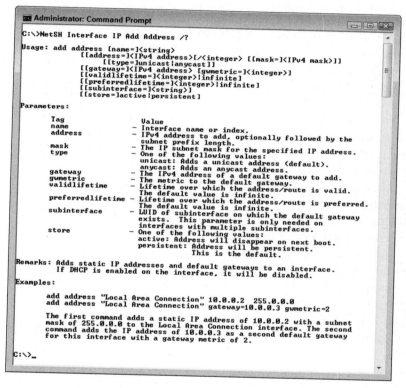

NOTE   This chapter doesn't discuss the specifics of each context because they vary according to operating system version and the helpers you have installed. Unfortunately, there isn't any documented resource from Microsoft for standard contexts in Windows Server 2008, Vista, or Windows 7, but you can use the Windows 2003 resource as a guideline. The contexts for Windows 2003 appear at http://technet.microsoft.com/library/cc778084.aspx. You can find additional NetSH utility documentation in the Microsoft Knowledge Base article at http://support.microsoft.com/?kbid=242468 and The Cable Guy article at http://technet.microsoft.com/library/bb878123.aspx.

Execute *NetSH* Commands

The NetSH utility provides access to a broad range of networking functionality using contexts. Each context represents a different functional network area such as configuring the firewall or modifying security. You can interact with NetSH at the command line, in an interactive environment, and using scripts. In this case, a script file is simply a list of commands that you want NetSH to perform. You place these commands in a text file and pass them to NetSH to execute.

To execute a NetSH command, you use the NetSH *Context Command [Arguments]* format, where *Context* is one or more levels used to access a specific NetSH context, *Command* is a command that the context supports, and the optional *Arguments* is one or more pieces of data that the command requires. For example, to see the interfaces supported by the local machine, you type **NetSH Interface Show Interface** and press Enter. In this case, Interface is the context, Show is the command, and Interface is an argument.

If you want to use a script to execute the commands, use the -f *ScriptFile* command line switch, where *ScriptFile* is the name of a file that contains one command per line. For example, if you want to execute a script named MyScript, you type **NetSH -f MyScript** and press Enter.

In some cases, you'll want to execute commands on another machine. Unlike most utilities, you can't specify the password for the remote system at the command line. Instead, you must provide the password when the command executes. In this case, you use the NetSH -r *RemoteMachine* -u *[DomainName\]UserName Context Command [Arguments]* format, where *RemoteMachine* is the UNC location of a remote system, *DomainName* is an optional domain name for the user account, and *UserName* is the name of the account you want to use for the connection. For example, to see the interfaces supported by MyServer using the Josh account, you type **NetSH -r MyServer -u Josh Interface Show Interface** and press Enter.

Understand the Basic *NetSH* Contexts

The various helper DLLs provide contexts that you can use to perform specific tasks. You can access some of these contexts directly from the command line using a command. Table 24.1 describes each of the top-level contexts.

Table 24.1: Standard NetSH Contexts

Context Name	Windows Version	Description
Bridge	Windows XP and above	Shows configuration information for network adapters that are part of a network bridge. You can also use this context to enable or disable Level 3 compatibility mode.
Diag	Windows XP and above	Performs network diagnostic commands. For example, you can use this context to display network service status information or perform diagnostics similar to the Ping utility. A special NetSH Diag GUI command displays information in the Help and Support Center that provides access to the network diagnostics.
Firewall	Windows XP and above	Provides complete access to the Windows firewall. You can use this context to add and remove configuration information, as well as display the current firewall state.
Interface	Windows 2000 and above	Provides access to the network interfaces installed on your machine, which normally include IP, IPV6 (Windows XP and above), and standard port proxies. You can use this context to configure the TCP/IP protocol including addresses, default gateways, DNS servers, and WINS servers.
RAS	Windows 2000 and above	Provides access to the Remote Access Server (RAS) and all of its configuration information. For example, this context provides access to the Authentication, Authorization, Accounting, and Auditing (AAAA) subcontext where you perform security setups.
Routing	Windows 2000 and above	Helps you configure the routing features of the system using a command line interface, rather than rely on the Routing and Remote Access console. The biggest advantage of the command line interface, in this case, is speed. You can access and manage remote servers over a large network, especially wide area networks (WANs) much faster using NetSH than you can the graphical equivalents. In addition, because these configuration tasks can become quite complex, you gain the advantage of scripting them once, rather than going through every required step each time you perform the task.
WinSock	Windows XP and above	Shows Windows Socket (WinSock) information for the current system. You can also use this context to dump the WinSock configuration script.

Creating Scripts

PART VIII

Use the Root Context Commands

The default context is the root context, the NetSH utility itself. You can use specific commands from this context to perform configuration tasks or access other contexts. The following list describes the command line arguments, which differ according to the version of Windows that you use and the networking features you have installed:

- **add:** Adds a configuration entry to the list of entries. When working at the root context, you can add new helper DLLs to the list.

- **delete:** Deletes a configuration entry from the list of entries. When working at the root context, you can remove a helper DLL from the list.

- **dump:** Displays a configuration script. The script is quite long, so you'll want to use redirection to store the script to a file.

- **exec:** Executes the specified script file.

- **interface:** Sets NetSH to use the interface context.

- **ras:** Sets NetSH to use the RAS context.

- **routing:** Sets NetSH to use the routing context.

- **set:** Updates the configuration settings. Most versions of NetSH only allow you to set the machine name when working at the root context.

- **show:** Displays NetSH configuration information. Most versions of NetSH provide commands to display both the list of aliases and the list of helpers installed on the system.

Windows XP and above provide additional functionality to support items such as the firewall. Here are the Windows XP additions:

- **bridge:** Sets NetSH to use the bridge context.

- **diag:** Sets NetSH to use the diag context.

- **firewall:** Sets NetSH to use the firewall context.

- **winsock:** Sets NetSH to use the WinSock context.

Windows 2003 and above supports still more commands. The following list describes the Windows 2003 additions.

- **cmd:** Creates a command window where you can enter NetSH commands manually.

- **comment:** Executes any commands accumulated in offline mode.

- **flush:** Discards the commands accumulated in offline mode.

- **online:** Sets the current mode to online. In online mode, which is the default for all previous versions of NetSH, the utility executes immediately any command you issue. Type **NetSH show mode** and press Enter to display the current mode.

- **offline:** Sets the current mode to offline. In offline mode, which was new for Windows 2003, the utility accumulates any commands you issue and executes them as a batch. Using this second approach on remote servers can greatly enhance performance without any loss of functionality. Use the show mode command to display the current mode.

- **popd:** Removes a context from the NetSH stack. Earlier versions popped the context from the system stack using the PopD command.

- **pushd:** Pushes a context onto the NetSH stack. Earlier versions pushed context onto the system stack by using the PushD command.

Newer Utilities Can Replace Older Equivalents

One of the tricks of the trade when working at the command line is to look for efficient replacements of old bulky commands. The NetSH utility is such a replacement. You can use it in place of a number of older utilities and graphical tools. For example, the NetSH utility replaces the older RouteMon utility. Even though you'll find the RouteMon executable on Windows XP and newer systems, the executable now tells you to use NetSH instead.

As part of keeping track of utility functionality, you must also monitor the services that Microsoft supports. For example, Windows 2000 supports the ReSerVation Protocol (RSVP), but Microsoft no longer supports this service on Windows XP and newer systems. The loss of this service affects the method you use to reserve network resources and, consequently, the use of utilities. See the MSDN article at http://msdn.microsoft.com/library/aa374137.aspx for details.

Of course, even if the latest version of Windows supports a particular service, you'll want to ensure the service runs automatically. As an example, Windows XP originally enabled the TelNet service but disabled it for the SP2 release. You'll often need to rely on third-party resources, such as the Web site at http://www.ss64.com/ntsyntax/services.html, to obtain information about services because Microsoft tends to hide this information (or not publish it at all).

Creating Scripts

PART VIII

Impersonate a User

It's important to set security on your machine to prevent outside sources, especially those from email or Web sites, from running scripts on your machine. Of course, setting security to prevent others from executing virus-laden code also tends to keep your scripts from running—at least with the credentials of the current user. The RunAs utility provides a way for you to have great security and still allow script execution too. You use this utility to run a particular application with credentials other than those used by the current user.

In the most basic form of this command, you type **RunAs / User:*UserName* *Command***, where *UserName* is the account you want to use in place of the current logon and *Command* is any executable that you want to run. When you use RunAs this way, RunAs will prompt you for a password to use to access the account.

If you use RunAs frequently with a particular account, you can add the /SaveCred command line switch to save the credentials you provide in the local password store. After the credentials are saved, RunAs won't ask you to provide a password every time you use a particular account. When a credential applies only for network access, use the /NetOnly command line switch so that the local store will record the password properly. If you have a smartcard that you use in place of a password, add the /SmartCard command line switch to the command.

Other accounts normally have an environment associated with them. Whenever you use RunAs, it configures the RunAs environment to match the account you're using to ensure the command works properly. If the account is for a user who doesn't have the same setup as you do, you can use the /Env command line switch to configure the RunAs environment the same as your own environment.

Likewise, RunAs normally uses the profile of the account you use to run a command. The /NoProfile command line switch specifies that you don't want to load the RunAs user's profile when running the application. The benefit of using this setting is that the application loads more quickly. In addition, this setting acts as a safety feature because the application you want to run is less likely to corrupt the RunAs user's settings. However, using this feature can prevent some applications from running, especially when they rely on settings in the user profile to perform certain tasks.

Change the Environment

Windows provides the means to control the user's environment with great accuracy through command line utilities. You can define whether the user can install applications, enable or disable session logons, and modify port configurations. The Change utility is the most powerful of the four because you can use it to perform any of these tasks. The other three utilities provide subsets of the Change functionality. The following sections describe these environment-changing utilities.

Change Logons, Ports, and Users

The Change utility helps you control the user's ability to install applications, enable or disable session logons, and control ports. You could consider each of these actions a specific utility mode, but the utility is quite simple, so the following sections describe all three tasks.

Define the User's Execution Rights

The Change User command specifies whether the user has execute or install privileges. To see the user's current rights, type **Change User / Query** and press Enter. The Change utility will show you the user's rights to execute and install applications.

If you want to keep the user from executing applications, type **Change User /Execute Disable** and press Enter. Likewise, when you want to enable this right, type **Change User /Execute Enable** and press Enter. This command is helpful when you want to ensure the user doesn't disturb the environment when you need to perform system updates. In addition, you could use it for remote sessions where the user should only access data and not execute applications.

To keep a user from installing applications, type **Change User / Install Disable** and press Enter. There are many situations where you don't want users installing any application that comes to mind, especially if you want to keep your network as virus free as possible. To re-enable this right, type **Change User /Install Enable** and press Enter.

Enable or Disable Session Logons Using Change

The Change Logon command determines whether Windows enables or disables session logons. Type **Change Logon /Query** and press Enter to display the current session logon status. If you want to disable logons, type **Change**

Logon /Disable and press Enter. A common reason to perform this task is to keep users from logging on to a server that's in a maintenance mode. When you finish maintaining the system, type **Change Logon /Enable** to let users start logging on to the system again.

Specify the Port Configuration

The Change Port command defines the port configuration. This command works with serial ports for the most part and you'll use other commands, such as WMIC, or a script to specific port assignments. To see the current port assignments, type **Change Port /Query** and press Enter. In most cases, you won't see a full list of port assignments—just the serial ports.

You can assign a port to a particular device. In this case, type **Change Port *LocalName* = *DeviceName*** and press Enter, where *LocalName* is the name of the device as you'd use it, such as AUX, and *DeviceName* is the name of the device, such as \DosDevices\COM1. Use the /D *LocalName* command line switch to remove the port assignment.

Enable or Disable Session Logons Directly

Use the ChgLogon utility to enable or disable session logons. To see the current session logon status, type **ChgLogon /Query** and press Enter. When you want to disable session logons, type **ChgLogon /Disable** and press Enter. Likewise, to enable session logons, type **ChgLogon /Enable** and press Enter.

List COM Port Mappings

The ChgPort utility controls port assignments on the current system. To see the current port assignments, type **ChgPort /Query** and press Enter. When you want to create a new port assignment, type **ChgPort *LocalName* = *DeviceName*** and press Enter, where *LocalName* is the name of the device as you'd use it, such as AUX, and *DeviceName* is the name of the device, such as \DosDevices\COM1. If you want to delete an existing port, type **ChgPort /D *LocalName*** and press Enter.

Modify the Install Mode

The ChgUsr utility controls the user's execute and install privileges on the system. To see the user's current rights, type **ChgUsr /Query** and press Enter.

When you want to change application execution rights, type **ChgUsr /Execute Enable** to enable the rights or ChgUsr /Execute Disable to disable the rights and press Enter. Likewise, when you need to change installation rights, type **ChgUsr /Install Enable** to enable the right or **ChgUsr /Install Disable** to disable the right and press Enter.

Map a Network Drive

You can map a network drive using a batch file, but it's more difficult and error prone than using a script. A script can provide one thing that a batch file can't in this case—great interactivity. Using a script lets you interact with the user in a way that would be difficult using a batch file. In addition, the script provides a modicum of additional error handling support that makes error handling easier. Listing 24.1 shows a typical example of how you can implement this functionality using JavaScript.

Listing 24.1: Mapping a Network Drive with JavaScript

```
// Define the network object used to map the drive.
var oNetwork = new ActiveXObject("WScript.Network");

// Detect a request for command line help.
if (WScript.Arguments.length == 1)
   if (WScript.Arguments(0) == "/?")
      {
          // Display the help information
          WScript.Echo("Usage: MapNetwork <letter> <UNC
target>\n");

          // Exit the script and provide an error level of 1
to
          // indicate a help request.
          WScript.Quit(1);
      }
   else
      {
          // Display an error message.
          WScript.Echo("Input argument is unknown.");
          WScript.Echo("Usage: MapNetwork <letter> <UNC
target>\n");
```

```
            // Exit the script and provide an error level of 2
to
            // indicate  a data entry error.
            WScript.Quit(2);
        }


// Create variables to hold the drive letter and the UNC
location.
var DriveLtr;
var UNCName;

// Detect the correct number of input arguments.
if ( WScript.Arguments.length < 2 )
{
    // Ask whether the user wants to continue.
    WScript.Echo("No input provided! Provide it
interactively? [Y | N]");
    var Answer = WScript.StdIn.ReadLine();

    // If the user doesn't want to continue, display help and
exit.
    // Use an exit code of 2 to indicate a data entry error.
    if (Answer.toUpperCase() == "N")
    {
        WScript.Echo("Usage: MapNetwork <letter> <UNC
target>\n");
        WScript.Quit(2);
    }

    // Input the drive letter.
    WScript.Echo("Type the local drive letter (X:).");
    DriveLtr = WScript.StdIn.ReadLine();

    // Input the UNC drive on the remote machine.
    WScript.Echo("Type the UNC location (\\MyServer\
MyDrive).");
    UNCName = WScript.StdIn.ReadLine();
}
else
{
    // Obtain the required inputs from the command line.
    DriveLtr = WScript.Arguments(0);
```

```
      UNCName = WScript.Arguments(1);
   }


   // Tell the user which drive is mapped.
   WScript.Echo("Mapping drive " + DriveLtr + " to " +
   UNCName);

   // Attempt to create the connection.
   try
   {
      // Perform the drive mapping function.
      oNetwork.MapNetworkDrive(DriveLtr, UNCName);
   }
   catch(e)
   {
      // Display an error when the task fails.
      WScript.Echo("Couldn't map the drive!\n" +
   e.description);
      WScript.Quit(3);
   }
```

The example begins by creating a network object to create the connection. In this case, the code uses the new ActiveXObject() method. You can also use WScript.CreateObject() to perform the same task. The method you use depends on personal taste in most cases. This example uses the ActiveXObject() method for the sake of completeness. If you want to use the other method, you would replace this line of code with var oNetwork = WScript.CreateObject("WScript.Network");.

The next section of code addresses the need to handle the /? command line switch. The help displayed in this example is decidedly weak. You'd provide a lot more help in a fully functional production script. The command and utility examples in this book provide you with a good idea of the kind of information you need to provide to make a script useful for everyone. Notice how the code detects the number of arguments first, and then handles the special case of the /? command line switch. Notice how the code exits with an error level of 1, so you can trap the help request in a batch file if desired.

Of course, you also need to handle the case where someone provides a single input, but it isn't the /? command line switch. The code displays a special error message along with the same help that you would normally display for the /? command line switch. Notice that in this case the script exits with an error level of 2. Using a different error level lets you trap this particular problem in a batch file.

At this point, the code begins looking at the input. The input must provide two arguments to map a network drive to a local drive letter. Consequently, when the script detects two input arguments, it places them in the appropriate variables and attempts to map the network drive. You might wonder why the script doesn't perform all kinds of odd error checking on the input arguments. The try...catch statement is the secret in this case. If the user provides incorrect input, the oNetwork.MapNetworkDrive(DriveLtr, UNCName) call fails and the catch part of the statement traps the error. The script displays an error message in this case and exits again. Because this is another kind of error, the script sets the error level to 3. Notice that the script conveniently disregards any more than two inputs.

Using Scripting Effectively

Sometimes you do need to use scripting techniques to ensure you get the right results from your command line activities. The best rule of thumb to follow is that anything that requires direct application access through something other than command line switches requires a script, rather than a batch file. In addition, if you've just spent five hours trying to get a batch file to work and feel that you still haven't made any progress, then perhaps you're not using the right tool for the job.

It's this second point where many people get into endless discussions about the suitability of one technique over another. In many cases, it's part personal preference and part skill or special need. For example, at one time some people tried to use spreadsheets in place of word processors (it really was common in the 1980s). However, anyone who has used both products today knows that each tool has a particular job to perform and it's better to use the right tool for the job. The same rule applies to scripts versus batch files. You might be able to use batch files to meet most of your needs, but eventually, you'll run into a complex task that simply requires a script to perform adequately.

At this point, all the code needs to handle is the case where the user doesn't provide any input arguments. This is where the interactive features of scripting pay off. The script begins by asking the user whether they want to provide the input interactively. If so, the code asks some simple questions and tries to map the drive. If not, the code exits with a help message and an error level of 2. The reason the script uses an error level of 2 is that this is the same kind of error as providing a single input that isn't the /? command line switch.

Create a .*CSV* File

Sometimes it's important to see the same example using two different techniques. The example in this section performs the same task as the batch file example in the "Use a Centralized Data Store" section of Chapter 21. When you compare the code in Listing 24.2 with the code in Listing 21.7, you'll notice that Listing 24.2 is significantly longer, even though it produces the same output. In addition, the code in Listing 24.2 is significantly more complex. However, if you perform just these two comparisons, you'll miss some of the reasons to use scripts. Mostly notably, the script version demonstrates the flexibility that this form of coding can provide. For example, you have more control over the files. The input files are read only, which means that the code can't damage them, even accidentally. Consequently, the files are safer than when you use a batch file to manipulate them. Listing 24.2 shows the script version of the CSV output example.

Listing 24.2: Creating CSV Output Using a Script

```
// Create a File System Object to work with files.
var FSO = WScript.CreateObject("Scripting.
FileSystemObject");


// Determine whether the Output2.CSV file exists and delete
it.
if (FSO.FileExists("Output2.CSV"))
   FSO.DeleteFile("Output2.CSV", false);


// Create a WshShell object to obtain environment variables.
var Shell = WScript.CreateObject("WScript.Shell");


// Create variables to hold the static data.
var CompName = Shell.ExpandEnvironmentStrings("%COMPUTERNAM
E%");
```

```javascript
var UserName = Shell.ExpandEnvironmentStrings("%USERNAME%");
var DateTime = new Date();

// Obtain the list of file specifications.
WScript.Echo("Locating temporary files to delete.");
var DirSpec = FSO.OpenTextFile("DelFiles.TXT", 1);

// Process each entry in the file.
while (!DirSpec.AtEndOfStream)
{
   // Get a single file specification.
   var ThisSpec = DirSpec.ReadLine();

   // Process the directory specification.
   WScript.Echo("Adding database values for " + ThisSpec);
   Shell.Run(
      "Cmd /C Dir " + ThisSpec + " /B /S > TmpDirFiles.TXT",
0, true);

   // Open the file containing the individual file entries.
   var Files = FSO.OpenTextFile("TmpDirFiles.TXT", 1);

   // Open the CSV file to accept the file entries.
   var Output = FSO.OpenTextFile("Output2.CSV", 8, true);

   // Process each of the file entries in turn.
   while (!Files.AtEndOfStream)
   {
      // Get an individual file entry.
      var File = Files.ReadLine();

      // Create the CSV file entry. Begin with the computer
name and
      // the username.
      Output.Write("\"");
      Output.Write(CompName);
      Output.Write("\",\"");
      Output.Write(UserName);
      Output.Write("\",\"");

      // Processing the date requires a little additional
work. You
```

```
        // must extract the individual elements and put them
together as
        // desired. Begin by converting the day number to a
day string.
        var DayNum = DateTime.getDay();
        switch (DayNum)
        {
           case 0:
              Output.Write("Sun ");
              break;
           case 1:
              Output.Write("Mon ");
              break;
           case 2:
              Output.Write("Tue ");
              break;
           case 3:
              Output.Write("Wed ");
              break;
           case 4:
              Output.Write("Thu ");
              break;
           case 5:
              Output.Write("Fri ");
              break;
           case 6:
              Output.Write("Sat ");
              break;
        }

     Output.Write(DateTime.getMonth() + 1);
     Output.Write("/" + DateTime.getDate() +
                  "/" + DateTime.getFullYear());
     Output.Write("\",\"");

     // Extract the time from DateTime.
     Output.Write(DateTime.getHours() + ":" +
                  DateTime.getMinutes() + ":" +
                  DateTime.getSeconds());
     Output.Write("\",\"");
```

```
        // Finally, add the filename to the output.
        Output.Write(File);
        Output.WriteLine("\"");
    }

    // Close the working files.
    Files.Close();
    Output.Close();
}

// Close the file containing the file specifications.
DirSpec.Close();
```

The code begins by removing any existing output file. JavaScript and VBScript lack file support. However, you have access to the Scripting. FileSystemObject object, which does provide full file system support. You can use this object to perform a multitude of tasks with files, including creating, deleting, and editing them. The FileSystemObject also includes functionality for working with folders.

The next step is to retrieve the username, computer name, date, and time. In many cases, you can simply use the ExpandEnvironmentStrings() method to obtain the information you need from the system. Notice that the example code uses the Date object in place of obtaining the date from the environment variables using the Shell.ExpandEnvironmentStrings ("%DATE%") method. When working with JavaScript, you can only access the environment variables that you can see with the Set command. JavaScript doesn't support the extended functionality that's available at the command line. In fact, you'll find that this general rule applies to both VBScript and JavaScript; neither scripting language supports the extensions that you can access from a batch file at the command prompt. The Date object also provides time support, so you don't need a separate Time variable.

At this point, it's time to begin collecting a list of temporary files on the system. This example, like its batch file counter, relies on an external file to hold the file specifications. The code opens the file and begins processing it one line at a time. The use of a constant value of 1 for the FSO.OpenTextFile() method opens the file in read-only mode. The code processes the file one line at a time (one file specification at a time) using the DirSpec.ReadLine() method. You can read one character at a time using the DirSpec.Read() method instead.

This example points out a very special feature of the scripting languages. Notice the use of the Shell.Run() method. You can use this method to run any application. To use this feature at the command prompt, you have to begin by creating a command processor using the CMD utility as shown. In this case, the code runs the Dir command with the file specification obtained from DelFiles.TXT. This line of code begs the question of why the code doesn't use the FileSystemObject. In this particular case, you can perform the task faster and without any loss of functionally by using the Dir command. The point is that you don't always have to use a scripting object; sometimes a command line tool works just as well or even better.

The code now has two files to work with. The first is an input file, TmpDirFiles.TXT, which contains the list of temporary files. The second is an output file, Output2.CSV, which contains the database of file entries. The FSO.OpenTextFile() constant of 8 opens the file in append (read/write) mode. If the file doesn't exist, the code raises an error unless you also set the third argument to True, which tells the method to create the file when it doesn't exist.

Now all the code needs to do is process the data and output it. The user and computer names are straightforward. Processing the date requires the most code because the code has to put the date string together. The downside of all this code is that it makes the example harder to read than the batch file. The plus side is that you can create a date string in any format required, even nonstandard formats.

As a final note on this example, make sure you close files when you finish working with them. Otherwise, the script raises an error when you try to open the file again. In some cases, the file could remain open until you reboot the system, making it inaccessible to everyone.

Creating Scripts

PART VIII

A

Alphabetical Command List

This appendix provides you with an alphabetical listing of all of the commands and utilities found in the book. You can use Table A.1 as a quick reference guide to make it easier to locate a particular command or utility. Given that the book provides you with details on using 149 different commands and utilities, locating a particular entry can prove difficult, which is why I included this appendix. If you can't find the command or utility you want, try the topical listing found in Appendix B. Please contact me at JMueller@mwt.net with any comments that will make this appendix more useful.

NOTE Remember that most commands and utilities support the /? command line switch. If you see a command or utility in this list that looks interesting, simply type *Name* **/?** and press Enter, where *Name* is the name of the command or utility, to get additional information.

Table A.1: Alphabetical Reference to Commands and Utilities

Command or Utility Name	Chapter	Section/Task
ANSI.SYS	19	Use ANSI.SYS to Control the Environment
Assoc	4	Determine File Associations Create File Associations
	19	Use Command Extensions
Attrib	4	Set File Attributes
AuditPol	16	Audit User Access
AutoChk	5	Manage the Volume Dirty Bit
BCDEdit	15	Manage the Boot Configuration
BlastCln	17	Remove Viruses
Call	19	Use Command Extensions
	21	Employ the Call Command
CD	4	View the Current Directory Change the Current Directory
	19	Use Command Extensions
Change	24	Change the Environment

Table A.1: Alphabetical Reference to Commands and Utilities *(continued)*

Command or Utility Name	Chapter	Section/Task
CHCP	19	Set the Code Page Number with the CHCP Utility
ChDir	4	View the Current Directory Change the Current Directory
	19	Use Command Extensions
ChgLogon	24	Enable or Disable Session Logons
ChgPort	24	List COM Port Mappings
ChgUsr	24	Modify the Install Mode
ChkDsk	6	Determine File and Directory Status Locate Bad Sectors
ChkNTFS	6	Perform Boot Time Disk Checks
Choice	21	Employ the Choice Command
Cipher	7	Protect Data
Clip	20	Redirect Command Line Output to the Clipboard
CLS	1	Clear the Display
CMD	19	Use the CMD Switches
CmdKey	20	Manage Usernames and Passwords
Color	19	Use Command Extensions
	20	Change Screen Colors
Compact	6	Save Hard Drive Space
Copy	4	Copy Files
CScript	2	Change Security and Basic Setup
	18	Use the SCRegEdit Script
	22	Use the Windows Scripting File Execute Scripts
	23	Use the WScript Object
Date	20	Configure the System Date

continues

Table A.1: Alphabetical Reference to Commands and Utilities *(continued)*

Command or Utility Name	Chapter	Section/Task
Defrag	6	Improve Disk Access Performance
Del	4	Remove a Directory Remove Files
	19	Use Command Extensions
Dir	4	Find Directories Find Directories Using Patterns Remove a Directory Find Files Find Files in Sorted Order Find Files by Attribute Find Files Using Patterns
	5	Employ Data Redirection Display Data One Page at a Time
DiskPart	6	Manage Partitions
DosX	19	Add DPMI Support Using the **DosX** Utility
DSAdd	11	Interact with Organizational Units
	12	Create New Objects
DSGet	11	Interact with Users
	12	Get Objects
DSMod	11	Reset a User's Password
	12	Edit Existing Objects
DSMove	12	Move Existing Objects
DSQuery	11	Manage Active Directory with the **DSQuery** Utility
DSRm	12	Delete Existing Objects
Echo	1	Display Environment Variables
	5	Execute Applications Anywhere
	21	Employ the **Echo** Command Perform Complex File Iteration Utilize Variable Substitution

Table A.1: Alphabetical Reference to Commands and Utilities *(continued)*

Command or Utility Name	Chapter	Section/Task
EMM.SYS	19	Control the Expanded Memory EMM Entry
EndLocal	19	Use Command Extensions
Erase	4	Remove Files
	19	Use Command Extensions
EventCreate	13	Create Simple System Events
EventTriggers	13	Trigger System Events
Exit	21	Employ the Exit Command
Find	5	Find Simple Strings
	11	Obtain a User's Full Name
	13	Enumerate the Logs
	17	List Services
FindStr	5	Find Complex Strings Display Files Containing Strings Perform Case Insensitive Searches
For	4	Find Files Using Patterns
	19	Use Command Extensions
	21	Employ the For Command
ForFiles	21	Employ the ForFiles Utility
Format	6	Format a Disk
FSUtil	4	Create Simple Hard Links View Simple Hard Links Delete Simple Hard Links
	5	Monitor the File System with the FSUtil Command
FType	4	Determine File Types Create File Types
	19	Use Command Extensions
GetMAC	8	Get the Media Access Control Information

continues

Table A.1: Alphabetical Reference to Commands and Utilities *(continued)*

Command or Utility Name	Chapter	Section/Task
Goto	4	Find Files Using Patterns
	19	Use Command Extensions
	21	Employ the GoTo Command
GPResult	16	Obtain Group Policy Results
GPUpdate	16	Manage Group Policies
GrafTabl	19	Enable Graphics Character Support with the GrafTabl Utility
Help	1	Obtain Command Line Help
HIMEM.SYS	19	Control Extended Memory with HIMEM.SYS
ICACLS	7	Change File and Directory Access
If	4	Find Files Using Patterns
	19	Use Command Extensions
	21	Employ the If Command
IPConfig	9	Manage the Internet Protocol
Label	6	Manage Volume Labels
LH	19	Save Memory Using the LH Command
LodCtr	14	Add Performance Counters
LogMan	14	Manage Performance Logs and Alerts
Logoff	2	Use the Logoff Utility
MD	4	Create Directories
	19	Use Command Extensions
Mem	19	Set the Command Interpreter Location
MkDir	4	Create Directories
MKLink	4	Create Hard Links Using the New Technique Create Symbolic Links Create Junctions

Table A.1: Alphabetical Reference to Commands and Utilities *(continued)*

Command or Utility Name	Chapter	Section/Task
MKLink	19	Use Command Extensions
More	5	Display Data One Page at a Time
	7	Use the Query Option
	11	Manage Directory Services Using the WMIC NTDomain Alias
	13	Display a List of Publishers Enumerate the Logs
	17	Use TaskKill and TaskList Filters
MountVol	6	Mount a Volume
Move	4	Move Directories Rename Directories Move Files
MRT	17	Detect and Remove Malicious Software
MSTSC	10	Create Remote Connections
Net	2	Change Security and Basic Setup
	8	Interact with the Network Using the Net Utility
	15	Configure a Time Source
NetDiag	9	Perform Detailed Network Diagnostics
NetSH	2	Change Security and Basic Setup
	24	Script Networking Solutions
NetStat	9	Get Network Statistics
NTDSUtil	11	Manage the Active Directory Database
OpenFiles	7	Detect Shared Open Files
Path	4	Find Files Using Patterns
	5	Execute Applications Anywhere
PathPing	9	Trace Transmission Paths

continues

Table A.1: Alphabetical Reference to Commands and Utilities *(continued)*

Command or Utility Name	Chapter	Section/Task
Pause	21	Employ the **Pause** Command
PING	9	Check Connections
PopD	19	Use Command Extensions
	21	Store and Retrieve Directories with the **PushD** and **PopD** Commands
Prompt	4	View the Current Directory
	19	Use Command Extensions
	21	Employ the Prompt Command
PushD	19	Use Command Extensions
	21	Store and Retrieve Directories with the **PushD** and **PopD** Commands
QProcess	10	Obtain Process Information
Query	16	Obtain Session Status Information
QUser	16	Obtain User Logon Information
QWinSta	10	Get Session Information
RD	4	Remove a Directory
ReDir	19	Install the Network Redirector Using the **ReDir** Utility
Reg	18	Manage the Registry
RegEdit	18	Perform Basic Registry Tasks
	19	Configure the Command Interpreter in the Registry
RegIni	24	Script Registry Entries
RegSvr32	22	Use the Windows Scripting File
ReLog	14	Create New Performance Logs from Existing Logs
Rem	21	Employ the **Rem** Command
Ren	4	Rename a File

Table A.1: Alphabetical Reference to Commands and Utilities *(continued)*

Command or Utility Name	Chapter	Section/Task
Rename	4	Rename a File
Reset	10	Terminate a Session
RmDir	4	Remove a Directory
Route	9	Manipulate the Network Routing Tables
RunAs	24	Impersonate a User
SC	1	Work with Services
	3	Configure the Task Scheduler
SCHTasks	3	Manage Tasks Using the SchTasks Command
SCRegEdit	18	Use the SCRegEdit Script
SecEdit	17	Configure Local Security Policies
Set	1	Manage Environment Variables with the Set Command
	19	Use Command Extensions
	21	Add Debug Information to Batch Files
SetLocal	19	Use Command Extensions
SetX	1	Manage Environment Variables with the SetX Utility
SFC	17	Verify System Files
Shift	19	Use Command Extensions
ShutDown	1	Shut Down the System
	2	Change Security and Basic Setup
SLMGR	2	Change Security and Basic Setup
	15	Activate Windows
Sort	5	Employ Data Redirection
Start	1	Start an Application
	19	Use Command Extensions

continues

Table A.1: Alphabetical Reference to Commands and Utilities *(continued)*

Command or Utility Name	Chapter	Section/Task
TakeOwn	7	Take Ownership of Files
TaskKill	17	Use **TaskKill** and **TaskList** Filters Terminate Tasks
TaskList	17	Use **TaskKill** and **TaskList** Filters List Applications List Services
TCMSetup	10	Set Up a Telephony Client
Time	20	Configure the System Time
TimeOut	21	Employ the **Choice** Command Employ the **TimeOut** Utility
Title	20	Change the Command Window Title
TraceRpt	14	Convert Event Trace Logs
TraceRt	9	Track the Network Path
Tree	4	Display a Directory Structure
TSDiscon	10	Disconnect an Active Session
TSKill	10	End Processes
TSShutDn	10	Shut Down the Terminal Server
Type	5	Display a Data File on Screen
UnlodCtr	14	Remove Performance Counters
Ver	1	Determine the Operating System Version
Verifier	17	Verify Drivers
Vol	6	Get Volume Information
W32Tm	8	Configure Time Synchronization
	15	Manage the System Time
WaitFor	21	Employ the **Choice** Command
WEvtUtil	13	Manage Event Information

Table A.1: Alphabetical Reference to Commands and Utilities *(continued)*

Command or Utility Name	Chapter	Section/Task
WhoAmI	16	Discover User Identity
WinRM	10	Perform Remote Windows Management
WinRS	10	Execute Commands on a Remote System
WMIC	2	Change Security and Basic Setup
	10	Define a URI
	11	Manage Directory Services Using the WMIC NTDomain Alias
	15	Configure the Server
WScript	22	Execute Scripts Configure the Host and Property Page Options
XCopy	4	Perform Bulk File Transfers
	21	Employ the If Command

B

Topical Command List

This appendix provides you with a topical (categorical) listing of all 149 commands and utilities found in the book. You can use Tables B.1 through B.14 to locate commands and utilities by topic (category). If you can't find the command or utility you want, try the alphabetical listing found in Appendix A. Please contact me at JMueller @mwt.net with any comments that will make this appendix more useful.

NOTE Remember that most commands and utilities support the /? command line switch. If you see a command or utility in this list that looks interesting, simply type *Name* /? and press Enter, where *Name* is the name of the command or utility, to get additional information.

Table B.1: Active Directory–Related Commands and Utilities

Command or Utility Name	Chapter	Section/Task
DSAdd	11	Interact with Organizational Units
	12	Create New Objects
DSGet	11	Interact with Users
	12	Get Objects
DSMod	11	Reset a User's Password
	12	Edit Existing Objects
DSMove	12	Move Existing Objects
DSQuery	11	Manage Active Directory with the DSQuery Utility
DSRm	12	Delete Existing Objects
NTDSUtil	11	Manage the Active Directory Database

Table B.2: Application Management–Related Commands and Utilities

Command or Utility Name	Chapter	Section/Task
Reg	18	Manage the Registry
RegEdit	18	Perform Basic Registry Tasks

Table B.2: Application Management–Related Commands and Utilities *(continued)*

Command or Utility Name	Chapter	Section/Task
RegEdit	19	Configure the Command Interpreter in the Registry
Start	1	Start an Application

Table B.3: Batch File and Script-Related Commands and Utilities

Command or Utility Name	Chapter	Section/Task
Call	19	Use Command Extensions
	21	Employ the Call Command
Choice	21	Employ the Choice Command
Clip	20	Redirect Command Line Output to the Clipboard
CLS	1	Clear the Display
CmdKey	20	Manage Usernames and Passwords
Color	19	Use Command Extensions
	20	Change Screen Colors
CScript	2	Change Security and Basic Setup
	18	Use the SCRegEdit Script
	22	Use the Windows Scripting File Execute Scripts
	23	Use the WScript Object
Date	20	Configure the System Date
DosX	19	Add DPMI Support Using the DosX Utility
Echo	1	Display Environment Variables
	5	Execute Applications Anywhere
	21	Employ the Echo Command Perform Complex File Iteration Utilize Variable Substitution

continues

Table B.3: Batch File and Script-Related Commands and Utilities *(continued)*

Command or Utility Name	Chapter	Section/Task
EventCreate	13	Create Simple System Events
EventTriggers	13	Trigger System Events
Exit	21	Employ the Exit Command
For	4	Find Files Using Patterns
	19	Use Command Extensions
	21	Employ the For Command
ForFiles	21	Employ the ForFiles Utility
GoTo	4	Find Files Using Patterns
	19	Use Command Extensions
	21	Employ the GoTo Command
GrafTabl	19	Enable Graphics Character Support with the GrafTabl Utility
If	4	Find Files Using Patterns
	19	Use Command Extensions
	21	Employ the If Command
LH	19	Save Memory Using the LH Command
Logoff	2	Use the Logoff Utility
More	5	Display Data One Page at a Time
	7	Use the Query Option
	11	Manage Directory Services Using the WMIC NTDomain Alias
	13	Display a List of Publishers Enumerate the Logs
	17	Use TaskKill and TaskList Filters
Net	2	Change Security and Basic Setup
	8	Interact with the Network Using the Net Utility

Table B.3: Batch File and Script-Related Commands and Utilities *(continued)*

Command or Utility Name	Chapter	Section/Task
Net	15	Configure a Time Source
NetSH	2	Change Security and Basic Setup
	24	Script Networking Solutions
Path	4	Find Files Using Patterns
	5	Execute Applications Anywhere
Pause	21	Employ the **Pause** Command
PopD	19	Use Command Extensions
	21	Store and Retrieve Directories with the **PushD** and **PopD** Commands
Prompt	4	View the Current Directory
	19	Use Command Extensions
	21	Employ the **Prompt** Command
PushD	19	Use Command Extensions
	21	Store and Retrieve Directories with the **PushD** and **PopD** Commands
Rem	21	Employ the **Rem** Command
RunAs	24	Impersonate a User
SCHTasks	3	Manage Tasks Using the **SCHTasks** Command
SCRegEdit	18	Use the **SCRegEdit** Script
Set	1	Manage Environment Variables with the **Set** Command
	19	Use Command Extensions
	21	Add Debug Information to Batch Files
SetX	1	Manage Environment Variables with the **SetX** Utility
Shift	19	Use Command Extensions
Start	1	Start an Application

continues

Table B.3: Batch File and Script-Related Commands and Utilities *(continued)*

Command or Utility Name	Chapter	Section/Task
Time	20	Configure the System Time
TimeOut	21	Employ the Choice Command Employ the TimeOut Utility
Title	20	Change the Command Window Title
Ver	1	Determine the Operating System Version
Vol	6	Get Volume Information
WaitFor	21	Employ the Choice Command
WhoAmI	16	Discover User Identity
WScript	22	Execute Scripts Configure the Host and Property Page Options

Table B.4: Command Line–Related Commands and Utilities

Command or Utility Name	Chapter	Section/Task
ANSI.SYS	19	Use ANSI.SYS to Control the Environment
CHCP	19	Set the Code Page Number with the CHCP Utility
Clip	20	Redirect Command Line Output to the Clipboard
CLS	1	Clear the Display
CMD	19	Use the CMD Switches
Color	19	Use Command Extensions
	20	Change Screen Colors
Date	20	Configure the System Date
EMM.SYS	19	Control the Expanded Memory EMM Entry
EndLocal	19	Use Command Extensions
EventCreate	13	Create Simple System Events

Table B.4: Command Line–Related Commands and Utilities *(continued)*

Command or Utility Name	Chapter	Section/Task
EventTriggers	13	Trigger System Events
Help	1	Obtain Command Line Help
HIMEM.SYS	19	Control Extended Memory with HIMEM.SYS
More	5	Display Data One Page at a Time
	7	Use the Query Option
	11	Manage Directory Services Using the WMIC NTDomain Alias
	13	Display a List of Publishers Enumerate the Logs
	17	Use TaskKill and TaskList Filters
Path	4	Find Files Using Patterns
	5	Execute Applications Anywhere
PopD	19	Use Command Extensions
PushD	19	Use Command Extensions
RunAs	24	Impersonate a User
Set	1	Manage Environment Variables with the Set Command
	19	Use Command Extensions
SetLocal	19	Use Command Extensions
SetX	1	Manage Environment Variables with the SetX Utility
Time	20	Configure the System Time
Title	20	Change the Command Window Title
TraceRpt	14	Convert Event Trace Logs
Ver	1	Determine the Operating System Version
Vol	6	Get Volume Information

Table B.5: Diagnostics-Related Commands and Utilities

Command or Utility Name	Chapter	Section/Task
EventCreate	13	Create Simple System Events
EventTriggers	13	Trigger System Events
NetDiag	9	Perform Detailed Network Diagnostics
PathPing	9	Trace Transmission Paths
PING	9	Check Connections
SFC	17	Verify System Files
TaskKill	17	Use TaskKill and TaskList Filters Terminate Tasks
TaskList	17	Use TaskKill and TaskList Filters List Applications List Services
TraceRpt	14	Convert Event Trace Logs
WEvtUtil	13	Manage Event Information
WinRM	10	Perform Remote Windows Management

Table B.6: Disk Management–Related Commands and Utilities

Command or Utility Name	Chapter	Section/Task
AutoChk	5	Manage the Volume Dirty Bit
CD	4	View the Current Directory Change the Current Directory
	19	Use Command Extensions
ChDir	4	View the Current Directory Change the Current Directory
	19	Use Command Extensions

Table B.6: Disk Management–Related Commands and Utilities *(continued)*

Command or Utility Name	Chapter	Section/Task
ChkDsk	6	Determine File and Directory Status Locate Bad Sectors
ChkNTFS	6	Perform Boot Time Disk Checks
Defrag	6	Improve Disk Access Performance
DiskPart	6	Manage Partitions
Format	6	Format a Disk
Label	6	Manage Volume Labels
MD	4	Create Directories
	19	Use Command Extensions
MkDir	4	Create Directories
	19	Use Command Extensions
MKLink	4	Create Hard Links Using the New Technique Create Symbolic Links Create Junctions
MountVol	6	Mount a Volume
Move	4	Move Directories Rename Directories Move Files
Path	4	Find Files Using Patterns
	5	Execute Applications Anywhere
RD	4	Remove a Directory
RmDir	4	Remove a Directory
TakeOwn	7	Take Ownership of Files
Tree	4	Display a Directory Structure

Table B.7: File Management–Related Commands and Utilities

Command or Utility Name	Chapter	Section/Task
Assoc	4	Determine File Associations Create File Associations
Assoc	19	Use Command Extensions
Attrib	4	Set File Attributes
Cipher	7	Protect Data
Compact	6	Save Hard Drive Space
Copy	4	Copy Files
Del	4	Remove a Directory Remove Files
	19	Use Command Extensions
Dir	4	Find Directories Find Directories Using Patterns Remove a Directory Find Files Find Files in Sorted Order Find Files by Attribute Find Files Using Patterns
	5	Employ Data Redirection Display Data One Page at a Time
Erase	4	Remove Files
	19	Use Command Extensions
Find1	5	Find Simple Strings
	11	Obtain a User's Full Name
	13	Enumerate the Logs
	17	List Services
FindStr	5	Find Complex Strings Display Files Containing Strings Perform Case Insensitive Searches

Table B.7: File Management–Related Commands and Utilities *(continued)*

Command or Utility Name	Chapter	Section/Task
FSUtil	4	Create Simple Hard Links View Simple Hard Links Delete Simple Hard Links
FSUtil	5	Monitor the File System with the FSUtil Command
FType	4	Determine File Types Create File Types
	19	Use Command Extensions
ICACLS	7	Change File and Directory Access
Move	4	Move Directories Rename Directories Move Files
OpenFiles	7	Detect Shared Open Files
Ren	4	Rename a File
Rename	4	Rename a File
SFC	17	Verify System Files
Sort	5	Employ Data Redirection
Type	5	Display a Data File on Screen
XCopy	4	Perform Bulk File Transfers
	21	Employ the If Command

Table B.8: Hardware Configuration–Related Commands and Utilities

Command or Utility Name	Chapter	Section/Task
Change	24	Change the Environment
ChgPort	24	List COM Port Mappings
Verifier	17	Verify Drivers

Table B.9: Networking-Related Commands and Utilities

Command or Utility Name	Chapter	Section/Task
GetMAC	8	Get the Media Access Control Information
ICACLS	7	Change File and Directory Access
IPConfig	9	Manage the Internet Protocol
MSTSC	10	Create Remote Connections
Net	2	Change Security and Basic Setup
	8	Interact with the Network Using the Net Utility
	15	Configure a Time Source
NetDiag	9	Perform Detailed Network Diagnostics
NetSH	2	Change Security and Basic Setup
	24	Script Networking Solutions
NetStat	9	Get Network Statistics
PathPing	9	Trace Transmission Paths
PING	9	Check Connections
ReDir	19	Install the Network Redirector Using the ReDir Utility
Route	9	Manipulate the Network Routing Tables
TraceRt	9	Track the Network Path

Table B.10: Remote Access–Related Commands and Utilities

Command or Utility Name	Chapter	Section/Task
QProcess	10	Obtain Process Information
Reset	10	Terminate a Session
TSDiscon	10	Disconnect an Active Session
TSKill	10	End Processes
TSShutDn	10	Shut Down the Terminal Server
WinRM	10	Perform Remote Windows Management
WinRS	10	Execute Commands on a Remote System

Table B.11: Server Configuration–Related Commands and Utilities

Command or Utility Name	Chapter	Section/Task
BCDEdit	15	Manage the Boot Configuration
Net	2	Change Security and Basic Setup
	8	Interact with the Network Using the Net Utility
	15	Configure a Time Source
NetSH	2	Change Security and Basic Setup
	24	Script Networking Solutions
Reg	18	Manage the Registry
RegEdit	18	Perform Basic Registry Tasks
	19	Configure the Command Interpreter in the Registry
RegIni	24	Script Registry Entries
RegSvr32	22	Use the Windows Scripting File
SC	1	Work with Services
	3	Configure the Task Scheduler
SCRegEdit	18	Use the SCRegEdit Script
ShutDown	1	Shut Down the System
	2	Change Security and Basic Setup
SLMGR	2	Change Security and Basic Setup
	15	Activate Windows
TCMSetup	10	Set Up a Telephony Client
W32Tm	8	Configure Time Synchronization
	15	Manage the System Time
WMIC	2	Change Security and Basic Setup
	10	Define a URI
	11	Manage Directory Services Using the WMIC NTDomain Alias
	15	Configure the Server

Table B.12: Session Management–Related Commands and Utilities

Command or Utility Name	Chapter	Section/Task
ChgLogon	24	Enable or Disable Session Logons
Logoff	2	Use the Logoff Utility
Query	16	Obtain Session Status Information
QUser	16	Obtain User Logon Information
QWinSta	10	Get Session Information
Reset	10	Terminate a Session

Table B.13: System Monitoring–Related Commands and Utilities

Command or Utility Name	Chapter	Section/Task
AuditPol	16	Audit User Access
BlastCln	17	Remove Viruses
EventCreate	13	Create Simple System Events
EventTriggers	13	Trigger System Events
FSUtil	4	Create Simple Hard Links View Simple Hard Links Delete Simple Hard Links
	5	Monitor the File System with the FSUtil Command
LodCtr	14	Add Performance Counters
LogMan	14	Manage Performance Logs and Alerts
Mem	19	Set the Command Interpreter Location
MRT	17	Detect and Remove Malicious Software
NetStat	9	Get Network Statistics
OpenFiles	7	Detect Shared Open Files
QProcess	10	Obtain Process Information

Table B.13: System Monitoring–Related Commands and Utilities *(continued)*

Command or Utility Name	Chapter	Section/Task
ReLog	14	Create New Performance Logs from Existing Logs
TaskList	17	Use TaskKill and TaskList Filters List Applications List Services
UnlodCtr	14	Remove Performance Counters
WhoAmI	16	Discover User Identity

Table B.14: User Management–Related Commands and Utilities

Command or Utility Name	Chapter	Section/Task
AuditPol	16	Audit User Access
Change	24	Change the Environment
ChgLogon	24	Enable or Disable Session Logons
ChgUsr	24	Modify the Install Mode
CmdKey	20	Manage Usernames and Passwords
GPResult	16	Obtain Group Policy Results
GPUpdate	16	Manage Group Policies
ICACLS	7	Change File and Directory Access
Net	2	Change Security and Basic Setup
	8	Interact with the Network Using the Net Utility
	15	Configure a Time Source
QProcess	10	Obtain Process Information
QUser	16	Obtain User Logon Information
SecEdit	17	Configure Local Security Policies
WhoAmI	16	Discover User Identity

C

Listing of Best Practices

IN THIS CHAPTER, YOU WILL LEARN TO:

M ost administrators are used to following best practices when
working with the Windows GUI. There are principles you follow
to ensure you get the right results, at least most of the time. Likewise,
when you work at the command line, you can follow best practices to
ensure you get good results, at least most of the time. This appendix
tells you about the best practices I've created while working at the
command line over the last 20 years. These are time-tested techniques
you can use to obtain good results. They won't always provide perfect
results; only practice on your part will produce the perfect results you
seek, but they'll help considerably. I'd love to hear your best practices as
well—feel free to contact me at JMueller@mwt.net.

Always Verify the Data

It always pays to verify the data you're going to use with a command
or utility. Unlike the GUI environment, the command line environment
doesn't ever provide you with a list of acceptable choices. Consequently,
you may find that something incredibly small can produce extremely
bad results. For example, you may have two employees and one is
named Newman, while the other is named Neumann. The difference of
two characters can make a huge difference. When working with a GUI,
you'd probably see both names and choose the right one or ask someone
if you weren't sure. When working at the command line you may not
ever know that both names exist. That's why you always want to verify
any data you use.

Get the data in written form whenever possible. Obtaining it in
a form that you can cut and paste to the command line is even better. Not only does such a practice save you typing time, but doing so
makes it considerably more difficult to make a mistake. Typos are
understandably a significant source of problems at the command line.
Anything you can do to verify data before you complete a command
is a plus. Copying and pasting are essential parts of working at the
command line.

NOTE   To copy any text in a GUI window, highlight the text and then press Ctrl+C. To paste the text from the clipboard into the command line window, right-click the command line window and choose Paste from the context menu. It's also possible to move information in the other direction. In this case, right-click the command line window and choose Mark from the context menu. Highlight the text you want to copy and then press Enter. To paste the text into any GUI window, place the cursor at the insertion point and press Ctrl+V.

Real Administrators Use Help

This book contains 149 commands and utilities. These are the commands and utilities that you find in most versions of Windows (depending on which version you use, you'll actually find considerably more commands and utilities). Add to these commands and utilities the commands and utilities that come with any applications you install, and it's pretty easy to see that you aren't going to memorize them all.

Unfortunately, some administrators don't want to admit that they lack a photographic memory and attempt to execute commands without looking at the help the command provides. No, this help isn't enough to help you learn how to use the command or utility in most cases, but it's enough to jog the memory of an experienced administrator. All you need to do is type the name of the command followed by the /? command line switch (in most cases) and the command will output help information for you.

Although this top-level help is enough to understand simple commands such as Dir, it's not enough to understand complex utilities such as WMIC. In this case, you have to drill down to the level of help you need. You can start by typing **WMIC /?** and pressing Enter to obtain a list of aliases. After you decide on something like the CPU alias, type **WMIC CPU /?** and press Enter to see the list of actions you can perform. After you decide on an action, such as GET, type **WMIC CPU GET /?** and press Enter to obtain the information you need about the GET action for the CPU alias. Of course, you can always save yourself a lot of time and simply look up the help for WMIC in this book (see Appendix A for an alphabetical list of commands and utilities).

Test Your Theories on a Test System

Nothing is as unforgiving as the command prompt when it comes to experimentation. You can completely trash your hard drive in a matter of seconds and may not even realize it. It's possible to kill groups, eliminate users, remove applications, destroy data wholesale, and completely ruin your career without a single word of warning from the command line.

This isn't the place to test out something without realizing that things can go horribly wrong dreadfully fast. In fact, the reason that many administrators moved from the command line to the GUI is to avoid such errors, but now many administrators are moving back to the command line because using a GUI is excessively slow and they simply don't have the time to wait for the GUI to get around to doing something. To try anything new, always use a test system that's configured like your real server. You'll appreciate the safety net that such an arrangement provides the first time you have to reformat the test machine drive due to unforeseen complications.

Write down absolutely everything as you test a new process. Don't use a file on the server to store this information—it may not be there in a few moments. If you don't have a secondary machine you can use, then write down your procedure on paper. Verify everything you write down to make sure you wrote it correctly. Execute a command only after you verify that you've written it down correctly and used help to ensure you've formatted the command correctly. If something does go horribly wrong, having a written record can make it possible for someone to help you fix the problem. Even if you can't get help, at least you know not to try that command line syntax again. In some cases, you have to be willing to fail in order to make progress. Of course, the safety net of your test system makes such failure nonfatal (but still aggravating).

Even after you create a complete procedure that works in every way, test it several more times on the test system before you begin using it in a production environment. Otherwise you may find that the procedure isn't as bug free as you anticipated.

Use Batch Files, Scripts, and Written Procedures

Documentation of all sorts will save you time and effort. A single command or utility probably won't do everything you want. Consequently, you need some method of documenting the command or utility sequence that helps you accomplish useful work on your server. Batch files, scripts, and written procedures all provide useful ways to record sequences that you'll use more than once.

Of course, you'll want to make sure that you write these items in a way that makes it easy to figure out what you did the next time you need to perform the task. Add copious comments to batch files and scripts to ensure they are documented fully. Make sure your comments are useful. Place an emphasis on what something does, why you did it that way, and how to work with it. Otherwise, the information you save is useless. Writing ideas down has a number of additional benefits that you should consider as part of the payback for the work you'll perform, such as:

- Any time you write down something, it makes it easier to perform the task again and it also reduces the time required to do it.

- You'll perform the task with fewer mistakes.

- The documentation also makes it possible for someone working for you to accomplish the task when you're not available—such as when you're home watching the game over the weekend and really don't want to hear about the latest network failure.

- You can document precisely what you have done when you do need outside help in fixing a problem.

- Approved procedures tend to reduce the risk of making the problem worse.

The one thing to avoid is using someone else's batch file, script, or written procedure without testing it first, especially if the item was written for another system. Yes, the information can be helpful, but your system is different from the one for which the batch file, script, or written procedure was designed. Differences between systems can cause significant damage, so you have to know that this external information is actually going to work. Of course, you don't want to reinvent the wheel either. Getting information from someone else can often help you create your own custom solution faster.

Make Backups

Before you begin any major configuration exercise on your server, make a backup. It seems like obvious advice, but administrators often fail to take it. They think that a little configuration job won't cause much trouble until they're picking up the pieces later. You should already have a good backup program in place because your server contains valuable data. If you aren't backing up your server regularly ("regularly" is defined as at least once a day and probably more often than that), then you're already setting yourself up for a major surprise at the worst possible moment. Don't cause that moment to occur by performing a task on a server that hasn't been backed up for the last month.

Try to perform any configuration tasks as soon as possible after the backup completes so that a disaster will cause as little loss as possible. In fact, if you can perform the tasks before anyone starts working with the server, you'll likely have better results.

Perform User-Specific Changes during Downtime

Some changes you make to a user account affect the user immediately; other changes wait until the next time the user logs onto the system. Think about this issue for a moment and you'll figure out that this scenario can create instabilities. The user is likely to become unhappy because their account won't work as anticipated. In fact, the account can become unstable. In a worst case scenario, the instabilities could cause system crashes and data loss (this scenario is rare, but you always have to work as if you'll be the unlucky individual who has it happen to them). If you can't make the changes before the user gets into work, specifically have the user log out of the system, perform the configuration task, and ask the user to log back on. Using this approach will reduce user frustration.

The same approach also applies to a group. Many group level changes can cause instabilities in the affected accounts. Normally, you'll want to make group changes when everyone is logged out to ensure that the changes take effect the next time the users of the group log back onto the system.

NOTE   Some users are invariably going to cheat. It's possible to stand behind the user, watch them log out, and then go back to your office to perform the reconfiguration while they log back onto the system. Inevitably the user will call back sometime later saying they were logged out, yet the instabilities that they're telling you about can only occur if they were logged on while you made the required account changes. If this occurs, have the user log back out and back onto the system again.

Index

Note to the Reader: Throughout this index **boldfaced** page numbers indicate primary discussions of a topic. *Italicized* page numbers indicate illustrations.

S